INSIDE CRIMINOLOGY

Ruth Masters, Ed.D.

Professor of Criminology
California State University, Fresno

Cliff Roberson, LLM, PhD.

Director, Justice Center
California State University, Fresno

Prentice Hall, Englewood Cliffs, New Jersey 07632

Library of Congress Cataloging-in-Publication Data
Masters, Ruth.
    Inside Criminology / by Ruth Masters and Cliff Roberson.
       p.   cm.
    Includes index.
    ISBN 0-13-463530-2
    1. Crime and criminals.   I. Roberson, Cliff,
II. Title.
HV6025.M364   1990   89-8407
364--dc20   CIP

Editorial/production supervision: **Lillian Glennon**
Interior design: **Suzanne Behnke**
Manufacturing buyer: **Dave Dickey**
Photo Researcher: **Barbara Scott**
Photo Editor: **Lori Morris-Nantz**
Cover Design: **Bruce Kenselaar**
Cover Art: **Myers Rohowsky,** *City Scene;* Grand Central, Art Galleries

©1990 by Prentice-Hall, Inc.
A Division of Simon & Schuster
Englewood Cliffs, New Jersey 07632

Printed in the United States of America
10 9 8 7 6 5 4 3 2 1

ISBN   0-13-463530-2

Prentice-Hall International (UK) Limited, *London*
Prentice-Hall of Australia Pty. Limited, *Sydney*
Prentice-Hall Canada Inc., *Toronto*
Prentice-Hall Hispanoamericana, S.A., *Mexico*
Prentice-Hall of India Private Limited, *New Delhi*
Prentice-Hall of Japan, Inc., *Tokyo*
Simon & Schuster Asia Pte. Ltd., *Singapore*
Editora Prentice-Hall Do Brasil, Ltda., *Rio de Janeiro*

Contents

2 Criminal Law and the Search for Crime Causation 48

3 Measuring Criminal Behavior 61

4 Classical Criminology 82

5 Early Positivist Criminology   102

PART II ∎ THE SOCIOLOGICAL THEORIES   117

6 Sociological Concepts and Crime Causation   120

7 Strain Theories   135

15 Nutrition and Criminal Behavior   264

PART IV ■ PSYCHOLOGICAL THEORIES   283

16 Psychological Theories of Crime Causation   285

17 Emotional Problems and Mental Disorder Theories   298

21   Crime Typologies   370

22   Conclusion   401

Glossary   412

Bibliography   430

Index   436

Preface

At one time not too long ago, the naive but widely held belief was that all social problems, including crime, could be solved and solved easily. This feeling probably reached its height in 1960 with the election of a young energetic president and the "Camelot" mood he symbolized for the United States. John F. Kennedy's election signified a new direction for the United States of America. The American people, however, were rudely awakened with President Kennedy's assassination in 1963. The Kennedy assassination created the realization that a "crime-free" society was an impossibility. Most criminologists now consider crime as a conflict-ridden, unresolvable problem that will continue to plague our society.

Accepting the fact that the crime problem is here to stay, society should seek to obtain a better understanding of the problem and work to reduce it. The crime problem affects every one of us, regardless of social status, educational attainment, or geographic location. No one in today's world is immune from crime. Crime is all around us. We read about it daily in our newspapers. We hear about it daily on the radio and we see it daily on television. Americans today are inudated with crime. Both the layman and the criminology student cannot help but have an awareness of crime.

An objective of this text is to provide a forum or mechanism that takes abstract criminological concepts and applies them to basic, contemporary criminal justice examples. Criminology is not an esoteric subject with little or no reference to today's world. Criminology is a more significant part of the world today than it was in 1763 when Beccaria's famous essay *On Crimes and Punishments* was written. The text is presented in a way that makes criminological theory both practical and current.

Criminology courses in colleges and universities are designed to provide the criminal justice student with a better understanding of the crime phenomenon. This book was developed with that goal in mind. One of our main objectives was to create a textbook for students that will be easily understood and thus enable instructors to focus on selected criminological issues and topics during class time. Too often textbooks can be understood only by instructors, and thus valuable class time must be used to explain the meaning of the concepts covered in the text. To overcome this problem we followed the example of Ernest Hemingway and used familiar, concrete words and short sentences whenever possible. This approach should allow valuable class time to be used in meaningful discussion. Thought-provoking questions are asked in the chapters to encourage critical thinking on the part of students and to enhance classroom discussions.

Most criminology textbooks currently used cover the entire spectrum of the criminal justice system, with chapters on police, courts, and corrections in addition to several chapters on crime causation. This book emphasizes crime causation and does not attempt to cover all the aspects of criminal justice system. The book is designed to be used in situations where crime causation is the main focus of the course.

It has been our experience that many students do not remember criminological theories after taking a semester's course in the subject. We designed this book with the idea of remedying this situation by giving the student exposure to the many interesting and practical theories of crime causation. The text is arranged so that the student will be able to glance at the beginning of each chapter to get acquainted with the chapter's highlights and key terms. At the end of each chapter there is a matching key terms and definitions section and a discussion questions section.

The book is divided into five major parts. In Part I we present an overview of the development of Western criminological thought. Chapters are included on the important issues and questions in the study of crime, the early administration of justice, and the classical and the positive schools of criminology. Selected personal information and little known facts about the early criminological theorists are presented to enhance students' understanding of concepts.

In Part II we discuss the sociological approaches to crime causation. A chapter on basic sociological concepts and crime causation is included first, to provide the student with an understanding of the fundamental sociological concepts. The sociological approaches are divided into five major categories and a chapter is devoted to each category. The five categories are strain theories, control theories, conflict/radical theories, cultural deviance theories, and symbolic interactionist theories.

In Part III we present the biological approaches to crime causation. We include chapters that deal with heredity and crime, biological inferiority and body-type theories, difference and defectiveness theories, and nutrition theories. Nutrition theories have been ignored in most criminology texts and are currently gaining credibility and interest.

In Part IV we describe the psychological approaches to crime causation. Chapter 16 deals with Freudian and psychoanalytic contributions to crime causation theories. Other chapters in Part IV cover emotional problem and mental disorder theories, sociopathic personality theories, and thinking pattern theories. In Part V we discuss various crime problems and typologies and present conclusions.

A few acknowledgments are appropriate: Paul Corey, our editor, for his encouragement and invaluable assistance; our colleagues at California State University, Fresno, Professors Max Futrell, Dean Ray, Les Pincu, Jack Quinn, Tom Dull, Doug Shannon, Ed Bates, and Caren Horowitz, for acting as sounding boards for our ideas; Susan Stirling, for her assistance in obtaining the vast collection of material on nutrition and crime; Professors Marianne Hopper, St. Edwards University; William Archambeault, Louisianna State University; M. Dwayne Smith, Tulane University; Thomas L. Zane, Daytona Beach Community College; Gwynne Peirson, Howard University (Retired); Lee Edmond, Fresno City College and Clemens Bartollas, University of Northern Iowa, for reviewing the manuscript and making valuable and critical comments to improve it and help eliminate inconsistencies; Robin Button for her administrative assistance; and Barbara Zeiders for an admirable job of copy-editing. Most of the credit for the development of the book should go to the persons named above. We, however, take full credit for any errors that are discovered.

Ruth Masters
Cliff Roberson

In Loving Memory
of our Parents

Beatrice Elkins
Robert Elkins
Sue Roberson
Burell Roberson

A Prelude To the Study of Criminology

As a prelude to the study of criminology, this section contains a brief overview of the criminal justice system. The general discussions on the police, courts, and corrections presented should provide the reader with sufficient information to facilitate the study of crime causation.

It is customary to refer to the police, courts, and corrections as the "criminal justice system." There is, however, no single criminal justice system in the United States. The word "system" implies an orderly arrangement of subsystems according to a general plan or design. The separate systems, police, courts, and corrections, have, for the most part, little or no effective working relationships with each other. The phrase "criminal justice system" is used to describe the hodgepodge of separate systems that are involved in the detection, apprehension, adjudication, and correctional phases of criminal behavior.

■ THE ROLE OF THE POLICE

There are over 40,000 police agencies in the United States. The agencies are federal, state, or local in their organization, duties, and powers. Local police agencies comprise approximately 90 percent of the total number. The local agencies range in size from a one-officer police force in some small towns to the present 30,000-officer force in New York City. Accordingly, the roles and functions of the various police departments vary. The general functions of police agencies can be divided into three basic functional categories; law enforcement, order maintenance, and service. In many cases, officer duties involve more than one of the basic functional categories. For example, a police officer directing traffic is performing both order maintenance and service functions.

FEDERAL LAW ENFORCEMENT AGENCIES. For historical and constitutional reasons, the United States does not have a national police force. Therefore, there is no single federal agency responsible for the enforcement of federal laws. There are approximately fifty federal agencies involved in the enforcement of federal criminal law. The most visible agencies are the Federal Bureau of Investigation (FBI), Drug Enforcement Administration (DEA), Border Patrol, Secret Service, Bureau of Postal Inspection, U.S. Coast Guard, and Bureau of Alcohol, Firearms and Tobacco Tax (AFT).

STATE LAW ENFORCEMENT AGENCIES. Most states maintain law enforcement agencies that have general police powers. The names of the agencies may be misleading. For example, in some states the "state highway patrol" is a statewide law enforcement agency with general police power. In addition, all states have state agencies with restricted police powers; for example, alcohol beverage control boards in several states have police powers to enforce the alcohol control statutes.

LOCAL LAW ENFORCEMENT AGENCIES. The traditional police power in the United States is with local law enforcement agencies. For the most part, when we refer to police officers or police action, we are referring to local agencies. The local agencies are either urban or rural. Approximately 8 percent of local agencies are rural in nature.

Law Enforcement Function

The law enforcement function pertains to the duties of the police in enforcing criminal laws, detecting breaches of the law, and apprehending persons suspected of criminal behavior. The law enforcement function is also known as the "crime-fighting" function of the police. Most of the time when people are considering law enforcement as a career, they think only of the law enforcement function. The majority of an officer's time may, however, be directed toward order maintenance and service functions.

Order Maintenance

"Order maintenance function" refers to the duties of the police agency in preserving peace and security. As noted earlier, emphasis during the law enforcement function is in preventing and detecting violations of our criminal laws. During the order maintenance function, emphasis is on the preservation of peace. In this function, violations of the law are often overlooked in the effort to maintain order. For example, if a fight breaks out and an officer arrests the persons involved, the officer is engaged in the law enforcement function. If, however, the officer simply breaks up the fight and requires the participants to disperse, the officer is involved in the order maintenance function. (*Note:* In the latter case, the officer ignores the violations of the law in order to facilitate the keeping of peace. Also note that the decision of the officer as to whether this situation should be treated as a law enforcement or an order maintenance function is an example of the personal discretion that an individual police officer has. The aspects of personal discretion of police officers are discussed later in this section.)

One of the factors considered by officers when using an order maintenance approach to community problems rather than the crime-fighting approach is that our criminal justice system is ill equipped to handle total enforcement of the law. Presently, the police, courts, and correctional institutions are overloaded and the backlog continues each year. If all persons who commit violations of criminal statutes were arrested and prosecuted, there would be a gridlock or logjam in the system, resulting in chaos. Accordingly, the police practice "selective enforcement" of the law.

Service Function

The service function of police activities has little relationship to "crime fighting." It consists of tasks that provide services to the community. Examples of service functions include providing emergency assistance for injured or sick persons, supplying funeral escorts, locating missing persons, checking on elderly citizens, and rescuing cats from trees.

Since the service function has little relationship to law enforcement, why are the police generally used for this function? First, they are available twenty-four hours a day, seven days a week. Accordingly, they are available with the necessary resources when needed. Second, the average person trusts the police. In addition, the historical development of the police in our country has traditionally included the service function.

Several reform efforts have advocated removal of the service function from the police. The reformers give as reasons the following:

- Inflates and distorts the police budget
- Diminishes the police's ability to respond to law enforcement efforts
- Makes a police career less attractive to many persons

Arguments in favor of retaining service functions in police agencies include:

- Helps the police generate goodwill in the community, which is essential in law enforcement
- Provides the police department with community information that is useful in combating crime
- No other governmental agencies can perform the service tasks economically

Police departments vary greatly in the effort expended on service functions. Some departments have established special units of civilian employees rather than sworn police officers to handle the bulk of the service functions. Others have transferred the primary responsibility for service functions to other community agencies and to private organizations.

Patrol Units

The key police unit involved in the law enforcement function is normally the patrol unit. Patrol officers are visible on the scene in the community to prevent criminal conduct and to take action when criminal conduct occurs. The objectives of a standard patrol unit include:

- To inforce the law and arrest offenders.
- To deny persons the opportunity to commit crimes.
- To influence conditions that are otherwise conducive to crime conduct.
- To protect lives and property from criminal conduct.
- To provide instant response for police help.
- To maintain the peace of the community.
- To encourage voluntary compliance with the law.

Although the primary emphasis of the patrol officer is on law enforcement, the majority of a patrol officer's time is taken up by other functions. It is estimated that in most police departments, patrol officers devote no more than 10 to 20 percent of their time to "crime fighting."

■ POLICE DISCRETION

Police officers, because of their role, normally initiate the criminal justice process with an arrest or citation of a criminal suspect. When a police officer discovers the commission of a crime and the identity of the offender, the officer can ignore it, informally counsel the offender, arrest the offender, or issue the offender a citation and release the offender. If the officer either ignores the offense or handles it informally, no official reports are made regarding the offense. It is as if the offense never occurred. Accordingly, police officers have considerable personal discretion in determining the reaction that the criminal justice system will take in individual cases. For example, two persons are stopped by an officer for speeding. In one case, the officer issues the driver a ticket. Once the ticket is issued, the person is now involved in the system. In the second case, the officer warns the driver and releases him. Since no formal report is made in the second case, the criminal process is never initiated. For minor crimes and misdemeanors, probably no one else has so much personal discretion as the police officer at the scene. The police officer's decision to book, cite, or take no official action in most cases depends on the personal discretion of the officer.

Several years ago in a small city in the midwest, the practice of the police when stopping a drunk driver (except in extreme cases) was to require the driver to park the car and call someone to come and get him or her. No official reports were made of the incidents unless the driver was arrested. Now because of the social movement against driving under the influence of drugs and alcohol, the police officers in this city presently stop and arrest all persons suspected of driving under the influence. Accordingly, the numbers of driving under the in-

IN FOCUS

Does the Racial Makeup of a Community Influence a Police Officer's Discretion?

Dennis Powell studied five adjacent police jurisdictions to determine if the community's racial makeup influences police discretion. He concluded that police in a predominantly black urban community were more punitive toward whites than toward blacks. Police in predominantly white areas were, however, significantly more punitive toward black offenders than toward white offenders. In a similar study, Douglas Smith and Jody Klein found that the socioeconomic status of the neighborhood had a great deal of influence on an officer's use of discretion in domestic violence cases. Police were more likely to use formal law enforcement procedures in lower-class neighborhoods than in middle- and upper-class neighborhoods [1].

fluence offenses (DUI) reported in crime statistics are now much higher than those reported in prior years. By this change in policy, there was an increase in the number of DUI offenses recorded for this city.

One of the problems with personal discretion on the part of individual police officers is that the officer's use of discretion may result in unfavorable discrimination toward various groups of our society.

Organizational Style and Discretion

Often the organizational style of the police agency has a direct impact on the amount and type of discretion used by individual officers. James Q. Wilson grouped police agencies into three major forms; watchman, legalistic, and service [2].

WATCHMAN STYLE. The organizational form of the watchman style is flat and narrow: flat in that there is little opportunity for advancement, and narrow because of limited differentiation in the types of work that each officer does. According to James Q. Wilson, the watchman style exists in cities with heavy political patronage and little response to community needs. This style also tends to experience more police corruption than other styles. Promotion is a function of "who you know" and inservice training is almost nonexistent. The pay is low and rewards for good work are limited. According to Wilson, in the watchman style of organization, "there will be few places in which he [the officer] can be transferred in the department and few incentives to seek transfer there. Most men will spend most of their police lives on patrol; unless they make detective" [3].

Since not much is expected of the officers, they have a wide range of discretion and tend to handle matters informally rather than invoking the system officially. The common practice is to keep drunks off the street and maintain a general appearance of order. In corrupt departments, discretion is often used as a weapon for shakedowns and bribes.

LEGALISTIC STYLE. In departments using the legalistic style, a high degree of control is maintained over individual officers. The high degree of control is accomplished by handling every call as a law enforcement matter. Accordingly, for every response the officer must make a report. For example, if an officer makes a traffic stop, the officer first calls in and reports the car and its license plate number and the reason for the stop. If the officer does not issue a citation, the officer must explain the reasons for not doing so. In lieu of relying on the officer's assessment of the situation and judgment, there are numerous regulations and controls (often referred to as standards) to guide the officer. In this style of organization, the individual officer has little personal discretion.

SERVICE STYLE. The service style, according to Wilson, is an attempt to combine the efficiency of the legalistic style and the broad informal discretion of the watchman style. Under the service style, the police take seriously all requests for assistance or service, but are less likely to respond by making an arrest or issuing a citation. The service-style organization is decentralized in order to maintain a sense of local community-oriented police. Community relations are a high priority with service-oriented police departments.

The service-style orientation does not measure an individual officer's performance on the number of arrests or citations issued, but on how appropriate the officer handles various situations. The individual officer has considerable personal discretion in responding to assistance or service requests.

Situational Elements of Discretion

In those police agencies where the officer has considerable personal discretion, the major variables that affect an individual officer's discretional decision during a typical encounter between an officer and an offender include the following factors [4]:

1. *Seriousness of the crime.* The most important variable is the seriousness of the crime. Major felonies (e.g., murder, rape, serious batteries) will in all likelihood be handled as crimes and will be treated as law enforcement functions.

2. *Demeanor of the offender.* In less serious crimes, the demeanor of the offender is often a significant factor in the officer's decision to handle the matter officially. Think about the last time that you were stopped for a traffic violation. When the officer first approached your automobile, why did you treat the officer with respect? Were you hoping that your pleasant demeanor would influence the officer not to write you a ticket?

3. *Offender's previous involvement in the criminal justice system as a client.* If the officer is aware that a person has a prior record, the officer is more likely to handle the matter as a law enforcement function (i.e., an arrest or citation).

4. *Presence of a victim who requests official action.* Studies indicate that officers are more likely to cite or arrest offenders if there is a

Who Is a Criminal?

After pleading "no contest" to charges of taking kickbacks on government contracts, a former governor of Maryland and U.S. vice-president stated: "Honesty is different things to different people."

An article in a Canadian prison newspaper stated: "There is only one difference between the men in this prison and a great number of your readers. We were caught" [5].

victim present who demands formal police action. (*Note:* One of the effects of the recent victims' rights movement is the limitation of police discretion when dealing with certain categories of crime.)

■ THE JUDICIAL SYSTEM

There are two basic criminal court systems in the United States, federal and state. The term "dual federalism" is often used to describe the concept of two separate court systems. Over 95 percent of the criminal cases, however, are tried in state courts. There are at least five counties in the United States whose courts each year prosecute more criminal cases than are prosecuted annually in the entire federal system. For example, the local state courts in Cook County, Illinois (Chicago), try twice as many criminal cases each year as are tried in the entire federal system.

Courts are classified as either trial or appellate. Trial courts are the courts where cases are originally tried. It is in the trial court that witnesses testify, evidence is presented, and findings of guilty or not guilty are made. An appellate court reviews cases that have been decided in a trial court. The appellate court makes its decision based on the record of trial in the trial court, trial briefs submitted by attorneys, and oral arguments presented by the attorneys. No witnesses or evidence is presented before an appellate court. Whereas the trial court makes findings of guilty or not guilty, an appellate court merely passes on the legal correctness of the trial as reflected in the documents before the court. If the appellate court determines that the accused was denied a fair trial, the appellate court will return the case to the original trial court for corrective action.

Under the protection of the U.S. Constitution, individuals tried in state courts have the right to a jury trial in all cases where they may receive six or more months confinement in jail or prison. In federal court, a person has the right to a jury trial in all criminal cases. (*Note:* A jury trial is available only in the trial courts.)

The phrase "courts of record" refer to those courts that keep a permanent record of their proceedings. Most felony trial courts and appellate courts are courts of record.

Federal System

> U.S. SUPREME COURT (USSC)   The judicial power of the United States shall be invested in one Supreme Court. . . .   (U.S. Constitution, Art. III, sec. 1)

The U.S. Supreme Court is the highest court in the federal system. The court is composed of one Chief Justice and eight associate justices. Justices are appointed by the President with the "advice and consent" of the U.S. Senate. Justices may be removed only by impeachment. The court always decides cases as one body. Except in unusual situations, the court acts as an appellate court and decides cases based on trial briefs, records of trial from the trial courts, and arguments of counsel.

> U.S. COURTS OF APPEAL (USCA).   The United States is divided geographically into twelve judicial circuits (including the District of Columbia,) which has its own circuit and is the only one not designated numerically. A U.S. Court of Appeal is located in each judicial "circuit." Like Supreme Court justices, courts of appeal judges are appointed by the President with the "advice and consent" of the Senate. The courts of appeal differ in the number of justices appointed to each. For example, the Court of Appeals for the 9th Circuit has twenty-eight judges. The courts of appeal normally hear cases in panels of three or five judges. In rare cases, a court of appeal will decide a case "in bank" (i.e., as a whole court).

> U.S. DISTRICT COURTS (USDC).   The basic trial court in the federal system is the U.S. District Court (USDC). There is at least one district court in each state. Most states have more than one district court. In those states, the state is divided geographically into federal judicial districts. For example, in New York, there is the U.S. District Court for the Southern District of New York.

District court judges are appointed by the President with the "advice and consent" of the Senate. District judges are appointed for life. In most judicial districts, there is more than one judge sitting as the district court. For example, the U.S. District Court for the Southern District of New York has over 100 judges each sitting as the District Court for the Southern District of New York.

In special cases (rarely) the USDC can sit and decide a case as a three-judge district court. The vast majority of cases are presided over by a single judge. In all criminal cases heard in the USDC, the accused has the right to a jury trial.

U.S. MAGISTRATES. U.S. magistrates are part of the federal judicial system but are not considered as separate courts. The magistrates are required to be attorneys and are appointed by the presiding judge of the judicial district for a specific term. Magistrates try minor offenses and perform pretrial matters and similar duties. They are considered as judicial officers and therefore can issue search and arrest warrants.

State Court Systems

State court systems are structured similar to the federal system. Lower trial courts (e.g., municipal and justice courts) are used to prosecute misdemeanors, and courts of record (e.g., district or superior courts) are used to prosecute felonies. In most cases, municipal courts are lower trial courts located in urban areas, and justice courts are lower trial courts located in rural areas. Most states have a state supreme court and intermediate courts of appeal for appellate functions. In two states, Oklahoma and Texas, the state supreme court handles only civil

IN FOCUS

U.S. Constitution, Sixth Amendment (enacted 1791)

In all criminal prosecutions, the accused shall enjoy the right to a speedy and public trial, by an impartial jury of the State and district wherein the crime shall have been committed, which district shall have been previously ascertained by law, and to be informed of the nature and cause of the accusation; to be confronted with the witnesses against him; to have compulsory process for obtaining Witnesses in his favor, and to have the Assistance of Consel for his defense.

matters. In those two states, the state court of criminal appeals performs the same functions in criminal matters as are performed by other state supreme courts.

Federal or State Action

If a person commits an offense that is a violation of a federal statute, he or she can be tried in federal court. If the offense is a violation of a state law, the state trial court will have jurisdiction. In some cases, the same act may be both a federal and state offense. For example, robbing a federally insured bank in Kansas City, Missouri, is a violation of the Missouri crime of robbery. It is also the federal crime of robbing a federally insured bank. In this example, since the person committed two crimes, he or she may be prosecuted in both federal and state court. In most situations such as this, one jurisdiction (state or federal) will defer prosecution if the other prosecutes. [*Note:* It is not double jeopardy to prosecute in both courts since there are two separate crimes involved (even though only one act) and two different jurisdictions (state and federal).]

State Issues in Federal Court

State courts try state crimes and federal courts try federal crimes. Also, the state high courts make final rulings on state issues and the U.S. Supreme Court makes final rulings on federal issues. How do the U.S. Supreme Court and other federal courts obtain jurisdiction to decide issues involving the trial of state criminal cases? The jurisdiction (power) of federal courts is limited to federal issues. Accordingly, for a federal court to decide issues involving state criminal cases, there must be a federal question involved. In most cases, the federal question is based on a claim by the defendant that his or her federal constitutional rights are being violated by the state court. An example of this is presented in the *Mapp* v. *Ohio* "In Focus" feature.

Prosecution of Criminal Cases

Federal cases are prosecuted in the name of "United States" versus the defendant (e.g., *United States* v. *Watson*). State cases are prosecuted in the name of the "People," "Commonwealth," or in the name of the state (e.g., *People* v. *Watson, Commonwealth* v. *Watson,* or *Iowa* v. *Watson*). In criminal cases, the prosecution must establish the guilt of the accused beyond a reasonable doubt.

IN FOCUS

Mapp v. Ohio

Dollree Mapp was convicted of knowingly having in her possession and under her control some lewd and lascivious pictures. The pictures, which were used as evidence in her conviction, were taken by police officers during execution of an illegal search.

Ms. Mapp lived alone with her 15-year-old daughter in a second-floor apartment in Cleveland, Ohio. On May 23, 1957, three police officers arrived at the home, rang her doorbell, and were asked the purpose of their visit. The police stated that they desired to talk to her. Ms. Mapp informed them that she would admit them only if they had a search warrant. The officers did not enter at that time but kept the home under observation for the next three hours. Other police officers arrived. The police then broke a glass to the rear door and entered the apartment. An officer waved a piece of paper, purporting to be a search warrant, at her. Ms. Mapp grabbed the paper and placed it down her dress. (There was no warrant.) The officer, after a brief struggle, was able to retrieve it. Ms. Mapp was then handcuffed and forced to sit on her own bed.

The officers searched her upstairs bedroom. In her dresser, a photo album and other personal papers were taken. A trunk was also searched and found to contain obscene materials. At Ms. Mapp's trial in a state court, her attorney objected to the introduction of the pictures and other obscene materials, taken from her apartment in violation of her rights under the Fourth and Fourteenth Amendments of the U.S. Constitution. She was convicted and the conviction was upheld (approved) by the Ohio Supreme Court. Ms. Mapp appealed to the U.S. Supreme Court, alleging that the conviction was in violation of her U.S. Constitutional rights as a U.S. citizen. The high court agreed with her and reversed her conviction. (*Note:* During the decision in this case, the Supreme Court instituted the "exclusionary" rule.)

The judge is the primary officer of the court. The judge is responsible for seeing that the case is resolved. Trial court judges also issue search warrants, arrest warrants, set bail amounts, and hold preliminary hearings. The judge decides on all issues of law; in trials without a jury, on the guilt or innocence of the accused; and in most states, the judge also decides on the appropriate sentence after a conviction. Judges are elected by the people in most states; in the other states, the judges are usually appointed by the governor and approved by the state legislature.

Federal cases are normally prosecuted by assistant U.S. attorneys. There is a U.S. Attorney's office in each federal judicial district. State prosecutors are normally assistant district attorneys or assistant state attorneys. The primary ethical obligation of the prosecutor is not to prosecute but to ensure justice. Accordingly, a prosecutor should not prosecute a person that the prosecutor believes is not guilty of the offense charged.

Defending the Accused

The U.S. Constitution guarantees every accused the right to the assistance of counsel in defending any criminal case. Even Ted Bundy, who brutally murdered over thirty young women, had a right to the assistance of counsel in his cases. Even if an attorney knows that his or her client is guilty, the attorney has a duty to use any legal methods or tactics to prevent the conviction of the accused. An attorney may therefore ethically plead the accused "not guilty" even though the attorney knows that the accused committed the crime charged. This is based on the concept that even the worst criminal has the right to the assistance of a counsel who will protect the interests of the accused. The adversary model of our criminal court process requires that the defense attorney represent the client's interest to the best of the attorney's ability. [Note: This means that in some cases the defense attorney should attempt to prevent conviction of the accused by protecting the client's constitutional and procedural rights. In others, the attorney should attempt to obtain the lightest sentence possible for the accused (in a negotiator role).]

Defense counsel are either retained (hired) by the accused or appointed by the state. If a person is being prosecuted for a crime for which he or she could be incarcerated, the accused has a right to an appointed counsel if he or she cannot afford to retain one. States use two basic methods to supply appointed counsel to accused who cannot afford to hire an attorney. A popular method is by the use of public defenders, who are attorneys employed by the state for appointment by courts as defense counsel. In the second method, the judge appoints a private attorney to defend the accused for a particular case only. In appointing private attorneys, judges usually rotate appointments among attorneys in active practice in the community.

IN FOCUS

Argersinger v. Hamlin
Supreme Court of the United States, 1972
(407 U.S. 25)

Mr. Justice Douglas delivered the opinion of the Court.

Petitioner, an indigent, was charged in Florida with carrying a concealed weapon, an offense punishable by imprisonment up to six months and a $1,000 fine. He was sentenced to serve 90 days in jail. . . . [He appealed his conviction claiming that he was deprived of his right to counsel. As an indigent he had requested the appointment of counsel, but the trial court denied the request.]

A person's right to reasonable notice of a charge against him, and an opportunity to be heard in his defense—a right to his day in court—are basic in our system of jurisprudence; and these rights include, as a minimum, a right to examine the witnesses against him, to offer testimony, and to be represented by counsel.

We hold . . . that absent a knowing and intelligent waiver, no person may be imprisoned for any offense, whether classified as petty, misdemeanor, or felony, unless he was represented by counsel at his trial.

. . . The requirement of counsel may well be necessary for a fair trial, even in a petty offense prosecution. We are by no means convinced that legal and constitutional questions involved in a case that leads to imprisonment, even for a brief period, are any less complex than when a person can be sent off for six months or more . . . The trial of vagrancy cases is illustrative. While only brief sentences of imprisonment may be imposed, the cases often bristle with thorny constitutional questions.

Plea Bargaining

Over 90 percent of the cases tried in criminal courts are guilty plea cases. An average guilty plea case takes only minutes of the court's time to complete. A not guilty plea case can take weeks and even months to complete. If every accused person pleaded not guilty and demanded a jury trial, our court system would be in total chaos. It is therefore to the government's benefit to encourage guilty pleas in criminal cases.

IN FOCUS

U.S. Constitution, Fourteen Amendment, Section 1 (enacted 1868)

All persons born or naturalized in the United States and subject to the jurisdiction thereof, are citizens of the United States and of the State wherein they reside. No State shall make or enforce any law which shall abridge the privileges or immunities of citizens of the United States; nor shall any State deprive any person of life, liberty, or property, without due process of law; nor deny to any person within its jurisdiction the equal protection of the laws.

One of the most controversial aspects of the criminal court process is the practice of "plea bargaining." A plea bargain is an agreement made between the prosecution and the defense whereby the accused pleads guilty in return for a lighter sentence, reduction in charges, or a recommendation for leniency. In most plea bargain situations, the guilt of the accused is taken for granted. The government saves resources and time by the plea bargain, and the defendant normally gets a lighter sentence. A major concern about plea bargaining is the feeling by many that because of the bargaining, many offenders receive light sentences for relatively serious crimes. Numerous reform movements have attempted to stop the practice of plea bargains. In general, the movements were unsuccessful.

▌ CORRECTIONS

There are four different rationales for punishing persons convicted of crimes: retribution, rehabilitation, incapacitation, and deterrence. Of the four, all but retribution are based on the concept of crime prevention. Often, the punishment imposed on an accused reflects a combination of two or more of these four rationales.

Retribution

Retribution is based on the concept of "just deserts." The person has committed a crime against society and therefore, he or she deserves to be punished. Under this rationale, if the crime is minor, the "just deserts" (punishment) should be minor. Accordingly, the death penalty is not justified for a parking ticket. The rationale could be expressed with the Biblical expression "an eye for an eye." For most of this century, this rationale was not very popular as a justification for sentencing convicted persons. One reason for its disfavor was the mistaken belief that it was a form of revenge. Revenge is punishment imposed based on the subjective passions of the punishers, whereas retribution is based on the principle of a debt owed to society. According to retributivists, society has a moral duty to punish because not to do so negates the very idea of crime [6].

In recent years, there has been an increase in the popularity of this rationale. According to present-day retributivists, there is only one possible justification for specific penalties for specific crimes. A specified punishment is justified when a convicted person has received a punishment that reflects the gravity of his or her offense. The punishment, therefore, should fit the crime. How do we make the punishment fit the crime? Possibilities for this include [7]:

- Make the punishment mirror the crime (an eye for an eye).
- Adjust the punishment according to the social harm resulting from the crime.
- Link the punishment to the moral outrage felt by a majority of the community affected by the crime.

Rehabilitation

Rehabilitation is based on the concept of what punishment is necessary to rehabilitate the offender. The punishment should not necessarily fit the crime. This rationale focuses on the fact that the offender has committed a crime and thus needs to be reformed. By turning the offender into a law-abiding citizen with treatment and reform, society will be protected from future crime being committed by this person. The punishment, therefore, should fit the criminal, not the crime. In the 1960s, this was a popular rationale for sentencing criminals. Criminals were to be treated, not punished. During this period, many of our prisons were renamed "correctional facilities."

Incapacitation

Incapacitation protects society by removing the offender from society to prevent him or her from committing additional offenses. The most common form of incapacitation is imprisonment. The death penalty is another form of incapacitation advocated by some. Under the extreme forms of this rationale, prisons should be only warehouses to keep criminals incapacitated and away from society.

A problem with incapacitation is the inability of society to predict who will commit crimes in the future. Accordingly, persons may be released from imprisonment who will commit future crimes and others may be retained in prison who would not commit future crimes when released. An additional problem is that the seriousness of the crime committed may bear no relationship to the likelihood of the person committing a future crime.

Deterrence

Deterrence is based on the concept of protecting society from further harm by the criminal. There are two types of deterrence, individual and general. Individual deterrence seeks to teach the offender a lesson and thus deter him or her from engaging in further illegal action. A parent spanking a child who has been naughty is one form of individual deterrence. General deterrence aims to discourage others from committing criminal offenses by making an example of the offender. For example, sentencing a person who commits a robbery to five years in prison may deter others from committing future robberies.

Sentencing Strategies and Goals

There are three primary sentencing strategies used by criminal courts when a sentence involving confinement is given: indeterminate sentences, determinate sentences, and mandatory sentences. Most states have a predominate orientation toward one of the three strategies. The most popular appears to be the determinate sentencing strategy.

INDETERMINATE SENTENCES. Indeterminate sentences normally place a maximum and minimum term of confinement (e.g., five to ten years). The exact period of confinement is determined by a decision of the parole authorities. Normally, it depends on the treatment success of the prisoner.

DETERMINATE SENTENCES. Determinate sentences provide fixed terms of confinements. The terms, however, may be reduced by good time or parole. Determinate sentencing systems usually provide for a base sentence that is increased or decreased for aggravating or mitigating factors. For example, if the base term for robbery is five years, the standard sentence for robbery would be five years. If the accused

used a firearm during the commission of the offense, it may be required that an additional two years be added to the base term, making the sentence seven years.

MANDATORY SENTENCES.   Mandatory sentences are established by statutes, and if a person is convicted of the crime, the sentence prescribed by the statute must be given. Crimes for which mandatory sentencing statutes have been used include driving under the influence of alcohol, murder, drug offenses, and robbery.

Confinement

Confinement is a popular method of punishing persons convicted of committing criminal offenses. It is also used to detain persons awaiting trial who do not qualify or cannot make bail. There are two basic types of confinement facilities: (1) jails or detention facilities and (2) prisons or correctional institutions.

JAILS AND DETENTION FACILITIES.   Jails and detention facilities are primarily the responsibility of local governmental units. There are three standard types of detention facilities:

- Pretrial detention facility used to confine persons who are awaiting trial
- Sentenced offender facility in which convicted persons serve sentences (usually for misdemeanors)
- Combined jail facility, used for both pretrial and convicted offenders (the most common type of jail in the United States)

PRISONS AND CORRECTIONAL FACILITIES.   Imprisonment as a means of punishment is a relatively modern practice developed in America. It was originally developed to replace the harsher penalties of death and torture. Presently, imprisonment in a prison or correctional facility is used only for persons convicted of felonies (serious offenses). Unlike jails, prisons and correctional facilities are primarily the responsibility of state governments.

Probation and Parole

Two popular alternatives to prison are probation and parole. The majority of persons convicted of felonies are placed on probation. Both probation and parole are forms of release to the community under supervision.

PROBATION. Probation originated with suspended sentences. A person given a probated sentence stays out of prison as long as he or she maintains good behavior. A person under probation is still under the jurisdiction of the court. The two chief factors that determine whether a person goes to prison or is placed on probation are (1) the seriousness of the offense and (2) the seriousness of the accused's prior record.

PAROLE. Parole is the process by which an imprisoned offender is released before the expiration of the sentence. The person is released under a conditional supervised plan. If the person fails to complete the plan, he or she may be returned to prison to serve the remainder of the sentence. The decision to grant parole is normally made by an administrative body known as a parole board. In some states, the decision of the parole board must be approved by the governor. The parole board also makes the decision to return a person to prison if the person has committed a new crime or violated the conditions of parole.

■ DISCUSSION QUESTIONS

1. What is the importance of police discretion in studying criminal behavior?
2. How do the duties of the prosecutor and defense counsel differ?
3. Should the government enter into contracts (plea bargains) with criminals?
4. Which rationale for sentencing should be used? Justify your answer.
5. What are the major differences between probation and parole?

Notes

1. Denis Powell, "Race, Rank, and Police Discretion," *Journal of Police Science and Administration*, vol. 9, 1981, pp. 383–89; and Douglas Smith and Jody Klein, "Police Control of Interpersonal Disputes," *Social Problems*, vol. 31, 1984, pp. 468–481.

2. James Q. Wilson, *Varieties of Police Behavior.* Cambridge, Mass.: Harvard University Press, 1968, p. 155.

3. Wilson, 1968:155–157.

4. Albert J. Reiss, Jr., *The Police and the Public.* New Haven, Conn.: Yale University Press, 1971.

5. Gwynne Nettler, *Criminology Lessons.* Cincinnati, Ohio: Anderson, 1988, p. 38.

6. See Stanley Grupp, ed., *Theories of Punishment.* Bloomington, Ind.: Indiana University Press, 1971.

7. See Don Gibbons, "Crime and Punishment: A Study in Social Attitudes," *Social Forces,* vol. 47, June 1969, pp. 391–397.

DEVELOPMENT OF WESTERN CRIMINOLOGY

In Chapter 1, analyses of the important issues in the study of crime are presented. The subject of crime causation and functions of crime are also discussed. Included in Chapter 1 is a discussion of the importance of criminological theory and how to evaluate theories. In Chapter 2 we trace the development of criminal law as a social control mechanism. Chapter 2 includes an examination of the influences of the Babylonians, Ancient Hebrews, Greeks, Romans, and the early Western Europeans. In Chapter 3 we discuss how criminal behavior is measured and some of the problems in determining the extent of crime in society. Chapter 4 deals with classical criminology and includes discussions on the importance of the contributions of Cesare Becarria and Jeremy Bentham. In Chapter 5 we examine the early positive approaches to crime causation and the contributions Cesare Lombroso and other early positivist theorists made to criminological theory.

The Study of Crime

CHAPTER HIGHLIGHTS

- Criminology is a study of people.
- Criminology is most often a practical and applied social science.
- Crime has a function in society.
- Defining the term "crime" is not simple.
- Modifications of criminal statutes change the definition of conduct considered to be criminal.
- Criminological theories tend to be descriptive and explanatory in nature.
- Criminological theories may be classified in many ways.
- Criminological theories tend to be stable and do not change frequently.

KEY TERMS

Applied Research	Macrotheories
Classical Theories	Microtheories
Conflict Theories	Multifactor Approach
Consensus Theories	Positive Theories
Criminal	Process Theories
Criminology	Pure Research
Durkheim	Social Definition of Crime
Etiology	Structural Theories
Legal Definition of Crime	

Criminology is the study of criminals, crime prevention, sociology of law, and the social processes involved in crime causation. Criminology is also the study of etiological (causal) variables related to criminal behavior.

The study of crime causation is exciting for several reasons. First, it is exciting because it is the analysis of human nature, people, drama, and how human beings solve problems. Second, crime is an underlying theme in much of our entertainment, such as our literature, movies, and television programs. All one need do is to visit a local bookstore and browse among the books on display. In how many books is crime the main plot? The answer is simple: most of them. An illustration of this point is that a major bookstore chain even publishes a complementary newsletter entitled "Crime Times" to encourage its customers to buy books about crime. We are inundated with crime in various forms and are intrigued by criminals and their antics. For most of us, we often see the criminal in diametrically opposed ways: exciting and despicable, repulsive and lovable. We are sometimes attracted to the criminal and, at the same time, recoil from him or her.

When introduced to the study of any theory, especially criminological theories, many students immediately think of a dry, abstract subject. They fail to realize that the study of theory is the study of dynamic, surprising, and ever-changing life. We use theory as a basic part of our everyday life [1]. Theory helps us in abstract reasoning. For example, if we go for a drive on a holiday weekend, we may theorize that there will be more traffic than normal on the highways and that the chances of encountering a drunk driver are higher than usual. This is an example of the use of theory in our reasoning process to alert us to be careful. As you read a murder mystery, you use your theoretical concepts of crime to help solve the questions of who committed the crime and why the murderer did it.

▌ A DEFINITION OF THEORY

Defining "theory" is a difficult task and any attempt to do so will include, of necessity, some degree of arbitrariness. Criminologists cannot agree among themselves as to what constitutes "theory." We have

FIGURE 1–1
Early forms of
punishment were very
cruel and inhumane.
Courtesy of the
Bettmann Archive

used a middle-of-the-road approach to defining "theory." We are aware
that some criminologists may criticize this approach for being too general; however, it provides a good working definition.

Theory is simply an explanation of a particular phenomenon.
Theory is also defined as a body of logically, empirically interrelated
propositions that permit explanatory statements to be made regarding
the phenomena being studied [2]. Theories refer to scientifically-based
explanations and must meet certain criteria requiring empirical verification. Theories are inclusive and general.

Scientific theories tend to make statements about the relationship
between two classes of phenomena. For example, a theoretical statement regarding the relationship between success in school and the
likelihood of involvement in juvenile crime is a statement regarding
the relationship between two classes of phenomena: education and
juvenile crime. An essential characteristic of a scientific theory is that
it makes assertive statements that can be proved or disproved [3]. If
an assertive statement cannot be proved or disproved, it is not a
scientific theory.

To gain acceptance, a theory should be consistent with the basic
facts of the phenomena it is trying to explain. A common criticism of
theory is that it narrows what we see. That when we accept a theory
as correct, we tend to see only those facts that support our theory. For
example, if we theorize that one ethnic group is more likely to be involved in organized crime than other ethnic groups, we tend to think
of involvement in organized crime as synonymous with that ethnic
group. Another criticism of theory is that it creates a tendency to generalize and oversimplify complex phenomena.

The study of crime causation is not the study of dry, abstract theories, but is the study of human nature, motives, psychology, and should have the same excitement as literature, movies, and television programs. Theory should be used and applied, not memorized and thrown away at the end of the semester.

■ MULTIFACTOR APPROACH

The multifactor approach is a popular research orientation in criminology today. This approach assumes that there are many different variables that contribute to criminality. The multiple-factor orientation, however, has not always enjoyed such popularity. The early biological and psychological theories centered around the idea of a single factor to account for all criminal behavior. The early criminological theorists did not entertain the idea that criminal behavior could be caused by two, three, or more factors working together.

The multifactor-approach orientation in criminology was largely the result of single-factor opponents conducting research and concluding that many different factors contribute to criminal behavior. All the single-factor critics had to do was to find the crime-causing single factor was found equally among criminals and noncriminals to discredit the position of the advocates of the single factor approach to the explanation of criminal behavior.

Today it is thought that psychological, biological, and sociological factors contribute to criminal behavior alone or in combination. Different crimes will therefore be the result of different combinations of factors. Accordingly, the logical approach in criminology is an eclectic one, emphasizing the identification and analysis of multiple factors.

The multifactor approach has been criticized on the following grounds:

1. Multifactor-approach advocates confuse explanation by use of a single theory with single-factor explanations. Theories tend to use a number of different variables, and a list of variables does not constitute a theory.

2. Multifactor-approach advocates forget that correlation does not mean causation. Just because certain variables are positively associated with crime, it does not mean that they cause it. For example, speeding and traffic accidents may be associated, but it does not mean that driving fast necessarily causes traffic accidents.

3. Multifactor-approach advocates fall into the "evil causes evil" fallacy. An evil outcome such as crime must be produced by evil causes.

When we analyze what causes crime, we must be eclectic and provide room for many different factors, all bearing a direct or indirect relationship to criminality. The truth is that psychological, biological, and sociological factors all contribute to criminality. Today, single- and multiple-factor explanations are used to explain criminal behavior. Multiple-factor orientations enjoy popularity today; however, most multiple-factor orientations tend not to be explanations at all, in that they are stated ambiguously and do not contain researchable propositions. A true explanation for criminal behavior and crime would exist if we could say with confidence that if conditions A, B, C, and D occurred, crime would result, and in the absence of conditions A, B, C, and D, crime would not occur. To date, we cannot predict crime with such accuracy.

The challenge for future criminologists is to develop clear, precise, unified theories of crime. If the theories of crime are to be unified, criminologists must become more precise and explicit in their

IN FOCUS

Crime—An Essential Industry?

Several years ago there was a study that examined the economic effects of an effective comprehensive arms-control treaty. The researcher concluded that if nations stopped spending money on defense, the loss of jobs would cause a worldwide depression. A similar situation exists within the criminal justice system. In many ways, the criminal justice system can be described as a "recession-proof" industry.

For example, in 1985, federal, state, and local governments spent $48.5 billion on the criminal justice system. In 1986, there were over 533,000 full-time police officers in the United States. In addition to the police officers, it was estimated that 1.1 million people were employed in security positions with private employers [5].

Is crime a necessary evil?

Is crime, like poverty, apparently always present in our society?

If we were to eliminate crime, how would we create enough new jobs to handle those formerly employed in the criminal justice system?

descriptions of the psychological, biological, and sociological factors of crime causation. To meet this challenge, not only is more in-depth knowledge regarding the phenomenon of crime required, but the organization and coordination of existing knowledge in a coherent theoretical framework must also occur [4].

■ FUNCTIONS OF CRIME IN SOCIETY

> The inescapable conclusion is that society secretly wants crime, needs crime, and gains definite satisfactions from the present mishandling of it.   (Karl Menninger, *The Crime of Punishment*)

Emile Durkheim, noted French sociologist, contended that crime was an integral part of all societies. (For more discussion on Durkheim's ideas, see Chapters 7 and 8.) He believed that a society totally devoid of crime was impossible to achieve and that such a society would not be an ideal or preferable one. According to Durkheim, the dominant group in society defines certain behavior as undesirable and, therefore, punishable. In any society where people are allowed to act as "individuals," it is inevitable that some acts will be labeled as deviant and/or criminal. A society where people are not allowed to act differently or to be "individuals" is clonelike and boring. According to Durkheim, this would be far worse than a society of people who act in unique, individual ways, even if it means that they commit crimes[6].

According to Durkheim and other theorists, the functions of crime in society include the following:

1. *Crime provides us with a method to measure the good and bad in the society.* Durkheim saw a need in society for the ability to deviate. By not committing criminal acts, we are considered as good and better than those who commit criminal acts. We use the criminal as a yardstick by which to measure ourselves. If no one committed any criminal acts, we would all be the same. There would be no good or bad citizens; everyone would be the same: colorless and boring. In summary, crime sets the "outer limits" for our behavior. If we go beyond such limits, society will take action against us. An example of this point is an unsigned article in a prison newspaper which stated: "No one is completely worthless—the worst member in society can at least serve as a bad example."

2. *Crime is a major industry.* Crime creates many jobs. If a genius discovered a method to end crime suddenly, think of how many people would be unemployed: police officers, correctional persons, lawyers, judges, security guards, criminologists, and so on. The economic impact on our economy would be catastrophic.

3. *Crime serves to unite various segments of the population.* It creates "social solidarity." People will unite against "bad guys." The two classic examples of criminals uniting a city are the "Boston Strangler" and the "Son of Sam" cases. Kai Erikson, professor of sociology at Yale University, holds the view that "deviant behavior is an ingredient in the glue that holds a community together." According to him, the criminal violates rules of conduct that the rest of the community hold in high respect [7]. When the citizens band together to express their outrage and to prosecute the offender, they develop a bond of solidarity.

4. *Crime can contribute to the efficiency of social life.* It provides for creativity. For example, in Los Angeles, two young computer wizards dissected telephone codes and were able to instruct the telephone company to deliver expensive equipment to selected addresses. They then sold the equipment. It was a considerable time before the telephone company discovered what was happening and proceeded to "catch" the criminals. Eventually, the youths were apprehended. The telephone company, however, could not figure out the actual procedures used by the criminals. As part of a plea bargain, the techniques used were demonstrated to the telephone company and the young criminals were hired by the telephone company as computer-crime prevention consultants[8].

5. *Crime can serve as a warning that something is wrong with society.* For example, increased criminal violations of the federal income tax

IN FOCUS

Society first creates thieves, then punishes them for stealing.   (Sir Thomas More, *Utopia*)

How does the quote above indicate the symbiotic relationship between the criminal and society?

Weisser states: "It is not so much that society tolerates crime; rather the structure of modern society inevitably creates situations and circumstances in which crime occurs" [9]. How are the two quotes by More and Weisser supportive of each other? How are they not supportive of each other?

statutes may indicate that our federal income tax law needs major revisions.

6. *Crime can serve as a warning that something is wrong with the social organizations within a community.* An increase in crime within a community may indicate that the community social organizations are disorganized and are failing its citizens.

7. *A certain amount of crime can serve as a safety valve for society.* It prevents an excessive accumulation of discontent and takes some of the strain off society. For example, the racial riots of the 1960s and 1970s tended to alert the mainstream society that there were significant societal problems that needed to be corrected.

■ NATURE OF LAW

Stephen Schafer defines ''law'' as the formal expression of the value system of the prevailing social power of the culture [10]. Law serves the purpose of affirming the values of the ruling social power. For example, one of the social values of the American culture is that our children should be educated. Accordingly, there are laws designed to encourage this value by restricting child labor and requiring compulsory school attendance. There are numerous conflicting opinions regarding the ''nature'' of the law. Listed below are five of the leading concepts.

1. *Law has a supernatural origin.* The authority to distinguish between right and wrong is based on the existence of supernatural beings. Under this concept, crime and sin are merged into a single phenomenon. There is little disagreement with the fact that early in our history, law and religion were interwoven into one concept. The Ten Commandments and the Code of Hammurabi were dominated by religious doctrines [11].

2. *Law is justice.* This concept is based on early Greek philosophy and the search for justice. Under this concept, the questions ''What is law?'' and ''What is justice?'' are the same. Plato's ideal world would be one ruled by philosophers who provided justice for all (an aristocratic form of rule).

3. *Law is a function of the sovereign.* Under this concept, law is not dependent on anything for its validity except the supreme power of the state.

4. *Law is a utilitarian concept.* This concept of law is based on the utilitarian principle that human conduct depends on the balance between pain and pleasure. People tend to maximize pleasure and minimize pain.

5. *Law is an instrument of the ruling class.* Under this concept, law is an economic tool of the ruling class used to retain power and further their own interests.

■ WHAT IS CRIME?

Most criminologists approach crime backwards. We try to explain criminal conduct but pay little attention to why certain acts are defined as crimes and why criminal responsibility is attached to some acts and not others [12]. To understand the causes of crime, we first must identify "crime." There is no general agreement as to the meaning of the concept of crime. Ernest Van den Haag defines crime as "conduct prohibited by law" [13]. Under his definition of crime, once certain conduct is forbidden, it becomes a crime regardless of its moral quality. The philosopher Thomas Hobbs would use the term "crime" only to describe "unjust" conduct [14].

In most of our attempts to define "crime," we look to the law for help. One reason for this is there is no "essence of criminology." In most criminal acts, there is no quality present that distinguishes them from noncriminal breaches of conduct norms [15]. There is no clear line between criminal and noncriminal conduct.

One definition states that crime is a violation of the primary personal rights of others and of the operations of public agencies that protect those rights [16]. This definition of crime includes murder, robbery, aggravated assault, rape, burglary, grand theft, and such acts as perjury, bribery, and insurrection; but excludes from the definition other violations of public order, such as traffic offenses and fire prevention laws. The latter offenses are excluded because "they are not true crimes and do not violate the universal law." Often when the term "crime" is used, the user is referring to one of three definitions: a social definition, a strict legal definition, or a less rigid legal definition.

Social Definition of Crime

The social definition of crime is broader than the legal definition. It includes acts that are "antisocial" and "unethical" and injurious to social interests. This definition allows for ethical considerations, whereas the legal definition does not. For example, if someone were drowning, it would be a social crime not to attempt a rescue if the rescue could be accomplished without endangering the rescuer's life.

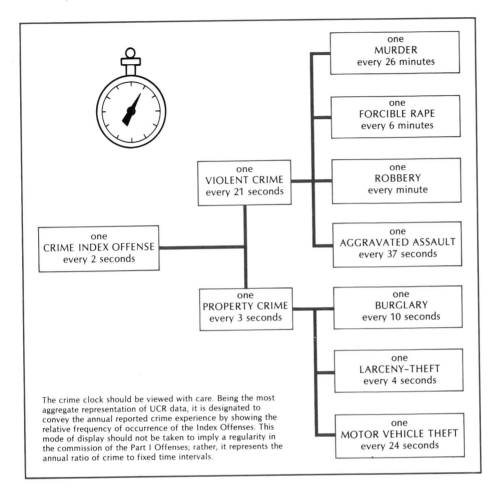

FIGURE 1–2
Crime is omnipresent in today's society.

Legal Definition of Crime

The legal definition of crime holds that behavior is a crime only when it violates criminal law. An act may be unethical, but it is not a crime unless it violates criminal law. In the example above, there may be no legal requirement to attempt to rescue the drowning person. Accordingly, it may not be a crime to watch the person drown without attempting to help the person.

Under a less rigid definition of crime, not only must the act be a violation of criminal law, but it must also be injurious to society. This definition would exclude many "victimless crimes" from being considered criminal behavior.

Most Often Used Definition of Crime

For purposes of this book, we will use Paul Tappan's definition of crime, but with the understanding that there are the problems discussed above in using any one definition of crime. Tappan's definition is the one most often used. It is as follows [17]:

> Crime is an intentional act or omission in violation of criminal law ... committed without defense or justification, and sanctioned by the state as a felony or misdemeanor.

This definition requires that the act or omission be a violation of the criminal statutes and committed without a legal excuse or justi-

IN FOCUS

The Challenge of Crime in a Free Society

Many Americans think of crime as having a very narrow range of behavior. It does not. An enormous variety of acts make up the "crime problem". Crime is not just a tough teenager snatching a lady's purse. It is also a professional thief stealing cars "on order." It is a well-heeled loan shark taking over a previously legitimate business for organized crime. It is a polite young man who suddenly and inexplicably murders his family. It is a corporation executive conspiring with competitors to keep prices high. No single theory, no single generalization can explain the vast range of behavior called crime.

The most understandable mood into which many Americans have been plunged by crime is one of frustration and bewilderment. For crime is not a single, simple phenomenon that can be examined, analyzed and described in one piece. It occurs in every part of the country and in every stratum of society. Its practitioners and its victims are people of all ages, incomes and backgrounds. Its trends are difficult to ascertain. Its causes are legion. Its cures are speculative and controversial. An examination of any single kind of crime, let alone of crime in America, raises a myriad of issues of the utmost complexity.

(President's Commission on Law Enforcement and Administration of Justice, Washington, D.C., 1967, pp. 3–5.)

fication. It is based on legal concepts and requires the existence of a penal code. It also depends on the penal code to define "defense or justification." The definition fails to explain why certain acts are treated as criminal, but others, equally antisocial, are not.

■ WHO IS A CRIMINAL?

Finding a good working definition of a "criminal" is even more difficult than defining "crime." The common definition of a "criminal"

FIGURE 1-3

How do crime rates compare with the rates of other life events?

Event	Rate per 1000 adults per year*
Accidental injury, all circumstances	242
Accidental injury at home	79
Personal theft	72
Accidental injury at work	58
Violent victimization	31
Assault (aggravated and simple)	24
Injury in motor vehicle accident	17
Death, all causes	11
Victimization with injury	10
Serious (aggravated) assault	9
Robbery	6
Heart disease death	4
Cancer death	2
Rape (women only)	2
Accidental death, all circumstances	0.5
Pneumonia/influenza death	0.3
Motor vehicle accident death	0.2
Suicide	0.2
Injury from fire	0.1
Homicide/legal intervention death	0.1
Death from fire	0.03

*These rates approximate your chances of becoming a victim of these events. More precise estimates can be derived by taking account of such factors as your age, sex, race, place of residence, and lifestyle. Findings are based on 1982–84 data, but there is little variation in rates from year to year. The rates exclude children from the calculations (those under age 12–17, depending on the series). Fire injury/death data are based on the total population, because no age-specific data are available in this series.

is one who has been convicted of a crime. The problem with this definition is that much crime is undetected and/or unsolved. However, the failure to convict a person who has committed a crime does not make his or her actions any less criminal. If we consider anyone who has committed a crime a criminal, most of us are criminals. There are very few people who have not committed, at least one criminal act in their lifetimes.

Another popular definition of a "criminal" is that it is a person who is given his or her status by those in society who have the legal or political power to establish the label as a social fact. The problem with this definition is that many people who commit criminal behaviors will not be labeled as criminal. In this book we concentrate on those who commit criminal acts rather than those who have been labeled as "criminals." We will, therefore, examine, to some extent and to some degree, the large percentage of offenders who have, at some time, committed criminal behavior. As a general rule, to be considered as a criminal, three conditions are necessary:

1. A criminal law must exist.
2. The person must violate the law without "defense or justification."
3. Some person or persons must demand enforcement of the law.

IN FOCUS

Who Is a Criminal?

Consider the following factual situations:

If in 1932, John and Joan Smith had walked down a street in New York City and John had a pint of whiskey in his pocket and Joan a gold coin in her pocket, John would be committing a criminal act because of the prohibition laws. Two years later under the same circumstances, John's act would not be a crime, but Joan's act would be. (*Note:* By 1934, the prohibition acts had been repealed in the United States and the possession of gold coins for currency had been made illegal.) Accordingly, was John a criminal in 1932 or in 1934? What about Joan?

In December 1955, Rosa Parks, a black seamstress in Montgomery, Alabama, refused to take a seat in the rear section of a public transit bus as required by state law. Was she a criminal? (*Note:* The law was later declared unconstitutional.)

California has a compulsory education statute that requires children 16 and under to attend school except in cases involving "home study." Failure of parents to take steps to ensure that their children aged 16 and under attend school or be actively enrolled in home educational study is punishable by criminal sanctions. In a recent case, a young male graduated from high school at age 12. He was refused admission to college because of his young age. His parents were faced with the following options:

1. Require him to attend junior high school. (*Note:* Because of his age, 12, a public junior high school would be required to enroll him.)
2. Establish a home study program. (*Note:* Neither parent had formal education beyond high school, and they were unprepared to establish an effective home study program.)
3. Commit criminal behavior by not requiring the child to attend school or be involved in a home educational study program.

Note: After this case received media attention, the student was accepted by a private college.

Is a person a criminal if no one labels him or her as such? (Note the discussion on labeling theory in Chapter 12.)

How long does a person remain a criminal after being convicted of a criminal offense?

Is a person a criminal only during the time that the criminal act is being committed, until the punishment has been served, or for the rest of the person's life?

■ IS CRIMINOLOGY A SCIENCE?

Is criminology a science? A science seeks to discover the consistencies and inconsistencies and causes of the consistencies and inconsistencies by the use of testing and verification procedures. According to this description, criminology is a science. It seeks to discover consistencies and inconsistencies and to find causes for them. If, however, we define a science as a "study using clinical perspectives," it is clear that criminology is not a true science. (*Note:* Since natural scientists do not use "clinical perspectives" under this definition, they also would not be considered true scientists.)

In most cases, criminologists cannot follow the scientific methods of research. Unlike laboratory scientists, one of the biggest problems facing criminologists is that most observations on which criminological theories are based are not the result of scientific experiments, but of selective, after-the-fact observations. From these selective observations, criminologists make broad generalizations about human nature.

Criminology is the study of crime and criminals in society. While criminologists attempt to analyze scientifically the causes of crime, their explanations are mainly sociological. Criminology is best described as a social science dealing with human behavior and employing scientific methods to discover causes and correlations.

Research is commonly classified as "pure" or "applied." Pure research is concerned with advancing the theoretical knowledge of a discipline. Applied research is concerned with finding practical solutions to present problems. The discipline of criminology is more often involved with applied rather than pure research. Accordingly, criminology can best be described as a functional study of human nature. Criminologists are, therefore, practical social scientists.

Reprinted later in the chapter as an "In Focus" feature is a journal article that deals with the question of whether criminology is a discipline or a field of study. There is considerable disagreement among criminologists in this regard. This may be caused by the multidisciplinary nature of criminology. Two of the leading criminologists of this area, Marvin Wolfgang and Franco Ferracuti, contend that criminology is a discipline consisting of integrated knowledge from many other disciplines [18]. Since criminology has a body of knowledge that is distinct and autonomous, its own professional organizations, and journals devoted to its study, criminology has evolved into a discipline.

▮ CONCERNS OF CRIMINOLOGICAL THEORY

Criminological theories tend to be descriptive and explanatory in nature. They either explain or describe certain aspects of criminal behavior. Criminological theories are normally concerned with:

1. The overall problem of crime
2. Patterns of crime
3. Explanations of crime in general
4. Explanations of individual criminal conduct
5. Prevention of crime
6. Punishment or treatment of criminals

Will a complete understanding of the causes of crime help prevent crime or reduce its effects? There seems to be a general assumption that if we understand the causation process, we will develop methods to prevent crime. Is this assumption valid?

CRIMINOLOGY AND THE INDIVIDUAL CRIMINAL

Criminological theories often imply more precise ability to predict than actually exists. For example, a theory dealing with why certain children become delinquent may fail to explain why one person who fits within the parameters of the theory does not become a delinquent. For the most part, criminological theories explain criminal conduct in general, not specifically, and should not be considered invalid because some persons do not fit the pattern.

CRIME AND SOCIAL MOVEMENTS

Since crime does not occur in a vacuum, the study of crime causation requires not only a study of crime but also of social movements and trends. In addition, study of the social movements and trends that were popular when a criminological theory developed helps us understand and evaluate the theory. Like other social sciences, criminology is closely tied to social values. These values often dictate the directions of research and, thus, criminological theories.

CLASSIFICATION OF THEORIES

There are a variety of schemes used to classify criminological theories. None of the classification schemes appears to have any great advantage over others. Even the most common classifications are more artificial than rational. (An excellent opportunity exists for a student to develop a comprehensive classification of criminological theories.) The most popular classifications are listed below.

   1. *Level of explanation.* Does the theory attempt to explain the criminality of classes of people, small groups, or individual criminals? Macrotheories are abstract and focus on crime rates, compared to mi-

A Theory of Theories

> There is no "theory of theories" to integrate the explanatory levels of theory in a coherent fashion. Accordingly, this is a promising area for research and development.

crotheories, which are more concrete in nature and focus on individual conduct.

2. *Classical–positive.* The oldest classification scheme is the classical–positivist scheme. Classical school theory focuses on rational conduct, criminal statutes, and governmental structures. The positivist school theory focuses on the individual, scientific method, and society's role in contributing to criminality.

3. *Structure–process.* Structural theories are those that focus on how society is organized. Process theories focus on how people become criminals.

4. *Consensus–conflict.* Consensus theories are based on the concept that there is general agreement within society concerning societal norms. Conflict theories emphasize the conflicts in norms and values that exist in society.

The classification scheme used in this book does not fit neatly into any of the foregoing schemes. Our primary purpose is to explain rather than to integrate or develop knowledge.

■ EVALUATION OF THEORIES

For a theory to have a practical value, it must be understandable to police officers, correctional personnel, professional criminologists, and others involved in the criminal justice system. In judging the usefulness of a theory, we should look at:

1. The value of the questions raised and usefulness to the development of knowledge
2. Whether or not the theory is capable of being falsified
3. The "generality" of the theory
4. Whether or not the theory is consistent with the known facts
5. The ability to translate the theory into real-life implications
6. Whether the theory has implications for change

IN FOCUS

Do Criminological Theories Have a Common Bias?

Criminological theories, for the most part, consider crime as a form of aberrant behavior, a brief departure from a lawful norm. Does this approach to the crime problem cause us to focus on "moments of crisis" and thereby create bias in our theories?

In evaluating a theory, the following should be considered:

1. Does the theory answer pertinent questions regarding the crime problem?
2. Is the theory capable of being tested by empirical research?
3. Is the theory understandable?

ARE THEORIES OUTDATED AND THUS IRRELEVANT?

Most theories were developed over forty years ago. Even the vast majority of the most recent theories were developed prior to 1980. The world has undergone many changes since 1980. Human nature and certain aspects of human behavior, however, never seem to change. Accordingly, when evaluating a theory, the crucial question should be: What relevance does it have to the present study of crime causation?

THEORY DOES NOT CONCERN ME!

Often, we feel that theory is for the "eggheads" and not for us. We are practical and functional rather than theoretical and abstract. This approach fails to consider that any decisions that we make are based on our theoretical foundations. To determine the correct approach to use in solving a particular problem, we need a theoretical foundation. Our theoretical foundations are the blueprints on which our actions are based. Theory and practical actions are not mutually exclusive. They are inseparable. For example, on April 14, 1988, Joe D., a 14-year-old high school student, killed his next-door neighbor. The reason that the

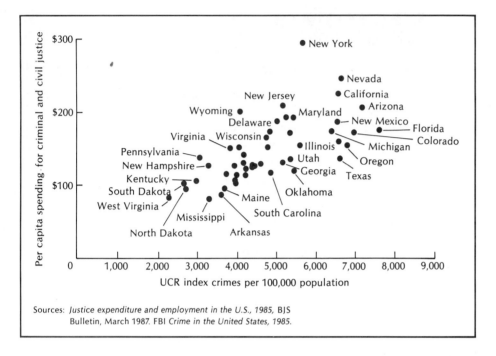

FIGURE 1-4
States with high crime rates tend to have high expenditures for criminal and civil justice.

student gave for killing the neighbor was that he was going to stop arguments between the neighbor and the neighbor's wife. As the judge in this case, what would you do with the student? Your theoretical foundations regarding the causes of crime will serve as a blueprint for your decision.

FRAMES OF REFERENCE USED IN STUDYING CRIMINAL BEHAVIOR

The four basic frames of reference used in studying the causes of criminal behavior are listed below.

1. Crime is caused by supernatural forces (e.g., "The devil made me do it").

2. The criminal is a rational human being with the ability to choose freely whether to commit or not to commit criminal behavior. (This

IN FOCUS

Criminology as a Discipline
THE INTEGRITY OF CRIMINOLOGY AS A DISCIPLINE

To the individual specifically trained as a criminologist, it is dismaying to find that the ongoing debate about whether criminology is "really" a discipline has become more heated as criminology has become more successful. Separate departments or schools of criminology and criminal justice (I use the terms interchangeably) now exist at about one thousand colleges and universities in the United States. Doctoral programs are established in Florida, Texas, Michigan, New York, New Jersey, Maryland and the District of Columbia. National, regional and state associations of professional criminologists enjoy growing membership and member participation. In short, all the basic external characteristics of a discipline exist. In academic organization and professional structure, criminology is as well established as any other discipline.

Arguments against according the status of a discipline to criminology ignore or discount such observables in favor of a focus on less tangible characteristics that "real" disciplines supposedly possess, and that criminology does not. In essence, the critics charge that criminology lacks "disciplinary integrity." By this they usually mean one or more of three things: (1) Criminology's subject matter is too specific and too much determined by events outside the discipline itself; (2) the theoretical and research literature that criminologists work with belongs to other disciplines; and (3) criminology is "too applied." I will consider each allegation in turn.

1. Whereas other disciplines take as their basic objects of study very broad and abstract concepts such as policy, society, humanity, the mind, or the economy, criminologists study crime. They do so not because crime is an essential or fundamental concept necessary for the understanding of how the world works, but because crime is an urgent social problem. Criminology has origins in a need to control events rather than understand them.

Several replies can be made to this assertion. First, it is based upon a faulty assumption about the historical purity of the basic concepts of other disciplines. All concepts mentioned above have traceable origins in the history of ideas. The categories of modern Western science seems to us to have lost their arbitrary and cultural specific character only as a result of a conscious effort to gain intersubjective agreement about their utility and generality. On reflection, the differentiation of the social sciences into its modern disciplines seems more of a historical accident than a natural and inevitable division of labor based upon some inherent characteristics of the concepts each discipline employs.

The concept of crime serves a similar purpose for criminologists as do the fundamental concepts of other disciplines. It acts as a "gateway" to a series of important questions about the nature and origins of human behavior and institutions. Other disciplines employ other gateways to get at the same questions. Another way of putting it is that the explanation of crime ultimately requires a general theory of behavior and less general theories that illuminate specific institutional contexts. Crime is a social, political, economic, psychological and moral phenomenon just as are morality, history, psyche, economy, polity and society. It is of general interest and is both concrete and abstract. Criminologists are interested in answering the same questions as other social and behavioral scientists.

Though the study of crime has very general implications, it is also the study of human problem. Criminologists are sensitive to demands that someone do something about crime and are often more eager than able to please. What criminologists desire to be true about crime often overshadows what is true; promises are made that cannot be kept. It is wrong and it is self-destructive to make such promises. When there is no defense for one's behavior, one can only plea that he who is without sin cast the first stone. The need to control events has always informed science (and the abuse of science) and is not safely ignored by anyone claiming to be a scientist.

2. Criminology is a "parasite" discipline. It borrows its substance from other disciplines but offers nothing in return.

At worst, this charge implies that the work of all those who call themselves (for example) anthropologists "belongs" strictly to other anthropologists, the work of political scientists belongs to political scientists, etc. I suspect that there are some people who actually hold such views, but I see no reason to dignify them by taking their ideas seriously.

A more cogent criticism is that the literature of criminology is mainly composed of pieces of the literature of other disciplines, especially sociology. It is related to the charge that many of the foremost "criminologists" primarily identify themselves with sociology, psychology, or some other discipline.

There is some truth to these charges. Precisely because crime is a problem of both intellectual and popular interest it attracts investigators from all fields. In the United States, criminology has traditionally been housed in sociology departments. It is likely that the majority of American criminologists identify themselves with other disciplines.

A number of comments are in order:

a. Criminologists are not alone in owning a debt to the great thinkers of the social sciences. Bentham, Comte, Marx, Lenin, Durkheim, Weber, Smith, Marshall, Malthus, Freud, Watson, Darwin and the other giants of science bequeathed a heritage of ideas shared by all students of humanity.

b. The contributions of American sociologists to the development of criminology are invaluable. But criminology has never been a strictly sociological discipline and it never will be. It has been housed in departments in every branch of the social sciences, as well as in schools of law and medicine.

To fulfill its promise, criminology must not be considered as a "sub-discipline" or specialty in other discipline. Instead, its position at the crossroads of many approaches to social sciences must be enhanced. Only as an independent discipline can criminology "pay back" its "debt" to other disciplines. A goal of criminology is the integration of a wide variety of ways to understanding human behavior. It is the criminologist who is mainly a criminologist, and not too closely tied to another discipline, who can best cope with the numerous theoretical and methodological strategies available in the social sciences. The independent criminologist enjoys a unique chance to bring together the best of other social sciences and humanities. In doing so, he can introduce the sociologists to the insights of the political scientists, political scientists to psychologists, and so on. A desire to claim criminology as part of one's turf is understandable but shortsighted.

c. Criminology is rapidly losing its parasite attributes, as professionally trained Ph.D's in the discipline begin to make their own distinctive contributions to the literature of the social sciences. However dependent criminology was on the contributions of others in the past, it is now developing its own literature. A criminological body of knowledge is gradually being defined and delineated.

3. Criminology is an "applied discipline" and not "academic." Criminologists are not interested in "pure" research.

No criticism infuriates criminologists as much as the complaint that their discipline is too applied. In the first place, their interests are much the same as those of the other social scientists, as I have argued above. In the second place, all the social sciences have a strong tradition of deriving knowledge from applied research, and of using their technologies in the services of policy-makers, businesses, non-profit organizations and others. If "applied" research is defined as research paid for by others and conducted for other's use, then a large portion of the literature of social science is applied.

I doubt that those who say criminology is not "academic" enough can provide a definition of academic that would allow them to demonstrate their claim. I suspect that "academic" is a codeword for "established." Criminology is in its youth as an autonomous discipline and attracts a greater diversity of faculty members and students that have traditionally been seen on college campuses. Criminologists and their students are often strangers to their better-established colleagues, and social scientists are as likely as anyone to be wary of strangers. The success of criminology programs in the last decade have made them upstarts as well, fueling even more suspicion and resentment.

The emotional reaction to the rise of criminology as an autonomous discipline is understandable. It is not often a source of constructive criticism. There are a host of practical and intellectual advantages for other social sciences in the establishment of criminology in its own right, as we have seen. An emotional reaction simply makes it less likely that those advantages will be properly appreciated. More importantly, the tolerance for diversity needed to achieve the goals of social science is dangerously compromised.

Source: This article was first published in the *Justice Professional,* vol. 2, no. 1, Spring 1987, and is reprinted with permission of *Justice Professional* and Professor Jerome McKean.

frame of reference, discussed in Chapter 4, is basic to the classical school.)

3. Criminal conduct is caused by forces beyond the control of the criminal. (This frame of reference, discussed in Chapter 5, is the foundation of the positivist theories of criminal behavior.)

4. Criminal conduct is primarily a function of the manner in which the criminal laws are written and enforced. This frame of reference focuses on the behavior that is a by-product of the criminal law rather than the behavior of the criminal.

■ SUMMARY

Criminology includes a practical study of why people commit criminal conduct. Criminological theories are, for the most part, practical and applied. Crime theories also tend to be descriptive and explanatory. Crime is a major industry in our society, and many criminologists contend that crime serves a functional role in our society. This raises the question: Since crime is functional, is complete elimination of it desirable?

The law is a formal expression of our value system. The leading concepts on the nature of law include: law has a supernatural origin, law is justice, law is a function of the sovereign, law is a utilitarian concept, and law is an instrument of the ruling class. There is no general agreement as to what constitutes a crime. Frequently used definitions of crime include the social definition, the strictly legal definition, and the less rigid legal definition. There is also a problem in defining who is a criminal. The common definition of a "criminal" is one who has been convicted of a crime. The problem with this definition is that much crime is undetected and/or unsolved. The failure, however, to convict a person who has committed a crime does not make his or her actions any less criminal.

Criminology is best described as a social science dealing with the functional aspects of human behavior. Since crime does not occur in a vacuum, the search for the causes of crime includes a study of social movements and trends.

∎ MATCHING KEY TERMS AND DEFINITIONS

Match each key term with the correct definition.

a. applied research
b. classical theories
c. conflict theories
d. consensus theories
e. criminal
f. criminology
g. Durkheim
h. etiology
i. legal definition of crime
j. macrotheories
k. microtheories
l. multifactor approach
m. positive theories
n. process theories
o. pure research
p. social definition of crime
q. structural theories

____ 1. Noted French sociologist who contended that crime was an integral part of our society.
____ 2. Crime consists only of behavior that violates criminal law.
____ 3. One who has been convicted of a crime.
____ 4. Behavior that is considered as "antisocial" and "unethical."
____ 5. A social science dealing with human behavior and employing scientific methods to discover causes and correlations of criminal behavior.
____ 6. Research that is concerned with developing the theoretical knowledge of a discipline.

___ **7.** Research that is concerned with solving practical problems.

___ **8.** Theories that are abstract and focus on crime rates.

___ **9.** Theories that are more concrete in nature and focus on individual conduct.

___ **10.** Theories that are based on the concept that there is a general agreement concerning societal norms within a society.

___ **11.** Theories that emphasize the conflicts within society.

___ **12.** Theories that focus on how people become criminal.

___ **13.** Theories that focus on how society is organized.

___ **14.** Theories that focus on rational conduct, criminal statutes, and governmental structures.

___ **15.** Theories that focus on the individual and his or her inability to make rational choices.

___ **16.** The study of causation.

___ **17.** An approach to the study of crime which assumes that crime is the result of many different factors.

■ DISCUSSION QUESTIONS

1. Explain the practical uses of theory.

2. Provide an explanation for the popularity of crime in our entertainment fare.

3. What considerations should be used when evaluating a theory?

4. At this point in your study, what do you feel explains criminal behavior?

5. What are some of the practical problems in developing a ''theory of theories'' to explain crime?

6. Is criminology a science? Explain your answer.

Notes

1. Frank P. Williams III and Marilyn D. McShane, *Criminological Theory.* Englewood Cliffs, N.J.: Prentice-Hall, 1988.
2. Ely Chinoy, *Society.* New York: Random House, 1962.
3. Arthur Stinchcombe, *Constructing Social Theories.* New York: Harcourt Brace & World, 1968, p. 5.
4. George B. Vold and Thomas J. Bernard, *Theoretical Criminology*, 3rd ed. New York: Oxford University Press, 1986.
5. U.S. Department of Justice, BJS *Report to the Nation on Crime and Justice*, 2nd ed. Washington, D.C.: U.S. Government Printing Office, 1988.

6. Emile Durkheim, *De la division du travail social.* Paris, 1893.

7. Kai Erikson, *Wayward Puritans.* New York: Wiley, 1966.

8. Donn B. Parker, *Crime by Computer.* New York: Scribner, 1976.

9. Michael R. Weisser, *Crime and Punishment in Early Modern Europe.* Atlantic Highlands, N.J.: Humanities Press, 1979.

10. Stephen Schafer, *Theories in Criminology.* New York: Random House, 1968, p. 1.

11. E. Adamson Hoebel, *The Law of Primitive Man.* Cambridge, Mass.: Harvard University Press, 1954.

12. Schafer, 1968:7.

13. Ernest Van den Haag, *Punishing Criminals.* New York: Basic Books, 1975.

14. C. Ray Jeffery, "The Development of Crime in Early English Society," *Journal of Criminal Law, Criminology and Police Science,* vol.. 47, 1957.

15. G. Williams, "The Definition of Crime," *Current Legal Problems,* vol. 8, 1955, pp. 107–130.

16. Macklin Fleming, "A Short Course in the Causes of Crime," *Prosecutor' Brief,* May–June 1979, p. 8.

17. Paul Tappan, "Who Is the Criminal?" *American Sociological Review,* vol. 12, 1947, pp. 96–102.

18. Marvin Wolfgang and Franco Ferracuti, *The Subculture of Violence.* London: Social Science Paperbacks, 1967.

2

Criminal Law
and the Search
for Crime Causation

CHAPTER HIGHLIGHTS

- The oldest known major set of laws is the Code of Hammurabi.
- The Code of Hammurabi was the first organized attempt to codify criminal laws.
- Criminology as a separate field of inquiry began in Europe in the late eighteenth century.
- The field of criminology evolved along with modern criminal law during the Age of Enlightenment.
- To the ancient Hebrews, law was an expression of God's command, and violation of it was a transgression against God.
- The Greek philosophers considered crime as an offense against society or the state.
- Plato taught that people have dual characters.
- Aristotle divided law into two classes: natural and man-made.
- In their search for the causes of crime, the Romans integrated the spiritualism of the Hebrews with the naturalism of the Greek scholars to develop laws that were based on the "nature of things."
- The early European churches equated crime with sin.
- St. Thomas Aquinas believed that the "soul" is implanted in the unborn child.
- One popular explanation of crime during the fifteenth and sixteenth centuries was that astral influences motivated both criminal and noncriminal behavior.
- There was a clear tendency in early America to equate crime with sin, pauperism, and immorality.

KEY TERMS

Code of Hammurabi   Freedom to Choose

Codification   Lunatic

Criminologist   Natural Law

Exorcism   Sin

T he development of criminology as a separate field of study and the development of modern criminal law are closely related. In this chapter we trace briefly both criminal law and criminology's ancient beginnings.

THE DEVELOPMENT OF CRIMINOLOGY AS A FIELD OF STUDY

Traditionally, the classical school of criminology is regarded as the beginning of the study of criminology as a separate field of study. The search for the causes of crime, however, started long before Beccaria's classical essay *On Crimes and Punishments* written in 1764. The term "criminology" was coined by Topinard, a French anthropologist. Earlier, J. Baptiste della Porta (1535–1615) studied criminals in an attempt to develop a relationship between physical characteristics and the type of crime the person committed [1]. For example, one of his conclusions was that men with small ears, bushy eyebrows, small noses, and long slender fingers were thieves. It was during this period (sixteenth century) that judging a person's character and qualities from his or her physical characteristics was popular in the search for "the correct location of responsibility" for criminal behavior. (It was not until the eighteenth century, however, that the study of physical characteristics as a cause of crime developed into popular criminological theories. This concept is discussed in Chapter 13.)

Criminology was originally the study of laws and their effects on society. The original researchers and writers in criminology were physicians, philosophers, physical scientists, and lawyers. The study of criminology evolved along with modern criminal law during the Age of Enlightenment. As noted in Chapter 4, it was the early writing of Cesare Beccaria in his famous essay *On Crimes and Punishments* that resulted in reform of Western European criminal law.

■ CODE OF HAMMURABI

The oldest known major set of laws (about 2100 B.C.) is the Code of Hammurabi. It is also known as the "Judgment of Righteousness." The Code was written on a seven-foot four-inch-high stone and contained 282 laws. The stated purpose of the Code was to "prevent the strong from oppressing the weak" and "to destroy the wicked," who threatened the organized social life at the time.

The Code of Hammurabi was the first organized social attempt to codify the criminal laws. (The codification of laws is the act of grouping them together in a unified general plan.) Prior to King Hammurabi, disputes and problems between people were decided by revenge and blood feuds. Clans were pitted against clans. If a member of one family wronged a member of another family, the wronged family would retaliate against the family it thought wronged them. One goal of the code was to prevent individuals from resorting to feuds and personal redress in settling disputes. At the time there was no state or mediator for such disputes. People took it on themselves to decide justice.

King Hammurabi was the sixth king of the First Dynasty of Babylonia. He was king for about fifty-five years. Historians cannot agree on the exact date when he became king, but it was approximately 2100 B.C. The king designed the code with five parts:

1. A penal code or code of laws
2. A manual of instruction for judges, police officials, and witnesses
3. A handbook of rights and duties of husbands, wives, and children
4. A set of regulations establishing wages and prices
5. A code of ethics for government officials, merchants, and doctors

Throughout the code, the particular obligation to be met, the particular action forbidden, and the precise punishment to be meted out to the offender were clearly delineated. The objectives of the code were as follows:

1. *Reinforcement of the power of the state.* The code was the beginning of state-administered punishments. Personal redress was taken out of the hands of citizens.

FIGURE 2–1
Upper part of the pillar on which the legendary Code of Hammurabi was inscribed. Photo by Art Resource

2. *Protection of the weaker from the stronger.* An example of this is the following: "The widow must be protected from those who exploit her, the distant or captured husband from the betrayal of the wife he left behind, the aged, impoverished father from the sons who would disown him, the pregnant slave from the beatings of the impatient master, the lessor official from the higher official."

3. *Restoration of equity between offender and victim.* The wrath against the offender and offense was to be wiped out and after the penalty was made, things were to be made as if the offense never occurred.

Punishments were harsh during King Hammurabi's day. For example, death, mutilation, branding, and banishment were common punishments. In the code, eight crimes punishable by mutilation were cited. They included disrespect by a slave, the fatal clumsiness of a physician, disrespect by an adopted son, and the false branding of a slave.

The code of Hammurabi, like other preclassical criminal codes,

Can we explain criminal behavior without first separating the criminal from the crime, examining each and their relationship to each other?

did not separate the crime from the criminal. There was an inherent connection between the evil act and the actor. The question "Why are some people criminal and others not?" would never be considered because criminal behavior was absolutely thought the result of "evil" or "wicked" forces. The concept that criminal behavior could be caused by different social values, economic conditions, psychological factors, and so on, did not exist.

The Code of Hammurabi was very protective of the crime victim. It was the first known set of laws that provided for victim compensation. Until the recent victim's movement in the 1980s, the "laws" that followed the Code of Hammurabi ignored the plight of victims and did not provide for victim compensation [2].

▌ THE HEBREWS

To the ancient Hebrews, law was an expression of God's command, and violation of it was a transgression against God. To the Hebrews, God was all knowing and jealous. Deviant behavior, at that time, was believed to destroy the bonds of society. It was also believed that antisocial acts caused dissension among the people of Israel. In addition, it was thought that deviant/criminal behavior on the part of any member of God's chosen people could incur God's wrath on everyone. Hebraic laws were therefore developed to appease God's displeasure. For example, consider the following quotation that explains how the ancient Hebrews dealt with homicide [3]:

> Israelite law demanded that one who killed should be put to death, a relatively harsh punishment principle that developed from the theological connection between the blood of the victim and the spirit of God. Yahweh (God) was believed to possess the blood of a man which, in turn contained the spirit given to the individual by the Creator. In shedding human blood, a murderer took what rightfully belonged to Yahweh (God), only his death and the shed-

ding of his blood was adequate compensation. If a murdered man should be found in a field, the nearby village was expected to sacrifice an animal if the culprit could not be found. . . .

The idea was that the blood of the animal and the animal's spirit would be returned to God, and thus "balance" would be restored. Until balance was restored, God would not be satisfied.

■ THE GREEKS

The Greek philosophers considered crime as an offense against the society or the state. They were also concerned about ameliorating a higher power, but they were convinced that the rule of the people was critical to the prevention of tyrannies. The Greeks believed that anyone who committed homicide was infected with corruption and evil. Merely being accused of homicide made a person corrupt, and his movements were sharply circumscribed to keep him away from places of assembly and from sites of religious significance. Later, however, the Greeks developed a naturalistic explanation of criminal behavior. Plato and Aristotle, for example, appeared to believe that the cause of criminal behavior was based on physical factors. As noted below, their concepts were very similar to those promulgated by the classical school discussed in Chapter 4.

Plato (428–348 B.C.) taught that man had a dual character. He believed that a person was rational and sought perfection but was limited by his or her own weakness and imperfections. Plato also contended that crime would always exist because of man's greedy nature. An examination of his *Republic* leads to the conclusion that he believed that we have the freedom to choose between right and wrong. He also contended that punishment was man's right to cleanse himself of evil. (*Note:* The concept of "freedom to choose" is similar to the classical concepts discussed in Chapter 4.)

Aristotle (384–322 B.C.) divided law into two classes, natural and man-made. Natural law concerns those values that are universally accepted as correct. Man-made laws were those that were created by man to promote equality and fairness. According to Aristotle, our ability to reason separates us from animals, and that crime is caused by our irrational acts. He was not clear on the cause of the irrational acts. He does appear, however, to have believed that the irrational acts (crimes) were the result of the individual's deliberate choices [4].

Did Aristotle mean that if we "reason," we will not commit crimes?

■ THE ROMANS

In their search for the causes of crime, the Romans integrated the spiritualism of the Hebrews with the naturalism of the Greek scholars to develop laws that were based on the "nature of things." The chief contribution of the Romans was their focus on "justice" and codes of law, not a search for crime causation [5].

■ THE EARLY WESTERN EUROPEANS

The early European churches equated crime with sin. Criminals were possessed by the devil. For example, St. Augustine (A.D. 354–430) contended that God gave Adam a choice between good and evil and that Adam chose evil. To St. Augustine, evil (crime) resulted from influences of the devil. Criminals therefore had to have the devil driven from them. The church rite of "exorcism" was used for this. If exorcism failed to drive the devil out of the "sinners," they were turned over to civil authorities, where capital punishment or other brutal punishments were used to eradicate the devil [6].

St. Thomas Aquinas (1225–1274) contended that the "soul" is implanted in the unborn child by God and that the "soul" is the source of our reasoning power. The conscience is that part of our soul that guides us toward rational and just behavior. It is our human appetite (influenced by the devil) that causes us to seek worldly pleasures. When the human appetite overrules our conscience, evil (crime) occurs [7]. (Note: The similarities to Sigmund Freud's theories discussed in Chapter 16.)

Another popular explanation of criminal behavior during the fifteenth and sixteenth centuries included astral influences (moon and stars). A Swiss physician, Hohenheim (also known as Paracelsus) (1490–1541), was a proponent of the idea that criminal behavior was caused by influences of the stars and the moon. According to this explanation, astral influences controlled human behavior and caused people to act in strange and irrational ways [8]. (Note: The word "lunatic" comes from the Latin word "luna," meaning moon.)

By the late sixteenth century, the authority of the European churches had declined and government had control of the administration of justice. The legal codes were confusing and inconsistent and procedures were incomplete. It was under these conditions that the classical theory of criminology developed. The classical school is discussed in Chapter 4.

As noted earlier in this chapter, it was during the late sixteenth

IN FOCUS

Lunar Cycles and Crime

Lunar cycles influence tidal changes in our oceans through the effects of the moon's gravitational forces on the earth. It is common to expect weird and unusual behavior of people during "full moons." A 1972 study of homicides occurring in Dade County, Florida, focused on the effects of lunar cycles and criminal behavior. The purpose of the study was to determine if a relationship existed between lunar synodic cycles and human emotional disturbance.

The major findings and conclusions of the study included the following [9]:

1. Homicides peaked at full moon and showed a trough leading up to a new moon, followed by a secondary peak just after a new moon.

2. There was a statistically significant grouping of criminal homicides around the full moon and new moon cycles.

3. The researchers suggested that a lunar influence on the frequency of criminal homicides may exist.

century and early seventeenth century that the early positive concepts developed. The concept of a relationship between the physical makeup of a person and his or her involvement in crime can be traced to J. Baptiste della Porte (1586), who studied the cadavers of criminals to determine the relationship between body form and type of crime.

■ CRIMINOLOGY IN EARLY AMERICA

There was a clear tendency in early America to equate crime with sin, pauperism, and immorality. The first explanations of crime in American colonies were linked to the devil [10]. For example, there were three "crime waves" during the first sixty years of the Massachusetts Bay Puritan Colony. All were blamed on the "devil." The most serious of the crime waves occurred in 1792 and was thought to be caused by witches [11].

Beccaria's *Essay on Crimes and Punishments* in 1766 marked the apex of the Age of Enlightenment. (His essay and the Age of Enlight-

IN FOCUS

The Capital Laws of Massachusetts In the years 1641–1643 (partial list)

1. If any man after legal conviction, shall have or worship any other God, but the Lord God, he shall be put to death.

2. If any man or woman be a Witch, that is, hath or consulteth with a familiar spirit, they shall be put to death.

3. If any person shall blaspheme the Name of God the Father, Son, or Holy Ghost, with direct, express, presumptuous, or high-handed blasphemy, or shall curse God in like manner, he shall be put to death.

4. If any person shall commit any willful murder, which is manslaughter, committed upon premeditate malice, hatred, or cruelty, not in a man's necessary and just defense, nor by near casualty, against his will; he shall be put to death.

5. If any person slayeth another through guile, either by poisoning, or other such devilish practice; he shall be put to death.

6. If any person shall slayeth another suddenly in his anger, or cruelty of passion, he shall be put to death.

7. If a man or woman shall lie with any animal, by carnal copulation, they shall surely be put to death and the animal shall be slain and buried.

8. If any person committeth adultery with a married, or espoused wife, the Adulterer and the Adulteress, shall surely be put to death.

9. If any man shall unlawfully have carnal copulation with any woman-child under ten years old, either with or without her consent, he shall be put to death.

10. If any man steals, he shall be put to death.

11. If any man rise up by false witness, he shall be put to death.

enment are discussed in Chapter 4.) At this time the colonies in North America were being settled. The Enlightenment and its reliance on the role of reason in understanding human behavior was very popular in the new world. The Age of Enlightenment made its influence felt throughout the Western world and led to the American Revolution and the adoption of a government marked by constitutionalism and limited

FIGURE 2–2
The Tower of London, a place where many English criminals were punished for their behavior.

political power. After the American Revolution our system of criminal justice expanded and developed its own unique identity [12]. The idea of clear and precise criminal laws (one of the hallmarks of the classical school discussed in Chapter 4) evolved at this time.

American criminology came into its own in the nineteenth cen-

IN FOCUS

The Relationship Between Sin and Crime

Before the American Revolution, the colonies were subject to the law handed down by the English judges. Accordingly, the common law of England with its Anglo-Saxon concepts became the basic criminal law of the colonies. After the revolution, the common law was modified and changed by state legislatures. During the modifications, the colonies' religious beliefs became a part of our criminal code, and criminal law was used to regulate morality. To some extent, we still use criminal law to regulate morality. According to Norval Morris and Gordon Hawkins, our present criminal codes in the United States are some of the most moralistic criminal laws in history.

Should we use criminal laws to regulate our concepts of morality? Can we separate crime and sin?

Source: Norval Morris and Gordon P. Hawkins, *The Honest Politician's Guide to Crime Control* (Chicago: University of Chicago Press, 1969).

tury. It developed from the fields of sociology and psychology and was directly influenced by the positive school and the Age of Realism [13]. Accordingly, American criminal law scholars embraced the classical school, and American correctional scholars embraced the positivist school. The result was a clear division between the legal and corrective aspects of our criminal justice system. The law tended to be based on the concept of "free will" and corrections were based on the "treatment" concept. This division was apparent until the late 1950s. Beginning in the late 1950s and the early 1960s, the "positive" influence on the penal aspects of our criminal justice system lost much of its influence [14].

■ SUMMARY

Criminology developed as a separate field of inquiry in Europe during the late eighteenth century. The early criminologists at that time were physicians, philosophers, physical scientists, sociologists, and so on. The Code of Hammurabi was the first major attempt to codify laws. It was also the beginning of state-administrated punishment. The ancient Hebrews, Greeks, Romans, and early Western Europeans made the initial theoretical contributions to the study of crime causation. Criminology in America was influenced by European Enlightenment ideas. American criminology came into its own in the nineteenth century. It evolved from the fields of sociology and psychology.

■ MATCHING KEY TERMS AND DEFINITIONS

Match each key term with the correct definition.

a. Code of Hammurabi   **e.** freedom to choose
b. codification   **f.** lunatic
c. criminologist   **g.** natural law
d. exorcism   **h.** sin

____ **1.** A person who studies crime.
____ **2.** The division of Aristotle's classification of law that reflects those values that are universally accepted as correct.
____ **3.** Plato's phrase which reflects that a person chooses to do right or wrong.
____ **4.** The act of driving the devil out of a criminal.

___ **5.** Behavior that was equated with crime in early America.

___ **6.** The grouping of criminal laws together in one unified code.

___ **7.** The oldest known major set of laws.

___ **8.** A term that means insane, mad, or crazy.

■ DISCUSSION QUESTIONS

1. Explain the importance of the Code of Hammurabi.
2. Compare the Greek concept of crime with that of the Hebrews.
3. Explain the difference between Aristotle's "natural law" and "man-made" law.
4. How did St. Thomas Aquinas explain crime?
5. Why was there a clear separation between the American legal and correctional parts of the criminal justice system?

Notes

1. J. Baptiste della Porte, *The Human Physiognomy*. 1586.
2. On the Code of Hammurabi, see Sir Henry Maine, *Ancient Law: Its Connection with the Early History of Society and Its Relation to Modern Ideas*. London: John Murray, 1861; Cyrus H. Gordon, *Hammurabi's Code: Quaint or Forward Looking*. New York: Rinehart, 1957; John Wilkinson, *The Ancient Egyptians*, Vol. III. London: John Murray, 1878; and Chilperic Edwards, *The Hammurabi Code*. New York: Kennikat Press, 1971.
3. See Edward Westermarck, *The Origin and Development of the Moral Ideas*, Vol. I, 2nd ed. London: Curzon Press, 1912; Herbert Johnson, *A History of Criminal Justice*. Cincinnati, Ohio: Anderson, 1988; Sir Henry Maine, *Ancient Law*, 10th ed. London: John Murray, 1905; and Richard R. Korn and Lloyd W. McCorkle, *Criminology and Penology*. New York: Holt, Rinehart and Winston, 1966.
4. See Maine, 1861; Lon Fuller, *The Morality of Law*, New Haven, Conn.: Yale University Press, 1964; George Calhoun, *The Growth of Criminal Law in Ancient Greece*. Berkeley: University of California Press, 1927; and F. M. Conford (translator), *The Republic of Plato*. New York: Oxford University Press, 1941.
5. See, generally, Rene A. Wormer, *The Story of Law*. New York: Simon and Schuster, 1962; and M. F. Morris, *The History of the Development of Law*. Washington, D.C.: John Byrne, 1909.
6. See Carl Joachin Friedrich, *The Philosophy of Law in Historical Perspective*. Chicago: University of Chicago Press, 1963; Paul C. Higgins and Richard R. Butler, *Understanding Deviance*. New York: McGraw-Hill, 1982; and St. Augustine's *On Christian Doctrine*, Library of Liberal Arts Series. New York: Bobbs-Merrill, 1961.
7. See Carl Joachin Friedrich, *The Philosophy of Law in Historical Perspective*. Chicago: University of Chicago Press, 1963.

8. See, generally, F. C. Copleston, *A History of Medieval Philosophy.* New York: Harper & Row, 1972; Arthur E. Fink, *The Causes of Crime: Biological Theories in the United States, 1800–1915.* Philadelphia: University of Pennsylvania Press, 1938; and Stephen Shafer, *Theories in Criminology.* New York: Random House, 1969.

9. Arnold Lieber and Carolyn R. Sherin, "Homicides and the Lunar Cycles: Toward a Theory of Lunar Influence on Human Emotional Disturbance," *American Journal of Psychiatry,* vol. 129, July 1972, pp. 101–116.

10. See Richard Quinney, *The Problem of Crime.* New York: Dodd, Mead & Company, 1971.

11. Kai Erikson, *Wayward Puritans.* New York: Wiley, 1966.

12. C. Ray Jeffery, "The Structure of American Criminological Thinking," *Journal of Criminal Law, Criminology and Police Science,* vol. 46, Jan.–Feb. 1956, pp. 663–674.

13. C. Ray Jeffery, "The Historical Development of Criminology," in H. Mannheim, ed., *Pioneers of Criminology.* London: Stevens, 1960.

14. Jeffery, 1960:489.

3

Measuring Criminal Behavior

CHAPTER HIGHLIGHTS

- The Uniform Crime Report (UCR) and the National Crime Survey (NCS) are the main sources of national crime statistics.
- The UCR indices show trends for eight serious crimes.
- The FBI receives their data for the UCR from over 15,000 law enforcement agencies.
- The UCR is prepared annually.
- Crimes are reported in the UCR as either index or nonindex crimes.
- Crime rates are statistics used by the UCR system to establish trends for the index crimes.
- Crime statistics are only as accurate as the data reported to the FBI.
- The National Crime Surveys (NCS) began in 1973 to learn more about crime, its victims, and its consequences.
- The data used by the NCS are based on random samples of U.S. households.
- NCS's inferences regarding crime and crime rates are made based on the random samples.
- Despite the extensive measures used to measure criminal activity, the fact remains that a substantial number of crimes are not reported or known to the police.
- According to the NCS, violence or theft touches about one-fourth of all households in the United States each year.
- Five percent of all households annually have at least one member who is a victim of rape, robbery, or assault.
- Property crimes outnumbered violent crimes by 9:1.
- According to the NCS, the percentage of households touched by crime has declined from 32 percent in 1975 to 25 percent in 1986.

- NCS data indicate that crimes against the person and crimes against the home are more likely to occur in warmer weather than in the winter.
- Most criminal activity takes place during evening or nighttime hours.
- According to NCS, the largest number of crimes occur within the general area where the victim lives.
- Persons who live in the central part of the city are more likely to be victimized than are suburban or rural residents.

KEY TERMS

Arson	National Crime Surveys
Assault	Nonindex Crimes
Burglary	Rape
Crime Rates	Robbery
Homicide	Self-reports
Index Crimes	Uniform Crime Reports
Larceny	

In this chapter, our main sources of national crime statistics are discussed. The problems of measuring criminal behavior and the rating of criminal behavior are included. Questions considered include: How much crime is there? Have crime rates gone up in recent years? When do crimes occur? Where do crimes occur? How do people rank the seriousness of different crimes?

■ UNIFORM CRIME REPORTS

The Uniform Crime Report (UCR) is one of the two major sources of national crime statistics. (The other source is the National Crime Surveys.) The UCR developed from a 1927 effort by the International Association of Chiefs of Police (IACP) to create a uniform system for gathering statistics on crimes known to the police. This effort was a continuation of a 1921 effort by the National Police Conference to develop a federal program for criminal identification. The goal of IACP

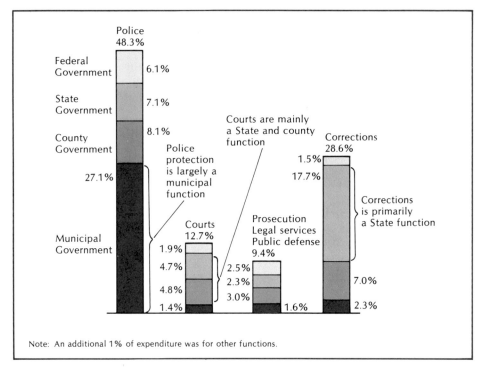

FIGURE 3–1
Crime is a growth industry. It provides many jobs for the American public. Forty-eight cents of every justice dollar is spent for police protection. Source: BJS *Justice expenditure and employment in the United States,* 1985.

was to develop a national system of crime statistics that would be uniform throughout the United States. In 1930, the U.S. Bureau of Investigation under J. Edgar Hoover [later renamed the Federal Bureau of Investigation (FBI)] was assigned the responsibility for gathering national crime statistics [1].

The FBI receives data for the UCR from over 15,000 law enforcement agencies. The agencies report the number of offenses that are known to them on a monthly basis to the FBI. The UCR is prepared annually. Crimes are reported as either index or nonindex crimes [2].

Seven crimes—based on their seriousness, frequency of occurrence, and likelihood of being reported to law enforcement agencies—were selected as index crimes. The seven crimes included: homicide, rape, assault, robbery, burglary, larceny/theft, and motor vehicle theft. In 1978, an eighth crime, arson, was added. The eight crimes are commonly known as index crimes. Presently, there are also twenty-one nonindex crimes recorded in the UCR.

Index crimes are reported in Part I of the UCR. Index crimes are recorded in two categories: (1) those known to the police (reported) and (2) those cleared by arrest, prosecution, or formally charged. Nonindex crimes (Part II crime data) are limited to those cleared by arrest, prosecution, or formally charged [3].

IN FOCUS

Characteristics of Index Crimes

Homicide

Definition: Causing the death of another person without legal justification or excuse, including UCR crimes of murder and nonnegligent manslaughter and negligent manslaughter.

Characteristics: Murder and nonnegligent manslaughter occur less often than other violent UCR Index crimes; about 58 percent of the known murderers are relatives or acquaintances of the victim; about 20 percent of all murders occur or are suspected to have occurred as the result of some felonious activity.

Rape

Definition: Unlawful sexual intercourse with a female, by force or without legal or factual consent.

Characteristics: Most rapes involve a lone offender and a lone victim; about 32 percent of the rapes recorded by NCS are committed in or near the victim's home; about 73 percent of the rapes occurred at night, between 6 P.M. and 6 A.M.; approximately 58 percent of the victims of rape are under 25 years of age.

Robbery

Definition: The unlawful taking or attempted taking of property that is in the immediate possession of another, by force or threat of force.

Characteristics: Robbery is the violent crime that most often involves more than one offender; about one-half of all robberies reported involve the use of a weapon.

Assault

Definition: Unlawful intentional inflicting, or attempted inflicting, of injury on the person of another. Aggravated assault is the unlawful intentional inflicting of serious bodily injury or unlawful threat or attempt to inflict bodily injury or death by means of a deadly or dangerous weapon with or without actual infliction of injury. Simple assault is the unlawful intentional inflicting of less than serious bodily injury without a deadly or dangerous weapon or an attempt or threat to inflict bodily injury without a deadly or dangerous weapon.

Characteristics: Simple assault occurs more frequently than aggravated assault; most assaults involve one victim and one offender.

Burglary

Definition: Unlawful entry of any fixed structure, vehicle, or vessel used for regular residence, industry, or business, with or without force, with the intent to commit a felony or larcency.

Characteristics: Residential property was targeted in two out of every three reported burglaries, nonresidential property accounting for the remaining third; approximately 42 percent of all residential burglaries occurred without forced entry; about 37 percent of the no-force burglaries were known to have occurred during the day, between 6 A.M. and 6 P.M.

Larceny/Theft

Definition: Unlawful taking or attempted taking of property other than a motor vehicle from the possession of another, by stealth, without force and without deceit, with intent to deprive the owner of the property permanently.

Characteristics: Less than 5 percent of all personal larcenices involve contact between the victim and offender; unlike most other crimes, pocket picking and purse snatching affect the elderly about as much as other age groups; pocket picking and purse snatching occur most frequently inside nonresidential buildings or on street locations.

Motor Vehicle Theft

Definition: Unlawful taking or attempted taking of a self-propelled road vehicle owned by another, with the intent of depriving him or her of it, permanently or temporarily.

Characteristics: Motor vehicle theft is relatively well reported to the police; approximately 89 percent of all completed thefts were reported; stolen vehicles are more likely to be recovered than in other property crimes.

Arson

Definition: The intentional damaging or destruction or attempted damaging or destruction by means of fire or explosion of property without the consent of the owner, or of one's own property or that of another by fire or explosives with or without the intent to defraud.

Characteristics: Single-family residences were the most frequent targets of arson; about 16 percent of all structures where arson occurred were not in use.

Source: U.S. Department of Justice, BJS, *Dictionary of Criminal Justice Data Terminology,* 2nd ed. (Washington, D.C.: U.S. Government Printing Office, 1981); and *Report to the Nation on Crime and Justice,* 2nd ed. (Washington, D.C.: U.S. Government Printing Office, 1988).

Crime Rates

Crime rates are statistics used by the UCR to reflect trends in index crimes. Rates are computed for each index crime and also for various groups of crimes. The crime rate is computed by dividing the annual number of crimes by total population and multiplying the results by 100,000. If we state that the homicide rate is 9.7 for 19xx, this means that for every 100,000 people, there were 9.7 homicides that year. The "In Focus" feature on homicide trends is an example of the use of crime rates to indicate crime trends [4].

Problems With UCR

The problems with UCR include:

1. Crime statistics are only as accurate as the data reported to the FBI. The inaccuracy in reporting has two causes (a) police agencies

IN FOCUS

Homicide Trends

The National Center for Health Statistics reports that there have been three major trends in homicide since 1903. From 1903 to 1933, the homicide rate rose from 1.1 to 9.7 homicides per 100,000 people. Between 1934 and 1958, the homicide rate fell to 4.5. From 1961 to 1980, it rose to 11. From 1980 to 1987, it fell to 8.3 per 100,000.

FIGURE 3–2
Prison yard on a weekend. State Prison of Southern Michigan at Jackson. Courtesy of
the Michigan Department of Corrections.

vary as to the regularity and accuracy of their reporting; and (b) crimes
not reported by victims to the police or other agencies.

2. Most federal crimes and white-collar crimes are excluded from
the UCR.

3. The UCR distorts the crime rates by focusing on index crimes
and ignoring nonindex crimes when computing crime rates.

4. Often, if several crimes are committed in one incident, only the
most serious one is reported.

5. The crime rates need refinement in many cases. The present rates
for total index crimes merely counts the number of crimes without
considering the seriousness of the various crimes.

6. In some crimes, the rates are misleading. For example, the crime rates for rape are reported based on total population. A more correct base would be one that is based only on the female population.

■ NATIONAL CRIME SURVEYS

The National Crime Surveys (NCS) were started in 1973 to learn more about crime, its victims, and its consequences. In the first crime survey, the National Opinion Research Center surveyed 10,000 households in Atlanta, Baltimore, Cleveland, Dallas, Denver, Newark, Portland, and St. Louis. One of the original purposes was to measure the extent of the "hidden crime" problem in the United States. The phrase "hidden crime" refers to crime that is unknown to authorities. As the result of this first survey, the research center concluded that the crime rates reported by the victims were much higher than the rates known by the police [5].

Presently, the NCS is conducted by the Census Bureau under the sponsorship of the U.S. Department of Justice's Bureau of Justice Statistics. The data used by the NCS are based on random samples of U.S. households. Inferences regarding crime and crime rates are then made based on random samples. The sampling techniques include face-to-face interviews in which family members are asked questions regarding crime victimization within the household during the past twelve months. Each year, the data are organized by cities and then subdivided into thirty-nine separate data sets. There is an average of forty-three variables for each household examined. The offenses surveyed are limited to serious crimes such as rape, robbery, burglary, assault, and thefts. (*Note:* The limited scope of crime coverage is a limitation of the NCS.) In 1987, 49,000 households were surveyed encompassing 101,000 persons age 12 and over [6].

Problems With the NCS

The major problems with the NCS include [7]:

1. The surveys are limited to street crimes.

2. The surveys concentrate on victims. One crime involving multiple victims would be reported as multiple crimes.

3. Victims in some cases exaggerate or distort the data.

4. Children under the age of 12 are not included in the victimization rates.

■ NCS AND UCR COMPARED

While the National Crime Surveys and the Uniform Crime Reports are both statistical measures of crime and tend to complement each other, there are distinct differences in the two. The major differences include [8]:

1. The UCR count only crimes known to the police. The NCS contains information on both reported and unreported crimes.

2. The UCR count crimes committed against businesses, organizations, agencies, and so on, in addition to crimes committed against people. The NCS counts only crimes against persons age 12 or older and their households.

3. Because of the design of each series, in some cases the UCR and NCS count crimes differently.

4. The two series use different population bases to compute crime rates.

5. Crime rates for rape in the UCR include both males and females, whereas the victim surveys limit rape crime coverage to females.

IN FOCUS

Explain the Difference in Crime Rates

Between 1973 and 1981, the NCS burglary rate decreased by 4 percent, but the UCR rate increased by 34 percent. There are two reasons for the differences:

1. The NCS base is household, whereas the UCR base is population. The number of households grew at a much faster rate than the general population.

2. The UCR measures all burglaries known to the police. The NCS measures both reported and unreported burglaries, but only those affecting households.

Interview form
version 01

U.S. DEPARTMENT OF COMMERCE
BUREAU OF THE CENSUS
ACTING AS COLLECTING AGENT FOR THE
LAW ENFORCEMENT ASSISTANCE ADMINISTRATION
U.S. DEPARTMENT OF JUSTICE

NATIONAL SURVEY OF CRIME SEVERITY
VERSION 01
NATIONAL CRIME SURVEY SUPPLEMENT

A. Sample (cc 4) JO ___

B. Control number (cc 5)   PSU | Segment | CK | Serial

C. H.H. No. (cc 2)

D. Version No. 01

E. Respondent Line No. | Name

F. Interviewer identification   Code | Name

G. Date completed

J. Reason for noninterview
1 ☐ Type Z noninterview on NCS
2 ☐ Proxy interview on NCS
3 ☐ Refused NSCS (supplement only)
4 ☐ Language difficulty
5 ☐ Could not understand instructions —*Explain on reverse side*
6 ☐ Other – *Specify*

H. Type of interview
1 ☐ Personal
2 ☐ Telephone
3 ☐ Not applicable
9 ☐ OFFICE USE ONLY

I. Was anyone else present during interview?
1 ☐ Yes – All
2 ☐ Yes – Part
3 ☐ No
4 ☐ Not applicable
9 ☐ OFFICE USE ONLY

OFFICE USE ONLY | K. | L. | M. | N. | O. | P.

INTERVIEWER INSTRUCTION ▶ *Interview all household members 18 years and over (proxy interview not acceptable)*

INTRODUCTION – I would like to ask your opinion about how serious YOU think certain crimes are.

The first situation is, "A person steals a bicycle parked on the street." This has been given a score of 10 to show its seriousness. *(PAUSE)* Use this first situation to judge all the others. For example, if you think a situation is **20 TIMES MORE** serious than the bicycle theft, the number you tell me should be around 200 *(PAUSE)* or if you think it is **HALF AS SERIOUS**, the number you tell me should be around 5 and so on. *(PAUSE)* There is no upper limit; use **ANY** number so long as it shows how serious **YOU** think the situation is. *(PAUSE)* If **YOU** think something should not be a crime, give it a zero. *(PAUSE)*

Consider the following situation: "A person robs a victim. The victim is injured but not hospitalized." What number would you give to this situation to show how serious **YOU** think it is compared to the bicycle theft with a score of 10? *(Obtain answer)* . . . .

"A person under 16 years old plays hooky from school." Compared to the bicycle theft with a score of 10, how serious do YOU think this is? *(Obtain answer)*

"A person stabs a victim to death." Compared to the bicycle theft with a score of 10, how serious do YOU think this is? *(Obtain answer)* . . . .

1. A person steals a bicycle parked on the street	10
2. A person robs a victim. The victim is injured but not hospitalized	
3. A person under 16 years old plays hooky from school	
4. A person stabs a victim to death	

Let's go over these first few answers to be sure I have recorded them correctly. You feel that a robbery in which the victim is injured but not hospitalized. You feel that a robbery in which the victim is injured is (more/less/as) serious (than/as) the bicycle theft, *(PAUSE)* and that playing hooky is (more/less/as) serious (than/as) the bicycle theft; is that correct? *(PAUSE)*

INTERVIEWER INSTRUCTION: Stop and resolve any misunderstandings about the instructions. Make any changes to the practice scores as needed.

Score the remaining situations in the same way by comparing each one to the bicycle theft. There are no right or wrong answers. Remember, you may use any numbers, as high or low as you wish. *(PAUSE)*

COMPARED TO THE BICYCLE THEFT SCORED AT 10, HOW SERIOUS IS . . .

5. A person kidnaps a victim. . . . .

COMPARED TO THE BICYCLE THEFT SCORED AT 10, HOW SERIOUS IS . . .

6. Several large companies illegally fix the retail prices of their products. . . . .

7. A person steals property worth $10 from outside a building. . . . .

8. A person robs a victim of $1,000 at gunpoint. The victim is wounded and requires treatment by a doctor but not hospitalization. . . . .

9. A person conceals the identity of others that he knows have committed a serious crime. . . . .

10. A company pays a bribe of $10,000 to a legislator to vote for a law favoring the company. . . . . . .

COMPARED TO THE BICYCLE THEFT SCORED AT 10, HOW SERIOUS IS . . .

11. A person takes part in a dice game in an alley. . . .

12. A person intentionally injures a victim. As a result, the victim dies. . . . .

13. A person walks into a public museum and steals a painting worth $1,000. . . . .

14. A man forcibly rapes a woman. No other physical injury occurs. . . . .

15. A person does not have a weapon. He threatens to harm a victim unless the victim gives him money. The victim gives him $10 and is not harmed. . . . .

COMPARED TO THE BICYCLE THEFT SCORED AT 10, HOW SERIOUS IS . . .

16. A person smokes marijuana. . . . .

17. A person breaks into a display case in a store and steals $1,000 worth of merchandise. . . . .

18. A person knowingly lies under oath during a trial.

19. A person, using force, robs a victim of $10. The victim is hurt and requires hospitalization. . . . . .

20. A person intentionally sets fire to a building causing $100,000 worth of damage. . . . .

COMPARED TO THE BICYCLE THEFT SCORED AT 10, HOW SERIOUS IS . . .

21. A factory knowingly gets rid of its waste in a way that pollutes the water supply of a city. As a result, 20 people become ill but none requires medical treatment. . . . .

22. An employer orders one of his employees to commit a serious crime. . . . .

23. A person steals property worth $1,000 from outside a building. . . . .

24. A man beats his wife with his fists. She requires hospitalization. . . . .

25. A person plants a bomb in a public building. The bomb explodes and 20 people are killed. . . . .

Q. To help us understand peoples' scores, I would like to ask an additional question. *(PAUSE)* **BEFORE** I gave you the last item to score, did you have an upper limit or a highest number in mind that you wouldn't go over?

1 ☐ No – End Interview
2 ☐ Yes – What was it? _____ *(Explain on reverse side any special circumstances, then end interview.)*

FIGURE 3–3
Sample copy of a National Survey of Crime Severity.

Interview form
version 02

U.S. DEPARTMENT OF COMMERCE
BUREAU OF THE CENSUS
ACTING AS COLLECTING AGENT FOR THE
LAW ENFORCEMENT ASSISTANCE ADMINISTRATION
U.S. DEPARTMENT OF JUSTICE

NATIONAL SURVEY OF CRIME SEVERITY
VERSION 02
NATIONAL CRIME SURVEY SUPPLEMENT

NOTICE – Your report to the Census Bureau is confidential by law (U.S. Code 42, section 3771). All identifiable information will be used only by persons engaged in and for the purposes of the survey, and may not be disclosed or released to others for any purpose.

A. Sample (cc 4)	B. Control number (cc 5)				C. H.H. No. (cc 2)	D. Version No.
JO___	PSU	Segment	CK	Serial		02

E. Respondent
Line No. | Name

F. Interviewer identification
Code | Name

G. Date completed

J. Reason for noninterview
1 ☐ Type Z noninterview on NCS
2 ☐ Proxy interview on NCS
3 ☐ Refused NSCS (supplement only)
4 ☐ Language difficulty
5 ☐ Could not understand instructions —Explain on reverse side
6 ☐ Other – Specify

H. Type of interview
1 ☐ Personal
2 ☐ Telephone
B ☐ Not applicable
9 ☐ OFFICE USE ONLY

I. Was anyone else present during interview?
1 ☐ Yes – All
2 ☐ Yes – Part
3 ☐ No
4 ☐ Not applicable
9 ☐ OFFICE USE ONLY

OFFICE USE ONLY	K.	L.	M.	N.	O.	P.

INTERVIEWER INSTRUCTION ▶ Interview all household members 18 years and over (proxy interview not acceptable)

INTRODUCTION – I would like to ask your opinion about how serious YOU think certain crimes are.

The first situation is, "A person steals a bicycle parked on the street." This has been given a score of 10 to show its seriousness. (PAUSE) Use this first situation to judge all the others. For example, if you think a situation is 20 TIMES MORE serious than the bicycle theft, the number you tell me should be around 200 (PAUSE) or if you think it is HALF AS SERIOUS, the number you tell me should be around 5 and so on. (PAUSE) There is no upper limit; use ANY number so long as it shows how serious YOU think the situation is. (PAUSE) If YOU think something should not be a crime, give it a zero. (PAUSE)

Consider the following situation: "A person robs a victim. The victim is injured but not hospitalized." What number would you give to this situation to show how serious YOU think it is compared to the bicycle theft with a score of 10? (Obtain answer)

"A person under 16 years old plays hooky from school." Compared to the bicycle theft with a score of 10, how serious do YOU think this is? (Obtain answer)

"A person stabs a victim to death." Compared to the bicycle theft with a score of 10, how serious do YOU think this is? (Obtain answer)

1. A person steals a bicycle parked on the street		10
2. A person robs a victim. The victim is injured but not hospitalized		
3. A person under 16 years old plays hooky from school		
4. A person stabs a victim to death		

Let's go over these first few answers to be sure I have recorded them correctly. You feel that a robbery in which the victim is injured is (more/less/as) serious (than/as) the bicycle theft, (PAUSE) and that playing hooky is (more/less/as) serious (than/as) the bicycle theft; is that correct? (PAUSE)

INTERVIEWER INSTRUCTION: Stop and resolve any misunderstandings about the instructions. Make any changes to the practice scores as needed.

Score the remaining situations in the same way by comparing each one to the bicycle theft. There are no right or wrong answers. Remember, you may use any numbers, as high or low as you wish. (PAUSE)

COMPARED TO THE BICYCLE THEFT SCORED AT 10, HOW SERIOUS IS . . .

5. A person breaks into a public recreation center, forces open a cash box and steals $1,000. . . . .

COMPARED TO THE BICYCLE THEFT SCORED AT 10, HOW SERIOUS IS . . .

6. A person intentionally hits a victim with a lead pipe. No medical treatment is required. . . . .

7. A person knowingly trespasses in a railroad yard. .

8. A person robs a victim of $1,000 at gunpoint. No physical harm occurs. . . . .

9. A person steals property worth $50 from outside a building. . . . .

10. A factory knowingly gets rid of its waste in a way that pollutes the water supply of a city. As a result, one person dies. . . . .

COMPARED TO THE BICYCLE THEFT SCORED AT 10, HOW SERIOUS IS . . .

11. A person picks a victim's pocket of $100. . . . . . .

12. A person smuggles marijuana into the country for resale. . . . .

13. A person steals a locked car and sells it. . . . . . .

14. A legislator takes a bribe of $10,000 from a company to vote for a law favoring the company. . . .

15. A man drags a woman into an alley, tears her clothes, but flees before she is physically harmed or sexually attacked. . . . .

COMPARED TO THE BICYCLE THEFT SCORED AT 10, HOW SERIOUS IS . . .

16. A person gives the floor plans of a bank to a bank robber. . . . .

17. A person steals property worth $1,000 from outside a building. . . . .

18. A person beats a victim with his fists. The victim is hurt but does not require medical treatment. . . .

19. An employer refuses to hire a qualified person because of that person's race. . . . .

20. A person stabs a victim with a knife. No medical treatment is required. . . . .

COMPARED TO THE BICYCLE THEFT SCORED AT 10, HOW SERIOUS IS . . .

21. A person breaks into a building and steals property worth $10. . . . .

22. A person intentionally injures a victim. The victim is treated by a doctor and hospitalized. . . . .

23. Two persons willingly engage in a homosexual act.

24. A parent beats his young child with his fists. As a result, the child dies. . . . .

25. A person plants a bomb in a public building. The bomb explodes and 20 people are killed. . . . . . .

Q. To help us understand peoples' scores, I would like to ask an additional question. (PAUSE) BEFORE I gave you the last item to score, did you have an upper limit or a highest number in mind that you wouldn't go over?
1 ☐ No – End Interview
2 ☐ Yes – What was it? _____ (Explain on reverse side any special circumstances, then end interview.)

■ SELF-REPORTS

An unofficial method of measuring crime is by self-reports. The self-report method was developed in an attempt to measure the extent of juvenile crime more accurately. There are three commonly used procedures for administrating self-reporting: (1) anonymous questionnaires with no check on validity, (2) sampling by use of structured or semistructured interviews, and (3) using questionnaires that can be checked against police reports and records. The problems with self-reports are numerous. They lack continuity. They are often not representative, and their accuracy is questionable [9].

■ DATA COLLECTIONS

In addition to the measures discussed earlier, there are numerous individual data collections that have been conducted by public institu-

FIGURE 3–4

Prisoner being escorted to disciplinary segregation. (Courtesy of the Washington State Dept. of Corrections.

tions, universities, and other research institutions. To provide an information network of data collections, the Criminal Justice Archive and Information Network (CJAIN) was established in 1977 at the Inter-University Consortium for Political and Social Research, Ann Arbor, Michigan, under a cooperative agreement with the U.S. Department of Justice, Bureau of Justice Statistics. CJAIN now publishes annual catalogs of all known data collections regarding criminal justice statistics. Subject categories included in CJAIN catalogs include attitude surveys, community studies, official statistics, victimization studies, and court statistics [10]. Also available from CJAIN are the British Crime Surveys, which are conducted periodically by the British Home Office Research and Planning Unit. Most of the data collections are maintained "on-line" and therefore may be retrieved by using a telecommunication network from a computer database called SPILES.

IN FOCUS

The Relative Severity of Criminal Conduct

Rank order the following cases as to their severity:

_____ 1. The individual who during a fight in a bar kills another person.

_____ 2. The public official who steals $300,000 from the school district's hot lunch program.

_____ 3. The person who cheats each year on his or her income tax.

_____ 4. The engineer who fails to report a safety problem with a new automobile being developed.

_____ 5. The male who rapes a 12 year old girl.

_____ 6. The robber who kills his only witness.

_____ 7. The contract killer.

_____ 8. The person who drives under the influence of alcohol and kills two people.

_____ 9. The person who drives regularly under the influence of alcohol, but has been lucky and hasn't hurt anyone.

_____ 10. The company executive who dumps chemical waste in a manner that causes a health hazard.

▌ RATING OF CRIMINAL BEHAVIOR

The rating of the seriousness of criminal behavior is highly subjective. Crime affects each victim differently. One famous study included an extensive survey to determine how people rank the severity of crime. Below is a selected list of crimes and the numerical rating given [11].

Rating	Situation
52.8	Forcibly raping and then murdering a woman
43.2	Armed robbery in which the victim is killed
33.8	Running a narcotics ring
25.9	Forcible rape
24.9	Arson where loss exceeds $100,000
21.2	Kidnapping a victim
20.7	Selling heroin
6.5	Using heroin
4.5	Cheating on income taxes
2.1	Prostitution

▌ CRIMINAL ACTIVITY

In this section we discuss the questions: How much crime is there? Have crime rates gone up in recent years? When do crimes occur? Where do crimes occur?

How Much Crime Is There?

Despite the extensive measures used to measure criminal activity, the fact remains that a substantial number of crimes are not reported or known to the police. This phenomenon is called the "dark side of crime" or "hidden crime." Since the NCS is based on victimization reports, it is apparently a more accurate measurement of actual criminal activity in society. As noted earlier, the scope of the NCS is limited. In addition, there is the contention by many that victims tend to overreport their involvement in criminal activity.

According to the NCS, violence or theft touches about one-fourth of all households in the United States each year. Approximately 5 percent of all households are burglarized each year. Five percent of all

IN FOCUS

How Do Crime Rates Compare With the Rates of Other Life Events?

Event	Rate per 1000 adults per year
Accidental injuries	242
Accidental injuries at home	79
Personal theft	72
Accidental injury at work	58
Violent victimization	31
Assault	24
Robbery	6
Cancer death	2
Rape (women only)	2
Suicide	0.2

Source: U.S. Department of Justice, BJS, The Risk of Violent Crime (Washington, D.C.: U.S. Government Printing Office, 1985).

households annually have at least one member who is a victim of rape, robbery, or assault. According to NCS, in 1985, 35 million persons were victimized [12].

The UCR indicates that there were 12 million index crimes reported to the police in 1985. Of those, 1.3 million were violent crimes of murder, rape, robbery and aggravated assault. In addition, there were almost 1 million businesses burglarized in 1985. Property crimes outnumbered violent crimes by 9:1 [13].

Has Criminal Activity Increased?

When crime rates soared in the 1960s and 1970s, it appeared that crime rates were increasing at an alarming rate. Beginning in 1980, however, the crime rates began to decline. By 1984, they appeared to have leveled off [14].

According to the NCS, the percentage of households touched by crime has declined from 32 percent in 1975 to 25 percent in 1986. The decline has, however, been greater for personal larceny without contact and burglary than for violent personal crimes [15]. Total UCR in-

IN FOCUS

Increased Efficiency of Police May Increase Crimes Rates

Much of the increase in crime rates from 1960 to 1980 may be attributed to the fact that more crime was known to the police because of increased and more comprehensive reporting procedures and increased professionalism on the part of the police. If the police are more professional and more efficient, they will detect more crime. In addition, if the public has confidence in the local police, they have a greater tendency to report crimes. Since the UCR is based on crimes known to the police, an increase in efficiency of the police may result in a rise in crime rates for that community.

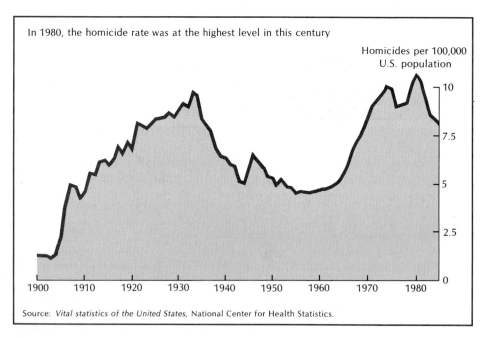

In 1980, the homicide rate was at the highest level in this century

Source: *Vital statistics of the United States,* National Center for Health Statistics.

FIGURE 3–5
In 1980, the homicide rate was at the highest level in this century.

dex crimes declined 2 percent from 1976 to 1985. There was, except for homicide, a 19 percent increase in violent index crimes. However, homicide decreased during that period by 10 percent [16].

Several different theories have been offered to explain the decline in crime rates [17]. The three most popular theories are as follows:

1. A larger number of career criminals are being incarcerated and are therefore unable to commit more crimes.

2. There is a decreasing percentage in our population of young adults, who are the most crime-prone.

3. The growth of citizen crime-prevention activities, such as neighborhood watch programs.

When Do Crimes Occur?

NCS data indicate that crimes against the person and crimes against the home are more likely to occur in warm weather than in the winter [18]. Several reasons have been advanced for this phenomenon:

1. People tend to spend more time outdoors during the warm months, making them more vulnerable to personal crimes.

2. Homes are more likely to be left open (doors and windows) during warm months than during cold months, making them more vulnerable to property crimes.

There are two exceptions to the trends noted above. First, robbery rates fluctuate but display no regular pattern of high and low months. Second, petty theft (larceny under $50) shows a regular decline during summer months. The drop in petty theft crimes may be based on the decline of school-related thefts during school vacations.

Most criminal activity takes place during evening or nighttime hours. For example, 63 percent of the motor vehicle thefts and 60 percent of the robberies with injuries in 1985 occurred during the hours of darkness. Homicide occurs most often during the "social hours" (7 P.M.–midnight).

Some crimes, such as simple assault, purse snatching, pocket picking, and personal larceny, are more likely to occur during daylight hours. Often, it is unknown when a burglary occurred. Among burglaries where time of occurrence can be established, they are almost equally divided between daytime and nighttime occurrences [19].

Where Do Crimes Occur?

According to NCS, the largest number of crimes occur in the general area where the victim lives. NCS reports that 88 percent of the violent victimizations of central city residents occurred in the central city, and 73 percent of the victimizations of suburban residents occurred in their suburban area [20]. The National Crime Survey for 1985 contained the following conclusions [21]:

1. Robbery and personal larceny with contact (purse snatching and pocket picking) are more likely to occur in cities.

2. Suburban dwellers are more likely to be victims of crime in the central city than are city dwellers to become victims in the suburbs.

3. Thirty-two percent of the rapes occurred in or around the home of the victim.

4. Twenty-six percent of the violent personal crimes occurred in or around the home of the victim.

5. Most of the violent personal crimes committed by strangers occurred away from the home of the victim.

6. Persons who live in the central part of the city are more likely to be victimized than are suburban or rural residents.

7. Residents of larger cities are more likely to be victimized than are residents of smaller cities.

IN FOCUS

Your Chances of Being Murdered on the Job

The odds are 2 in 100,000 annually that a male worker will be murdered on the job. According to researchers Jess Kraus and Harold Davis, only motor vehicles kill more people than guns at work. The *American Journal of Public Health* states that murder is a vocational peril that the Occupational Safety and Health Administration has failed to address. Women are less likely than men to be murdered at work because few toil in the most hazardous jobs.

Source: The Wall Street Journal, Sept. 8, 1988

■ SUMMARY

The Uniform Crime Reports (UCR) and the National Crime Surveys (NCS) are the main sources of national crime statistics. The UCR indices show trends for eight serious crimes. The FBI receives their data for the UCR from over 15,000 law enforcement agencies. The UCR is prepared annually. Crimes are reported as either index or nonindex crimes. Crime rates are statistics used by the UCR system to establish trends for the index crimes. Crime statistics are only as accurate as the data reported to the FBI.

The National Crime Surveys (NCS) were started in 1973 to learn more about crime, its victims, and its consequences. The data used by the NCS are based on random samples of U.S. households. NCS's inferences regarding crime and crime rates are based on the random samples. Despite the extensive measures used to measure criminal activity, the fact remains that a substantial number of crimes are not reported or known to the police. According to the NCS, violence or theft touches about one-fourth of all households in the United States each year. Five percent of all households annually have at least one member who is a victim of rape, robbery, or assault. Property crimes outnumber violent crimes by 9:1. According to the NCS, the percentage of households touched by crime has declined from 32 percent in 1975 to 25 percent in 1986.

NCS data indicate that crimes against the person and crimes against the home are more likely to occur in warm weather than in the winter. Most criminal activity takes place during evening or nighttime hours. According to NCS, the largest number of crimes occur within the general area where the victim lives. Persons who live in the central part of the city are more likely to be victimized than are suburban or rural residents.

■ MATCHING KEY TERMS AND DEFINITIONS

Match each key term with the correct definition.

a. arson
b. assault
c. burglary
d. crime rates
e. homicide
f. index crimes
g. larceny

h. National Crime Surveys
i. Nonindex Crimes
j. rape
k. robbery
l. self-reports
m. Uniform Crime Reports

——— **1.** This crime is defined as the unlawful taking or attempted taking of property from the possession of another, by stealth, without force and without deceit, with intent to deprive the owner of the property permanently.

——— **2.** This crime is committed by causing the death of another person without legal justification or excuse.

——— **3.** A series of crime statistics developed from a 1927 effort by the International Association of Chiefs of Police (IACP) to create a uniform system for gathering statistics on crimes known to the police.

——— **4.** The act of unlawful sexual intercourse with a female, by force or without legal or factual consent, is a description of this crime.

——— **5.** This crime consists of the intentional damaging or destruction or attempted damaging or destruction by means of fire or explosion of property without the consent of the owner.

——— **6.** This series of crime statistics was started in 1973 to learn more about crime, its victims, and its consequences.

——— **7.** Statistics used by the UCR to reflect trends in index crimes.

——— **8.** This crime is committed by the unlawful taking or attempted taking of property that is in the immediate possession of another, by force or threat of force.

——— **9.** Unlawful intentional inflicting, or attempted inflicting, of injury upon the person of another is a violation of this crime.

——— **10.** The crimes of arson, homicide, rape, assault, robbery, burglary, larceny/theft, and motor vehicle theft are included in this group of crimes.

——— **11.** This crime is the unlawful entry of any fixed structure, vehicle, or vessel used for regular residence, industry, or business, with or without force, with the intent to commit a felony or larceny.

——— **12.** Crimes reported in this category are limited only to those cleared by arrest, prosecution or those formally charged.

——— **13.** This class of crime statistics was developed in an attempt to measure the extent of juvenile crime more accurately.

∎ DISCUSSION QUESTIONS

1. What are some of the major problems in measuring the extent of criminal activity in society?

2. What are the bases for inclusion of crimes in the UCR?

3. What are the deficiencies of the NCS?

NOTES

1. U.S. Department of Justice, BJS, *Report to the Nation on Crime and Justice*, 2d ed. Washington, D.C.: U.S. Government Printing Office, 1988.

2. U.S. Department of Justice, FBI, *Uniform Crime Reporting Handbook*, Washington, D.C.: U.S. Government Printing Office, 1980.

3. U.S. Department of Justice, FBI, *Crime in the Untied States, 1986*. Washington, D.C.: U.S. Government Printing Office, 1986.

4. U.S. Department of Justice, BJS, 1988.

5. U.S. Department of Justice, BJS, *National Crime Surveys: National Sample, 1973–1983*. Washington, D.C.: U.S. Government Printing Office, 1985.

6. U.S. Department of Justice, BJS, *National Crime Survey, 1980–1984*. Washington, D.C.: U.S. Government Printing Office, 1985.

7. Wesley G. Skogan, *Issues in the Measurement of Victimization*. Washington, D.C.: U.S. Government Printing Office, 1981.

8. Robert Lehnen and Wesley G. Skogan, eds., *The National Crime Survey: Working Papers*, Vol. II, Washington, D.C.: U.S. Government Printing Office, 1984.

9. Lehnen and Skogan, 1984.

10. Inter-University Consortium for Political and Social Research, *Data Collections Available from the CJAIN*. Ann Arbor, Mich.: ICPSR, 1988.

11. *The Seriousness of Crime: Results of a National Survey*. Philadelphia: Center for Studies in Criminology and Criminal Law, University of Pennsylvania, 1983.

12. U.S. Department of Justice, BJS, 1988.

13. U.S. Department of Justice, FBI, *Crime in the United States, 1985*. Washington, D.C.: U.S. Government Printing Office, 1985.

14. U.S. Department of Justice, BJS, 1988: 14–15.

15. U.S. Department of Justice, BJS, 1988: 14.

16. U.S. Department of Justice, FBI, 1986.

17. U.S. Department of Justice, BJS, 1988: 14.

18. U.S. Department of Justice, BJS, 1988: 17.

19. U.S. Department of Justice, BJS, *National Crime Survey*, 1985.

20. U.S. Department of Justice, BJS, *Criminal Victimization in the U.S.*, Washington, D.C.: U.S. Government Printing Office, 1985.

21. U.S. Department of Justice, BJS, *Criminal Victimization, 1985*: 19; and BJS Special Report, *Locating City, Suburban, and Rural Crime*. Washington, D.C.: U.S. Government Printing Office, 1985.

4

Classical Criminology

CHAPTER HIGHLIGHTS

- The classical school is considered one of the first attempts to organize a view of crime causation.
- The classical school was a product of the Age of Enlightenment.
- The writings of the classical school were philosophical and nonempirical.
- The classical school's concepts were based on social contract theory.
- The doctrine of free will is used to explain human behavior.
- The pleasure–pain concept is inherent in classical school theory.
- Criminals are solely responsible for their behavior.
- Crime reduction can be accomplished by inflicting a sufficient amount of pain upon the offender.
- The type and amount of punishment imposed upon the offender should be determined by focusing only on the crime itself.
- There should be similar punishments for all persons who commit the same crime under similar circumstances.
- The purpose of punishment is to deter both the criminal and noncriminal from committing criminal acts.
- Offender treatment is not considered by classical thinkers.
- The classical concept of punishment was that it should be fast, certain, and serve a useful function.

KEY TERMS

Age of Enlightenment	Despotic Spirit
Beccaria	Free Will
Bentham	Neoclassical
Classical School	Utilitarian Principle

The collection of ideas known as the classical school of criminology is considered one of the first attempts in the modern Western world to organize a view of crime causation and pinpoint the significant concepts in understanding the crime problem. (A "school of criminology" is a system of thought and includes those persons who advocate that system of thought.) The term "classical" refers to the fact that the school was one of the first to develop an organized perspective of the criminal's nature. "Classical" is used as a descriptive term, alluding to being the first, similar to Latin's reference as a classical language. The classical theory was dominant for almost a century until it was replaced by positivist theory (see Chapter 5).

In the late 1970s and early 1980s there was a revival of classical school thinking. As will be discussed later in this chapter, the classical theme is alive and well today in the American administration of justice.

▌ BACKGROUND

The classical school is an outgrowth of the Age of Enlightenment. The Enlightenment movement dominated European thinking for three-quarters of the eighteenth century. Prior to the Age of Enlightenment was the Age of Science, during which scientists and mathematicians such as Copernicus, Descartes, Newton, Galileo, Locke, Rousseau, and others discovered new ideas that revolutionized human thinking.

The Age of Enlightenment promoted optimism, certainty, reason, toleration, humanitarianism, the belief that all human problems could be solved, and a belief in human progress. The philosophers and theorists were of the opinion that they could discover the laws governing human institutions and behavior. The heroes of the Enlightenment period were philosophers, who with logic and rationality, attempted to rid the world of its problems.

The Enlightenment movement influenced all aspects of European and early American life, including social thinking, the arts, literature, and politics. Its influence is noted in the U.S. Constitution and is especially prominent in the Bill of Rights. This was the environment in which Cesare Beccaria and Jeremy Bentham flourished and developed their ideas on crime causation, and thus the classical school evolved.

IN FOCUS

(Cesare Bonesana, Marchese de Beccaria; (Cesare Beccaria); 1738–1794)

Cesare Bonesana, Marchese de Beccaria, considered one of the founders of the classical school of criminology, has been described as lazy and easily discouraged. His short essay on penal reform is apparently his only work of distinction. It was published during his lifetime and after his death, made him famous.

Beccaria was born in Milan, Italy, on March 15, 1738. His parents were members of the aristocracy and both had distinguished professional careers. He attended college at Jesuit College in Parma and studied economics. Later, he studied law at the University of Pavia. Except for a brief interest in mathematics, Beccaria found his schooling a drudgery.

Beccaria returned to Milan after completing his education. There he developed into an avid reader of literature and philosophy. He joined a group of young men dedicated to the study of literary and philosophical subjects. While a member of this group, he published his first work, a short, unimportant essay on the plight of the monetary system in Milan.

Two brothers who were members of the group turned Beccaria's attention to the subjects of penology and crime. The two men, Pietro Verri, a distinguished economist, and Allessandro Verri, a creative writer, provided Beccaria with heated debates on the social issues of the time. They assigned him the task of analyzing the Italian penal system. Prior to this, Beccaria knew little about penology. After studying the issues, Beccaria presented his arguments for reforming the Italian penal system. The brothers encouraged him to put his thoughts and ideas into writing.

In July 1764, at the age of 26, Beccaria published his famous essay, *On Crimes and Punishments.* He had started writing it in March 1763 and completed the manuscript in January 1764. It was originally published anonymously. The essay was an immediate success. At the time it was published, the existing system of criminal law was repressive and barbaric. His essay was considered a blueprint for reform. It advocated changes that were quickly supported by public opinion.

After his essay was published, Beccaria visited Paris in 1766, where he gave lectures on political economy. In 1768 he was appointed as a professor of political economy at the Palatine School of Milan. Ten years after his death, a collection of his essays were published. This collection represents his only other major creative work.

In his essay, Beccaria adopted the "social contract" theory which was sweeping Europe at the time, and applied it to penology. According to him, a person was bound to society only by his consent, and there-fore, this made society responsible to him as well. One of his most fa-mous recommendations was that all social actions should be based on the greatest happiness for the greatest number. Beccaria's influence can be noted in Blackstone's *Commentaries on the Laws of England,* which is the basis for modern English law.

(*Source:* Coleman Phillipson, *Three Criminal Law Reformers* (London: Dutton, 1923).

Whereas the leaders of the seventeenth century were scientists and mathematicians, the leaders of the eighteenth century were phi-losophers. The scientists and mathematicians were unable to solve the human problems that existed at the time. Accordingly, the philoso-phers proceeded with a mandate to solve them. Such problems, the philosophers maintained, could be eradicated only if the concept of reason was applied. The application of pure reason was considered the answer to all societal problems. Rationality was itself considered curative. The "light of pure reason" was exhaulted.

The philosophers' writings were abstract, global, and had a phil-osophical, nonempirical tone. They came to conclusions by trusting their instincts and intuition regarding events and ideas. At this time scientific research methodology with the use of random sampling, sta-tistical tests, and so on, had not been perfected. Working under these conditions, it is a tribute to one of the founders of the classical school, Cesare Beccaria, that his famous essay *On Crimes and Punishments* is considered an excellent critique of our criminal justice system today.

▌ CONCEPT OF HUMAN NATURE

The classical school's concept of human nature marked a shift in the-oretical concepts from that of the divine rights of kings to the intel-lectualism and rationalism of the social contract followers. It repre-sented an abandonment of the supernatural as an explanation of crime and criminal behavior. Human beings were seen as governed by the doctrine of "free will" and rational behavior [1].

According to the classical school:

- All human beings, including criminals, will freely choose either criminal paths or noncriminal paths, depending on which path they believe will benefit them.

FIGURE 4–1
The electric chair, modern science's answer to the gallows, has been replaced in some states by lethal injection, the gas chamber, or a firing squad. UPI/Bettman Newsphotos

- Criminals will avoid behaviors that will bring pain and will engage in behaviors that will bring pleasure.
- Prior to deciding which course of action to take, criminals will weigh the expected benefits against the expected pains.
- Criminals are responsible for their behaviors. They are seen as human beings who are able to interpret, analyze, and dissect the situations in which they find themselves.
- Criminals act over and against their environments. They are not victims of their environments.
- Criminals go through a thinking process whereby they take a variety of factors into account before they make a final decision on whether or not to commit a criminal act.
- Criminals are totally responsible for their behavior.
- Environmental forces do not push, pull, or propel individuals to act. An individual acts willfully and freely.

- Offenders are not helpless, passive, or propelled by forces beyond their control.
- Each criminal act is a deliberate one, committed by a rational, choosing person who is motivated primarily by the pleasure–pain principle.

The classical school's concept of human nature is summarized as follows:

- The criminal takes a variety of factors into account before freely choosing to commit a criminal act.
- Accordingly, the criminal should be held responsible for his or her behavior.

▌ CRIME CAUSATION

Crime is related to the inequities in the criminal justice system. The criminal, a rational and logical person, sees inconsistencies in the administration of justice process. There is a general awareness that punishments are not administered rationally and fairly. Criminals understand that judges have different biases and that these biases are often reflected in sentencing practices. Offenders understand that a "good" attorney can often make the difference as to whether or not punishments will be harsh.

In eighteenth-century Italy there were many inequities in the administration of justice. Judges had great autonomy and did what they wanted. There was no consistency or uniformity in sentencing. Each jurisdiction was an island unto itself. This lack of logic and rationality in the administration of justice was thought to be related to the cause of crime.

▌ PURPOSES OF PUNISHMENT

There was no room for the individual offender's reformation or cure in original classical school thinking. The idea of individual treatment of the offender was not present in the eighteenth century. Individualized treatment would not emerge until the second half of the nineteenth century. (It would come about with the birth of positivism.) The classical concept was that punishment should be fast, certain, severe, useful, and fit the crime. A punishment such as cutting off a thief's hands because the thief stole a loaf of bread would be wrong because it did not fit the crime. It was too harsh. The punishment must be proportional to the crime. No consideration is given to the person who committed the act.

Punishment should also be only as severe as is necessary to deter. For the classical school, the function of punishment was to deter crime. It would be considered as a deterrent only if the punishment was perceived as fair and in proportion to the crime committed. If the punishments were too severe, they would cause people to commit other criminal acts solely to avoid punishment.

The only purpose of punishment was to protect society. The concept of crime prevention as we know it today was nonexistent. The classical concept of justice included an exact scale of punishments for acts without reference to the criminal's circumstances.

THE THEORY OF CESARE BECCARIA AS CONTAINED IN *ON CRIMES AND PUNISHMENTS*

Cesare Beccaria's revolutionary essay *On Crimes and Punishments* was published in 1764. His essay was a revolt against despotism, absolutism, and the Italian administration of justice practices. The highlights of Beccaria's essay are discussed next.

Origin of Punishments

Beccaria was a believer in the social contract theory. He believed that people gave up certain individual freedoms to live collectively within a society. The individual gained certain advantages and protections living in a group that he or she would not have living an isolated existence.

Human nature is such, however, that some people will always try to take more than is rightfully theirs and will behave as if they had no regard for the group unless checked by society. Beccaria called this the "despotic spirit" which he felt was within every human being. He was also of the opinion that if the despotic spirit was not checked, society would be plunged into chaos. Accordingly, it was necessary to create laws and punishments to protect the group against the individual's innate despotic spirit.

Results of Punishment and the Role of Legislatures

Beccaria was firm in his belief that punishment should be determined by legislatures, not judges. He reacted against the widespread practice of his day. Judges were autonomous and did what they pleased. They would augment statutory punishments with whatever they saw fit at the time. The concept of due process did not exist. The status, money, and power of the accused often affected sentencing. Punishments were arbitrary and inconsistent.

Interpretation of the Law by Judges

Beccaria was of the belief that the judge should not interpret laws but rather, should carry out the letter of the law. He felt that the problems that occur from "rigorous observance of the letter of penal law are hardly comparable to the disorders that arise from interpretations." Beccaria concluded that people would be able to understand the consequences of specific criminal acts, and this would make the administration of justice process rational.

Incarceration

Beccaria reacted to judges institutionalizing prisoners on bogus pretexts and on flimsy evidence. In Beccaria's day, judges, at their pleasure, tended to imprison citizens. According to Beccaria, the law alone should determine the cases in which imprisonment should be the penalty.

Torture

Torture was a common practice in Beccaria's day and was used routinely to force a person to confess, to clear up inconsistencies, or to discover accomplices. Beccaria considered that a person was not guilty until he or she was sentenced. He felt that torture was inhuman, and hence wrong. He also considered torture to be irrational. To Beccaria it was difficult to tell if people were telling the truth when they were comfortable, let alone when they were in pain.

Mildness of Punishments

Beccaria was of the opinion that a punishment should be only slightly harsher than the advantages that were derived from the crime. It was

IN FOCUS

An American Indian Precept

According to an American Indian precept, if the child is naughty, do not hit it. Make the child fast. When the child is hungry, it will remember its past misconduct. Beating a child makes it more naughty. What classical concepts are present in this precept?

more important for punishment to be certain. Any harsh punishment was considered cruel and superfluous. Severe punishments could backfire, Beccaria reasoned, in that they could cause people to commit additional crimes, such as perjury to avoid harsh punishment.

Capital Punishment

Beccaria indicated that when people formed a social contract, they did not give the group the right to kill a person. Such an act would not be rational. The sacrifice of individual liberty did not include the sacrifice of the greatest good of all, life.

Beccaria was opposed to capital punishment except in two instances:

1. In the case of an imprisoned person who could endanger the security of the nation

2. In the case of an imprisoned person who could still cause other serious crimes to be committed

Beccaria thought that life imprisonment was a greater deterrent than capital punishment. He saw the death penalty, in most cases, as barbaric.

Promptness of Punishment

Beccaria indicated that the swiftest punishment was the most useful to society. Although behavior modification theory and practice were several centuries in the future, Beccaria did understand and write about the importance of the association and linkage of ideas regarding

A Chinese Proverb

There is an old Chinese proverb that states: "It is better to hang the wrong fellow rather than no fellow." This is based on the classical concept that certainty of punishment is an important variable in reducing crime. How does this proverb support the classical concept of punishment? How does it differ?

crime and punishment. As one reads this section of his essay, one is impressed at his primitive understanding of behaviorist principles.

Certainty of Punishment

Certainty of punishment was an absolute necessity, according to Beccaria. As long as punishment would result from a criminal act, it did not matter if punishment was mild. The follow-through was the important variable.

FIGURE 4-2
Serious crime arrest rates are highest in young age groups. Source: FBI Uniform Crime Reports, three-year averages, 1983–1985.

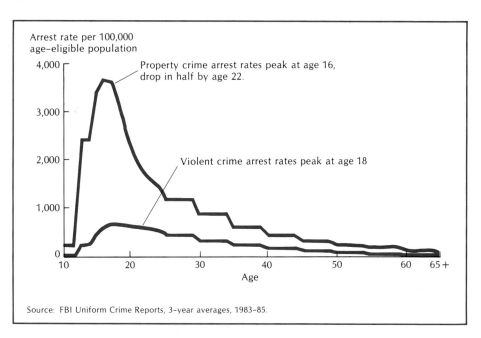

Arrest rate per 100,000 age–eligible population

Property crime arrest rates peak at age 16, drop in half by age 22.

Violent crime arrest rates peak at age 18

Age

Source: FBI Uniform Crime Reports, 3-year averages, 1983-85.

FIGURE 4–3
Hard work on a Georgia road gang was one method used to correct criminals in the 1940s. Courtesy of Danny Lyon/Magham

Proportion Between Crimes and Punishment

Punishments should fit crimes. Punishment should make sense in relation to the offense committed. The greater the harm done to society by the act, the more severe the punishment should be. The less the harm to society, the milder the punishment should be.

Crime Prevention

Beccaria acknowledged that it was better to prevent crimes than to punish the criminals. However, he saw crime prevention occurring as a result of a rational legal system, not as a result of neighborhood watch programs, secured homes, and the education of the public as to criminal behaviors and practices. The best way to prevent crimes was to make the laws clear, simple, unbiased, well publicized, and not to allow corruption in the administration and enforcement of laws.

Summary

Beccaria concluded his essay with this statement:

> In order for punishment not to be, in every instance, an act of violence of one or many against a private citizen, it must be essentially public, prompt, necessary, the least possible in the given circumstances, proportionate to the crimes, dictated by the laws.

Jeremy Bentham (1748–1832)

Jeremy Bentham was a prolific writer and has been described as an "armchair philosopher" whose writing covered a variety of topics, such as the purpose of law and prison building. A contemporary of Beccaria, Bentham has been called the greatest legal philosopher and reformer the world has ever seen. He was also considered one of the founders of the classical school.

Bentham's great grandfather was a prosperous pawnbroker in London. His father and grandfather were attorneys. He also studied law and was admitted to the bar. However, he had great scorn for the legal profession. One of the rare humorous comments in his writings is: "Only the lawyer escapes punishment for his ignorance of the law."

Whereas Beccaria enjoyed being with people, Bentham was ill at ease with a group and preferred books to people. Bentham's mother died when he was young. He did not get along with his stepmother. He had his first and only relationship with a woman at the age of 57. When she refused his offer of marriage, he had nothing further to do with women.

Bentham developed the Panoptican plan for prisons. This prison plan was meant to be a rational, humane environment for offenders. It was to be the answer to the human warehouses that existed at the time. The Panoptican prison was a circular building with a glass roof. It was designed so that every cell was visible from a central point. The prison inspector would be kept from the sight of the prisoners by the use of blinds. If the prisoner thought that he was fit to be observed, the prisoner could show himself by raising the blinds. The person in charge of the prison would be the manager. The manager was liable if a certain number of the prisoners under his supervision died. The prisoners would be contracted out, with the manager receiving a percentage of the money earned by the prisoners. The manager would, however, be held liable if prisoners, under his supervision, later committed additional crimes.

Jeremy Bentham died in 1832. In accordance with his will, his body was dissected. His skeleton was dressed in his usual attire and is on display at the University College in London. For over 150 years, the fully dressed skeleton has attended the college faculty assemblies. Speakers at the assembly traditionally first voice recognition to Mr. Bentham and then to the other members of the assembly and guests.

Source: Charles Milner Atkinson, *Jeremy Bentham: His Life and Work,* 1905.

■ THE THEORY OF JEREMY BENTHAM

Jeremy Bentham was also a major contributor to the classical school of criminology. He wrote *An Introduction to Principles of Morals and Legislation* in 1789 [2]. Bentham was called a utilitarian because of his practical approach to philosophy in human nature and psychology. Bentham's major contributions to the classical school are as follows.

Utilitarian Principle

Bentham believed that an act had utility if it produced happiness or prevented pain. He also believed in the greatest happiness for the greatest number of people in a society. He was considered practical and emphasized the problem of eliminating crime by a system of social control. He attempted to rationally assign weights to various behaviors and motivations.

Bentham felt that all behavior could be tagged and weighted. A good portion of his life's work was cataloging crimes and their motivations. Bentham's criteria to judge the utility of an act was his own subjective feelings.

Motivation Behind Criminal Acts

According to Bentham, people act rationally and deliberately. Modern psychiatry has undermined Bentham's work in that today it is known that not all people act deliberately or consciously. Bentham was also of the opinion that people are motivated by the pursuit of pleasure and the avoidance of pain. Accordingly, he saw people as hedonistic and believed that criminal behavior was learned.

Current Evaluation

Bentham's ideas are currently viewed as faulty. He did, however, exert a major influence on the classical school of criminology. Bentham's ideas were revolutionary for his time. Bentham and others provided the early concepts and foundations that paved the way for the development of the insanity defenses used today [3[.

■ THE INSANITY DEFENSE

The insanity defense is based on the classical concept that man has "free will" to choose between good and bad behavior. Therefore, if someone lacks the ability to choose (i.e., no free will), that person should not be punished for his or her criminal behavior. The two leading tests for insanity used in the United States today are the M'Naughten and American Law Institute tests.

The M'Naughten test developed out of a famous English case in 1843. Under this test, a defendant is not culpable for his or her conduct if he or she was "laboring under such a defect of reason, from disease of the mind, as not to know the nature and quality of the act he was doing; or, if he did know it, that he did not know he was doing what was wrong." The American Law Institute Test (ALI Test) was developed in 1962. Under this test, a defendant is not guilty who lacks "substantial capacity" either to know right from wrong or to conform to the law. Both of the tests require that the defendant have the ability to choose between right and wrong before the defendant may be convicted of a crime. Accordingly, a person must have free will in order to be a criminal [4].

THE NEOCLASSICAL SCHOOL

The neoclassical school is based on the concept of free will. People are guided by reason. People are responsible for their acts, punishment can control people. The pain from one punishment must exceed the pleasure that comes from committing a criminal act. These are neoclassical premises. The neoclassical school differs primarily from the classical school in that it incorporated the practical modifications necessary for the administration of criminal law and justice [5]. For example, the neoclassical school recognizes differences in criminal circumstances; that is, some people, such as juveniles and persons with unstable mental conditions, cannot "reason" or have limited ability to reason. Wilson and Herrnstein hold that people choose to commit crime when they are impaired psychologically or biologically [6]. In those special cases, the criminal justice system should look at the needs of the offender in determining the appropriate punishment for the offense.

The application of criminal codes based on classical thinking without regard to the circumstances of the crime creates an inflexible system of justice. The neoclassical school advocated providing limited discretion to the judges in their sentencing process, while still supporting the concept that criminals are responsible for their acts.

Neoclassical thinking is present in many of our current theories dealing with the handling of criminals. As exemplified in the recent statements of public officials, note the following:

> The notion of choice is important. Nobody is inevitably going to commit a crime. Even a person who sneezes on a subway would

probably not sneeze if the penalty was 10 years in prison or immediate execution.   (James Q. Wilson, Chairman of the White House Task Force on Crime)

Today's neoclassical thinking also points to irrationality in the administration of justice as a major causative factor in controlling criminal behavior. Many present-day criminal justice professionals contend that if our criminal justice punishments were quicker, certain, and appropriate to the crime, many criminals would not commit crimes. According to these professionals, there are severe overcrowding problems in today's jails and prisons. Criminals also know that when they commit certain types of crimes, they may only receive warnings. The return to fixed and inflexible punishments advocated by many contemporary criminal justice professionals and laypersons alike is based on classical and neoclassical thinking. This thinking centers on the notion that the offender has a freedom of choice and has deliberately chosen the criminal path.

Case of DANIEL M'NAGHTEN (1843)

[The prisoner, Daniel M'Naghten, was indicted for the murder of Edward Drummon, private secretary to the Prime Minister, Sir Edward Peel.] In his instructions to the jury, Lord Chief Justice Tindal stated:

> The question to be determined is, whether at the time the act in question was committed, the prisoner had or had not the use of his understanding, so as to know that he was doing a wrong or wicked act. If the jurors should be of opinion that the prisoner was not sensible at the time he committed it, that he was violating the laws of both God and man, then he would be entitled to a verdict in his favor: but if, on the contrary, they were of the opinion that when he committed the act he was in a sound state of mind, then their verdict must be against him.

The jury after listening to the above instructions, entered a verdict of not guilty. The forgoing instructions were the subject of debate within the House of Lords. The result was that England adopted the M'Naghten rule for the test of criminal responsibility (insanity defense). The M'Naghten test is currently used by many states to determine criminal responsibility.

■ REALISM ORIENTATION

A new orientation in criminology is emerging. As of this date, there is no widely accepted name for it. The label "realism" was introduced by Lincoln Steffens and other "muckrakers" in the 1920s. The muckrakers used a realistic approach in investigating corruption in government. Like the movement during the time of the muckrakers, the present realism orientation takes a "no-nonsense" approach to crime and an attitude that society is imperfect. The general concept is that we should take a "realistic approach" to society's problems and forget the dream of a "crime-free" society. (The term "muckraker" originally referred to the workers in the peat moss bogs in Ireland, who continued to rake up dirt and kept their eyes down toward the muck rather than up toward the blue sky.) The realism orientation differs from the classical and positivist approaches in its premises and assumptions.

FIGURE 4–4
Cell blocks in an unidentified prison.

The realism orientation has gotten its impetus primarily from criminal justice theories and practices that originated in the Scandinavian countries. This is not to say that the United States and other Western European countries have not contributed to the development of this orientation, which is most clearly observed in Scandinavia.

The orientation rejects the treatment ideology on three grounds. First, treatment is ineffective. The magic pill to cure criminal behavior and recidivism cannot be found because the ailment (criminality as a disease) does not exist. Second, true successes in rehabilitation have been nonexistent. Studies have shown that with offenders within the criminal justice system treatment often does not work. Some studies have shown that one correctional alternative is not better than another in preventing recidivism. Third, research dealing with "hidden" or "undetected" crime within the past 30 years has challenged our ideas about the criminal. We now know that those who come to our attention as criminals are merely a small biased sample of the criminal universe. Most criminals are never caught.

The realism orientation is also concerned with the civil liberties of offenders. Many voices today are indicating that practices such as legally enforced treatment can be more punitive for the offender than classical school punishment. Treatment of the offender today has not resulted in more humane handling of offenders.

The realism orientation also focuses on the role of society in creating and maintaining crime and criminals. It maintains that society is criminogenic and that society promulgates the values that lead to criminal behavior. Under this orientation, trying to eliminate the crime problem by controlling the behavior of specific potential lawbreakers is like trying to control yellow fever by swatting mosquitoes rather than by draining the swamp.

As noted earlier, the precepts of the realism orientation are not fully developed as of this date. The basic precepts that are emerging are listed below.

1. The causes of crime are varied. Crime has no one single cause. Accordingly, any approach to solving the crime problem must take a multifaceted approach.

2. The traditional forms of corrections/punishments do not work. Innovative programs to replace our present methods of handling criminals is necessary to reduce the crime problem.

3. Some crime in society is inevitable. The cost, both economical and noneconomical, of eliminating all forms of crime would destroy society.

4. The focus should be on reducing the violence in society rather than entirely eliminating crime.

5. Crime is a social problem.

6. To help solve the crime problem, we need to change society.

7. Specific crimes should be evaluated by the amount of harm caused society. For example, the Love Canal chemical dumping should be considered a far greater crime than a robbery of a convenience store.

IN FOCUS

Comparison of the Classical School of the Past With Today's Neoclassical School

Classical	Neoclassical
1. The individual is motivated by free will.	1. The person is motivated at times by free will and at other times by forces beyond his/her control (i.e., psychological, physical, and social forces).
2. A primary cause of crime was the harsh, barbaric nonhumane legal system.	2. A primary cause of crime is that the criminal justice system is soft on criminals.
3. Punishment should be public to be effective.	3. There should be public punishments (i.e., public executions, etc.).
4. Punishment should be prompt to be effective.	4. We should revive the concept of prompt punishments and eliminate long trials and lengthy appeals.
5. Punishment should be proportionate to the crime.	5. They support popular movements to increase punishments for certain crimes.
6. No attempt should be made to treat or rehabilitate the criminal.	6. Treatment and rehabilitation are not effective and are a waste of money.
7. Eliminate capital punishment.	7. Revive capital punishment.

■ SUMMARY

The classical school is considered one of the first attempts to organize a view of criminal causation and pinpoint the significant concepts in understanding the crime problem. The classical school was an outgrowth of the Age of Enlightenment. The Age of Enlightenment promoted optimism, certainty, reason, toleration, humanitarianism, and the belief that all human problems could be solved. Its influence is noted in the U.S. Constitution. The leaders of the classical school were Cesare Beccaria and Jeremy Bentham. The main points of the classical school are as follows:

- The doctrine of free will is used to explain human behavior.
- Criminals are responsible for their behavior.
- Crime reduction can be accomplished by inflicting a sufficient amount of pain upon the offender.
- The purposes of punishment should be to deter others from committing criminal acts.
- The type and amount of pain to impose on the offender should be determined by focusing only on the crime itself.
- Punishment to be effective should be prompt, certain, and serve a useful function.

Although based on the concept of free will, the neoclassical school of criminology recognizes that some people, such as juveniles and persons with unstable mental conditions, cannot reason. Accordingly, these people may not be completely free to make a choice and this should be considered when determining and imposing punishment. Neoclassical thinking is alive and well in many of our present criminological theories.

■ MATCHING KEY TERMS AND DEFINITIONS

Match each key term with the correct definition.

a. Age of Enlightenment   **e.** despotic spirit
b. Beccaria   **f.** free will
c. Bentham   **g.** neoclassical
d. classical school   **h.** utilitarian principle

_____ **1.** One of the first organized systems of thought, which viewed the criminal as having free will and individual choice.

    2. The movement that dominated European thinking for most of the eighteenth century.

    3. The writer of the famous essay *On Crimes and Punishments*.

    4. The doctrine that supports the ideas that the individual is considered rational and is free to choose his or her behavior.

    5. The aspect of human nature that is a part of every human being and if left unchecked would plunge society into chaos.

    6. A prolific writer, "armchair philosopher," and utilitarian.

    7. The principle that an act has utility if it produces happiness or prevents pain.

    8. The school of criminology that is based on the concept of free will, but which recognizes that some people cannot reason.

DISCUSSION QUESTIONS

1. How do the "use a gun, go to prison" laws reflect classical school theory?

2. If we consider parole and probation as attempts to adjust societal responses to the circumstances of the offender, how do parole and probation conflict with and/or support classical precepts?

3. How are offenders motivated by pleasure and the avoidance of pain?

4. Today the average prisoner spends only a short period of time in prison. How does this fact reflect the ideas that punishment should be fast, certain, and serve a useful function?

Notes

1. Cesare Beccaria, *On Crimes and Punishments*, The Library of Liberal Arts Series (translated by Henry Paolucci). New York: Bobbs-Merrill, 1963; and Cesare Beccaria, *Dei delitti e délle pene, 1776* (An Essay on Crime and Punishments; translated from the Italian with the commentary by Voltaire), 5th ed. London, 1804.

2. Jeremy Bentham, in John Bowring, ed., *An Introduction to the Principles of Morals and Legislation*. New York: Russell & Russell, 1962.

3. Charles Milner Atkinson, *Jeremy Bentham: His Life and Work*, Kelly, 1905.

4. Bennett H. Beach, "Picking between Mad and Bad," *Time*, Oct. 12, 1981, p. 68.

5. Ernest Van den Haag, *Punishing Criminals*. New York: Basic Books, 1975.

6. James Q. Wilson and Richard J. Herrnstein, *Crime and Human Nature*. New York: Simon and Schuster, 1986.

Early Positivist Criminology

CHAPTER HIGHLIGHTS

- The positive school of criminology was the leading school of criminology during the latter half of the nineteenth century.
- The positive school was a product of the realism movement and a reaction to the harshness of the classical school.
- For the positivists, science was supreme.
- Crime, according to the positivists, could be studied as an empirical science and the causes of crime could be determined.
- Auguste Comte is considered the founder of positivism.
- Comte's positivism repudiated the metaphysical and speculative methodology of classical thinking.
- Cesare Lombroso is known as the father of modern criminology.
- Lombroso considered the criminal as a subhuman "throwback."
- The concept of social determinism is an important part of the positive theory.
- Positivists believed that a person was propelled by social or biological forces beyond his or her control.
- The positivists believed that the offender was ill, sick, and/or deprived, and they believed in a treatment approach rather than a punitive approach to crime.
- Punishment should be individually tailored to meet the needs of the offender.

KEY TERMS

Atavism

Born Criminal

Determinism

Empiricism

Positivism   Sociology
Realism

▌ BACKGROUND

The leading school of criminology in the latter half of the nineteenth century was the positivist school. Just as the classical school was a product of the Age of Enlightenment, the positivist school was a product of the "realism" movement. Realism was the prevailing intellectual temper of the third quarter of the nineteenth century. It touched every area of life, including literature, philosophy, religion, and social thought. The realism movement placed a high value on action, power, and success. The movement discounted sentiment, idealism, mysticalism, and the belief in the supernatural [1].

The "realism" movement encouraged an attitude of "matter-of-fact detachment" and encouraged a close precise description of various phenomena, including the rigorous use of the scientific method. In describing the mood of that time, Barlow stated: "The armchair philosophy that for centuries had dominated learned discourse on the nature of man and society was replaced by the logic and methodology of objective, empirical science. . . . Crime became one of the phenomena newly placed under the microscope" [2].

Positivist thinking represented a major shift from classical thinking in that the concept of free will was replaced by the concept of determinism. Determinism was based on the notion that behavior is governed by physical, mental, environmental, and social factors beyond the offender's control. Determinists were also of the opinion that heredity could influence an offender's behavior [3].

Auguste Comte (1798–1857) is considered the founder of the positivist school. Comte ambitiously attempted to apply methods of science to the study of society. He originally labelled his methods "social physics." When the Belgian social statistician, Adolphe Quetelet also referred to his work as "social physics," Comte quickly abandoned the label. Using a hybrid term compounded of Latin and Greek parts, Comte coined the term "sociology" to describe his methodology [4].

According to Comte, there were three stages in the evolution of human thinking [5]:

1. Theological or fictive stage that was characterized by mythological thinking.
2. Metaphysical or abstract stage that was characterized by classical thinking.

IN FOCUS

Auguste Comte (1798–1857)

Auguste Comte was born in southern France near the city of Montpelier in January 1798. His father was a low-level government employee and a devoted Catholic. His father despised the French Revolution and its attack on the Catholic church.

As a young boy, Auguste Comte was frail and in poor health. He was, however, an outstanding student in the school, which he entered at the age of 9. During his early education, he became disillusioned with his parents' teachings on the evils of a republican form of government and the supremacy of the church. Comte, then, developed a strong belief in the republican form of liberty. He advocated a return to the glorious days of the French Revolution and the renewal of the republican principles of government.

In 1814, he entered a prestigious university, the Ecole Polytechnique in Paris. In protest, he left the institution in 1816. He was upset about the handling of six students who objected to antiquated methods of administrating examinations. In the summer of 1817, he met Henri Saint-Simon, who was director of the periodical *Industrie*. Saint-Simon became a close friend and advisor to Comte. Comte's major ideas were developed during his association with Saint-Simon. In 1825, he married Caroline Massin, the owner of a small bookstore. The marriage was an unhappy one and ended several years later. During this period, his major preoccupation involved the elaboration of his positivist philosophy.

Comte had a mental collapse in 1827 while presenting a series of lectures on his philosophy. He later tried to commit suicide. He resumed his lectures in 1829 and attempted several times, unsuccessfully, to obtain an appointment to the university. Finally, in 1832, he received an appointment as external examiner to the Ecole Polytechnique. This position paid only 2000 francs a year. Accordingly, he lived on the verge of poverty most of his academic career. He died in 1857.

3. Scientific or positive stage that was considered the highest stage in human thinking.

Comte's positivism repudiated the metaphysical and speculative. He envisioned a society in which all social problems were solved by scientific methods and research. He believed in studying large groups of people to discover specific laws. Empiricism was born. It was thought that all social sciences could be dealt with by empirical research and scientific methods, not by abstract intuitive philosophy, which was the hallmark of the classical thinkers [6].

▌ SUPREMACY OF SCIENCE

Science was supreme, according to the positivists. The positivists rejected the legal definition of crime developed by the classical thinkers and, instead were concerned with the person as sick and/or deprived. The positivists believed in social determinism as the primary controller of human actions and discounted free will and personal choice as a factor in human behavior.

The socialization process was important in the determination of the individual's personality. Positivists believed that a person was propelled by social, biological, psychological, and/or emotional forces beyond his or her control. They also believed that animal experimentation was an acceptable way to learn about human physiology, medicine, psychiatry, and psychology. The "In Focus" feature presents a comparison of ideas regarding the classical and positive schools of criminology.

Treatment of the offender was a concept that emerged with positivism. The clinical approach was a positivist concept. Treatment, however, should fit the offender. The positivists believed in punishment; however, the main goal of punishment was to "cure" the offender. Also, the indeterminant sentence was a positivist intervention that allowed the person to remain incarcerated until he or she was cured. The major tenets of positivism can be summarized by the following:

1. Superiority of science and experimentation in solving problems of criminality.

2. Social determinism; people are governed by social laws that can be unraveled through scientific inquiry.

3. Good of the individual is of larger interest than the good of society.

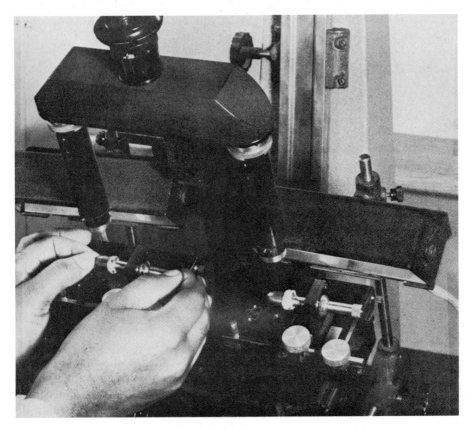

FIGURE 5–1
**One important contribution of the positivist's approach to crime causation was
the introduction of science to the field.**

IN FOCUS

Comparison of the Classical and Positive Schools of Criminology

Classical School

1. Free will/man is hedonistic/ pleasure–pain formula
2. Cause of crime related to inequities in legal system

Positive School

1. Social determinism
2. Cause of crime related to a myriad of factors such as poor environments

3. No treatment consciousness	3. Treatment consciousness clinical approach/treatment must fit criminal
4. Abstract/philosophical method	4. Scientific method
5. Overriding concern with social system inadequacies	5. Overriding concern with the person as sick and/or deprived
6. Punishment is only what is necessary to deter	6. Punishment individually designed to cure
7. Abstract/global focus	7. Specific answers to the problems of crime and the criminal based on the study of large groups

THE POSITIVIST SCHOOL OF CRIMINOLOGY

The positive school of criminology (sometimes called the Italian School) is often associated with Cesare Lombroso, Enrico Ferri, Gabriel Tarde, and Raffaele Garofalo. The religious leaders at the time referred to Lombroso, Ferri and Garofalo as the "unholy three" because of their belief in evolution as opposed to Biblical interpretation of the origin of men and women. The three have also been called the "holy three of criminology" because their emergence "symbolized clearly that the era of faith was over and the scientific age had begun" [7].

THE THEORY OF CESARE LOMBROSO

Cesare Lombroso is known as the father of modern criminology, although most of his ideas have been discredited today. It is interesting to examine the chain of events that caused Lombroso, rather than Beccaria or Bentham, to be credited with this title.

As explained in Charles Darwin's *Descent of Man*, the theory of organic evolution was largely responsible for Lombroso's popularity and for his theory's success and acceptance. Darwin's theory of evolution was, beyond doubt, the major scientific theory of the nineteenth century [8].

In the nineteenth century, the predominant influence on social science came from the biological sciences, which affected it by:

1. Providing analogies and terminology.
2. Providing the principle of evolution.

Society came to be viewed as an organism, and the principle of organic evolution was applied to it.

Lombroso applied Darwin's theory of evolution to the explanation of the criminal's nature. Lombroso postulated that just as human beings evolved from nonhuman animal forms, the criminal was a primitive, atavistic, throwback, or mutant who never fully evolved. The criminal was product of biology and not much could be done for this "born criminal." (The term "born criminal" was actually coined by Enrico Ferri [9].) Lombroso's popularity was a direct result of Darwin's popularity and ideas. Had the theory of evolution not been so

FIGURE 5–2
Crime in paradise? Hawaii State Prison, Honolulu. Courtesy of Hawaii Department of Social Services and Housing.

popular, Lombroso would probably not have been considered the father of modern criminology.

Lombroso was a medical doctor, scientist, and clinician. He applied the scientific method to the measurement of criminal craniums. He was a pathfinder in his time. His emphasis and focus was on the hereditary components of criminal behavior, although he also acknowledged the role of social factors. Lombroso's major contributions to criminological theory can be summarized as follows:

1. *The theory of atavism.* Lombroso was of the opinion that criminals were evolutionarily primitive or subhuman individuals who were characterized by certain "inferior" physical and mental characteristics. These physical characteristics were identifiable. He spent much of his life considering these "biological throwbacks" and trying to identify their physical characteristics [10].

2. *The application of the experimental or scientific method to the study of the criminal.* He was the first clinical criminologist who "got his hands dirty" by spending numerous hours measuring criminally insane persons and epileptics' skulls. Some have referred to Lombroso as a "scientific Columbus" [11].

3. *The development of a criminal topology.* Although Lombroso's system of classification is considered crude and discredited today, Lombroso attempted to categorize and classify types of offenders. Lombroso classified criminals as follows:

    a. Epileptic criminal
    b. Insane criminal
    c. Born criminal
    d. Occasional criminal

He also identified the various types of occasional criminals as:

    a. Pseudocriminals
    b. Criminaloids
    c. Habitual criminals
    d. Passionate criminals
    e. Political criminals

Lombroso also studied female criminals. He viewed prostitution, for example, as an atavistic phenomenon [12].

4. *The belief in the indeterminant sentence.* Penalties should be indeterminant so that those other than "born" criminals who were incorrigible could be worked with and perhaps redeemed.

5. *The application of statistical techniques to criminology.* Although crude and with the use of questionable control groups, Lombroso used statistical techniques to make criminological predictions.

Cesare Lombroso (1835–1909)

Cesare Lombroso was born in 1835 in Verona, which was, at the time, under Austrian rule. He was of Jewish descent, but attended public schools that were controlled by the Jesuits. At the age of 15, he had two noteworthy historical papers published. At age 16, he published a review of Paolo Marzolo's *An Introduction to Historical Monuments Revealed by Analysis of Words.* Marzolo, a leading philosopher and physician, was impressed by the review and requested an interview with Lombroso. Marzolo was shocked to learn that a 16-year-old schoolboy had written a comprehensive review of his works.

Under Marzolo's influence, Lombroso at the age of 18 enrolled as a medical student at the University of Pavia. He eventually received his degree in medicine from the University in 1858 and a degree in surgery from the University of Genoa in 1859. During his studies, Lombroso discounted the free-will philosophy that dominated Italian academic circles. He also began to support the views of the French positivists and the English evolutionists.

After graduating from school in 1859, Lombroso volunteered for medical service in the Army. While serving as an army physician, he began systematic measurement and observation of over 3000 Italian soldiers. His purpose was to ascertain and analyze the physical differences that he had noted among Italian soldiers from various regions of Italy. During this time, he concluded that the practice of tattooing was a characteristic of criminals.

Later, after he was released from the army, Lombroso was in charge of several hospital wards for the criminally insane. During this time, he continued his systematic measurement and observation of patients.

In 1876, Lombroso was appointed to a professorship at the University of Turin. While at the university, he published *Legal Medicine of the Corpse* in 1877. This publication set forth scientific methods of identifying dead bodies and was a significant contribution to pathology and police work. In 1880, with the assistance of Ferri and Garofalo, he founded the "Archivio di Psichiatria e Antropologia Criminale" (Archives of Criminal Psychiatry and Anthropology).

Lombroso's personal life was apparently normal. At the age of 34, he married a young Jewish girl. They had two daughters. Both daughters married professional men who were involved with Lombroso's work. With his daughter Gina's husband, G. Ferrero, he spent many hours examining criminal skulls. Together, Ferrero and Lombroso published *The Female Offender.*

FIGURE 5-3
Cesare Lombruso.
Courtesy of the
National Library of
Medicine.

■ THE THEORY OF GABRIEL TARDE

Whereas Lombroso emphasized the biological and physical components of criminality, Gabriel Tarde (1843–1904) emphasized the sociopsychological factors. Tarde was of the opinion that society played
an important role in creating the criminal; however, individual choice
and chance were also important to him [13].

A major contribution of Tarde was his concept of the criminal as
a professional type. He was of the opinion that most criminals went
through an apprenticeship before becoming criminal and it was an
accident of birth or chance that put them in an atmosphere of crime.

Tarde also attempted to classify crime. He analyzed rural and urban crime and attacked vigorously Lombroso's idea of the "born"
criminal. Biological and physical factors, according to Tarde, might
influence the offender; however, they were only partially important and
should not prevent individuals from being held responsible for their
crimes.

Tarde proposed some radical reforms for his day, among them
the following:

1. A committee of experts comprised of doctors and psychologists to be set up to determine the responsibility of the accused for his conduct.

2. Punishment should be meted out on a psychological basis. He felt that it was important for the offender to feel deprivation, and if two offenders committed the same crime with the same circumstances, their punishments would be individually designed to "balance or equalize deprivations." For example, a rural criminal would experience greater deprivation from incarceration than an urban criminal. Therefore, the rural criminal needs to have a specially designed punishment to equalize the deprivation.

3. Elimination of the jury system. he felt that juries were unprepared to make professional decisions regarding the guilt and punishment of offenders.

4. Special schools for criminal judges to ensure better administration of criminal laws.

5. He supported the idea of parole or "conditional liberty."

Like Lombroso's work, Tarde's work advanced the idea of the criminal as an individual. Another contemporary who furthered the idea of the criminal as an individual was Raffaele Garofalo (1852–1934).

■ THE THEORY OF RAFFAELE GAROFALO

Raffaele Garofalo's theories on criminology and/or his contributions to the field are as follows:

1. The concept of "natural crime," which referred to any crime against persons or property that was offensive and repulsive to a society's moral sensibilities.

2. The criminal had a "moral" deficiency that had an "organic" basis and was hereditarily transmissible. He believed in the biological transmission of criminality but not necessarily in the physical manifestation of criminality, as Lombroso did.

3. Garofalo classified criminals as:
   a. Murders
   b. Violent criminals
   c. Thieves
   d. Lavicious criminals

4. Garofalo also relied on Darwin's theory of survival of the fittest. He felt that if the criminal did not adapt to society, he should be eliminated or incapacitated. Garofalo believed in capital punishment and life imprisonment to deal with those who would not adapt.

5. Like Lombroso, Garofalo viewed criminality as something organic and innate; however, he did not believe that criminality was manifested physically. His views represented a different path from Tarde's views. Tarde, his contemporary, viewed criminality solely from a social perspective [14].

■ THE THEORY OF ENRICO FERRI

Enrico Ferri's (1856–1929) major contribution to positivist theory was his rejection of the free-will doctrine. He felt that free will had no place in criminal law. Ferri was an adamant believer in social determinism as the primary cause of criminality. Ferri, however, did believe that for some offenders there was a hereditary basis for criminality, and he referred to these people as "born" criminals. He was also responsible for a classification system [15]. Ferri classified criminals as:

1. Born criminals
2. Insane criminals
3. Passionate criminals
4. Occasional criminals
5. Habitual criminals

Ferri was also a social reformer in his day [16]. He believed that criminal justice personnel should be trained. This special training should also include judges. In addition, he recommended that juries be abolished and cellular isolation during the day be eliminated for prisoners.

While Lombroso is considered the father of modern criminology and Comte is considered the founder of the positivist school, Ferri is the person who made the positivist school popular. He delineated the basic concepts of the school and broadened its depth and scope. His advocacy of offender treatment and individually designed sentences was widely accepted in the United States and Europe until the 1970s. For example, until July 1977, California had an indeterminate sentencing procedure that individually tailored sentences to fit offenders' needs.

▮ IMPORTANCE OF POSITIVISM

The positivists were reacting to the harshness of the classical school. The realism movement borrowed from the fields of medicine and biology and aided the development and evolution of theories about crime causation. The early positivists, like Lombroso, focused on biological causes; the later positivists focused on psychological and social causes.

The positivists emphasized not the crime (as had the classical thinkers) but the criminal as an individual. The central theme of positivism is determinism and not free will. Where the classical theorist stated that the criminal by use of his or her free will made a voluntary choice to commit the criminal act, the positivist contended that because of determinism the criminal had no choice in the crime decision. Only by treating the criminal could the "illness" of crime be eliminated.

The positivists advocated scientific methodologies for studying the cause of crime. Accordingly, by careful study and scientific observation the causes of crime could be determined and thus eliminated. This dream was never realized.

One of the most important contributions of the positivists is evidenced in today's juvenile justice system, where treatment and punishment is directed toward "what's best for the juvenile delinquent" rather than the "just deserts" punishment concept (classical thinking) that dominates today's adult criminal courts.

▮ SUMMARY

The positivist school of criminology was the leading school of criminology during the latter half of the nineteenth century. The school was a product of the realism movement and a reaction to the harshness of the classical school. Auguste Comte is considered the founder of the positivist school. According to this school, crime can be studied as an empirical science and the causes of crime can be determined. The most famous of the positivist theorists was Cesare Lombroso, who is considered to be the "father of modern criminology."

The concept of determinism is an important part of the positivist theory. The theory is based on the concept that a person is propelled by social, biological, emotional, and/or spiritual forces beyond his or her control. The school discounts the punitive approach to crime and instead advocates treatment. In addition, treatment should be individually tailored to meet the needs of the individual offender.

▪ MATCHING KEY TERMS AND DEFINITIONS

Match each key term with the correct definition.

a. atavism
b. born criminal
c. determinism
d. empiricism

e. positivism
f. realism
g. sociology

____ **1.** The positivist school of criminology was a product of this movement.

____ **2.** This concept is based on the premise that behavior is governed by physical, mental, environmental, and social factors beyond the offender's control.

____ **3.** One of the major tenets of this school is the superiority of science.

____ **4.** A term coined by Ferri to indicate that the criminal is a product of biology and that treatment cannot change the criminal.

____ **5.** This concept held that the criminal was a "throwback" or subhuman being.

____ **6.** The concept that all social sciences could be dealt with by empirical research and scientific methods.

____ **7.** The study or science of the origin, development, organization, and functioning of human society.

▪ DISCUSSION QUESTIONS

1. If the criminal's behavior is determined by factors beyond his control, what is the role of punishment in the positive school?

2. Joe, a hardened criminal, is arrested for driving his automobile without a license. What factors would the positive criminologists consider in determining the appropriate sentence for this crime? How would they differ from the position of the classical theorist?

3. Two female defendants appear for sentencing before the judge. One is a 30-year-old drug addict who has committed numerous robberies. The other is a 17-year-old drug dealer with several arrests for peddling drugs to junior high school students, who occassionally uses drugs herself. How would a positivist handle each case?

4. According to researchers, heavy drug abusers commit crimes as much as ten times more frequently than if they were not actively using drugs. What would the positivist do with heavy drug users?

Notes

1. Marvin E. Wolfgang, "Cesare Lombroso," in Hermann Mannheim, ed., *Pioneers in Criminology*. Montclair, N.J.: Patterson Smith, 1973, pp. 232–291.
2. Hugh D. Barlow, *Introduction to Criminology*. Boston: Little, Brown, 1984.
3. See Cesare Lombroso, *Crime: Its Causes and Remedies* (translated by H. P. Horton). Boston: Little, Brown, 1911.
4. Lewis A. Coser. "The Sociology of Poverty," *Social Problems*, vol. 13, Fall 1971.
5. Julius Gould, "Auguste Comte," in T. Raison, ed., *The Founding Fathers of Social Science*. Harmondsworth, England: Penguin, 1969.
6. C. R. Jeffery, "The Historical Development of Criminology," in Mannheim, 1973.
7. Stephen Schafer, *Theories in Criminology*. New York: Random House, 1969, p. 123.
8. Charles Darwin, *Descent of Man*. London: John Murray, 1871; and George B. Vold and Thomas J. Bernard, *Theoretical Criminology*; 3rd ed. New York: Oxford University Press, 1986.
9. Wolfgang, 1973:251.
10. G. Lombroso-Ferrero, *The Criminal Man according to the Classification of Cesare Lombroso*, Montclair, N.J.: Patterson Smith, 1972.
11. Wolfgang, 1973:287.
12. Lombroso-Ferrero, 1972.
13. G. Tarde, *Social Laws: An Outline of Sociology*. New York: Macmillan, 1907; and Schafer, 1969: 238–239.
14. Raffaele Garofalo, *Criminology*. Boston: Little, Brown, 1914; and Francis A. Allen, "Raffaele Garofalo," in Mannheim, 1973:318–340.
15. Enrico Ferri, *Criminal Sociology*. Boston: Little, Brown, 1917; Enrico Ferri, in Phillip Grupp, ed., *The Positive School of Criminology*. Pittsburgh: University of Pittsburgh Press, 1968; and Thorsten Sellin, "Enrico Ferri," in Mannheim, 1973:361–384.
16. Schafer, 1969.

THE SOCIOLOGICAL THEORIES

The sociological theories of crime causation are popular in the United States. The psychological and biological theories have not met with the widespread acceptance that the sociological theories have enjoyed. The United States, a great sociological experiment herself, was a country that accepted the sociological theories as making the most sense in explaining and understanding crime. A number of factors present in the United States caused us to focus on and generally embrace social explanations for criminal conduct.

The social climate in the United States is one of the primary reasons that we have embraced the sociological explanations for crime causation. After World War I, the United States experienced many social changes. A new middle class of salaried professionals emerged. These people were concerned with efficiency and reshaping urban environments. During the time following World War I, cities in the United States were disorganized. There was inadequate housing, unemployment, health problems, delinquency, and crime. The new salaried professionals were not totally altruistic. They wanted to clean up the disorganized urban cities, but they also wanted cities that were more hospitable to their professional interests.

Another force that caused Americans to embrace the sociological theories of crime causation was the depopulation of farms and small towns in the United States. Between World War I and the Depression, many people left their rural environments and went to the urban areas looking for jobs, a better way of life, and the American Dream. These new city residents found disorganized cities that were ill-equipped to support their needs.

The growth of the cities by immigration was another factor at work that contributed to the American penchant toward sociological solutions to their crime problems. The influx of people from rural United States and immigrants from foreign shores created concentrations of peoples with different backgrounds, beliefs, and values in American's cities. The conflict in human values and economic beliefs led to hostility against particular cultural groups and to the development of urban ghettos. People flooded the urban areas so quickly that the cities did not have the ability to handle the numbers. For example, between 1910 and 1930 Chicago gained over a million immigrants. The new Americans were often viewed as ignorant, contemptible, and evil.

The solutions to environmental problems such as crime appeared to best be answered by the sociological theorists who conducted extensive research in the cities. It was thought that the researchers who would look into the social environment would be able to find the answers to the problems facing urban America.

All the sociological theories of crime causation include as a major assumption the idea that crime is caused by factors such as poor education, poverty, inadequate housing, inadequate socialization, broken families, delinquent peer relations, poor parenting, family difficulties, and criminogenic social conditions. The cause of crime is located outside the person, lying instead within the social environment. The factors in the offender's social environment push or pull the person toward crime and are often viewed as being beyond his or her control. The criminal is viewed as a passive person who is being propelled by factors beyond his or her control. In Chapter 6 we present several basic sociological concepts utilized by criminologists who study crime causation. This chapter is designed to provide the student with an introduction to the study of crime causation from a sociological viewpoint. In Chapters 7–11 we address the sociological theories of crime causation from a logical categories perspective as opposed to the standard chronological perspective. This should be valuable to the student because many theories were developed by a haphazard method which makes it difficult to find similarities in theories. The sociological theories are grouped in commonly known categories. There is, however, some overlapping of groups. The common categories and the theorists who are associated with the categories presented in Chapters 7–11 are as follows:

1. *Strain theories:* Emile Durkheim, Robert Merton, Albert Cohen, Richard Cloward, and Lloyd Ohlin

2. *Control theories:* Emile Durkheim, Albert Reiss, David Matza, Gresham Sykes, Walter Reckless, and Travis Hirschi

3. *Conflict/radical theories:* Jeffrey Reiman, Austin Turk, Karl Marx, Friedrich Engels, Willem Bonger, Richard Quinney, William Chambliss, and George Vold

4. *Cultural deviance theories:* Ernest Burgess, Robert Park, Clifford Shaw, Henry McKay, Frederic Thrasher, Walter Miller, Robert Redfield, Robert Faris, Thorsten Sellin, Marvin Wolfgang, Franco Ferracuti, Donald Taft, Ralph England, and Milton Barron

5. *Symbolic interactionist theories:* Herbert Blumer, Edwin Sutherland, Frank Tannenbaum, C. H. Cooley, Erving Goffman, and Edwin Lemert

6

Sociological Concepts and Crime Causation

CHAPTER HIGHLIGHTS

- Sociologists generally view deviant, delinquent, and criminal behavior as learned social behavior.
- Human beings are gregarious and are dependent on other human beings to fulfill their needs.
- The terms "society" and "social group" can be applied to no other species because human beings are the only ones that have the capacity to enter into abstract social relationships.
- Society is crucial in making the person human and in sustaining human qualities.
- The absence of society and group relationships can be a variable behind the commission of a crime.
- The norm is one of a number of basic sociological concepts used to explain human behavior and crime causation.
- Norms can be prescriptive, proscriptive, formal, and/or informal.
- Mores, customs, and folkways are types of norms.
- Laws are formal, proscriptive norms that when violated cause a formal and punitive reaction.
- Socialization involves learning how to live and function in a society.
- Culture gives meaning to a society.
- Subcultures are found in modern, heterogeneous societies.
- Countercultures are subcultures that are considered deviant by the dominant culture's standards.

KEY TERMS

Counterculture	Customs
Culture	Folkways

Formal Norm   Resocialization
Informal Norm   Secondary Group
Mores   Secondary Socialization
Prescriptive Norm   Socialization
Primary Group   Social Norm
Primary Socialization Subculture
Proscriptive Norm

   I n this chapter we identify and explain selected basic sociological concepts that are related to the topic of crime causation. The sociological concepts are important in understanding why people become criminal, deviant, and/or delinquent. The following sociological concepts are the focus of Chapter 6: (1) significance of society and group relationships; (2) social norms; (3) primary and secondary groups; (4) socialization; (5) culture, subculture, and counterculture.

■ SIGNIFICANCE OF SOCIETY AND GROUP RELATIONSHIPS

The discipline of sociology provides us many concepts that aid in understanding why a person becomes a criminal, delinquent, or deviant. Sociologists generally classify deviant, delinquent, or criminal behavior as social behavior (i.e., behavior that is learned in society's groups) [1]. Human beings are gregarious and dependent on other human beings to fulfill their needs even before they are born. Human beings rely on others to satisfy physical, mental, financial, spiritual, and social needs. Even before a person is born, the baby is dependent on the mother for nourishment, and the mother must eat and drink the things that will increase the probability of the baby being born healthy.

   The terms "society" and "social group" can be applied to no other species than humans, for only human beings have the capacity to enter into abstract social relationships [2]. Humans are also the only species that possesses sophisticated forms of language, awareness, and consciousness. It is these characteristics that allow human beings to develop abstract social relationships.

   Abstract social relationships or group relationships are highly

FIGURE 6–1
People with norms that radically differ from what society considers normal often end up behind bars. Courtesy of Laima Druskis.

significant for the human's personal development. Without the society or group the human being would be little more than a "featherless biped" or a purely biological being moving through life in a haphazard manner. If one doubts the significance of society's role in shaping the individual and determining if the individual will commit criminal conduct, let's look at some cases in which society has been absent.

There are several cases in the literature of feral children. The term "feral" is defined as wild, untamed, and characteristic of wild animals. Feral children are children who have been isolated from society, and therefore society has been absent in their lives. The personality development of feral children suggests that children who are victims of social isolation behave in subhuman ways. Since few examples of feral children cases exist and most of the cases have only been documented or recorded, not scientifically studied, the conclusions that we make based on the feral children cases should be cautious. However, they do raise interesting questions about the role that society and human groups play in the development of the human being.

Isabelle and Anna, studied by Kingsley Davis, are perhaps the most scientifically studied cases. Kingsley Davis studied these young girls shortly after they were found on a Pennsylvania farm in 1938. Both girls were illegitimate and confined to an upper chamber in a house. They were kept barely alive by being given the minimum of food and water. Isabelle was approximately 6 years old when she was found. She was shut up in the dark with her deaf and mute mother. Her behavior was like that of a 6-month-old child when she was found. Those that worked with her thought that she, too, was deaf, but after some education she became fairly normal. Isabelle learned with excessive rapidity. Anna, at 6, could not talk or walk, and did not show any signs of what would be considered intelligence. Anna died at the age of 10, but did learn to do simple tasks [3].

Two other female feral children were supposedly found in India by local villagers [4]. Their names were Kamala and Amala. Kamala was found at approximately age 8. Amala was found at approximately age 2. The villagers supposedly found the children in a wolf den and brought them to the local clergymen, who took it on himself to educate them. When they were found they crawled on all four legs, growled, snarled, scratched, and groomed themselves like wolves. Their sense of smell was so highly developed that they could smell meat at a distance of seventy-five yards. One girl died after capture and the other girl responded to simple training and behavior-modification techniques of reward and punishment. The girl who lived did learn to do simple tasks, but at age 17 could speak only fifty words.

Another example of a feral child is the Wild Boy of Aveyron, supposedly found by hunters in 1799 at approximately age 10 [5]. The boy apparently had lived by himself in the woods since early childhood. When he was found he walked on all fours and was terrified by other humans. He was reared by a doctor. He learned to eat with utensils, sleep on a bed, and generally to accommodate himself. However, he barely learned to talk and was never fully assimilated into society.

The Nuremberg Boy is another example of a feral child. He was found in a dungeon in 1828. He, too, was deprived of human society, but at one time may have learned to talk because when he was found, he attempted to interact with his captors. The Nuremberg case seems to indicate the need for persistent social interaction if human characteristics are to be preserved.

Another example of a case that illustrates the human's extreme dependence on society and human groups is the case of Admiral Richard E. Byrd, who voluntarily isolated himself for a few months in the Antarctic to collect scientific information [6]. Admiral Byrd collected data in an uninhabited area of the Antarctic and was miles away from any other human being. He kept a diary of his experiences and the following is a personal accounting of what happened to him [7].

10 p.m. Solitude is an excellent laboratory in which to observe the extent to which manners and habits are conditioned by others. My table manners are atrocious—in this respect I've slipped back hundreds of years; in fact, I have no manners whatsoever. If I feel like it, I eat with my fingers, or out of a can, or standing up—in other words, whichever is easiest. What's left over, I just heave into the slop pail, close to my feet. Come to think of it, no reason why I shouldn't. It's rather a convenient way to eat; I seem to remember reading in Epicurus that a man living alone lives the life of a wolf.

A life alone makes the need for external demonstration almost disappear. Now I seldom cuss, although at first I was quick to open fire at everything that tried my patience. Attending to the electrical circuit on the anemometer pole is no less cold that it was in the beginning; but I work in soundless torment, knowing that the night is vast and profanity can shock no one by myself.

FIGURE 6–2
Lonely inmate at the State Prison of Southern Michigan.
Courtesy of the Michigan Department of Corrections.

The feral children cases and the Admiral Byrd example are important in illustrating the role that society plays in normal human development. Society is important in making the person human and in sustaining human qualities. Without societal and group influences the person would not learn to talk or behave socially. When a person is deprived of society and group contact, either forcibly or voluntarily, his or her development will be impaired. We know that placing a prisoner in solitary confinement for prolonged time periods can produce dramatic behavior changes. Also, the absence of society and group relationships can be a variable as to why a person commits crime. Although a person may not be literally isolated from society, a person may be alienated from society and society's groups. This may also result in antisocial or asocial behaviors and attitudes that may be a factor in crime causation (see Chapters 7 and 8).

IN FOCUS

Regina v. Machekequonabe (High Court of Justice for Ontario, 1897) (28 Ont. 309)

Chief Justice Armour:

It appeared that the prisoner was a member of a tribe of pagan Indians who believed in the existence of an evil spirit clothed in human flesh, or in human form called a Wendigo which would eat a human being.

That it was reported that a Wendigo was seen in the neighborhood of the Indian camp desiring to do them harm.

That the accused saw what appeared to him to be a Wendigo. The accused and another Indian gave chase, and after challenging three times and receiving no answer fired and killed the "object". It was then discovered that the "object" was the accused's foster father.

This homicide appears to have been committed by Machekequonabe in the genuine belief that it was justified. Had it been a Wendigo, the accused would have been a hero.

Questions: Does the presence of a belief mitigate the homicide? Does it matter that the belief may appear to be unreasonable to the majority of society?

Periodically, the criminal justice system comes in contact with adults and juveniles who have been isolated from society. Usually, these cases take the form of child abuse and/or kidnapping. The criminal law will take care of those who abuse or kidnap. However, how do we deal with the person who has been isolated from society? He or she is often traumatized for life, and if isolated for long periods, the person may not be capable of full assimilation back into society. To compound an already difficult situation, the person who has been isolated will often exhibit antisocial and/or criminal behavior.

■ SOCIAL NORMS

The norm is one of a number of basic sociological concepts frequently used to explain human behavior and crime causation. Norms are rules that govern our behavior in a given situation and at a given time. Norms can also be defined as socially accepted and expected conduct in society. Sociologists have referred to norms in a number of ways. They have called norms "rules of conduct," "blueprints for behavior," and "specifications for appropriate and inappropriate behavior" [8]. A more formal definition of a norm is a shared standard of behavior which in turn entails certain expectations of behavior in a given situation.

Norms have great power to motivate behavior. They carry with them positive and negative sanctions. Norms are important agents in social control. When we behave according to norms, we are rewarded. When we behave in ways that do not meet normative expectations, we may be punished. We do not have to agree with norms to obey them, and we do not have to disagree with norms to be deviant. Most people do not obey norms just because of the sanctions. We usually live up to norms when nobody would be aware that we violated them. Most people wish to obey norms most of the time. There would never be enough police to enforce all laws if everyone were determined to break them. Law and order is possible in society because people police themselves. Norms can be prescriptive, proscriptive, formal, and informal. Proscriptive norms forbid actions. They involve the "thou shalt not's." Our penal code is an example of formal proscriptive norms. Prescriptive norms, on the other hand, tells what we can do and should do.

Formal norms are imposed on us from above or outside and often codified or written down. Examples of formal norms are organizational policies or laws. Informal norms are created out of face-to-face interaction with others. They spring from the social interactions of people and often are not written down. A classic example of the emergence of informal norms comes from the Hawthorne or Western Electric studies. During the 1920s through 1932, the Western Electric Company conducted a number of studies designed to increase production in their company. The researchers studied a small group of 14 workers whose duties involved the assembly of switches for use in telephone switchboards. The company established a normal day's output at 6600 wiring connections (formal norms). The group of fourteen men shared a set of norms that were not officially defined by the company (informal norms), in that they defined a reasonable day's output as only 6000 wiring connections. The workers felt that no one should be a "rate buster" or squeal to management. The workers also devised ways to enforce the informal norms. If a person became a rate buster, the workers would become hostile, criticize, ostracize, and use violence to keep the person in line, and if none of these methods worked, they would go to management and complain about the person in question. Management did not want the morale of the majority of the workers to suffer because it meant that production might suffer, so they would eventually terminate the rater buster's employment [9]. In this case the informal norms became more important than the formal norms of the organization.

William Graham Sumner was responsible for developing three categories of norms [10]. Sumner's three categories of norms include mores, customs, and folkways, defined as follows:

1. Mores are behaviors that arouse intense feelings and are subject to extreme consequences. They involve the basic moral judgments and ethical rules of a society. They are the strongest norms and have great power over us. An example of a more is the belief that we should not kill other people.

2. Customs do not arouse the intensity of feelings that mores do, and generally their violation will result in less severe reactions. Usually, people react with disgust, repulsion, and shock to the violation

IN FOCUS

The Hawthorne study is also an interesting study of group pressure. For adolescents, perhaps more than adults, peer group approval is critical. Could this be why so many delinquent and criminal acts are committed by gangs rather than by individuals alone?

of a custom. An example of a violation of a custom would be a person who at a luncheon proceeds to file his or her nails.

3. Folkways are norms that when violated carry with them the least intense feelings. Folkways are trivial conventions and are generally not taken as moral imperatives. They are generally concerned with taste and good manners, dress, politeness, and speech. They do not involve feelings of disgust or repulsion.

Laws are formal proscriptive norms that when violated cause a formal and punitive reaction that could result in a person's arrest. Two major questions that concern criminologists who study crime causation are what causes people to break the norms that we call laws and how law violations are handled.

▪ PRIMARY AND SECONDARY GROUPS

The concept of primary and secondary groups was originally conceived by C. H. Cooley. Cooley defined a primary group as a group that forms the person's character and makes society an integral part of the person. The primary group is characterized by feelings of closeness, consensus, and "we-ness." In a primary group members interact in a personal intimate, and emotional way. Some examples of primary groups are families, gangs, and peer groups.

The primary group also has important social functions. Primary groups provide for the person's need for intimate association. They are also important in socializing the person. As a result of the close ties that bind the primary group together, the primary group also serves as an instrument of social control. Finally, primary groups teach the person how to perform social roles.

The secondary group, according to Cooley, was characterized by bureaucracy, organization, heterogeneity, complexity, nd impersonality. In short, all groups that were not bound together by intimate ties were considered by Cooley to be secondary groups. In a secondary group, members interact in an impersonal, businesslike, and unsentimental way. Some examples of secondary groups are trade unions, business associations, corporations, factories, universities, and government offices [11].

Primary groups are of particular interest to the criminologist who is concerned with crime causation. It appears that a significant number of criminals lack strong family bonds when growing up. If they do not get their needs for intimate association met in their families, they will go to other sources. Many will satisfy their need for intimate association in gangs. The gang then becomes the major socialization force for the youngster. (See Chapter 7 for criminological theories related to the juvenile gang.) The primary group is also important in controlling the individual. (See Chapter 8 for criminological theories related to social control.)

■ SOCIALIZATION

The concept of socialization refers to the learning process by which the person learns and internalizes the ways of society so that he or she can function and become an active part of society [12]. Most people usually behave in law-abiding and proper ways because they have incorporated the ways of society into their own personalities. The process of becoming socialized is a result of interaction with people and social groups (see the section "Significance of Society and Group Relationships"). The socialization process begins at birth and continues throughout life. The newborn is born unsocialized, helpless, and fully dependent on others. The newborn is a blank slate, and what he or she becomes in terms of skills, knowledge, attitudes, values, and behaviors is a result of the socialization process.

There are a number of agencies of socialization. The primary agency of socialization is the family. Our parents and parental surrogates provide for our primary socialization. They teach us the basic aspects of life and are our primary socializers until we enter school. There are other agencies of socialization that become important after we enter school (at approximately age 5). School, church, peer groups, television, radio, films, magazines, and newspapers are all examples of agencies that carry out secondary socialization. Secondary socialization involves learning more complex, abstract cultural knowledge. Secondary socialization occurs through interaction with friends, teachers, clergy, and so on.

Resocialization is a concept that is related to socialization. It refers to an extreme change or shift in values, attitudes, and behaviors that were once an integral part of a person's life. Examples of resocialization are the shift from civilian to military status, conversion to a religious or political group, and the shift from a criminal lifestyle to a noncriminal lifestyle. The corrections system is responsible for the latter.

The major goals of the socialization process can be summarized as follows [13]:

1. To teach self-control
2. To teach values

```
IN FOCUS
```

Regina v. Dudley and Stephens
Queens Bench, 1884

Decision by Lord Coleridge, Chief Justice:

Two prisoners, Thomas Dudley and Edwin Stephens were indicted for the murder of Richard Parker on the high seas on the 25th of July in the present year. The special verdict of the jury was as follows:

> That on July 5, 1884, the prisoners, with one Brooks, all able-bodied English seamen, and the deceased, also an English boy between seventeen and eighteen years of age, the crew on an English yacht, were cast away in a storm on the high seas 1600 miles from the Cape of Good Hope, and were compelled to put to sea in an open boat. In this boat, they had no water supply and no food. For three days, they had nothing to eat or drink. On the fourth day, they caught a small turtle, upon which they subsisted for a few days. They had no fresh water, except such rain as they from time to time caught in their oilskin capes. That on the eighteenth day, when they had been seven days without food and five without water, the prisoner Dudley proposed to the others that lots should be cast to decide who should be put to death to save the rest. They could not agree on this. Next it was agreed that since all but the youth had family in need of support, that the boy should be killed. On the next day, Dudley with the consent of Stephens, went to the boy, and telling him that his time had come, put a knife into his throat and killed him then and there; the three men fed upon the body for three days and were rescued on the fourth day. That the boy because of his weakened condition would not have lived for two more days, and had the others not fed upon the body of the boy . . . would have within four days died of starvation.

The real question in this case is whether the killing under the circumstances set forth in the verdict be or be not murder . . . if a person, being under necessity for want of food or clothes . . . steal another man's goods, it is a felony and punishable by death. . . . If, therefore, that extreme necessity of hunger does not justify larceny, . . . necessity would not justify murder.

It must not be supposed that in refusing to admit temptation to be an excuse for crime it is forgotten how terrible the temptation was; how awful the suffering; how hard in such trials to keep the judgment straight and the conduct pure. We are often compelled to set up standards we cannot reach ourselves, and to lay down rules which we could not ourselves satisfy. But a man has no right to declare temptation to be an excuse, though he might himself have yielded to it, nor allow compassion for the criminal to change or weaken in any manner the legal definition of the crime . . . in our unanimous opinion the prisoners are upon this special verdict guilty of murder. [The court then proceeded to pass sentence of death upon the prisoners. The sentence was later commuted by the crown to six month's imprisonment.]

Questions: Does a verdict of death in a situation as described above, serve any purpose? Is it likely to prevent criminal behavior in the future?

3. To teach useful life skills
4. To teach role behavior

The socialization and resocialization process is of major interest to the criminologist who studies crime causation. Many criminologists believe that the answer as to why a person becomes criminal is connected to the criminal's socialization process. (See Chapter 8 for criminological theories related to the socialization process.)

Many types of deviancy and criminality are thought to be the result of inadequate socialization experiences during childhood. Children who are close to their parents are less likely to misbehave than children who are not close to their parents. Delinquents also say that their childhood was unpleasant, that their parents never understood them, and that their parents were too strict [14].

▋ CULTURE, SUBCULTURE, AND COUNTERCULTURE

Culture refers to the system of values and meanings shared by a group, including the embodiment of those values and meanings in material objects [15]. Culture gives meaning to a society. Society is often distinguished from culture and defined as the social structure of a group. Culture involves a way of life, modes of thinking, acting, and feeling. Culture is a design for living that is transmitted from one generation to another.

In any culture there are subcultures that have been described as "cultures within cultures." Subcultures are groups whose mores differ significantly from those held by the wider society of which they are a part. Many subcultures are found in modern, heterogeneous societies. For example, there are many different ethnic groups represented in the United States. Each ethnic group has an identity and traditions different from the dominant American culture. Each ethnic group could be called a subculture.

There are also countercultures [16]. Countercultures are subcultures whose mores run counter to the mores of the rest of society. The values and norms of countercultures are often opposed to the dominant culture and its subcultures. Countercultures are often considered deviant by the dominant culture's standards. Many countercultures are organized and resist the values of the dominant culture. They are also of particular interest to the criminologist who studies crime causation.

∎ SUMMARY

Sociology gives us many concepts that help us understand why people become criminals and/or delinquents. Human beings are highly dependent on other human beings to meet their basic needs. The social relationships that people form are significant for their personal development. In cases where social relationships are absent, human personal development is retarded. This is illustrated by the example of feral children. Social relationships are important not only in making people human but are also important in sustaining human qualities.

The sociological concepts of social norm, more, custom, folkway, primary group, secondary group, socialization, culture, subculture, and counterculture are important in the explanation of delinquent and/or criminal behavior. These concepts are used repeatedly by criminologists who develop theories about criminal behavior.

∎ MATCHING KEY TERMS AND DEFINITIONS

Match each key term with the correct definition.

a. counterculture   g. mores
b. culture   h. prescriptive norm
c. customs   i. primary group
d. folkways   j. primary socialization
e. formal norm   k. proscriptive norm
f. informal norm   l. resocialization

m. secondary group   **p.** social norm

n. secondary socialization   **q.** subculture

o. socialization

____ **1.** A "culture within a culture."

____ **2.** Rules or standards that forbid actions.

____ **3.** A group that is characterized by intimacy, close bonds, and "we-ness."

____ **4.** The learning process by which human beings learn the ways of society so that they can function within it.

____ **5.** A subculture whose mores are opposed to the mores of the dominant culture.

____ **6.** The learning process that refers to an extreme change or shift in values, attitudes, and behaviors that were once an integral part of a person's life.

____ **7.** The basic sociological concept used to explain human behavior.

____ **8.** Rules or standards that involve the basic moral judgments of a society and that arouse intense feelings and reactions when broken.

____ **9.** A rule that is imposed on us by those in greater authority.

____ **10.** A term used to describe the process whereby we learn the basic aspects of life.

____ **11.** Rules and standards that tell us what we can and should do.

____ **12.** A group characterized by heterogeneity, impersonality, and bureaucracy.

____ **13.** Rules that when broken result in disgust, repulsion, and shock.

____ **14.** Rules that spring from the social interaction of people and are not written down.

____ **15.** The process whereby we learn complex, abstract cultural knowledge.

____ **16.** Norms that deal with manners, speech, and etiquette.

____ **17.** A term that refers to the system of values and shared meanings of a group.

▌ DISCUSSION QUESTIONS

1. How do culture, norms, and socialization interact to produce a criminal?

2. How are mores and laws related?

3. What type of countercultures are considered illegal in the United States?

4. Discuss the significance of human group life for human development.

Notes

1. Marshall B. Clinard, *Sociology of Deviant Behavior.* New York: Holt, Rinehart and Winston, 1968; and George Homans, *The Human Group.* New York: Harcourt Brace, 1950.

2. Clinard, 1968.

3. Kingsley Davis, "Extreme Isolation of a Child," *American Journal of Sociology,* vol. 45, Jan. 1940, pp. 554–565; and "Final Note on a Case of Extreme Isolation," *American Journal of Sociology,* vol 52, Mar. 1947, pp. 432–437.

4. A. L. Singh and R. M. Zingg: *Wolf Children and Feral Man.* New York: Harper, 1942.

5. Jean Marc Itard, *The Wild Boy of Aveyron.* New York: Appleton-Century-Crofts, 1962.

6. Richard E. Byrd, *Alone.* New York: G.P. Putnam's Sons, 1938.

7. Byrd, 1938:139–140.

8. Arnold Birenbaum and Edward Sagarin, *Norms and Human Behavior.* New York: Praeger Publishers, 1976, p. 10.

9. Fritz J. Roethlisberger and William J. Dickson, *Management and the Worker.* Cambridge, Mass.: Harvard University Press, 1939.

10. William G. Sumner, *Folkways: A Study of the Sociological Importance of Usages, Manners, Customs, Mores, and Morals.* Boston: Ginn, 1906.

11. Charles H. Cooley, *Social Organization,* Part I. New York: Scribner, 1909.

12. John A. Clausen, ed., *Socialization and Society.* Boston: Little, Brown, 1968, p. 18–72.

13. David Popenoe, *Sociology,* 3rd ed. Englewood Cliffs, N.J.: Prentice-Hall, 1977, p. 120.

14. Gwenn Nettler, *Explaining Crime,* 2nd ed. New York: McGraw-Hill, 1978, pp. 144–145.

15. Popenoe, 1977:75.

16. Theodore Roszak, *The Making of a Counter Culture.* New York: Anchor, 1969.

7

Strain Theories

CHAPTER HIGHLIGHTS

- Strain theories assume that excessive pressures or strain on the person often results in criminal conduct.
- Anomie is a result of widespread changes and transition within a society.
- Anomie is the condition whereby norms have lost their meanings and have become inoperative for individuals.
- The degree of integration in a society is inversely related to its rate of suicide.
- Durkheim believed that crime was normal and a necessary part of society.
- Punishment is a social reaction used to preserve society as we know it.
- Mechanistic and organic societies have different forms of punishment.
- Anomie is greatest when goals are coveted by people and the means to achieve goals are thwarted or limited.
- Norms and values taught to working- and middle-class youths may be different and conflicting.
- Middle-class values are emphasized in the American system of education and justice.
- Juvenile gang behavior is a result of young people experiencing anomie.
- Not everyone can become criminal. Criminal behavior is based on the opportunities the person has to be exposed to crime.

KEY TERMS

Anomie	Homogeneous
Collective Conscience	Mechanical Society
Ethic of Reciprocity	Organic Society
Goals–Means Dysjunction	Short-Run Hedonism
Heterogeneous	Social Solidarity

T he strain theories have certain basic, common assumptions. The assumptions include:

1. If the criminal fails to conform to social norms and laws, it is because there is excessive pressure or strain that propels him or her to commit the criminal behavior.

2. Law breaking and deviance are not normal.

3. Such behavior is caused by immense pressures on the individual.

4. People are basically moral and desire innately to conform to society's laws.

The critical question that strain theorists try to answer is: What is the nature of the strains and/or pressures on an offender that causes him or her to commit criminal behavior? The strain theorists who have contributed greatly to criminological theory include Emile Durkheim, Robert Merton, Albert Cohen, Richard Cloward, and Lloyd Ohlin.

∎ EMILE DURKHEIM

Emile Durkheim (1858–1917), a French sociologist, contributed several seminal theories to the field of criminology. His theory of "anomie," which was originally developed to explain suicide, his theory of suicide, his explanation of the crime phenomenon, and his thoughts on punishment are best known. Durkheim also contributed much to the field of sociology. His theories of social solidarity are most noteworthy and are presented here and also in Chapter 8. It was Talcot Parson's analysis of Durkheim that appeared in 1937 that introduced Durkheim to a wider reading public. Because Parsons and his student Robert Merton were both at Harvard University, the American anomie theorists have been called the "East Coast School of Deviance."

Anomie

Durkheim is credited with introducing the term "anomie" into the literature in his 1893 book *The Division of Labor in Society* [1]. Like other European social scientists, Durkheim was concerned primarily with the transformation of folk societies to modern ones and the attendant problems that resulted from the transformation, including social disorganization. During such change a number of core institutions, such as government, church, and extended family, disappear and/or are eliminated and lose their meanings for the people.

Durkheim defined "anomie" (a Greek term defined as "lawlessness") as a state or a condition that exists within people when a society evolves or changes from a primitive to a modern entity. Anomie occurs as a result of wide-sweeping scientific, technological, and social changes. Simplistically speaking, anomie is the condition of normlessness—not lack of norms, but the condition whereby norms have lost their meaning and become inoperative for large numbers of people. Other ways of describing anomie would be fragmentation or disassociation from one's center; atomization; the feeling of being a number, not a person; rootlessness; aimlessness; frustration; normlessness; hopelessness; collective sadness; social isolation; or social loneliness. This state or condition develops in people when societies grow larger, become heterogeneous (comprised of many different groups of people), develop a complex division of labor, and lose tradition directiveness. Anomie has been the subject and focus of modern poets, artists, and philosophers.

Durkheim believed that anomie was the product of societal transition and that in the course of a society's development, it was possible for anomie to emerge. He also believed that anomique states were only temporary and that once social solidarity was achieved again, anomie within a society would decrease and dissipate. In short, anomie was the result of rapid change within a society.

During such a transitional period in society, not just a few but many people are afflicted by the condition. As such, anomie refers to a disordered relationship between the individual and the society. The traditional institutions of society lose their meaning for people. When society is in transition and anomie is high, institutions and laws become meaningless to people and crime results. Durkheim thought that crime was functional in that it was a measure of societal transition. (A discussion of the functions of crime is set forth in Chapter 1.)

Durkheim On Suicide

As noted earlier, Durkheim's theory of anomie was introduced to explain the phenomenon of suicide. In 1897, Durkheim published his book *Suicide* [2]. Durkheim believed that the degree of integration of a society was inversely related to its rate of suicide. To support his theory, Durkheim noted that there were low suicide rates in predominantly Catholic countries, where religion provided a unifying theme. He also noted that there is increased social solidarity during wartime and in prolonged economic depressions. Whenever there is unification and high social solidarity within a society, anomie is low or non-existent and suicide rates are also low. Durkheim indicated that there were four distinct types of suicide.

1. *Altruistic suicide.* This occurs when an individual is closely identified with a social group and the person feels that it is necessary to sacrifice his or her life for the higher goal. Such people experience extreme solidarity with the system. Examples of altruistic suicide would be the religious monks who immolated themselves to draw attention to the atrocities of the Vietnam war, Japanese pilots who committed hara-kiri, and the Christian martyrs.

2. *Egoistic suicide.* This occurs when an individual is inadequately integrated into society and when the person perceives that society rejects him or her. An example would be a person who does something totally out of character and loses face. Another example would be a person who has what is known as "the beautiful life" but is still unhappy.

3. *Fatalistic suicide.* This occurs when the individual feels that he or she is backed into a corner and that there is no way out. An example

FIGURE 7–1
Anomie and loneliness are a part of modern society. (Photo by Michael Glennon)

would be a young person who is placed in prison for the first time and hangs himself or herself, or a person who loses his or her life savings in a stock market crash.

4. *Anomic suicide.* This occurs when the person is totally alienated from society. The person lives in a world where norms are not meaningful. It is characteristic of disorganized societies that lack unity and cohesion.

Durkheim's Thoughts on Crime

Durkheim's thoughts on crime were unique for his time. He took a broad approach. Before Durkheim, scholars attempted to attribute the cause of crime in factors such as climate or weather. Durkheim, however, attempted to find the answer to the explanation of crime in the very nature of society itself. It was thought that if an explanation for crime could be found, the search for causation would be easier.

Durkheim thought that crime was imminent in society [3]. He was also the first to maintain that crime was a normal and necessary phenomenon in any society. It was not abnormal, pathological, or an imperfection of human nature as other theorists stated and implied. Only when crime increases to 300 percent does it become abnormal. (Note: Durkheim did not state that the criminal was normal, only that crime was normal.) Durkheim also believed that crime played a useful social role in that it stimulated society to develop ways of dealing with crime [4].

Durkheim On Punishment

Durkheim believed that any punishment imposed should be only to the degree that it sustains and reinforces society's collective conscience. Punishment is a social reaction to preserve society. He noted that punishment was different in large, heterogeneous, organic societies and in small, homogeneous, mechanistic societies.

Mechanistic societies are homogeneous societies. They are preliterate, preindustrial, and orderly. Norms and values are shared by all the society's members. People in such a society have a high consensus about issues and events. People are not allowed to be different or march to the tune of their own drummers. There is only a slight division of labor. The mechanistic society is stable, rigid, and tradition-directed. People are clear about their purposes, and deviance and crime are rare. Anomie does not exist in this society. Durkheim indicated that when crime or deviant behavior did occur, punishment was a mechanical reaction to preserve the social solidarity and bonds of the group. Therefore, punishment was usually a harsh and public affair. There was no thought of reforming the offender, only of preserving the social solidarity. In this type of society, the criminal was not seen as bad. Only the act was perceived as bad, because it had the potential to destroy social bonds. The criminal was usually given punishment that resulted in death. However, if the offender survived the punishment, he or she was permitted to continue being a fully functioning member of society. (In mechanical societies, each member's contribution was important for the society's survival.) Punishment served as a message to each person in the society that such behavior would not be tolerated.

Organic societies have dense populations and are heterogeneous (populated by many different ethnic, religious, and racial groups). In these societies there is a complex division of labor. There are many subcultures and contra-cultures. There is low consensus and often disagreement among citizens. The person who marches to the tune of his or her own drummer is found in this type of society. It is in the organic society that chronic anomie is found, and anomie is considered pathological [5]. We also find a great deal of deviance and crime in organic societies. Instead of punishing only the criminal act as in the mechanical society, the entire person is called into question and stigmatized. Punishment is not concerned with preserving social solidarity. Wrong is measured only in terms of how much damage is done to the victim. Society is not concerned with social solidarity but with restitution and reinstatement to the victim. Punishment is also meant to reform, change, and correct the criminal. The shift in the way punishment was administered was a result of the complex division of labor.

▌ ROBERT MERTON

In 1938, Robert K. Merton wrote an article called "Social Structure and Anomie" and applied Durkheim's term "anomie" to deviant behavior [6]. Merton's paper is perhaps the single most frequently quoted paper in modern sociology and criminology. Merton's basic question was: How is malintegration in society related to deviance? Merton used the value of economic success in the United States as an example and tried to relate this example to institutionalized ways of achieving economic success, such as getting an education and speculation with stocks. His premise was that anomie is greatest in societies where certain ends or goals are elevated but there are no means, or limited means (access), to the institutionalized cultural goals or ends. Merton referred to the person's acceptance of society's goals and the blocked access to achieving society's goals as the "goals–means dysjunction." The goal–means dysjunction is the essence of Merton's theory. When there is a dysjunction between cultural goals and the means to achieve them, Merton postulated that specific and predictable adaptations would develop. Merton theorized that there were five adaptations that could develop. The adaptations can also be viewed as five ways that a person could deal with anomie.

1. *Conformity:* acceptance of cultural goals and institutionalized means. Conformity as an adaptation does not usually lead to deviance and is a middle-class response.

2. *Innovation:* acceptance of cultural goals and rejection of institutionalized means. Innovation is like taking a shortcut. Merton believed that this adaptation was greater among lower-socioeconomic status groups, but also felt that this could apply to white-collar crime.

3. *Ritualism:* rejection of cultural goals and acceptance of institutionalized means. Merton believed that this was a lower–middle socioeconomic status group response. Like conformity, ritualism does not seem to be a deviant response, unless overcompliance with the rules is considered deviant. (The Mai Lai massacre and Nuremburg could be examples of overcompliance with the rules and thus considered criminal.)

4. *Retreatism:* rejection of cultural goals and institutionalized means. Retreatism is an escapist response. Addicts, alcoholics, vagrants, and people who become mentally ill and immobilized could be viewed as retreating.

5. *Rebellion:* acceptance and rejection of cultural goals and institutionalized means. Rebellion is an angry, revolutionary response. It differs from retreatism in that goals are not desired secretly by the rebel. However, rebels generally do care and have strong feelings about their goals.

Merton, in contrast to Durkheim, did not see anomie as a temporary state. He saw anomie as a permanent feature of all modern industrial societies. As long as a society elevates certain cultural goals and values, such as financial success or any other value, and there are limited means, access, or inability to achieve goals and values, there will be anomie. In a 1957 presidential address to the American Sociological Society, Merton demonstrated how deviance develops among scientists because of pressures to be original. Since originality is not common and the opportunities for realizing it are limited, deviance occurs in the form of scientists only reporting data that support their research hypotheses; secrecy; stealing ideas; fabricating data; and so on. Merton's theory has been critiqued on the following points:

1. Merton's framework is amenable to and in need of expansion and revision. As such, his ideas have limited application.

2. Merton has no specific research hypothesis about forms of deviant conduct.

3. The question of whether anomie is an explanation of all forms of deviance or relevant only to some kinds of deviance and not to others has not been answered.

■ ALBERT COHEN

Albert Cohen, another strain theorist, in 1955 published his book *Delinquent Boys: The Culture of the Gang* [7]. In the book Cohen applied the anomie theory to delinquency. He also suggested that the theory could be applied at the national level if the national climate were right.

In the 1950s the political and social climate of the United States turned its attention to young people. There were greater numbers of professionals than ever before who were interested in working with youth. The U.S. government also turned its attention toward youth problems, and funding was made available to those who were interested in doing research on juvenile delinquency. Cohen's ideas were well accepted in this climate.

Cohen's Theory of Delinquency

Cohen saw American society as being comprised primarily of the middle and working classes. However, American society tended to place high premiums on ambition, getting ahead, achievement, and education. Getting ahead and making something of oneself were values that transcended one's class and were therefore coveted by all. He believed that the two dominant classes were in conflict due to the different values in which they believed and by which they socialized their children.

Cohen stated that both the middle classes and the working classes tended to teach certain values to their young. The values that each class taught their children were not necessarily the same, although persons in both classes believed in getting ahead and making something of themselves. Since lower-class boys are taught a different value system, they are not properly socialized to meet the requirements of middle-class society. Nevertheless, lower-class boys are measured or evaluated by the standards and aspirations of the middle class, which they cannot fulfill.

The middle classes, according to Cohen, tended to emphasize the following values in socializing their children:

1. Self-control
2. Postponement of immediate gratification and self-indulgence in favor of long-term goals
3. Planning for the future
4. Orderliness
5. Punctuality/time consciousness
6. Individual responsibility
7. Ambition
8. Cultivation of skills and tangible achievements
9. Cultivation of manners and courtesy
10. Respect for property
11. Wholesome recreation
12. Control of aggression and violence

The working classes, according to Cohen, tended to emphasize the following values in socializing their children:

1. Nonchalantness/easygoingness
2. Spontaneity
3. Lack of order
4. Lack of punctuality/different perception of time (*Note:* An example of this would be an offender who is given work release or home furlough from prison and is told to be back before 5:00 P.M. on a certain date. The offender comes back at 6:25 P.M. and does not understand why he or she is put on escape status. "After all, I'm here!" the offender exclaims, "I didn't escape!")
5. Ethic of reciprocity (*Note:* This is defined as the tendency of coming to the aid and assistance of friends, family, and casual acquaintances before meeting one's vocational, social, and financial responsibilities.)

Cohen's point was that the school system in America emphasizes middle-class values. For a child to compete in school successfully, he would have to embrace middle-class values. What does this do to the working-class child? He or she would be at a definite disadvantage in the school environment. Cohen stated that "all children were subject to the middle class measuring rod." According to Cohen, working-class children learn early that they are at a disadvantage in the school environment. They know that they have a handicap and become anxious. They are afraid that they will become lost in the struggle and this produces pressures and strains on them. Another way of describing what happens to working-class children is that they become anomique and often react with violence.

The working-class boy seeks out others who are experiencing what he is. As a group working-class youth reject all symbols of the middle-class system and a delinquent gang emerges to deal with anomie and as a collective protest against a status system that places working-class boys at the bottom. According to Cohen's theory, gang activity is determined primarily by flouting middle-class values. To use Robert Merton's terminology, the gang members rebel.

Cohen described the characteristics of the delinquent gang:

1. There exists a strong sense of gang solidarity with hostility to the outside world. There is also an in-group solidarity free of adult interference.

2. Gang acts are committed that do not bring financial gain. Delinquent activity is "purposeless." Acts are engaged in for immediate pleasure. Cohen calls this "short-run hedonism."

3. The gang possesses malice and negativism toward the middle class.

Cohen studied males; however, he did believe that the patterns he studied were more likely to develop among boys than among girls. He also believed that delinquent subcultures emerged among boys whose status, power, and income were relatively low but whose aspirations were high. In short, such boys cared about being at the bottom.

Evaluation of Cohen

Cohen has been criticized on the following points:

1. Cohen's critics claim that many working-class boys accept and are taught middle-class values and do not accept working-class values and goals as Cohen theorizes.

2. Empirical studies fail to show that delinquent gangs reject middle-class values and goals.

3. Much of what delinquent gangs do, according to Cohen's critics, has been labeled "for kicks" and is not done against middle-class or mainstream American society as Cohen theorizes.

4. Cohen makes no attempt to explain middle-class delinquency, which later works using self-reported delinquency found to be quite extensive.

CLOWARD AND OHLIN'S OPPORTUNITY STRUCTURE

Richard Cloward and Lloyd Ohlin were also contributors to strain theory [8]. They offered an explanation of subcultural delinquency by using "opportunity theory." Ohlin states:

> We [Ohlin and Cloward] scrounged around and got all of the kinds of information we could find to help test the plausibility of the theory, but it was essentially a theory. What we wanted to explore was the linkage between the socially structured patterns of youth opportunity in the community and the dominant patterns of subcultural formation among youth which would occur in response to that system. In short, we hypothesized that the community had sets of legitimate and illegitimate opportunities that conditioned the shape of the deviant subcultures that developed.

In their research they found that lower-class boys also share the American dream for success. Success is a value to them and they measure it materially. However, lower-class boys do not have access to legitimate means to attain success goals as do middle-class youth. They also perceive their chances of success as limited. Lower-class boys, according to Cloward and Ohlin, have a severe gap between their aspiration levels and expectations. These pressures and strains cause anomie and result in deviancy and crime. The boys will handle the strain and pressure in some way. Some boys go in the direction of crime and delinquency by using illegitimate means to achieve goals. The theorists indicate that three basic types of subcultures emerge [9]:

1. *Criminal subculture.* Criminal subcultures primarily conduct illegal activities such as drug sales and auto theft. A new opportunity structure emerges that provides an alternative way for the subculture's members to achieve success.

2. *Conflict subculture.* Conflict subcultures are characterized by violent and aggressive gangs in unstable transient neighborhoods to gain status. Members of conflict subcultures feel great pressure and perceive that legitimate and illegitimate opportunities are blocked for them.

3. *Retreatist subculture.* Retreatist subcultures have members who have failed to find a place for themselves in the criminal and conflict subcultures and have withdrawn.

Cloward and Ohlin also believe that the particular deviant adaptation that develops is a function of opportunity structures for deviant behavior. For example, in some areas gangs steal. In other areas gangs fight. The theorists state that some boys are failures in both legitimate and illegitimate opportunity structures and engage in retreatist behavior and become alcoholics and/or addicts.

Cloward and Ohlin believed that there were varied illegitimate and legitimate opportunity structures. Deviancy and criminality were conditional based on opportunities to engage in deviance and crime. For example, not everyone could become a drug dealer or an addict. The use of drugs and selling drugs depends on contact with people who are suppliers. Professional mercenaries need contact with those who will induct the individual into such behavior. In short, it may be more difficult than meets the eye to engage in certain types of criminal behavior.

■ PUBLIC POLICY AND STRAIN THEORY

Strain theory has had public policy ramifications. Strain theory fit American thinking. America was a great "melting pot" and all Americans should be given the opportunity to succeed [10]. In 1961 the Kennedy Administration created the President's Commission on Juvenile Delinquency and Youth Crime. Cloward, Ohlin, and Cohen's ideas appealed to the Kennedy administration, which supported the idea of opportunities for lower-class youth. New delinquency legislation was passed that smacked of strain theory. Opportunity theory became the primary rationale for Kennedy's War on Poverty [11]. The War on Poverty gave rise to a number of opportunity programs, such as Head Start, Job Corps, Vista, Neighborhood Legal Services, and the Community Action Program.

■ SUMMARY

Strain theories of criminology assume that people commit crimes as a result of extreme pressures or strains on them. Some strain theorists

FIGURE 7–2
Juvenile behavior is often gang related.
UPI/Bettman Newsphotos

believe that people are innately moral and want to be be law abiding. Other strain theorists believe that people are subject to external social forces that may alter their risks of engaging in crime. It is the structural factors that can produce strains that enhance the likelihood of criminal offending. Strain theorists want to isolate the type of strain that causes people to break laws.

Emile Durkheim, one of the first strain theorists, contributed theories on anomie, suicide, criminality, and punishment to the field of criminology. These theories have withheld the test of time, for they are taught in contemporary criminology, sociology, and political science courses.

Robert Merton believed that the goals–means dysfunction caused strain or pressure on the individual. He also believed that people responded to strains and pressures in different ways. They could conform, innovate, engage in rituals, retreat, and/or rebel.

Albert Cohen applied anomie theory to delinquency. He believed that boys from working classes had strains and pressures on them that were products of being taught values different from middle-class boys. The working-class boy had a disadvantage in middle-class schools. This resulted in the working-class boy joining gangs to relieve the pressures or strains on them.

Cloward and Ohlin also offered an explanation of subcultural delinquency. They believed that lower-class boys did not have the same opportunity structures or access to legitimate means to attain their goals as did middle-class boys. This produces frustration and pressure which makes them look for illegitimate opportunity structures to deal with their frustrations and pressures.

Strain theory found public policy support in the Kennedy administration. Numerous programs were initiated that gave lower-class youths the opportunity to succeed in the American Dream.

■ MATCHING KEY TERMS AND DEFINITIONS

Match each key term with the correct definition.

a. anomie

b. collective conscience

c. ethic of reciprocity

d. goals–means dysjunction

e. heterogeneous

f. homogeneous

g. mechanical society

h. opportunity structure

i. organic society

j. short-run hedonism

k. social solidarity

—— 1. The tendency to come to the mutual aid of relatives and casual acquaintances before attending to one's social, employment, and financial responsibilities.

—— 2. Destructive behavior that brings here-and-now pleasure.

—— 3. A term that describes a situation where ends or goals are elevated but there is only limited access to the means to achieve the goals.

—— 4. A term used to describe the degree of cohesion present in a society.

—— 5. A small, tradition-directed society with slight division of labor, high consensus, and little crime.

—— 6. A large, heterogeneous society with great division of labor, low consensus, and much crime.

—— 7. A term that refers to everyone in a society being similar in beliefs, values, creeds, and so on.

—— 8. A term that refers to a society being comprised of many different subcultures and countercultures.

____ **9.** A term that refers to a person needing to have the opportunity to become criminal.

____ **10.** A state or condition whereby societal norms and values have lost meaning for the person.

____ **11.** A term that refers to the way many people in a society experience and feel about situations.

▌ DISCUSSION QUESTIONS

1. What are the different ways people respond when legitimate and illegitimate opportunities are cut off?

2. How are anomie and opportunity theories similar? Different?

3. Do the different socioeconomic status groups in the United States teach different values to their children? Give examples.

4. Robert Merton discusses five ways in which people attempt to deal with anomie. Are there any other ways that people use to deal with anomie?

5. How can parents be helped to prevent delinquency in their children?

6. How can the government best support families and aid parents in dealing with children whose characteristics place them at high risk of becoming delinquents?

Notes

1. E. Durkheim, *The Division of Labor in Society* (translated by George Simpson). New York: Free Press, 1965.

2. E. Durkheim, *Suicide* (translated by J. A. Spaulding and G. Simpson ed.). New York: Free Press, 1951.

3. W. A. Lunden, "Emile Durkheim," in H. Mannheim, ed., *Pioneers in Criminology*. Montclair, N.J.: Patterson Smith, 1972; p. 390.

4. Lunden, 1972:391.

5. George B. Vold and Thomas J. Bernard, *Theoretical Criminology*. New York: Oxford University Press, 1986, p. 150.

6. Robert K. Merton, *Social Structure and Anomie*. New York: Free Press, 1938.

7. Albert K. Cohen, *Delinquent Boys: The Culture of the Gang*. New York: Free Press, 1955.

8. R. A. Cloward and L. E. Ohlin, *Delinquency and Opportunity*. New York: Free Press, 1960.

9. J. H. Laub, *Criminology in the Making: An Oral History*. Boston: Northeastern University Press, 1983, p. 211.

10. Lamar T. Empey, *American Delinquency: Its Meaning and Construction*. Homewood, Ill.: Dorsey Press, 1982, p. 240.

11. Empey, 1982:243.

Control Theories

CHAPTER HIGHLIGHTS

- Social control theorists contend that criminal behavior occurs when a person's bonds to society are weakened or severed.
- According to control theorists, if socialization is effective, people will not normally become criminal.
- Control theorists believe that people are amoral by nature and will commit deviant acts if they have the chance.
- Social controls are often stronger on people who live in small, homogeneous communities than on people who live in larger, heterogeneous population centers.
- Most offenders are not committed to either criminal or conventional society's norms. They fluctuate or drift back and forth between criminal and conventional society's norms.
- Internal and external containments prevent people from committing criminal acts.
- Social bond theory holds that people are born to break laws but will refrain if attachment, commitment, involvement, and belief (social bonds) are present.

KEY TERMS

Criminogenic	Outer Containment
Drift	Social Bond
Inner Containment	Socialization Process
Mechanical Society	Subterranean Values
Organic Society	Techniques of Neutralization

The major assumption of the control theories of crime causation is that delinquency or criminal conduct occurs when an individual's bonds to society are weak or severed. The socialization process (how we come to fit in and live harmoniously in society) is the key to whether we become criminal. It controls us. If our socialization is effective, our control mechanisms will prevent us from becoming deviant. If our socialization is inadequate, our control mechanisms will not connect us to society and we may become criminal.

Control theory deals with order and conformity to rules. It is concerned with what causes human beings to conform. Control theorists believe that human beings are amoral by nature and have the proclivity to commit crime; however, society requires social order and demands people to conform, and most people do conform because they are restrained by their relationships to conventional institutions and individuals, such as family, school, and peer groups [1]. The major question that control theories should ask: Why does anyone conform; that is, why are we not all deviants? [2]. In this chapter we discuss the crime causation theories of the major control theorists; Emile Durkheim, Albert Reiss, Gresham Sykes and David Matza, Walter Reckless, and Travis Hirschi.

■ EMILE DURKHEIM

Some of Emile Durkheim's theories are classified as control theories because they are concerned with the breakdown of society's restraints on individuals' behaviors. Durkheim's strain theories dealing with anomie are presented in Chapter 7. Durkheim's theory is classified in the control perspective because it describes the driving forces behind criminal behaviors (unlimited human needs) as the same at all times and places, and explains differences in the amount of crime on the basis of differences in the restraining forces (societal restraints) [3]. Accordingly, Durkheim believed that mechanical societies controlled people better than did organic societies. (See also Chapter 7 for his discussion on anomie.) In the mechanical society, which was small and tradition-directed, people knew each other by face. Everyone knew what the other person was doing. Each person in the society served as a police officer and provided surveillance. It was difficult for people under such close scrutiny to commit transgressions. Similar conditions sometimes exist in today's small towns. Everyone knows everyone else's business and the pressures are greater to conform.

In contrast to mechanical societies, organic societies do not control people as well. Organic societies are large, heterogeneous, and people can easily disappear in the group. In such societies, people rarely know their neighbors and do not serve as surveillance officers for each other. Most people do not want to get involved. For example, it is not uncommon for people to see others assaulted or even shot before their eyes. They do not interfere because they do not want to get involved. In organic societies, therefore, people lack significant bonds to society.

ALBERT REISS

Albert Reiss conducted a Chicago study dealing with the characteristics of 1110 working-class boys between the ages of 11 and 17 who were on probation [4]. He classified the juveniles according to psychological types. Reiss's theory is derived from psychiatry but has a sociological basis and was the first of the self-described control theories of delinquency [5].

Reiss found that revocation of probation was more likely when boys had weak ego and superego controls which prevented them from internalizing society's norms. In short, such youth had weak personal control mechanisms. Reiss believed that control was related to the attachment people had for others [6]. People were controlled by the norms held by those to whom they were attached. Hopefully, such persons were law abiding. Reiss contended that delinquency emerges from the "failure of personal and social controls to produce behavior in conformity with the norms of the social system to which penalties are attached" [7].

SYKES AND MATZA

David Matza and Gresham Sykes are two of the leading control theorists. Matza in *Delinquency and Drift* indicates that delinquents have no commitment either to societal norms or to criminal norms [8]. Instead, delinquents drift in and out of crime. Matza indicates that delinquents tend to spend most of their time in law-abiding activities. Matza takes the position that delinquents are not immune from the

FIGURE 8-1
Albert Reiss. Courtesy of
Professor Albert J. Reiss, Jr.

demands made by society and that delinquents do have values that support the dominant society. He believes that delinquents are flexible in their commitment to the values of the dominant society and that the majority of delinquents are drifters who are not committed to the norms of mainstream or criminal groups. Most delinquents are not wholly committed to delinquency but are dabbling in it. Delinquents are acting out society's "subterranean values," values that exist in conventional society but are not approved by that society except in the proper time and place. Subterranean values refer to such things as morality with a wink and slick business practices [9]. Matza concluded that "drift" made delinquent behavior possible and that it occurs in segments of society where control is loosened.

Sykes and Matza contend that people do not commit crimes when they are controlled by morals; however, when the morals can be neutralized, the controls lessened and then people are more apt to commit crimes [10]. To commit crimes, people need to neutralize their morals before violating laws in which they believe. People need to make acceptable, behavior that they know is wrong before they will so behave. The theory of Sykes and Matza is popularly known as "techniques of neutralization," rationalizations or justifications that allow a person to commit acts that he or she knows are wrong. Additionally, techniques of neutralization facilitate a person's drift into criminal behavior. Sykes and Matza developed five techniques of neutralization that enabled delinquents to break laws in which they believed.

1. *Denial of responsibility.* The delinquent defines himself or herself as lacking responsibility for behavior. When this happens the delinquent's disapproval of himself or herself does not act as a mechanism leading to socially controlled behavior. Delinquent acts are a result of outside forces such as unloving parents, bad companions, and slum housing. The person tends to view himself or herself as a "poor thing" propelled like a billiard ball in new situations.

2. *Denial of injury.* Injury refers to injury or harm to victims. Vandalism is perceived as "mischief." Auto theft is viewed as "borrowing." Gang fighting is seen as a private quarrel and no one else's business. The delinquent feels that his or her behavior does not cause any great harm despite the fact that it runs counter to the law.

3. *Denial of the victim.* The injury is not wrong in light of the circumstances. Injury becomes rightful retaliation or well-deserved punishment. The victim deserves to have something happen to him or her. A subtle alchemy transforms the victim into the wrongdoer in the offender's mind and the offender becomes the Robin Hood. Hence vandalism is justified as revenge on an unfair teacher. Thefts are justified on crooked, corrupt store owners. Rape is justified because the woman is really asking for it. If the victim is physically absent, unknown, or a vague abstraction, the offender can more easily justify and rationalize his or her actions.

4. *Condemnation of the condemners.* This technique involves a shift in focus. It is a rejection of rejecters. For example, to the offender the police are corrupt, stupid, and brutal. The offender thinks that criminals are hypocrites or deviants in disguise.

5. *Appeal to higher loyalties.* The delinquent sacrifices the demands of society for the gang or peer group and the group becomes more important than the individual. The norms of the gang or peer group are considered more pressing, important, and involving a higher loyalty than the societal norms. Examples of this abound. War is justified for God and country. G. Gordon Liddy, a key figure in the Watergate affair, kept his mouth shut to protect President Nixon from criminal wrongdoing. A large number of high school students in Milpitas, California, were shown the dead body of a classmate by a student who committed the murder and decided not to tell authorities because it was squealing on a friend.

In short, techniques of neutralization are critical in lessening the effectiveness of social controls that lie behind a large share of criminal and delinquent behavior. It should be noted that support for the existence of neutralization theory is mixed. Some of the criticisms of neutralization theory are that it fails to show whether neutralizations occur before or after the criminal act, fails to show why some kids drift and others do not, and does not explain self-destructive acts such as heroin addiction[11].

■ WALTER RECKLESS'S CONTAINMENT THEORY

Containment theory holds that people have a number of social controls, containments, or protective barriers which help them in resisting pressures that draw them toward crime. Walter Reckless felt that we all have pushes and pulls toward crime; however, not all people with the same pushes and pulls become criminal [12]. His containment theory attempted to answer why some people succumbed to the pushes and pulls and why others did not.

There are two kinds of containments: inner/internal containments and outer/external containments. External containments are strong social bonds and ties that prevent a person from committing criminal behavior. External containment comes from peers, family, schools, churches, and the like. Internal containments are such things as good self-image, conscience, strong ego, goal-directedness, and all the things that give a person inner strength and self-control. Reckless defines inner and outer containment as follows [13]:

> Inner containment consists mainly of self components, such as self-control, good self-concept, ego strength, well-developed superego, high frustration tolerance, high resistance to diversions, high sense of responsibility, goal orientation, ability to find substitute satisfactions. tension-reducing rationalizations, and so on. These are the inner regulators.

> Outer containment represents the structural buffer in the person's immediate social world which is able to hold him within bonds. It consists of such items as a presentation of a consistent moral front to the person, institutional reinforcement of his norms, goals, and expectations, effective supervision and discipline (social controls), provisions for reasonable scope of activity (including limits and responsibilities) as well as for alternatives and safety-valves, opportunity for acceptance, identity, and be-

longingness. Such structural ingredients help the family and other supportive groups contain the individual.

Reckless was of the belief that the internal containments provided the most effective controls on the person. Together the internal and external containments prevent people from becoming criminal. The theory also holds that people have many social pressures that pull and push them and interact with their containments. The pulls are environmental factors such as poverty, poor family life, and deprived education. The pushes are individual factors such as hostility, personality, and aggressiveness. Hopefully, inner and outer containment interacts with the pushes and pulls on a person to prevent criminal behavior.

▌TRAVIS HIRSCHI

Travis Hirschi believes that people are born to break the law and will refrain from doing so only if special circumstances exist. This is known as his "social bond theory" and was presented in 1969 in *Causes of Delinquency* [14]. The special circumstances exist only when a person's bond to mainstream society is strong. Hirschi believes that a person's bond to mainstream society is based on four elements [15].

1. *Attachment.* Attachment refers to the person's ability to be sensitive to thoughts, feelings, and desires of others. It refers to the emotional or affective involvement the person has with others. If a person has faulty affective involvement with others, attachment could be affected and the person would have a higher probability of committing criminal acts. If the person cares and values relationships with others, he or she is less likely to commit criminal acts.

2. *Commitment.* According to Hirschi, commitment is the rational component in conformity. For example, the authors' have invested a great deal of time and energy going to school and obtaining degrees. Before we would commit a crime we would have to go through a rational process of weighing the costs and benefits of committing a crime compared to our investment in conformity. Hirschi states: "The concept of commitment assumes that the organization of society is such that the interests of most persons would be endangered if they were to engage in criminal acts" [16].

3. *Involvement.* Hirschi indicates that the more a person is involved or engrossed in conventional things, the less the opportunity the person has to commit criminal behavior. One person has only a limited

FIGURE 8–2
Do prisons like the one illustrated control? Louis P. Carney, *Corrections: Treatment and Philosophy,* © 1980, p. 189. Reprinted by permission of Prentice Hall, Inc., Englewood Cliffs, NJ.

amount of time and energy. Hirschi states: "The person involved in conventional activities is tied to appointments, deadlines, working hours, plans, and the like, so the opportunity to commit deviant acts rarely arises" [17].

4. *Belief.* Hirschi indicates that when the person's belief in the values of the society or group are weakened, criminal behavior is more likely to occur [18].

When belief in the values of society are present in conjunction with involvement, commitment, and attachment, deviancy is rare [19].

Hirschi has been criticized because he fails to explain differences in crime rates, fails to indicate whether a weakened social bond can be strengthened, and fails to distinguish the importance of different elements of the social bond. Hirschi has been touted because he drew attention to the importance of intrafamilial relationships as the primary factor in contributing to delinquency, and research on the family increased after the publication of Hirschi's theory. Authorities found Hirschi's control theory logical and appealing and many interventions have been based on it [20]. Hirschi's social control theory is considered by some as one of the most preeminent social theories of crime in the 1980s.

■ EVALUATION OF CONTROL THEORY

The social control theorists do not view human nature as inherently evil, a blank slate, or inherently good. They see the human being as a "free spirit," free to do whatever is most convenient and advantageous at a given time. All people have nonconformist impulses. In short, all people would deviate if given the chance. The social control theorists do not see deviant behavior as problematic and therefore do not feel the need to explain it [21]. Control theorists are not interested in people's motives. They assume that all people would deviate if they did not have controls to stop them. Additionally, social control theories account for criminogenic factors (crime-producing factors inherent throughout society) and individual responses in crime [22]. However, if socialization is effective, a social bond will result, giving the person a stake in conformity and preventing him or her from committing crime. If socialization is ineffective, a social bond will not result, thus the person will not have a stake in conformity and will commit criminal acts.

■ SUMMARY

The control theorists hold that crime occurs whenever a person's bonds to society become weak or severed. Our societal bonds are formed primarily by our socialization experiences. Control theorists also believe that people are not born good or bad but rather, have the inclination to do whatever they can get away with. People are prevented from doing anything they like by their bonds to family, friends, school, church and similar groups.

Emile Durkheim believed that there were greater controls on human deviance in small, homogeneous, mechanistic societies where people knew each other and were able to keep an eye on everyone, as opposed to larger, heterogeneous organic societies where people were anonymous. Albert Reiss believed that control was related to the attachment people had for others to whom they were attached. David Matza postulated that delinquents do not have a particularly strong commitment to delinquent/criminal or conventional norms and values. Instead, delinquents adhere to the norms and values in both groups and pick and choose norms and values that are convenient. In short, Matza postulated that delinquents drift from one set of norms and values to other sets of norms and values.

Sykes and Matza developed the idea that to commit crimes criminals know are wrong, they have to rationalize, justify, and make the wrong behavior acceptable before they can go through with it. This is known as "techniques of neutralization" theory. Techniques of neutralization are critical in lessening the effectiveness of social controls that lie behind a large amount of criminal and delinquent behavior.

Walter Reckless's containment theory holds that people have a number of containments or protective barriers that help them in resisting pressures that attract them to crime. Travis Hirschi's social bond theory maintains that only when a person has attachment, involvement, commitment, and belief in people and society's institutions will he or she not break the law.

■ MATCHING KEY TERMS AND DEFINITIONS

Match each key term with the correct definition.

a. criminogenic
b. drift
c. inner containment
d. mechanical society
e. organic society

f. outer containment
g. social bond
h. socialization process
i. subterranean valves
j. techniques of neutralization

____ 1. The way in which we learn the things that we need to know in order to fit and live in society.

____ 2. A term that refers to the idea that delinquents do not have commitment to either conventional or criminal norms.

____ 3. A term that refers to crime-producing flaws that are inherent within the structure of society.

—— 4. Devices that allow people to rationalize and justify their involvement in criminal acts that they know are wrong.

—— 5. A phrase that refers to strong social bonds such as those that are fostered in school, church, family, and with peers.

—— 6. A small, homogeneous, tradition-based society.

—— 7. A term that refers to the things that give people self-control and strength.

—— 8. A large, heterogeneous society characterized by low consensus among its members.

—— 9. Values that exist in conventional society but are not openly approved of by society's members.

——10. The social feelings that constrain a person to a certain line of behavior.

■ DISCUSSION QUESTIONS

1. If both the deviant and nondeviant believe that their acts are wrong, why does one commit the act and the other not?

2. Are there cases where attachment, belief, commitment, and involvement on the part of an offender were present but the offender committed crimes anyway? Explain.

3. Can a weakened social bond be strengthened? How?

4. If people's social controls were sufficiently powerful as to prevent all delinquent behavior, does it mean that people would not turn to other deviant responses, such as suicide and acting crazy?

Notes

1. J. J. Senna and L. J. Siegal, *Introduction to Criminal Justice,* 4th ed. St. Paul, Minn., West Publishing 1987, p. 71.

2. Sue Titus Reid, *Crime and Criminology,* 3rd ed. New York: Holt, Rinehart and Winston, 1982, p. 160.

3. George B. Vold and Thomas J. Bernard, *Theoretical Criminology,* 3rd ed. New York: Oxford University Press, 1986, p. 232.

4. Albert J. Reiss, "Social Correlates of Psychological Types of Delinquency," *American Sociological Review,* vol. 17, 1952, pp. 710–718.

5. Vold and Bernard, 1986:233.

6. Albert J. Reiss, "Delinquency and the Failure of Personal and Social Controls," *American Sociological Review,* vol. 16, 1951, pp. 196–207.

7. Reiss, 1951:196.

8. David Matza, *Delinquency and Drift,* New York: Wiley, 1964.

9. Matza, 1964:63–64.

10. Gresham M. Sykes and David Matza, "Techniques of Neutralization: A Theory of Delinquency," *American Sociological Review*, vol. 22, Dec. 1957, pp. 667–670.

11. Senna and Siegel, 1987:79.

12. Walter Reckless, *The Crime Problem*, 5th ed. Englewood Cliffs, N.J.: Prentice-Hall, 1973.

13. Reckless, 1973:55–56.

14. Travis Hirschi, *Causes of Delinquency*, Berkeley: University of California Press, 1969.

15. Hirschi, 1969.

16. Hirschi, 1969:19–21.

17. Hirschi, 1969:23.

18. Hirschi, 1969:23–26.

19. Hirschi, 1969:27–30.

20. Lamar T. Empey, *American Delinquency: Its Meaning and Construction*. Homewood, Ill.: Dorsey Press, 1982, p. 275.

21. F. T. Cullen, *Rethinking Crime and Deviance Theory: The Emergence of a Structuring Tradition*. Totowa, N.J.: Rowman & Allanheld, 1983, p. 137.

22. F. E. Hagan, *Introduction to Criminology: Theories, Methods, and Criminal Behavior*. Chicago: Nelson-Hall, 1987, p. 450.

The Conflict
and Radical Theories

9

CHAPTER HIGHLIGHTS

- Conflict theories focus on the political nature of crime.
- There are two major approaches used by sociologically based criminological theorists when considering societal norms; (1) the consensus approach and (2) the conflict approach.
- According to the consensus approach, society is based on a consensus (general agreement) of values among its members and the state is organized to protect those collectively held values.
- Conflict theorists contend that there is an implicit ideology within our criminal justice system which conveys a subtle, powerful message in support of our present criminal justice system.
- Austin Turk contended that criminologists should study the differences between the status and role of legal *authorities* and *subjects*.
- According to the conflict theorists, by concentrating on individual wrongdoers, we are diverted away from consideration of whether our society is just or unjust.
- Radical criminology is but one of a new group of criminological theories that is based on the economic determinism thesis of Karl Marx.
- The central theme of radical and conflict theories is that criminal behavior can be explained in terms of economic conditions and is an expression of class conflict.
- Karl Marx and Friedrich Engels believed that crime is a product of capitalism.
- According to the radical theorists, the capitalist economic system encourages people to be greedy and selfish and to pursue their own benefits without regard to the needs and wishes of others.
- Radical criminologists contend that the criminal justice system criminalizes the greed of the poor but allows the rich to pursue their selfish desires.

- Richard Quinney believes that the traditional notion of the causes of crime should be abandoned and we should attempt to understand what "could be," not "what is."
- Quinney contends that criminology, as the scientific study of crime, has served a single purpose: legitimation of the existing social order.
- Radical criminologists believe that the question "What causes crime?" has focused criminology on the criminal rather than understanding that crime is a product of the authority that defines behavior as criminal.
- The criminal justice system, according to the critical criminologists, is used for the purpose of maintaining the status quo for the powerful members of society or as a means of serving the self-interests of those who operate the criminal justice agencies.

KEY TERMS

Conflict Approach

Consensus Approach

Cubidity

Economic Determinism

Material Forces of Production

Norms of Deference

Norms of Domination

Schedules of Reinforcement

Social Reality of Crime

Social Relations of Production

■ TWO CONTRASTING VIEWS

There are two major approaches used by sociologically based criminological theorists when considering societal norms: (1) the consensus approach and (2) the conflict approach. According to the consensus approach, society is based on a consensus of values among its members and the state is organized to protect those collectively held values. The conflict approach holds that society is composed of groups of people with conflicting values and interests. According to the conflict approach, the state does not represent the values and interests of society as a whole, but rather the values and interests of those groups with sufficient power to control the state (e.g., the rich and powerful). Often, the conflict orientation is divided into two general approaches: the conservative conflict perspective and the critical or radical approach. In this chapter we use "conflict criminology" to refer to the conservative conflict perspective approach, and "radical criminology" to refer to the radical or critical approach. Conflict theories focus on the political nature of crime and seek to examine the development and application of criminal law [1].

   While the consensus approach holds societal norms and laws as being representative of the general and common view of what behaviors are right and wrong, the conflict approach views values, norms, and laws as creating dissention and conflict [2]. At first, the conflict perspective was restricted to political conflicts. Presently, its focus is broader than the class struggle. The conflict may be between cultures, subcultures, interest groups, or others. In this chapter, the traditional conflict and radical theories are discussed. Culture- and subcultural-based conflict theories are discussed with the cultural deviance theories in Chapter 10.

FIGURE 9–1
The fact that property crimes outnumber violent crime by 9:1 strengthens the conflict criminologist's positions.

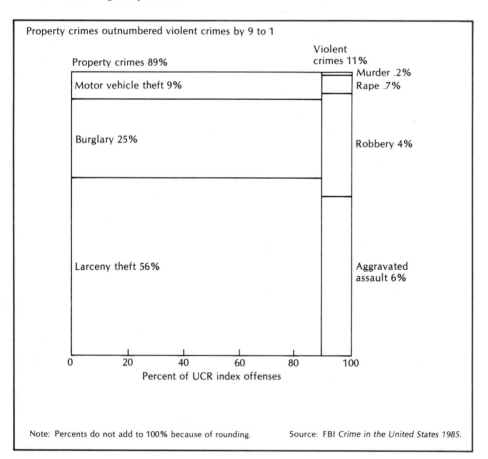

▌IMPLICIT IDEOLOGY

Conflict theorists contend that there is an implicit ideology of our criminal justice system which conveys a subtle, powerful message in support of our present criminal justice system. A similar contention is present in Plato's *Republic* as noted by the following passage:

> In every case the laws are made by the ruling party in its own interest; a democracy makes democratic laws, a despot autocratic ones and so on. By making these laws they define as "just" for their subjects whatever is for their own interest, and they call anyone who breaks them a "wrongdoer" and punish him accordingly.

Jeffrey Reiman states that the system conveys this message for two interconnected reasons [3].

1. By concentrating on individual wrongdoers, we are diverted away from consideration of whether our society is just or unjust.

IN FOCUS

Designed to Fail

Reiman, in one of his graduate seminars at American University, had his students design a penal/correctional system that would encourage the existence of a stable and "visible" class of criminals. The basic principles developed by his students are as follows:

1. Have a number of laws on the books which punish acts that have no clear victims.

2. Give prosecutors, police, and judges broad discretion in deciding who are arrested, prosecuted, and punished.

3. Make the prison experience not only painful, but also demeaning.

4. Do not provide prisoners with training in marketable skills.

5. Use prison records as perpetual stigma.

How do the foregoing principles compare with those being practiced in our present penal/correctional system.

2. The criminal law is put forth as the "minimum neutral ground rules for social living." (Reiman uses this phrase to describe those societal rules that are neutral as to culture bias and are necessary for society to function.) By use of this mask of neutrality, the established institutions divert our attention away from the injustice of our social institutions.

Reiman contends that the effect of focusing on individual guilt and diverting our attention from the possible evils of the established institutions is that we put forth half the problem of justice as if it were the whole problem. The other half of the problem is the issue of whether fellow citizens have fulfilled their obligations toward the offender. Reiman states that by looking only at individual responsibility, we treat the system as a one-way street. According to him, justice is a two-way street.

■ THE CONFLICT APPROACH

The political conflict theorists can be divided into two groups: the more radical and less radical groups. The more radical group contends that a revolution is necessary to cure the ills of society. The less radical group (critical theorists) contends that reforms in the capitalist economic system will result in a true consensus-based state.

McCaghy contended that conflict criminology has two important advantages over the traditional crime causation theories [4]. First, unlike the traditional theories, conflict criminology acknowledges that a relationship exists between deviant behavior and the process of making and enforcing laws, and second, again unlike traditional theories, conflict criminology recognizes that many acts of rule breaking are committed in the name of a group or cause.

Austin Turk

Austin Turk, a modern conflict theorist, viewed the conflicts of society as the result of political organizations and their exercise of control [5]. Turk contended that criminologists should study the differences between the status and role of legal *authorities* and *subjects*. According to him, in all social arrangements, there are norms of domination (established by those in authority) and norms of deference (established by those subject to the authorities). (*Note:* He does not view conflict over social norms in the traditional sense that some persons have internalized the norms and others have not. He stated that people react

FIGURE 9-2
Boredom: a cause of crime? (Photo by Michael Glennon)

differently to societal norms. They react according to their own social perspective.)

Some behavioral norms we accept and others we perceive as "norms of domination" (i.e., they are imposed on us). Whether or not we comply with the norms that we perceive as "norms of domination" depends to a great extent on our deference to authority (i.e., "our norms of deference"). Turk views lawbreaking as an indicator of a failure or lack of "authority" of the system. It is also a measure of the extent to which the subjects and those in authority are not bound together in a stable authority relationship.

Turk suggests that control is exercised through the use of power [6]. He classified power into five classes based on the type of resources controlled by each group. The classes are as follows:

1. Police power, which is based on control of the means of direct physical violence

2. Economic power, which is based on control of material resources

3. Political power, which is based on control of the political decision-making processes

4. Ideological power, which is based on control of definitions, beliefs, and values

5. Diversionary power, which is based on control of human attention and "living times"

Turk has been criticized for ignoring the evidence that there is considerable normative consensus in society that cuts across classes and power groups (e.g., norms that reject rape, murder, etc.).

▌ RADICAL CRIMINOLOGY

Radical criminology is but one of a new group of criminological theories that is based on the economic determinism thesis of Karl Marx. In addition to radical criminology, the new group of theories include the "new conflict approach," "new" criminology, "Marxist" criminology, "materialist" criminology, and "socialist" criminology. The central theme of these theories is that criminal behavior can be explained in terms of economic conditions and is an expression of class conflict [7]. Since there is divergence among these theories, it is not practical in this book to discuss the subtle nuances and differences. The theories are based, however, on Marx and Engels's economic determinism and are treated as one theoretical concept in the following sections.

Marx and Engels

Beginning as early as the sixteenth century, criminologists have attempted to link economic conditions to criminal causation [8]. Karl Marx and Friedrich Engels originated the idea that crime is a product of capitalism. To them, the criminal was a person who had been brutalized and demoralized by capitalism.

In attempting to explain the social changes caused by the industrial revolution (1760–1840), Karl Marx (1818–1883) linked economic development to social and political changes. Marx based his theories on the conflict between the material forces of production and the social relations of production [9]. Material forces of production, according to Marx, referred to the society's ability to produce material goods. Social relations of production referred to the relationship between people involved in producing and consuming the material goods and included property relationships.

FIGURE 9-3
**Karl Marx. Courtesy of
the Library of Congress**

Marx suggested that the development of material forces of production was relatively continuous throughout history. Social relations of production, however, tended to remain stable for long periods. At some point, then, would social relations have to change abruptly and violently. Marx predicted that as the material forces of production continued to develop under capitalism, the social relations would restrict them until eventually there would be a violent restructuring of society. When this occurred, he predicted that capitalism would be replaced by socialism.

During Marx's time, the classical school was the dominant school of criminological theory. Marx contended that the classical concept of "free will" ignored the fact that individuals had unequal power and wealth. To Marx, crime was not the result of willful violations of criminal law, but the "struggle of the isolated individual against the prevailing conditions" [10]. The criminal was not attempting, therefore, to redistribute wealth by his or her criminal conduct, but was merely reacting as a demoralized victim of the capitalist society. While Marx failed to develop a specific theory of crime causation, he saw the mode of production as the causative element in social, political, ethical, and religious life [11].

In his study of the conditions of the working class in mid-nineteenth century England, Friedrich Engels saw crime as a response to the oppression of the working class. He stated [12]:

> Crime is a primitive form of insurrection, driven by need and deprivations, an incomplete but not altogether mistaken response to a bad situation, and coming into active existence only by overcoming the resistance of inherited values and internalized sanctions. . . .

Marx and Engels' economic determinism is summarized as follows:

1. Private ownership of property results in poverty.
2. Private ownership distinguishes those who own the means of production from those whom they exploit for economic reasons.
3. The exploited turn to crime as the result of poverty and exploitation.
4. The economic system, therefore, is the sole determinant of crime.
5. Social revolution is the only way to bring about necessary changes in the economic system.

Engels, in *The Condition of the Working Class in England*, summarizes his beliefs on crime as follows:

> If one individual inflicts a bodily injury upon another which leads to the death of the person attacked we call it manslaughter; on the other hand, if the attacker knows beforehand that the blow will be fatal we call it murder. Murder has also been committed if society places hundreds of workers in such a position that they inevitably come to premature and unnatural ends. Their death is as violent as if society knows perfectly well that thousands of workers cannot avoid being sacrificed so long as these conditions are allowed to continue.

Whereas Marx and Engels contended that criminal behavior is caused by rebellion against oppression and exploitation, later Marxist theorists attempted to explain criminal behavior in terms that are similar to the concepts used by strain and labelling theorists (i.e., the special strains placed on the lower class by society and the concept of stigma).

Willem Bonger

Although Marx and Engels did not devote a great deal of time and study to the relationship between criminal behavior and economic conditions, a disciple, Willem Bonger, made this relationship his life work. Bonger, a Dutch criminologist, studied primitive societies and concluded that primitive societies were characterized by altruism. He concluded that the altruism can be explained only by examining the mode of production. People in primitive societies produce goods for personal consumption only. In these societies there is neither wealth nor poverty. It is only when a society begins to produce goods for exchange that society loses its altruistic nature and replaces altruism with selfishness. Bonger called this selfness "egoism." When this occurs, social irresponsibility results and people become criminals. The capitalistic economical system therefore provides a "climate of motivation" for criminal behavior [13].

To Bonger, the definition of crime was social in nature. For certain behavior to be considered criminal in a capitalistic society, the behavior must be harmful to those in power. Bonger also studied the motives associated with different types of criminal behavior. He divided crime into four types based on the motivation of the criminal.

1. *Economic.* These crimes Bonger viewed as resulting from poverty, cubidity (a desire for inordinate wealth), white-collar crime, and acts of professional criminals.

2. *Sexual.* Rape and related crimes are a consequence of living conditions in the lower classes, which teach children to view sex from an animalistic point of view.

3. *Political.* Political crimes are those crimes that are directed toward the ruling class in order to aid an oppressed class.

4. *Vengeful.* Vengeful crimes result from the conditions created by an economic system that encourages strife and competition.

Bonger considered social and economic conditions as the cause of degeneracy. The pressures created by the desire to maintain or improve one's economic position often result in mental problems. Bonger defined degenerates as people who suffer from mental diseases or diseases of the nervous system. According to Bonger, even biological degeneracy that could be heredity is caused by unfavorable environmental circumstances (economic conditions) suffered by earlier generations [14]. Bonger's theory is summarized as follows:

1. The capitalist economic system encourages people to be greedy and selfish and to pursue their own benefits without regard to the needs and wishes of others.

2. The criminal justice system criminalizes the greed of the poor but allows the rich to pursue their selfish desires.

3. A socialist society would eliminate crime because it would promote a concern for the welfare of society as a whole, not just the privileged class.

Richard Quinney

The leading modern spokesperson for radical criminology is Richard Quinney. Quinney's thesis is that the state is a political organization that serves to maintain the interests of the ruling class over and against those of the ruled class. Quinney stated [15]:

> Criminal law is used by the state and the ruling class to secure the survival of the capitalist system, and, as capitalist society is further threatened by its own contradictions, criminal law will be increasingly used in the attempt to maintain domestic order.

Quinney stated that the traditional ideas about the causes of crime should be abandoned and we should attempt to understand what "could be," not "what is." He stated that criminology, as the scientific study of crime, has served a single purpose: legitimation of the existing social order [16]. By asking the question "What causes crime?" we have focused our study on the criminal rather than understanding that crime is a product of the authority that defines behavior as criminal.

Quinney accuses the media of disseminating to the American public the dominant ruling class's position on crime and control. According to Quinney, the media, as a major industry, is not separate from the interests of the state and thus of the ruling class [17]. The themes used by the media to disseminate the dominant ruling class's position are as follows:

1. The "forces of evil" are to be wiped out.
2. In the "Dick Tracy mentality," the crime fighter is no mere mortal but rather, a super crime fighter.
3. Good always triumphs over evil; crime does not pay.
4. Violence is central to the crime problem.
5. The criminal is a distinctive, unique, readily identifiable, and different (subhuman) person.
6. There are two types of people in society—good and bad.
7. Operating outside the law is appropriate when dealing with major crimes and criminals.

Quinney developed six propositions regarding the "social reality of crime" [18]:

IN FOCUS

Do the *Dirty Harry* movies by Clint Eastwood and movies like *Rambo* and *Death Wish* support Quinney's theory that the media disseminates the view of the dominant ruling class?

1. Crime as a legal definition of human conduct is created by agents of the dominant class.

2. Definitions of crime are composed of behaviors that conflict with the interests of the dominant class.

3. Definitions of crime are applied by the class that has the power to shape the enforcement and administration of criminal law.

4. Behavior patterns are structured in relation to definitions of crime, and within this context people engage in actions that have relative probabilities of being defined as criminal.

5. An ideology of crime is constructed and diffused by the dominant class to secure its position of dominance.

6. The social reality of crime is constructed by the formulation and application of definitions of crime, the development of behavior patterns to these definitions, and the construction of an ideology of crime.

One of the problems that radical criminologists have is explaining "personal crimes" (e.g., rape, murder, and assault). Quinney attempts to explain them as "crimes committed by those who are already brutalized by the conditions of capitalism" [19]. Quinney also stated

IN FOCUS

Essence of Radical Theory

The essence of the radical theory is that crime is simply behavior that threatens the ruling class. Does this mean that the protection of others is coincidental to the extent that they fall under the umbrella of the protection of the status of the ruling class?

that personal crimes were the result of "the social psychological effect of the contradictions of capitalism" [20]. This may explain why the "nonruling" class commits those crimes, but it fails to explain why members of the "ruling" class also commit crimes of rape, murder, and so on.

Critique of Radical Criminology

Some of the popular criticisms of radical theories are as follows:

1. Contemporary radical criminologists are incorrect in alleging that earlier generations of criminologists were oblivious to the origin of criminal laws in social and economic conflicts.

2. The radical position exaggerates the political nature of crime.

3. The radical position is surrounded by mystification. Radical criminologists use terminology such as "exploitation," "monolithic" power, and "structures of corporate capitalism."

4. Radical theories lack comprehensive and rigorously stated theoretical bases.

5. Radical theories are a modern version of conspiracy theories.

■ CRITICAL CRIMINOLOGY

Critical criminology developed from the social turbulence of the 1960s. The reaction to American involvement in the Vietnam war and the development of the drug counterculture caused many people to question the traditional assumptions of the criminal justice system [21]. Critical criminology may be described as a mixture of the labeling and radical theories. Gresham Sykes, the theory's leading spokesperson, lists the three major themes of critical criminology as follows [22]:

1. Critical criminologists take issue with theories that view crime as a result of biological and psychological maladjustments and with sociological theories that rely on such factors as inadequate socialization and peer group pressure. Criminologists should focus on why some people and not others are labeled as criminal rather than focusing on the characteristics that distinguish criminals from noncriminals.

2. The criminal justice system is used for the purpose of maintaining the status quo for the powerful members of society or as a means of serving the self-interests of those who operate the criminal justice agencies.

3. Present criminal laws reflect not the morality of our society, but the desires and interests of only a small segment of our society. They reject the concept that criminal law is the collective moral judgment of the society and contend that "law" should be considered as rules imposed by the ruling "regime."

William Chambliss

Another leading spokesperson for critical criminology is William Chambliss [23]. Chambliss's theory is summarized as follows:

1. In every historical era, societies and human groups in the struggle to survive invariably create contradictory forces and tendencies that serve as unseen forces moving the groups toward new social, political, and economic relations.

2. In the movement, contradictions tend to intensify with time and cannot be resolved within the existing social framework.

3. The contradictions lead to conflicts between groups, classes, and strata.

4. Criminal behavior is generated because of the contradictions and conflicts that inevitably arise in the course of life. The type of crime and the amount depends on the nature of existing contradictions, the conflicts that develop as people respond to the contradictions, and the mechanisms institutionalized for handling the conflicts and dilemmas produced by the contradictions.

Chambliss contends that criminologists should be "critical" of traditional concepts and ask questions regarding them [24]. He states that the questions we ask will shape our knowledge far more than the theories we propose. According to Chambliss, the questions that we ask should include:

1. Why are some acts defined by law as criminal, whereas others are not?

2. Why, given the definition of certain acts as criminal, are some people arrested, prosecuted, convicted, and sentenced, whereas others are not?

3. Why is crime distributed as it is by social class, race, and gender?

▮ GROUP CONFLICT THEORY

Using conflict theorists' precepts, George Vold developed a group conflict theory of criminal causation [25]. (*Note:* The theory could also be classified as a cultural deviance theory.) The key points of Vold's theory are as follows:

1. The conditions of one's life determine the "schedules of reinforcement" that one experiences.

2. "Schedules of reinforcement" include a person's values and interests.

3. Complex societies are composed of groups with widely different life conditions and widely different schedules of reinforcement.

4. Behavior is acquired and persists to the extent that it is reinforced over alternative behavior. Behavior is also evaluated as desirable or undesirable, depending on our schedules of reinforcement.

5. Since persons' values and interests tend to remain stable, groups tend to develop relatively stable behavior patterns that differ in varying degrees from the behavior patterns of other groups.

IN FOCUS

The Union Carbide Case

During the night of December 3, 1984, at the Union Carbide plant in Bhopal, India, methyl isocyanate leaked into the air, causing a posionous vapor to cover the city. Somewhere between 2000 and 5000 victims died. Over 200,000 persons were injured. Investigation reports of the disaster include the following allegations against Union Carbide:

1. Management was lax

2. Workers were poorly trained

3. Many defective instruments and "safety valves" were in use

If these allegations are correct, are management officials guilty of mass murder? Using a conflict orientation, compare punishment that should be given if the allegations are correct to a situation involving a bar fight resulting in a single murder.

■ SUMMARY

There are two major approaches used by sociologically based conflict criminological theorists when considering societal norms: (1) the consensus approach and (2) the conflict approach. Conflict theorists contend that there is an implicit ideology of our criminal justice system which conveys a message in support of the existing social structure. Austin Turk held that criminologists should study the differences between the status and role of legal *authorities* and *subjects*. According to the conflict theorists, by concentrating on individual wrongdoers, we are diverted from consideration of whether our society is just or unjust.

Radical criminology is but one of a new group of criminological theories that are based on the economic determinism thesis of Karl Marx. The central theme of the radical theories is that criminal behavior can be explained in terms of economic conditions and is an expression of class conflict. Karl Marx and Friedrich Engels believed that crime is a product of capitalism. The capitalist economic system encourages people to be greedy and selfish and to pursue their own benefits without regard to the needs and wishes of others. The criminal justice system criminalizes the greed of the poor but allows the rich to pursue their selfish desires.

Richard Quinney stated that the traditional notion of the causes of crime should be abandoned and we should attempt to understand what "could be," not "what is." He stated that criminology, as the scientific study of crime, has served a single purpose: legitimation of the existing social order. According to Quinney, by asking the question "What causes crime?" we have focused our study on the criminal rather than understanding that crime is a product of the authority that defines behavior as criminal.

The criminal justice system, according to the critical criminologists, is used for the purpose of maintaining the status quo for the powerful members of society or as a means of serving the self-interests of those who operate the criminal justice agencies.

■ MATCHING KEY TERMS AND DEFINITIONS

Match each key term with the correct definition.

a. conflict approach

b. consensus approach

c. cubidity

d. economic determinism

e. material forces of production   h. social reality of crime
f. norms of deference   i. social relations of production
g. norms of domination

___ 1. Society is based on a consensus of values among its members
       and the state is organized to protect those collectively held
       values.
___ 2. Society is composed of groups of people with conflicting val-
       ues and interests.
___ 3. Norms that are imposed on us.
___ 4. Our established deference to authority.
___ 5. Society's ability to produce material goods.
___ 6. The relationship between people involved in producing and
       consuming the material goods.
___ 7. Quinney's six propositions regarding crime.
___ 8. A desire for inordinate wealth.
___ 9. It is determined by the condition of one's life and includes our
       values and interests.

▌ DISCUSSION QUESTIONS

1. What are the basic tenets of radical criminology?
2. How would Marx and Engels explain corporate crime?
3. How do the radical theorists explain sadistic crimes?
4. Do the radical and conflict theories provide explanations for all
   forms of criminal behavior?

Notes

1. Frank P. Williams and Marilyn D. McShane, *Criminological Theory*. Englewood Cliffs, N.J.: Prentice-Hall, 1988, p. 96.
2. C. Ronald Hull, "Conflict Theory in Criminology," in James A. Inciarci, ed.,
   Radical Criminology: The Coming Crises. Beverly Hills, Calif.: Sage, 1980, pp.
   61–78.
3. Jeffery H. Reiman, *The Rich Get Richer and the Poor Get Prison: Ideology, Class
   and Criminal Justice*. New York: Wiley, 1979.
4. C. H. McCaghy, *Deviant Behavior: Crime, Conflict, and Interest Groups*. New
   York: Macmillan, 1976.
5. Austin T. Turk, *Political Criminology: The Defiance and Defense of Authority*.
   Beverly Hills: Sage, 1982.
6. Turk, 1982:15.

7. Ronald Akers, "Theory and Ideology in Marxist Criminology: Comments on Turk, Quinney, Toby, and Klockers," *Criminology*, Feb. 1979, pp. 442–444.

8. G. S. Beccker, "Crime and Punishment: An Economic Approach," *Journal of Political Economy*, vol. 76, 1968, pp. 169–217.

9. Ian Taylor, Paul Walton, and Jock Young, *The New Criminology*. New York: Harper & Row, 1973, pp. 209–236.

10. Paul Phillips, *Marx and Engels on Law and Laws*. Totowa, N.J.: Barnes & Noble, 1980.

11. Sue Titus Reid, *Crime and Criminology*, 4th ed. New York: Holt, Rinehart and Winston, 1982, p. 169.

12. As reported by Steven Marcus, *Engels, Manchester, and the Working Class*. New York: Random House, 1974.

13. Willem Bonger, *Criminology and Economic Conditions*, Boston: Little, Brown, 1916.

14. Bonger, 1988.

15. Richard Quinney, *Critique of Legal Order: Crime Control in Capitalist Society*. Boston: Little, Brown, 1973.

16. Quinney, 1973:267.

17. Quinney, 1973:158.

18. Richard Quinney, *Criminology: Analysis and Critique of Crime in the United States*. Boston: Little, Brown, 1974, p. 38–42.

19. Carl B. Klockars, "The Contemporary Crises of Marxist Criminology,"*Criminology: An Interdisciplinary Journal*, vol. 16, no. 4, Feb. 1979, pp. 477–526.

20. Klockars, 1979:500.

21. A. Platt, "Prospects for a Radical Criminology," in I. Taylor, P. Walton, and Jock Young, eds., *Critical Criminology*. London: Routledge & Kegan Paul, 1975.

22. Quinney, 1973:160.

23. William J. Chambliss, *Exploring Criminology*. New York: Macmillan, 1988, pp. 38–42.

24. Chambliss, 1988.

25. George B. Vold, *Theoretical Criminology*. New York: Oxford University Press, 1958.

10

Cultural Deviance Theories

CHAPTER HIGHLIGHTS

- Cultural deviance theories assume that people are not capable of committing deviant acts; acts are deviant only by mainstream standards, not by offenders' standards.
- The Chicago School researchers studied people in their own natural habitats in an attempt to understand their behavior.
- Social disorganization theorists hold that there is a relationship between increasing crime rates and social disorganization caused by increasing complexity of society.
- Ecological theorists assume that crime rates are highest in the center of the city, where there is greatest social disorganization.
- Culture conflict theorists hold that if a person's norms conflict with society's conventional norms, culture conflict will occur.
- Subculture theorists contend that there are subcultures with value systems different from the mainstream or parent value system in society.
- Cultural deviance theorists hold that lower classes have a separate identifiable culture that is distinct from the middle-class culture.
- Subculture of violence theorists contend that lower classes in the United States have a value system that emphasizes aggression and violence in resolving problems.
- Criminogenic culture theorists hold that certain inherent social values and factors encourage criminal behavior on the part of society's members.

KEY TERMS

Chicago School

Concentric Circle Theory

Conduct Norms

Criminogenic

Culture Conflict

Focal Concerns

Subculture of Violence   Value Pluralism
Tautology

The criminological theories that are based on cultural deviance, cultural conflict, and cultural disorganization are discussed in this chapter. Sir Thomas More, Lord Chancellor to Henry VIII of England, was one of the first major intellectual figures to consider culture as a causative factor in criminal behavior. In his *Utopia,* More was skeptical of the then widely accepted doctrine of retributive justice as a deterrent to crime. More suggested that we should examine the "conditions" that helped to produce criminal behavior. (*Note:* Culture is included within his definition of "conditions." His ideas, including those on criminology, were too advanced for his time and did not gain acceptance or creditability in his day [1].

The underlying premise of the cultural deviance theories is that human beings are incapable of deviant behavior: People commit acts that are deviant by middle-class, mainstream standards but not acts that are deviant by their own standards. For example, if a person were raised by parents who belonged to the Nazi party, the person would normally accept or hold beliefs supported by that party. A person therefore becomes deviant by being socialized with nonmainstream values.

■ CHICAGO SCHOOL

No study of sociological theories of crime causation would be complete without considering the influence of the University of Chicago. The first department of sociology established in an American school was at the University of Chicago in 1892 [2]. The first major effort to compile research on criminal statistics took place in the sociology department of the University. The Chicago School dominated the American Sociological Movement from its founding until as late as the 1950s, and it still has a major influence on American criminology. This time span has also been referred to as the "Golden Age of American Sociology." The one recurring theme of the Chicago School was that human behavior was shaped by social and physical environments, not simply by genetic structure. The phrase "Chicago School" is used to identify a collection of various sociopsychological and urban sociological theories that were developed by or under the direction of the faculty of the University of Chicago. (*Note:* The phrase is also used by some criminologists to identify what is known as the "ecological school.") The major criminological theories developed under the Chicago School's influence include the ecological, culture conflict, social disorganization, subcultural, and symbolic interaction theories (discussed in Chapter 11).

The following list includes significant points in the Chicago School's development and contributions to criminological theory:

1. Prior to the development of the Chicago School, most research on criminal behavior attempted to link criminal behavior to biological causes.

2. The leading figures in the early sociology movement at the University of Chicago studied in Germany and France and were influenced by the German and French approaches, which placed emphasis on social and cultural aspects of human behavior.

3. The University of Chicago faculty used the scientific study of social problems to enhance their academic and scientific credibility and to rebut the image of sociology as a speculative endeavor [3].

4. The two major methods of study used by the Chicago School were as follows:

    a. The use of official data (i.e., crime reports, census reports, welfare records, etc.) to support assumptions regarding crime and criminal behavior patterns.

    b. The use of individual case studies. The Chicago School developed the methodology of studying individual personal histories to seek the cause of behavior. The practice of studying individuals in their natural habitats was developed to determine how people behave in their own time and space. Accordingly, addicts, bums, and others were observed and studied in their own environments. The Chicago School researchers believed that "human beings group themselves by categories or learned influences." During research projects, many of the researchers actually lived in the same environments as their subjects. This is one of the reasons the school is often referred to as the "ecological school" [4].

5. One central theme of the Chicago School was that people are social animals and human behavior is a product of our social environment. The cultural values and definitions that direct our behavior are therefore shaped by our social environment.

6. The Chicago School theorists were predominantly process orientated: that is, they stressed the ways that people came to act in a certain manner.

■ ECOLOGICAL SCHOOL

The first large-scale research project in criminology was conducted by the Department of Sociology at the University of Chicago in the 1920s [5]. This project was probably an outgrowth of public reaction to the crime problem in Chicago in the 1920s. The Prohibition Era had started in 1919 and continued until 1933. In addition to the economic problems, there was a heavy demand for beer in Chicago, and supplying beer became a major industry. Many researchers attribute the heavy demand for beer in Chicago on the presence of a large foreign-born population. An oversupply of "bootleggers" developed and gang

FIGURE 10-1
Old and new construction exists side by side in the center of a city. (Jan Lukas/Photo Researchers)

FIGURE 10-2
Al Capone. UPI/Bettman
Newsphotos.

warfare erupted. Crime quickly emerged as a major social problem.
(*Note:* Many historians credit Al Capone and his flagrant lawbreaking
for directing the nation's attention to crime as a major social problem.)

In developing the first major research project in criminology, the
university was responding to the social problems present in Chicago.
Researchers involved in the project included Ernest Burgess, Clifford
Shaw, Robert Park, Henry McKay, and Frederic Thrasher. Two of the
researchers, Park and Burgess, focused their attentions of the characteristics of neighborhoods and their relationship to crime rates. Park
and Burgess's ideas became known as "ecological" theory because they
studied the community as if the community were a body with inter-
relating organs. (*Note:* Ecology is the study of the patterns of relations
between organisms and their environment. It appears that Park and
Burgess borrowed their methodological approach from the field of biology.)

Park and Burgess developed a model of the city that divided it
into zones by using a series of distinctive concentric circles radiating

from the center of the city outward. Their theory is also known as "the concentric circle theory" because of the radiating circles. The first zone was the "central business district." It had businesses and factories but few residences. The next zone was the "zone of transition," also known as the "zone of deterioration." This was the area next to the central business district that at one time, when the city was smaller, was the primary residential area. As the city grew, however, businesses began to encroach into the zone of transition and the families who could afford to move, moved to newer neighborhoods. As the area declined, it was not a desirable location in which to live. It was, however, inexpensive and thus attracted new immigrants. The zone of transition thus consisted of a mixture of businesses, factories, and low-income families. The next zone was the "zone of workingmen's homes." In this zone, the homes were nicer and the income of the families tended to be higher than those in the zone of transition. Other zones radiating out were more expensive to live in and the income of the families tended to be higher.

Park and Burgess noted that the rates of delinquency, tuberculosis, infant mortality, and so on were the highest in the central business district and next highest in the zone of transition. They concluded that most delinquents and criminals were concentrated in areas of physical deterioration, congested population, economic dependency, rented homes, and minority populations. The crime rates declined as one moved from the center of the city to the outer zones. Based on these facts, Park and Burgess concluded the following:

1. The primary social controls were weakest in the center of the city because of the lack of social organization. As one moves away from the center of the city toward the newer neighborhoods, social controls on human behavior become stronger because of the increasing social organization present in the outer zones.

2. The high crime rates in the central business district and the zone of transition were caused by the weakening of primary social bonds in those zones.

3. As the city grows, the central business district and the zone of transition expand and replace the areas now included in other zones. Accordingly, as the city grows, what was once the zone of workingmen's homes becomes part of the zone of transition and the better residential areas become the zone of workingmen's homes. During this process, the higher-income families move farther away from the city. Park and Burgess considered this changing pattern as the normal developmental pattern of American cities.

■ SHAW AND MCKAY

Clifford R. Shaw and Henry D. McKay compared juvenile court records of Cook County, Illinois (includes the city of Chicago), for the period of 1900–1906 to those of 1917–1923 and 1927–1933. Their purpose was to determine the extent to which changes in delinquency rates are related to changes in the physical or social characteristics of the neighborhood [6]. They compared the delinquency rates of the city for each time period (1) by zones, (2) by area, and (3) by extent of concentration. Each of the comparisons is discussed below.

To compare the rates of delinquency by zones, Shaw and McKay started at the center of the city and drew five circles of increasing size around the city at two-mile intervals. For each zone, they computed the rate of delinquency based on the number of delinquents and the male population between 10 and 16 years of age within the zone. For the area comparisons, the city was divided into twenty-four geographical areas and the rates of delinquency were computed.

The comparison by extent of concentration was accomplished by dividing the population of the city in four equal parts on the basis of the magnitude of rates of delinquency. Then Shaw and McKay calculated the percentage of the total number of delinquents and total city area for each population quartile.

Based on the results of their research, Shaw and McKay reached the following conclusions:

1. There is a direct relationship between conditions existing in local communities and differential rates of delinquency and criminal behavior.

2. Communities with the highest rates of delinquency had social and economic characteristics that were different from communities with the lowest rates.

3. Higher-economic-status communities tended to be more stable because the norms and values were more uniform and consistent. As a result, delinquency rates were lower.

4. In lower-economic-status communities, norms and values lack consistency. In these communities, youths encounter competing systems of values. Careers in delinquency and crime are tempting alternatives.

5. Communities that are stable and have conventional value systems have lower rates of delinquency.

6. In low-income areas where there is greatest deprivation and frustration, there is also the widest variety of divergent cultural traditions and high rates of delinquency.

7. Delinquency had its roots in the dynamic life of the community. In slum areas, for example, delinquent traditions were often transmitted to children who were exposed to a variety of contradictory standards.

8. The high degree of consistency in the association between delinquency and other characteristics of the community not only sustains the conclusion that delinquent behavior is related dynamically to the community but also appears to establish that all community characteristics are products of the operation of general processes more or less common to American cities. [*Note:* The "general processes" refers to the developmental patterns described by Park and Burgess (see the section "Ecological School").]

■ JUVENILE GANGS

The classic study on juvenile gangs is Frederic Thrasher's study of 1313 gangs in Chicago in the 1920s [7]. Thrasher's conclusions were as follows:

1. Gangs are merely loose federations of individual boys who are trying to work out emotional problems.

2. There is little consensus, little identification, and rapidly changing leadership in the gangs.

3. Most gangs are really "cliques" involving quasi-permanent relationships between individuals interacting frequently as a social unit.

4. Most gangs form in the transition areas of the city, where the social controls are the weakest.

5. The gang becomes the primary group and replaces the family in the psychosocial development of the person, who feels the need for acceptance and finds it in the delinquent gang.

■ WALTER MILLER

Walter Miller studied the diffusion of delinquent values in the lower class [8]. Miller explained delinquency as caused by the fact the lower class had a separate, identifiable culture distinct from the middle-class culture. The lower-class culture, he contended, also had a tradition as old as the middle class. Miller saw society as a collection of groups without a general consensus of values and norms. The lower class has different values and norms from the middle class. Since the middle class is the dominant class, it can enforce its values on the lower class. Miller contended that "working-class" values included a delinquent subculture. According to Miller, the primary motivation involved in delinquent behavior is an attempt to meet norms of conduct as they are defined in lower-class urban areas. Miller characterized the value system of the lower-class male as emphasizing certain "focal concerns." The focal concerns are a generating milieu for gang delinquency and are as follows:

1. Trouble
2. Toughness
3. Smartness
4. Excitement
5. Fate
6. Autonomy

■ SOCIAL DISORGANIZATION

Social disorganization theorists contend that there is a relationship between increasing crime rates and increasing complexity of our society. Social disorganization as a causative factor in criminal behavior had its greatest popularity in the early 1920s and 1930s. The 1920s and 1930s were periods of marked changes in our society and also periods in which the crime rates appeared to increase significantly.

Social disorganization can be defined as a breakdown in the bonds of relationship, coordination, teamwork, and morale among different groups in society so as to impair the functions of society. Disorganization theorists have accepted the following basic propositions and concepts:

1. Society is a complex whole whose parts are interdependent, and society needs to maintain basic equilibrium.

2. Social organization exists when there is a high degree of harmony and internal cohesion in the society.

3. Harmony unites a society and creates common goals and values that are reflected in a high degree of behavioral predictability.

4. Internal cohesion consists of general acceptance by people in society of goals worth striving for (values) and rules on how to behave (norms).

5. When the consensus of values and norms is disrupted, traditional rules do not apply and social disorganization occurs.

6. When social disorganization occurs, social controls will be lax or nonexistent and deviant behavior will increase.

Robert Redfield described the folk society as the antithesis of the modern, urban criminalistic society as a way of indicating that there was little social disorganization in folk societies compared to modern societies [9]. Redfield indicated that folk societies used informal social controls as opposed to formal codes of law to control personal behavior. Also, there was little nonconformity or deviance in folk societies because goals and means were in harmony. People in folk societies did not seem to be confused or insecure and did not have many mental problems. There was little, if any, social disorganization present. There are few folk societies present today. Today, folk societies are generally found in underdeveloped agrarian nations. American society probably never approached an ideal folk society; however, recently, American society has become more unlike folk society organization.

Robert Faris described the characteristics of successful social organizations compared to disorganized social organizations in much the same terms as Redfield. Faris found that there is high morale, little personal deviation, and informal control over behavior in nondisorganized societies. He contended that the United States was a complex, dynamic, materialistic, impersonal disorganized society that produces crime and deviance [10].

Robert Park attempted to specify various stages of social organization and reorganization. He concluded that there were four processes [11]:

1. Change in spatial and food relationships in a community. This results in population, cultural, and division-of-labor changes. People in a community become competitive.

2. Conflict in lifestyles as different people are thrust into contact with each other.

3. Accommodation and adjustment made to situations created by competition and conflict.

4. Assimilation and the development of new consensus, customs, and mutual expectations of people in the community.

Park's theory provided a framework for criminologists to understand crime rates among newcomers to urban areas.

Critique of Social Disorganization Theory

Any evaluation of social disorganization theory should include the following:

1. The concept of social disorganization is itself disorganized, vague, ambiguous, and subjective.

2. Examples of social disorganization are not clearly recognizable.

3. Application of social disorganization theory to real life tends to be tautological; that is, the same behavior that is explained by disorganization is being used to demonstrate disorganization.

4. The concept of social disorganization is judgmental.

5. Social disorganization's bias is in favor of homogeneity and against heterogeneity.

6. The concept of disorganization is equated with its consequences of social problems. Not all social disorganization results in social problems.

■ CULTURE CONFLICT

Many of the concepts held by the cultural conflict theorists can be traced to the Chicago School. Thorsten Sellin is credited with publishing the first systematic discussion of the relationship between culture conflict and crime [12]. Sellin defined crime as a violation of group conduct norms [13].

According to Sellin, different cultures have different "conduct norms," rules that reflect the attitudes of a group about the manner in which a person should behave in a given situation. He contended that the conduct norms of the dominant class decide which conduct is criminal and which is not. As Sellin stated: "Values which receive the protection of the criminal law are ultimately those which are treasured by the dominant interest groups" [14].

At the time that Sellin was developing his theoretical concepts (1937–1938), there was an increase in fascism in Europe and in cultural conflicts in America brought about by immigration in the late nineteenth century. Sellin cited studies on crime and economic conditions in Europe in the nineteenth century to support his theory. One study he cited was Georg von Mayr's study of the correlation between the fluctuations in the price of rye and criminal behavior in Bavaria for the years 1836–1861. It appeared that with a half-penny rise in the price of rye, crime rose an average of 20 percent. When the price dropped a half-penny there was a corresponding 20 percent reduction in crime [15]. (*Note:* An increase in rye prices indicated favorable times for the people of Bavaria, whereas a price decrease indicated a depressed economy.) Another study cited by Sellin was by Clay, who examined the commitments to the Prestion House of Corrections in London from 1935 to 1954. Commitments were lower during "normal times," higher during "hard times," and even higher during "good times" [16]. (*Note:* It was during this period that European societies were being transformed from simple societies to complex ones.) Sellin contended that the fluctuations in the economy and the changing nature of the European societies resulted in groups with different conduct norms.

Sellin's theory is summarized as follows [17]:

1. For every person, there is a right or wrong way to act in each given situation, according to the conduct norms of the group to which he or she is a member.

2. The conduct norms of one group may allow a person to act in one way, whereas the conduct norms of another group would prohibit such conduct.

3. Problems occur when a person acts in a manner permitted by his or her conduct norms but not permitted by the conduct norms of the groups in control of political organizations.

4. There are two types of culture conflicts:

a. *Primary.* A primary culture conflict occurs when one's native cultural conduct norms conflict with those of the new culture. An example of a primary culture conflict is a case that occurred in New York in 1965. In that case, an Albanian immigrant shot and killed the father of a young woman whom he wanted to marry. Apparently, the immigrant had entered into a traditional Albanian marriage contract and paid the woman's family money to obtain the right to marry the woman. Later the woman's father canceled the contract and attempted to return the money. In Albania, this violation of the contract is an affront to the man's honor. The young man was therefore within the conduct norms of his native culture when he killed the person who had caused him dishonor. The killing, however, was a violation of the cultural norms of his new culture, America.

b. *Secondary.* A secondary culture conflict occurs in complex societies comprised of a variety of groups when the behavior required by one group's conduct norms violates the conduct norms of another group. For example, during the 1960s smoking marijuana and protesting the war in Southeast Asia was expected behavior by conduct norms of some groups. The conduct, however, was a violation of the conduct norms of the dominant culture that controlled the criminal justice system. (*Note:* Sellin did not suggest that primary or secondary culture conflicts were the only causes of criminal behavior.)

Sellin therefore contended that crime must be analyzed in terms of conflict among norms. If the norms of the individual conflict with the norms of society, culture conflict will occur.

Criticisms of Culture Conflict Theory

The criticisms of culture conflict theory include the following:

1. In regard to primary culture conflict, it is difficult to determine the specific contributions of the culture conflict to any criminal behavior because of the other variables that are always present.

2. Culture conflict theorists fail to consider that individuals who commit criminal behavior may have the same conduct norms as those of the dominant class.

3. The conflicts noted by Sellin are not with our goals, since we all have the same goals (i.e., to have a good life, a new car, etc.), but with the means that are acceptable to attain those common goals.

■ SUBCULTURE THEORIES

Edwin Lemert suggests that American values are not always clear and that Americans tend to be "value plural," (i.e., Americans believe in many different values). Lemert also suggests that criminality is the result of a positive response to one set of subcultural values that happen to be out of tune with another set of subcultural values [18].

The subculture theories are based on the general assumption that there are subcultures with value systems different from conventional value systems in society. In the delinquent subcultures, criminal values are normal and criminal behavior is a legitimate means of attaining desirable goals. (*Note:* In both the culture conflict theories and the subculture theories, the general theme is that differences in norms and values are a factor in the causation of deviant behavior.

Albert Cohen also contended that lower-class delinquent youths belong to a subculture that has different value systems from those of society in general [19]. According to him, the delinquent subculture is a mode of reaction and adjustment to the dominant middle-class society that discriminates against the youths because of their lower-class status. Cohen's middle class measuring rod theory is discussed in Chapter 7.

Marvin Wolfgang and Franco Ferracuti

Marvin Wolfgang and Franco Ferracuti's "subculture of violence" theory was developed in an attempt by them to integrate a wide range of disciplinary approaches to understanding deviant behavior [20]. Using

FIGURE 10–3

Some motorcycle gangs promote images of themselves as deviants; others define that deviance as a social problem. UPI/Bettman Newsphotos

findings from Wolfgang's 1958 study of criminal homicides in Chicago as a framework, they used the following disciplinary approaches to constitute the "subculture of violence" theory:

1. *From psychology:* learning, conditioning, developmental socialization, and differential identification theories.

2. *From sociology:* culture conflict, differential association, and personality theories.

The researchers found that in lower-class social structure in the United States there is a value system that emphasizes aggression and violence in resolving problems. They state that this constitutes a subculture of violence. The lower classes tend to use physical aggression as a demonstration of masculinity and toughness, whereas aggression in the middle class is turned inward.

Wolfgang's theory is summarized as follows:

1. Members of the subculture hold values different from those of the dominant parent culture.

2. Those who belong to the subculture of violence have values that are not, however, totally different from those of the dominant culture.

3. Individuals who belong to the subculture of violence have a favorable attitude toward the use of violence and learn a willingness to resort to violence.

4. Members of the subculture of violence have different psychological traits from those who are not members of the subculture of violence.

5. Persons who commit violent acts are distinctly more pathological and display more guilt and anxiety that are those persons who do not commit violent acts.

Wolfgang and Ferracuti also established the following seven corollary propositions to the subculture of violence theory [21]:

1. No subculture can be totally different from or totally in conflict with the society of which it is a part.

2. The existence of a subculture of violence does not require that the actors sharing these basic value elements express violence in all situations.

3. The potential resort or willingness to resort to violence in a variety of situations emphasizes the penetrating and diffusive character of this culture theme.

4. The subcultural ethos of violence may be shared by all ages in a subsociety, but this ethos is most prominent in a limited age group, ranging from late adolescence to middle age.

5. The counter norm is nonviolence.

6. The development of favorable attitudes toward, and the use of, violence in a subculture usually involves learned behavior and a process of differential learning, association, or identification.

7. The use of violence in a subculture is not necessarily viewed as illicit conduct and the users therefore do not have to deal with feelings of guilt about their aggression.

■ SOCIAL THEORY OF CRIME

Using the culture conflict framework, Donald Taft and Ralph England developed a social theory of crime. According to Taft and England, criminal behavior is caused by a combination of certain aspects of our culture [22]. They contend that selected aspects of our culture cause America to have a high incidence of crime:

1. Our culture is dynamic. Our standards are constantly changing. What was unacceptable behavior yesterday is acceptable today.

2. Our culture is complex. Culture conflict is present in America because of immigration and migration.

3. Our culture is materialistic. Generally, we all have the same goals (i.e., to attain material goods). The underprivileged, however, have a more difficult time attaining material goods.

4. Our social relations are increasingly impersonal. Our primary relationships to our family and neighborhoods have declined. Anonymity breeds alienation.

5. American culture fosters restricted group loyalties. We show preferences for people because of the groups they belong to, not for what they are. This creates feelings of rejection among people, and rejection, in turn, causes conflict and hostility.

6. Frontier values have survived. Our frontier values have survived along with the emphasis on individualism and the tendency to take the law into our "own hands."

▌ CRIMINOGENIC CULTURE

Milton Barron contends that our culture is criminogenic [23]. According to Barron, the societal values and factors listed below encourage criminal behaviors:

1. *Success.* We place a high value on achieving success and a lower value on the means by which the success is achieved. As coach Lombardi of the Green Bay Packers once stated: "Winning isn't everything, it is the only thing." If a person realizes that he or she will not achieve success by traditional and legitimate methods, the societal value placed on the results (i.e., success) may encourage the person to use illegitimate means to achieve success.

2. *Status.* Money and material goods have value in themselves, and the attainment of them automatically gives a person high social status in our society. People without money and material goods are often tempted to use illegitimate means to get them and thereby attain higher social status.

3. *Individuality.* We are encouraged to be independent and nonconformist. Americans tend to ridicule literal observance and strict compliance with the law. (A review of the present television and movie heros supports this concept.)

4. *Toughness.* Although there are class differences in the value of toughness, a large portion of our society values "toughness." (*Note:* Toughness is emphasized in most popular television programs and movies that we watch.)

5. *Getting the better of others.* We are proud of getting the best of others. The statement "There is a sucker born every minute" has widespread acceptance in our society.

6. *Our culture is dynamic and often with conflicting values.* Our culture changes so rapidly that differences between right and wrong are often not clearly delineated. In addition, as values change, conflicts are created between those who hold older values and those who hold new values.

7. *Our society is impersonal.* We barely know our neighbors today. Accordingly, traditional informal neighborhood controls are nonexistent.

8. *We have a duality of loyalty and ethics.* Many of us have one set of ethical codes for members of our "in group" and another set for others in society.

▌ SUMMARY

Cultural deviance theories assume that people are not capable of committing deviant acts; acts are deviant only by mainstream standards, not by the offender's standards. The Chicago School researchers studied people in their own natural habitats in an attempt to understand their behavior. Social disorganization theorists indicate that a positive relationship between crime rates and social disorganization exists and is caused by increasing complexity of society. Ecological theorists hold that crime rates are highest in the center of the city, where there is greatest social disorganization. Culture conflict theorists contend that if a person's norms conflict with society's conventional norms, culture conflict will occur.

Subculture theorists believe that there are subcultures with value systems different from conventional value systems in society. Cultural deviance theorists hold that lower classes have a separate identifiable culture that is distinct from the middle-class culture. Subculture of violence theorists hold that lower classes in the United States have a value system that emphasizes aggression and violence in resolving problems. Criminogenic culture theorists believe that certain inherent social values and factors encourage criminal behavior on the part of its members.

▌ MATCHING KEY TERMS AND DEFINITIONS

Match each key term with the correct definition.

a. Chicago school

b. concentric circle theory

c. conduct norms

d. criminogenic

e. culture conflict

f. focal concerns

g. subculture of violence

h. tautology

i. value pluralism

_____ **1.** A term used to refer to faculty from the University of Chicago who attempted the first major compilation of crime and delinquency statistics.

_____ **2.** The concept that the lower classes are socialized to solve their problems by aggression and violence.

_____ **3.** The idea that a city can be divided into radiating zones emanating from the center of the city to the outer limits.

_____ **4.** The same behavior that is being explained by an idea is used to demonstrate the idea.

_____ **5.** The clash between individual norms and mainstream society's norms.

_____ **6.** The belief in many different and often conflicting values.

_____ **7.** Core values and norms that different classes possess.

_____ **8.** Societal values and factors that encourage criminal behavior.

_____ **9.** Rules that reflect the attitudes of a group about the manner in which a person should behave in a given situation.

■ DISCUSSION QUESTIONS

1. What are some of the common attributes of most culture-oriented theories?

2. What are five criminogenic values present in mainstream society?

3. Do the ecological theories make sense when considering modern American cities?

Notes

1. Stephen Schafer, _Theories in Criminology,_ New York: Random House, 1969; and Sir Thomas More, _Utopia,_ Louvain, 1516 (there are numerous English editions).

2. Martin Blumer, _The Chicago School of Sociology,_ Chicago: University of Chicago Press, 1984; and Robert Faris, _Chicago Sociology: 1920–1932,_ Chicago: University of Chicago Press, 1970.

3. Frank P. Williams and Marilyn McShane, _Criminological Theory._ Englewood Cliffs, N.J.: Prentice-Hall, 1988, p. 36.

4. Williams and McShane, 1988:37.

5. Martin Blumer, 1984.

6. Clifford R. Shaw and Henry D. McKay, *Juvenile Delinquency and Urban Areas*. Chicago: University of Chicago Press, 1942.

7. Frederic M. Thrasher, *The Gang*. Chicago: University of Chicago Press, 1927.

8. Walter B. Miller, "Lower-Class Culture as a Generation Milieu of Gang Delinquency," *Journal of Social Issues*, vol. 14, 1958, pp. 5–19.

9. Robert Redfield, *The Primitive World and Its Transformation*. Ithaca, N.Y.: Cornell University Press, 1953.

10. Robert Faris, *Social Disorganization*, 2nd ed. New York: Ronald Press, 1955.

11. Robert E. Park and Ernest Burgess, *Introduction to the Science of Sociology*, 2nd ed. Chicago: University of Chicago Press, 1924; and Robert E. Park, *Human Communities: The City and Human Ecology*. Glencoe, Ill.: Free Press, 1952.

12. George B. Vold and Thomas J. Bernard, *Theoretical Criminology*, 3rd ed. New York: Oxford University Press, 1986.

13. Thorsten Sellin, *Culture Conflict and Crime*. New York: Social Science Research Council, 1938.

14. Sellin, 1938:34.

15. Sellin, 1938:104.

16. Sellin, 1938:105.

17. Sellin, 1938:63.

18. Edward M. Lemert, *Human Deviance, Social Problems, and Social Control*. Englewood Cliffs, N.J.: Prentice-Hall, 1967.

19. Albert Cohen, *Delinquent Boys*. New York: Macmillan, 1955.

20. Williams and McShane, 1988:79.

21. Marvin E. Wolfgang and Franco Ferracuti, "The Subculture of Violence," in L. D. Savitz and N. Johnson, eds., *Crime in Society*. New York: Wiley, 1978.

22. Donald R. Taft and Ralph W. English, Jr., *Criminology*, New York: Macmillan, 1964.

23. Milton L. Barron, "The Criminogenic Society: Social Values and Deviance," in, Abraham S. Blumberg, ed., *Current Perspectives on Criminal Behavior*. New York: Alfred A. Knopf, 1974, pp. 68–87.

11

Symbolic Interactionist Theories

CHAPTER HIGHLIGHTS

- The two leading symbolic interactionist (SI) theories of crime causation are differential association and labeling.
- The symbolic interactionist theories examine the process of becoming a criminal.
- According to the SI theorists, the symbols we learn and use become our social reality.
- Our primary socialization force consists of people with whom we associate.
- Symbolic interactionism locates the causes of our behavior in our interpretations of reality.
- According to symbolic interactionism, the meanings that things have for human beings are central in their own right.
- Differential association has been the most influential social-psychological theory of crime causation for the past sixty years.
- According to the differential association theory, criminal behavior is learned.
- Criminal behavior is learned by the process of communication.
- A person, according to differential association, becomes delinquent because of an excess of definitions favorable to violation of the law compared to definitions unfavorable to violation of the law.
- The process of learning criminal behavior by association with criminal and noncriminal patterns involves all the mechanisms that are involved in any other learning.
- According to the labeling theory, no act is intrinsically criminal.
- The labelists contend that a person does not become a criminal by violation

of the law alone, but becomes criminal only by the designation of criminal by authorities.

- The phrase "degradation ceremony" is used by labelists to describe the process whereby one is separated from the rest of us and labeled a criminal.

- The "looking-glass self" is a concept used by labelists to explain criminal behavior.

- Stigma is a discrediting mark that tends to discredit a person and set him or her apart from the legitimate public.

KEY TERMS

Culture Conflict	Neutral Associations
Degradation Ceremony	Primary Deviance
Differential Association	Primary Socialization Force
Differential Association Reinforcement	Secondary Deviance
Labeling	Stigma
Looking-Glass Self	Symbolic Interactionism

■ SYMBOLIC INTERACTIONISM

The two leading symbolic interactionist (SI) theories of crime causation are differential association and labeling. Both theories are very popular in the United States today. The two theories examine the process of becoming a criminal; differential association by the influence of one's associations with peers, family, and so on, and labeling by the behavioral effects of contacts with the criminal justice system [1].

The general principles of SI theories are as follows:

1. The symbols we learn and use become our social reality.
2. We become socialized by the people with whom we associate.
3. Individuals' definitions and perceptions of their situations are the sources of their behaviors. (Another way of stating this principle is that symbolic interactionism locates the causes of our behavior in our interpretations of reality.)

The interactionist crime theories focus on situations and inter-actions with society leading up to the crime rather than differences or defectiveness present in offenders [2]. Although symbolic interactionism originated with the work of George Herbert Mead, the phrase "symbolic interactionism" was coined by Herbert Blumer in 1937. It is presently used as a label for a "relatively distinctive approach to the study of human group life and human conduct" [3].

The position of symbolic interactionism is that the meanings that things have for people are central in their own right. Symbolic interactionism rests on three basic principles:

1. People act toward things on the basis of the meanings that things have for them.

2. The meanings that things have are derived from, or arise out of, the social interaction that one has with others.

3. The meanings that things have are handled in, and modified through, an interpretative process used by a person in dealing with the things that he or she encounters.

Blumer summarizes symbolic interactionism as follows [4]:

The meaning of a thing for a person grows out the ways in which other persons act toward the person with regard to the thing. . . . Symbolic interactionism sees meanings as social products, as creations that are formed in and through the defining activities of people as they interact.

■ DIFFERENTIAL ASSOCIATION

Edwin Sutherland's theory of differential association was developed in an attempt to explain career criminal behavior [5]. "Differential association" is not a good descriptive title for his theory. The title sounds as though it refers to people in association, but it does not refer to who associates with whom. What is differentially associated are "definitions of situations" [6].

Differential association has been the most influential sociopsychological theory of crime causation for the past sixty years [7]. After Sutherland's death in 1950, his student, friend, and longtime associate Donald Cressey continued to advocate and explain differential association theory. The theory's present popularity is due in large part to Cressey's ability to explain the theory. Gibbons pointed out that Suth-

FIGURE 11–1
Edwin H. Sutherland. *Source:* From *The Sutherland Papers* by Albert Cohen, et al. © 1956, Indiana University of Chicago.

erland clearly touched all involved in the formation of criminology as a distinct intellectual discipline [8]:

> The evidence is incontrovertible that Edwin Sutherland was the most important contributor to American criminology to have appeared to date. Indeed, there has been no other criminologist who even begins to approach his stature and importance. Moreover, it is extremely unlikely that anyone will emerge in future decades to challenge Sutherland's position in the annals of this field.

Sutherland had a conflict orientation to society. He contended that there are a number of societal values from which we can choose and that these values influence our behavior. According to him, we learn to accept antisocial values and thus commit antisocial acts because of the people with whom we associate. Sutherland does not see social factors as being innately good or bad, but simply present to be acted upon by others [9].

According to Sutherland, the individual does have limited choice regarding his or her conduct. The choice, however, is influenced by

—DONALD R. CRESSEY—

FIGURE 11-2
Until his death in 1987, Don Cressey was a proponent of differential association theory. Courtesy of Donald R. Cressey

our associations and situational definitions. This limitation of "free choice" has caused some criminologists to contend that Sutherland is as much a positivist as was Lombroso [10].

Sutherland's Propositions

1. *Criminal behavior is learned.* Sutherland rejected the concepts that crime was a necessary outcome of our socially disorganized society and the positivist approach that criminals are different from noncriminals. Criminal behavior, according to his theory, is learned, not inherited, and anyone can learn to be a criminal. In classifying criminal behavior as learned behavior, Sutherland suggests that it is like any other learned behavior, such as writing or painting. According to him, a person who is not already trained in crime does not invent criminal behavior, just as a person does not make mechanical inventions unless he or she has had training in mechanics [12]. A person, however, can

IN FOCUS

Edwin H. Sutherland, "Dean of American Criminology"

Edwin H. Sutherland (1883–1950) was born in Grand Island, Nebraska. Contrary to popular belief, Sutherland did not come from a poor background. His father was an educator and later president of a small college in Nebraska. Edwin Sutherland received a bachelor's degree from Grand Island College. He taught Latin, Greek, and geometry for several years at a Baptist college in South Dakota before going to the University of Chicago for graduate study. At Chicago, he was a student of George Herbert Mead, who developed symbolic interactionism as a theory. After receiving his Ph.D., Sutherland taught for six years at William Jewell College, a small Baptist college in Missouri. His title at William Jewell was "Professor of Christian Socialism." In 1919, he joined the faculty at the University of Illinois.

It was at the University of Illinois in 1924 that Sutherland published his first textbook on criminology. The textbook was published as a result of the insistence of his department chair. His primary interest in writing the text was to comment on the controversy that was raging at the time between theories of environment and theories of heredity.

Sutherland's differential association theory was first proposed in 1928. He mentioned it briefly in his 1934 text, but did not present it formally until the 1939 edition. Sutherland expanded and clarified the theory for the 1947 edition. In the 1939 edition, differential association theory was applied only to systematic criminal behavior. In the 1947 edition, it was expanded to explain criminal behavior in general. It has remained basically unchanged since that date. Sutherland first developed the differential association theory while studying white-collar crime. His classic study of professional criminals is discussed in Chapter 20.

Sutherland was described as a very poor teacher. In his undergraduate classes, he would mumble and look out the window when he talked. He was noted for being boring. His seminars were somewhat better but were still disjointed. He was, however, always gently pushing his students to do better [11]. He has been described by many of his ex-students as a simple and modest person who did not constitute himself as an authority.

IN FOCUS

If criminal behavior is learned, how did Richard Speck, who killed eight nurses in Chicago in cold blood, obtain the essential learning elements that resulted in his murders?

Did Sutherland actually mean that we act based on our attitudes, beliefs, and values, and that those attitudes, beliefs, and values are learned?

learn criminal skills at any point in his or her life. The people who have the greatest impact on the individual are those with whom the person has strong emotional bonds and/or who satisfy the person's emotional needs. If parents and other members of the family do not satisfy the person's emotional needs, the person will get his or her satisfaction in any way possible. Examples of this are the "Jonestown

FIGURE 11-3
There is considerable evidence that children learn violent behavior through observation of adult models. (Photo by Michael Glennon)

Massacre" and the resurgence of juvenile gang behavior throughout the United States.

2. *Criminal behavior is learned with other persons in the process of communication.* According to Sutherland, behavior (both criminal and noncriminal) is learned from our associations with others. Simply living in a criminogenic environment does not cause criminal behavior. The person actively participates in the processes with others, who serve as teachers and guides to delinquent behavior [13]. Sutherland uses "communication" to mean the sum total of our interactions with others, including the "communication of gestures" [14].

3. *The principal part of learning criminal behavior occurs within intimate personal groups.* Impersonal agencies of communication (i.e., movies, newspapers and television) have a relatively small role in the genesis of criminal behavior. We identify with our reference groups, and they, in turn, guide our values. The reference group includes all groups with which we really identify, but the impact of each association depends to some extent on the degree of association involved. Thus the contacts that a juvenile has with his or her peers, family, and friends have the greatest influence on the juvenile's behavior only if the contacts have significance and meaning for the juvenile.

4. *When criminal behavior is learned, the learning includes (a) techniques of committing the crime, which are sometimes very complicated, sometimes very simple; and (b) the specific direction of motives, drives, rationalizations, and attitudes.* Our associations with others influence not only whether or not we commit criminal acts, but also the techniques and methods used to commit the acts. Thus a criminal learns not only to commit the crime, but also the proper way to commit it, from his or her more experienced companions. A juvenile therefore learns to steal cars in the same manner that the juvenile learns to play baseball.

5. *The specific direction of motives and drives is learned from definitions of the legal codes as favorable or unfavorable to violation of the law.* Since the definitions of what is right or wrong are extremely var-

IN FOCUS

Does this mean that a juvenile who spends many hours watching TV rather than playing with or associating with peers, family, and so on, can adopt TV characters as his or her primary reference group?

ied, people have different views regarding moral and immoral behavior. A person's attitude regarding "right or wrong" is greatly influenced by the attitude of those the person considers to be important and those that have meaning to him or her. Thus, if the "important people" have an attitude favorable to violation of the law, the person will be more likely to commit criminal behavior. Since our definitions are almost always mixed with the consequences, we often have "culture conflict" with our legal codes.

6. *A person becomes delinquent because of an excess of definitions favorable to violation of the law over definitions unfavorable to violation of the law.* This proposition states that the theory is a ratio between associations with attitudes favorable and unfavorable to the violation of criminal law. Therefore, if the ratio is toward an attitude favorable to the violation of the law, the person will violate the law. A definition toward the violation of social norms occurs when juveniles discuss the benefits of illegally buying alcoholic beverages and getting drunk. A definition favorable to law-abiding behavior occurs when peers and "significant others" indicate disapproval of criminal conduct. (*Note:* Many of the associations are neutral as far as crime is concerned and have little or no effect on the genesis of criminal behavior (e.g., learning to tie shoes). Sutherland sees neutral behavior as an important occupier of time, and during the time as such, the person is not engaged in criminal behavior [15].)

7. *Differential associations vary in frequency, duration, priority, and intensity.* Priority refers to how early in life the associations occur. Intensity refers to prestige, emotional impact, significance, and meaning of the associations (intensity is not precisely defined by Sutherland). Therefore, associations that occur early in life and which are frequent, intense, and have duration will have the greatest impact on our behavior. The influence of a close personal friend, close relative, and so on, thus have far more influence on behavior than will the influences of a distant but socially prominent figure (e.g., "hard-rock singer").

8. *The process of learning criminal behavior by association with criminal and anticriminal patterns involves all of the mechanisms that are involved in any other learning.* This proposition states that criminal behavior patterns are learned by processes similar to those involved in learning other behavior patterns. (*Note:* While the processes are similar in criminal and noncriminal behavior, as noted in Proposition 9, Sutherland suggested that the motives are different.)

Proposition 8 does not mean that the learning of criminal behavior is restricted to the process of imitation. While imitating others is an important aspect of our learning processes, often the associations motivate us to act in an entirely different manner. For example, if our parents were very frugal when we were growing up, this could cause us to rebel against fiscal restraint. An example that Sutherland used, in explaining that the learning was not restricted to the process of imitation, was: "A person who is seduced, for instance, learns criminal behavior by association, but this process would not ordinarily be described as imitation" [16].

9. *Although criminal behavior is an expression of general needs and values, it is not explained by those general needs and values since noncriminal behavior is an expression of the same needs and values.* Sutherland contended that the motives that cause criminal behavior are different from those that cause conventional behavior. He discounted the desire to accumulate money or property, personal frustration, low self-esteem, and similar motives as causes of criminal behavior. According to him, it is only the learning of deviant norms through differential associations with an excess of definitions toward criminality that causes criminal behavior. This aspect of his theory has a "cultural conflict" bias. Does this indicate that criminals are not "bad," but just have different cultural norms?

Evaluation and Critique of Differential Association Theory

Being very general in nature, differential association can account for most types of criminal behavior. The theory has been called "the most truly sociological of all theories which have been advanced to explain criminal and delinquent behavior" [17]. Presently, it is probably the most popularly accepted theory in the United States. One reason for its popularity is that it provides a consistent explanation for all types of criminal behavior [18]. It explains criminal behavior of middle-class juveniles as well as of street gangs. It also explains white-collar crime.

A question that should be considered when evaluating any theory is: Do the facts that we know about criminal behavior and crime fit the theory? Chambliss states that differential association theory explains a wide range of behaviors in a single and straightforward generalization [19]. He also states that the theory has generated more empirical research than any other theory in criminology. However, it has never been adequately tested. The problem with testing differential association theory is that Sutherland's propositions are difficult to conceptualize in a manner that leads to empirical measurement.

Additional criticisms of the theory are the following:

1. It cannot account for the fact that most people involved in crime become less involved as they grow older.

2. The theory has no independent measure of whether a particular association or behavioral experience is reinforcing.

3. All the theory really states is that people are apt to behave criminally when they do not respect the law.

4. It neglects individual differences in people.

5. It regards opportunity as being constant.

6. Differential association theory does not explain crimes of passion.

7. The theory is concerned only with the mechanism by which criminal attitudes and techniques are acquired by individuals.

8. The theory fails to consider the role of "free will" in criminal behavior.

Differential Association Reinforcement

In an attempt to provide a more adequate specification of the learning process under differential association, Robert Burges and Ronald Akers formulated the differential association-reinforcement theory. Their purpose was to merge Sutherland's theory with the more general theory of behaviorism and the works of B. F. Skinner [20]. The key points of their theory are as follows:

1. The primary learning mechanism in social behavior is operant conditioning, in which behavior is shaped by the stimuli that follow, or are consequences of, the behavior.

2. Direct conditioning and imitation of others are important in determining this behavior.

3. Rewards, or positive reinforcement, as well as avoidance of punishment, strengthen this behavior.

The Case of Richard Miller

While a student at Brigham Young University, Richard Miller was very religious and had a conservative political ideology, and for twenty years he was considered a good FBI agent. In 1985 he was arrested for spying. After his arrest, he confessed to numerous petty crimes. Does differential association theory explain his criminal behavior? Did he associate with too many criminals while an FBI agent? (Note: If this were true, every police, probation, parole, and correctional officer would eventually become a criminal.)

4. The determination of whether the behavior is deviant or conforming depends on differential reinforcement.

5. People learn norms, attitudes, and so on, from those who are important to them; that is, our associations with the people who are important to us provide the stimuli for shaping our behavior.

■ LABELING

The labeling theory is based on the concepts developed and expanded upon by Frank Tannenbaum, David Matza, Edwin Lemert, Howard Becker, Austin Turk, and Edwin Shur. In explaining labeling concepts, Frank Tannenbaum stated [21]:

> The process of making the criminal . . . is a process of tagging, defining, identifying, segregating, describing, emphasizing, making, conscious and self-conscious; it becomes a way of stimulating, suggesting, emphasizing, and evoking the very traits complained of. . . . The person becomes the thing he is described as being.

Degradation Ceremony

When a person commits a crime, there is no automatic labeling process that labels the person a criminal. Labeling theory therefore shifts the emphasis from why or how a person comes to commit a criminal act to how he or she becomes defined as a criminal. This problem is the central focus of the labeling theory. Harold Garfinkel used the phrase "degradation ceremony" to describe the process whereby a person is separated from the rest of us and labeled a criminal. According to him, there are eight steps involved in the "degradation ceremony" [23]:

1. The actor and the act must be defined as being different.

2. The actor must be denounced as being a certain type (criminal) and that the act and motives cannot be better defined or justified in any other way.

3. The denouncer must have public stature (e.g., judge).

4. The denunciation must be seen in support of public values.

5. The denouncer must appear not to have any personal vendetta against the actor.

6. The denouncer must appear to be a supporter of public values.

IN FOCUS

Hypotheses of Labeling Theory

1. No act is intrinsically criminal.

2. Criminal definitions are enforced in the interest of the powerful.

3. A person does not become a criminal by violation of the law but only by the designation of criminal by authorities.

4. Due to the fact that everyone conforms and deviates, people should not be dichotomized into criminal and noncriminal categories.

5. The act of "getting caught" starts the labeling process.

6. "Getting caught" and decision making in the criminal justice system are a function of the offender as opposed to offense characteristics.

7. Age, socioeconomic class, and race are the major offender characteristics that establish patterns of differential criminal justice decision making.

8. The criminal justice system is predicated on a free-will perspective that allows for the condemnation and rejection of the identified offender.

9. Labeling is a process that eventually produces identification with a deviant image and subculture, and a resulting "rejection of the rejecters" [22].

7. The denouncer must be seen as detached from the person being denounced.

8. The person being denounced has to be set apart from the legitimate public (i.e., he or she is not one of us).

The Looking-Glass Self

One concept used in labeling theory to explain criminal behavior is the "looking-glass self." This concept, developed by Cooley, defines the social self as made up of what a person sees others seeing him or her to be [24]. Others are a mirror (looking-glass) to one's self. Therefore, if a person sees that others view him or her as lazy, the person will tend to act lazy. If a person sees that others consider him or her to be a criminal, the person will commit criminal behavior. According to this concept, the way we perceive others seeing us dictates our behavior. This concept is similar to the "self-fulfilling prophecy" concept: We act out our view of how others think of us. In describing this concept, Cohen states [25]:

> The self is built up in the process of interacting with others. In doing business with them, we discover what we are—i.e., the categories to which we have been assigned—and what to some extent we determine that we shall be. We may lay claims to being a certain sort of person, but this claim must make sense in terms of the culture of those we are dealing with, and we must make these claims stick. To lay a claim is to say, in effect: "I am such-and-such a sort of person: I invite you to deal with me on this basis; you may expect certain things of me."

Stigma

Another key concept in the labeling theory is "stigma." The concept was developed by Erving Goffman [26]. Stigma refers to discrediting marks (e.g., tattoos or deformities) that tend to belittle a person. It is the opposite of a status symbol. Not all stigmas are physical marks on a person (e.g., a criminal record). When visible (or known) to the public, the stigma sets the person apart and he or she is viewed by the legitimate public as being different. Once the person is viewed as different, the public tends to label him or her as undesirable. Once stigmatized, new restrictions are then placed on his or her legitimate opportunities. (*Note:* The person is also shunned by the legitimate public and forced to associate with other "undesirables".)

Primary and Secondary Deviance

Edwin Lemert used the classifications "primary" and "secondary" to explain the relationship between criminal behavior and labeling [27]. Primary deviance is any norm violation that occurs prior to a person being labeled as a criminal. Secondary deviance is deviance that is caused by a reaction to the labeling process. Therefore, if one commits a crime because he or she had previously been labeled as a criminal, this would be an example of secondary deviance. Lemert contended that there was a process involved that changed a person's identity from noncriminal to criminal. He used the term "degradation ceremony" (e.g., a court trial) as one example of the processes involved in changing one's identity from noncriminal to criminal. (*Note:* Lemert did not contend that all primary deviance would eventually lead to secondary deviance, only that it was a process involved in changing a person's identity from noncriminal to criminal.)

Evaluation of the Labeling Theory

Labeling theory calls for the focus of attention to shift from the criminal to the society that labels him or her a criminal. Vold and Bernard point out that under the labeling theory, one would expect that people who commit criminal behavior would think of themselves as criminal (looking-glass self) [28]. Vold and Bernard state that many criminals do not see themselves as being criminal and that the maintenance of a noncriminal self-image is very important to most people, including criminals. Yochelson and Samenow also concluded that even the most hardened criminals do not consider themselves as criminal (see Chapter 19). One of the authors once taught a criminology course to prisoners in a federal prison. He noted that while each student (prisoner) considered criminals as bad, each had a particular reason or justification for why he was not a criminal.

In evaluating labeling theory, Vold and Bernard contend that the more practical question is not whether the labeling process causes crime, but whether it creates more crime than it eliminates [29]. As they point out, average persons are deterred from committing most crimes not because of fear of punishment associated with conviction, but because of the stigma of conviction. (*Note*: Since convictions for traffic offenses lack the stigma associated with other criminal convictions, most people are deterred from committing traffic violations by punishments and by the increased cost of car insurance associated with bad driving records.)

Criticisms of labeling theory include:

1. Empirical testing of the theory is difficult and almost impossible.

2. Labeling theory avoids the question of causation of the first series of deviant acts that lead to the criminal label.

3. There is a lack of attention given to the personal characteristics of the individual.

4. Labeling theory assumes that the labeling processes produce only negative behaviors.

5. Labeling theory is a study of the sociology of law rather than a study of why people commit criminal acts.

■ SUMMARY

The two leading symbolic interactionist theories of criminal causation are differential association and labeling. Both theories examine the process of becoming a criminal and locate the cause of our behavior in our interpretations of reality. Differential association has been the most influential sociopsychological theory of crime causation for the past sixty years. According to differential association theory, criminal behavior is learned. It is learned with others in the process of communication. A person becomes a criminal, according to differential association, because of an excess of definitions favorable to violation of law compared to definitions unfavorable to violation of law. The processes of learning criminal behavior involve all the mechanisms that are involved in any other learning.

According to the labeling theory, no act is intrinsically criminal. A person becomes a criminal not by violation of the law alone, but by the designation of criminal by authorities. The degradation ceremony is used by labelists to describe the process whereby a person is separated from the rest of us and labeled a criminal. Lemert differentiates between primary and secondary deviance to explain the direct relationship between criminal behavior and the labeling processes. Primary deviance is that deviance committed prior to being labeled a criminal. Secondary deviance is deviance that is caused by the reaction to the labeling process.

■ MATCHING KEY TERMS AND DEFINITIONS

Match each key term with the correct definition.

a. culture conflict
b. degradation ceremony
c. differential association
d. differential association reinforcement
e. labeling
f. looking-glass self

g. neutral associations
h. primary deviance
i. primary socialization force
j. secondary deviance
k. significant others
l. stigma
m. symbolic interactionism

—— 1. The theory that is based on the concept that a person does not become a criminal by violation of the law but only by being designated criminal by authorities.

—— 2. The most influential sociopsychological theory for the past sixty years.

—— 3. A phrase that means "the people with whom we associate."

—— 4. A term "coined" by Herbert Blumer in 1937 and currently used as a label for a "relatively distinctive approach to the study of human group life and human conduct."

_____ 5. The phrase used to describe the process of labeling a criminal.

_____ 6. A theory that is based on both Sutherland's differential association and Skinner's behaviorism.

_____ 7. Associations that have little or no effect on the genesis of criminal behavior.

_____ 8. A discrediting mark that tends to set a person apart from the legitimate public.

_____ 9. The condition caused by mixed definitions of "right or wrong" in a society.

_____ 10. Those people with whom we closely associate and who have the greatest influence on our behavior.

_____ 11. This concept defines the social self as being made up of what a person sees others seeing him or her to be.

_____ 12. Deviance that occurs prior to a person being labeled as a criminal.

_____ 13. Deviance that is caused by a reaction to the labeling process.

∎ DISCUSSION QUESTIONS

1. Do the SI theorists see people as basically good or bad? Explain.

2. Explain the difference between primary and secondary deviance.

3. Explain the concept of "looking-glass self." Why is it important to the labeling theorists?

4. According to differential association theory, what is involved in learning to be a criminal?

5. What are the key theoretical differences between the two SI theories?

6. What are the theoretical similarities between the radical theories discussed in Chapter 9 and the labeling theories?

Notes

1. Edwin H. Sutherland, "The Differential Association Theory," in Stephen Schafer and Richard D. Knudten, eds., *Criminological Theory*, Lexington, Mass.: Lexington Books, 1977.

2. William B. Sanders. *Criminology*. Reading, Mass.: Addison-Wesley, 1983.

3. Herbert Blumer, *Symbolic Interaction: Perspective and Method*, Englewood Cliffs, N.J.: Prentice-Hall, 1969.

4. Blumer, 1969:4–5.

5. Sutherland, 1977.

6. Gwynn Nettler, *Explaining Crime*, 2nd ed. New York: McGraw-Hill, 1978.

7. William J. Chambliss, *Exploring Criminology*. New York: Macmillan, 1988, p. 234.

8. Don Gibbons, *The Criminological Enterprise: Theories and Perspectives*. Englewood Cliffs, N.J.: Prentice-Hall, 1979, p. 65.

9. William V. Pelfrey, *The Evolution of Criminology*. Cincinnati, Ohio: Anderson, 1980, p. 45.

10. C. Ray Jeffery, "The Historical Development of Criminology," in Hermann Mannheim, ed., *Pioneers in Criminology*, 2nd ed. Montclair, N.J.: Patterson Smith, 1973.

11. John H. Laub, "An Interview with Donald R. Cressey," in John H. Laub, ed., *Criminology in the Making: An Oral History*. Boston: Northeastern University Press, 1983:136.

12. Sutherland, 1977:187.

13. Jeffery, 1973.

14. Sutherland, 1977:187.

15. Sutherland, 1977:189.

16. Sutherland, 1977:188.

17. Sue Titus Reid, *Crime and Criminology*, 4th ed. New York: Holt, Rinehart and Winston, 1982, p. 180.

18. Reid, 1982.

19. Chambliss, 1988:235.

20. Reid, 1982:183.

21. Frank Tannenbaum, *Crime and the Community*. Boston, Ginn, 1938, p. 20.

22. C. Schrag, *Crime and Justice: American Style*. Washington, D.C.: U.S. Government Printing Office, 1971.

23. Harold Garfinkel, "Conditions of a Successful Degradation Ceremony," *American Journal of Sociology*, vol. 61, Mar. 1956, pp. 420–424.

24. Charles Horton Cooley, *Human Nature and the Social Order*. New York: Charles Scribner's, 1902.

25. Albert K. Cohen, *Deviance and Control*. Englewood Cliffs, N.J.: Prentice-Hall, 1966.

26. Erving Goffman, *Stigma*. Indianapolis, Ind.: Bobbs-Merrill, 1963.

27. Edwin Lemert, *Social Pathology*. New York: McGraw-Hill, 1951.

28. George B. Vold, and Thomas J. Bernard, *Theoretical Criminology*, 3rd ed. New York: Oxford University Press, 1986.

29. Vold and Bernard, 1986:256.

PART

III

THE BIOLOGICAL THEORIES

The biological theories have not enjoyed the popularity in the United States that they have enjoyed in Europe. The Europeans grew up with the rich traditions of the phrenologists—Charles Darwin, Cesare Lombroso, and the like—and are much more willing to embrace the biological explanations of crime causation. The United States, in contrast, has been cautious in its acceptance of biological explanations of crime causation. Chapters 12 to 15 deal with various groupings of biological theories of crime causation. Chapter 12 deals with the idea of inherited criminality. Chapter 13 deals with biological inferiority and body-type theories, Chapter 14 deals with difference and defectiveness theories, and Chapter 15 deals with nutrition and vitamin theories.

All of the biological theories of crime causation are joined by a common assumption: Crime is caused by a biological process. This biological process could be a result of our genetic makeup or brought on by the things we eat. We may be able to control the biological process in some cases, and in other cases we may not be able to alter the biological process.

Chapter 12 contains a discussion of the "bad seed" concept and deals with criminological theories stemming from twin research. Theories relating to phenology, physiognomy, atavism, IQ, and body types appear in Chapter 13. Crime causation theories related to PMS, hormones, chromosome abnormality, learning disabilities, and the central nervous system are discussed in Chapter 14. In Chapter 15 we describe criminological theories related to nutrition, vitamins, low blood sugar, alcohol, and allergies.

12

Heredity and Crime

CHAPTER HIGHLIGHTS

- Biological theories of crime causation tend to give us hope that crime can be reduced to simple cause and solution.
- Medical science has given us the ability to modify and control to some extent human behavior.
- Sociobiology is devoted to genetic explanations for social behaviors.
- Biosocial criminology is the study of crime from a biological perspective.
- Biological theories of criminal behavior are based on the assumption that structure determines function.
- Heredity and environment are intertwined and it is impossible to separate their contributions to behavior.
- The idea that offenders inherit general tendencies to break laws is contrary to modern genetic theory.
- "Bad seed" refers to antisocial and criminal proclivities supposedly inherited by a person.
- Identical-twin research supports the idea that a person could be born a criminal.
- Evidence of hereditary factors in criminality is also found in research on adoptees.
- Some criminologists believe that biology and genes set the limits of human behavior.

KEY TERMS

Bad Seed	Discordance	Monozygotic
Biosocial Criminology	Dizygotic	Phenotype
Concordance	Genotype	Sociobiology

The biological explanations of criminal behavior are intriguing and popular. They have been around a long time. They began before the emergence of the positive school of criminology and gained greater acceptability with the positivist school's emphasis on empirical research. However, the biological theories have been absent from most current criminological theories because of the interest the sociological theories hold for Americans [1]. Nonetheless, we continue to demand that crime be reduced to a simple cause and solution. The biological theories of crime causation give us hope that we can isolate simple concrete causes of crime and find fast, effective solutions. Technological advances in biology and medicine have also given us the ability to modify and control human behavior by intervention into the mind and body. Some of the biological techniques used today to control antisocial behavior are psychosurgery, drug therapy, genetic engineering, and shock therapy [2].

A relatively new field called "sociobiology" gained a great deal of attention in 1975 with the publication of Edward O. Wilson's book *Sociobiology: The New Synthesis*. Wilson's book created great interest by laying the foundations for a new science that provided a biological basis for human social behavior [3]. Sociobiology is devoted to genetic explanations for such behaviors as altruism, homosexuality, male dominance, and conformity. The field of sociobiology is constantly expanding to include other behaviors, including crime. Now there is a new subdivision of criminology known as "biosocial criminology" [4]. Biosocial criminology deals with the study of crime from a biological perspective. Biosocial criminologists believe that the way to control crime is to apply science and technology to criminal behavior and social environments. Biosocial theories assume that criminal behaviors cannot be understood unless the interaction between the offender's biology and his or her environment is understood.

Biological explanations of criminal behavior are based on the assumption that structure determines function. People behave differently because they are structurally different. This structural difference may be the result of chromosomes, genes, chemistry, hormones, or even body type. The biological theories assume that something is happening inside the person, often beyond his or her control, to cause criminal behavior.

Fundamental difficulties plague all attempts to discover heredi-

tary influences on behavior, criminality included. The theoretical issues that must be unraveled before hereditary influences can be identified are as follows:

1. Heredity and environment interact from the point of conception.
Today it is thought that if expectant parents talk to, play music to, and
interact with the fetus, the newborn will be ahead of other infants de-
velopmentally. The separation of the unique contribution heredity
makes to behavior is almost impossible, even under ideal conditions.

2. Criminals engage in a large assortment of activities. A particular
criminal may rob, burglarize, forge, and embezzle. Modern genetic
theory indicates that inherited traits are specific in nature. We inherit
blue eyes, red hair, small bones, prominent facial features, and so on.
Criminal behavior is not specific in nature. It is general. The argument
that offenders inherit general tendencies to break laws is contrary to
modern genetic theory.

∎ THE "BAD SEED" CONCEPT

The concept of the "bad seed" has been around for a number of years.
The concept was popularized by a movie, *The Bad Seed*. The story was
about an angelic little girl whose parents were homicidal, antisocial
people. She had no contact with her biological parents and was raised
by a model citizen. Her behavior appeared to progress normally and
she behaved in model ways. However, the bad seed or the aberrant
gene eventually took control and she committed deceptive, shocking,
atrocious criminal acts.

The film was fiction. However, some research has supported the
bad seed concept, the idea that criminality is inherited and that a per-

FIGURE 12–1
**Are criminals physically different from noncriminals? Can you pick the criminals
out of the list of photographs on the left? (Answers on page 228).**

FIGURE 12–2
Bank surveillance camera records robbery in progress.
Curt R. Bartol, *Criminal Behavior: A Psychosocial Approach,* © 1980, p. 323. Reprinted permission of Prentice Hall, Inc., Englewood Cliffs, NJ.

son is born a criminal. Presented below are some of the research studies that have supported the bad seed concept.

The Jukes and Kallikaks

Two studies that emerged in the early twentieth century that attempted to prove that antisocial behavior was genetic were the Juke and Kallikak family studies. Dugdale studied the famous Juke family and Goddard studied the famous Kallikak family [5]. Dugdale concluded in his study of the Jukes that certain people have bad genes and are born to be criminals. Such bad genes could be transferred from generation to generation.

Goddard studied the Kallikak family, which was traced back to a Revolutionary War soldier who married a good Quaker woman and was also joined with a feebleminded girl. Both women had children. The offspring from the Quaker woman were considered good by Goddard, and the offspring from the feebleminded girl were considered antisocial and produced a long line of social misfits. The thought of

FIGURE 12-3
A bad seed? Courtesy of
the Kentucky Department
of Corrections

the day was that feeblemindedness was inherited and produced social
inadequacy, deviation, and criminality. At the time that these studies
were published they were considered evidence of the hereditary transmission of criminality, even though there was little evidence that these
families committed actual crimes.

Twin Research

Other research that supports the theory that criminality is inherited is
twin research, involving a comparison of identical (one-egg or monozygotic) twins with fraternal (two-egg or dizygotic) twins. Identical
twins are alike genetically, whereas fraternal twins are unlike genetically; therefore, identical twins should be more alike behaviorally than
fraternal twins. If crime were inherited, there should be a high rate of
association of criminal behavior in identical twins and a low rate of
association in fraternal twins. The association of criminal behavior is
called concordance. The lack of an association of criminal behavior
is called discordance. There are also half-identical twins, a rare type,
which are formed when a precursor to an egg splits evenly and is fertilized by two sperm. The fetuses have half of their genes in common,

those from their mother. There are also twins from different fathers. In rare situations, an egg can be released the month after a woman has gotten pregnant. If the second egg is fertilized by another man, the fetuses may be born together but are like half-siblings genetically. Twin research has focused on identical and fraternal twins.

In twin research criminals are identified with known twins and researchers attempt to identify whether the other twins are also criminals. Lange; Newman, Freeman, and Holzinger; and Christiansen have studied twins and have found that in identical twins,concordance is almost twice as high as discordance, supporting the idea that criminal behavior is a result of biology [6]. Rowe also found concordance for self-reported delinquent behavior to be higher for identical twins than for fraternal twins [7].

An ongoing study of twins by Bouchard at the University of Minnesota has studied identical twins who were separated shortly after birth and raised apart. Many of the twins separated early in life did not know that they had an identical twin until the University of Minnesota's twin project contacted them. Bouchard found some uncanny coincidences that occurred with identical twins. One reported case involved Bridget Harrison and Dorothy Lowe, identical sisters separated shortly after birth. Reunited at the University of Minnesota twins project, each arrived—not having seen each other for thirty-four years—wearing rings on seven fingers, a bracelet on each wrist, and a watch. Bridget's children were named Richard Andrew and Karen Louise; Dorothy's, Andrew, Richard and Catherine Louise.

Bouchard stated [8]:

> No scientist would seriously argue that somewhere in our chromosomes lies a gene for ring wearing or child naming. But Bridget and Dorothy's similarities nevertheless suggest that behavior patterns seemingly remote from the influence of heredity may in fact be genetically based. The women, for example, might have inherited genes that gave them attractive fingers, eliciting complements from their friends. Then, independently, they might have come to wear numerous rings to show off their hands. And their children's names? The chance of any two people choosing the same names is high enough that statisticians just label it coincidence.

In 1986, Bouchard announced the preliminary results of a study of 350 pairs of identical twins reared apart. The twins were given a battery of physical and psychological tests. It was found that leadership ability, capacities for imaginative experiences, vulnerability to stress, alienation, and desire to shun risks were 50 to 60 percent inherited.

"Aggression, achievement, orderliness and social closeness were all more strongly influenced by upbringing, with genetic components of 48 percent to 33 percent" [9]. In short, Bouchard's preliminary findings support the idea of genetic influence on behavior.

The twin studies have been criticized on the following grounds:

1. Conclusions were based on small samples.

2. Differentiation of identical from fraternal twins was done by visual observation, not by blood testing in most studies. If the twins looked similar, they were considered identical. Mistakes were often made in the direction of misidentifying fraternal twins as identical, so observations were biased in favor of the hereditary hypothesis.

3. Environmental influences were not controlled.

Adoptee Research

Evidence of hereditary factors in criminality is also apparent in adoptee research conducted in Scandinavia and the United States. In a study where female criminals had given their babies up for adoption, it was found that a significant number of their biological children had been arrested and in trouble for antisocial behavior compared with a control group of adoptees whose biological mothers were not offenders [10]. In another study it was found that if the biological father had a criminal record, the sons who were adopted were more likely to exhibit criminal behavior [11]. In summary, adoptee research suggests that there is a strong biological resemblance between parents and children who are given up for adoption with regard to proclivity toward criminal behavior.

Genotype/Phenotype Research

Shah and Roth's research also support the theory of biological factors involved in criminality [12]. Shah and Roth have charged that contemporary criminologists have minimized the role of biology in criminal behavior. They conclude that biological factors are influential in criminal behavior. Their position is that the genotype and phenotype interact. The genotype is defined as the totality of factors that make up the genetic complement of a person. The phenotype is the totality of that which can be observed about the person. The phenotype is not inherited but rather evolves as a product of the interactions between genotype and the environment. Human traits evolve from this interaction. Shah and Roth concluded that genes fix a range within which human behavior patterns can develop, rather than leading directly to particular behavior and characteristics. According to them, our biology and genes set the limits of our behavior.

▋ CLASSIFICATION OF BIOLOGICAL THEORIES

Biological theories of crime causation can be categorized for easier understanding as follows:

1. *Biological inferiority theories.* These theories assume that the criminal's biology is inferior to the biology of noncriminals. They assume that the offender's inferior biology causes criminal behavior.

2. *Body-type theories.* These theories assume that the criminal's constitution or physique is different from the constitution or physique of a noncriminal and that constitution or physique influences behavior.

3. *Difference and defectiveness theories.* These theories assume that there is something physiologically different or wrong occurring within the criminal's body. Something within the body has gone awry. (Note: These theories do not assume that the person's biology is inferior or that the difference or defect is a result of biological inferiority.)

4. *Nutrition and vitamin theories.* These theories assume that what a person eats or does not eat affects his or her behavior and thus causes criminal behavior.

FIGURE 12–4
Biological theories of
crime causation.

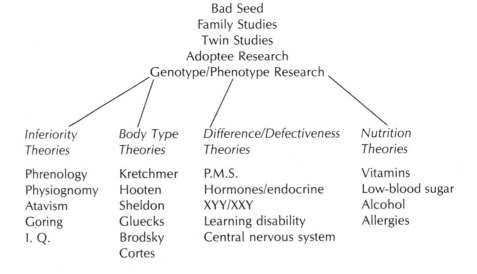

Bad Seed
Family Studies
Twin Studies
Adoptee Research
Genotype/Phenotype Research

Inferiority Theories	*Body Type Theories*	*Difference/Defectiveness Theories*	*Nutrition Theories*
Phrenology	Kretchmer	P.M.S.	Vitamins
Physiognomy	Hooten	Hormones/endocrine	Low-blood sugar
Atavism	Sheldon	XYY/XXY	Alcohol
Goring	Gluecks	Learning disability	Allergies
I. Q.	Brodsky	Central nervous system	
	Cortes		

■ SUMMARY

The biological theories of crime causation are popular because society is interested in concrete, simple, cause-and-effect answers to the crime problem. In the twentieth century alone there have been awesome technological and medical breakthroughs that have prolonged and saved lives. Medical techniques and drugs have also been discovered that have allowed us to alter antisocial behavior. Under these circumstances, why shouldn't we look toward biology for the answer to the crime problem?

Sociobiology is a relatively new field that looks toward genetics for the answers to social problems. Biosocial criminology looks toward the interaction of biology and environment for the answers to the crime problem.

The biological explanations of criminal behavior are based on the assumption that chromosomes, genes, chemistry, hormones, and/or body type can affect behavior, possibly causing antisocial or criminal behavior. There are four subdivisions of the biological theories: (1) inferiority theories, (2) body-type theories, (3) difference and defectiveness theories, and (4) nutrition and vitamin theories.

Two problems that plague any attempt to discover hereditary influences on criminal behavior are (1) keeping separate hereditary and environmental influences and (2) understanding modern genetic theory. Much of the biological research focuses on twin, adoptee, and genotype/phenotype studies.

■ MATCHING KEY TERMS AND DEFINITIONS

Match each key term with the correct definition

a. bad seed
b. biosocial criminology
c. concordance
d. discordance
e. dizygotic

f. genotype
g. monozygotic
h. phenotype
i. sociobiology

___ **1.** A relatively new science devoted to genetic explanations for social behavior.

___ **2.** A new subdivision of criminology that deals with genetic explanations for criminal behavior.

_____ **3.** A person who supposedly inherits criminal genes.

_____ **4.** The lack of an association of similar behavior between one identical twin and another.

_____ **5.** Two-egg twins.

_____ **6.** One-egg twins.

_____ **7.** An association of the like behavior between one identical twin and another.

_____ **8.** A term that refers to the genetic complement of a person.

_____ **9.** A term that refers to the totality that can be observed about a person.

■ DISCUSSION QUESTIONS

1. If criminality is the result of biological factors beyond a person's control, is the criminal responsible for his or her behavior? How can we control the criminal's behavior? What is the role of treatment? Is culpability a meaningless concept?

2. Suppose we found that criminality was genetically transmitted from parent to offspring and that the only way society could ensure that criminality could be stopped was mandatory sterilization of criminals. How would you feel about this? What societal issues would be raised?

3. If criminality is biologically determined, is it not justifiable to forcibly alter the biochemical or genetic makeup of criminals?

4. If human behavior is biologically determined, should we use our biological knowledge to fashion law-abiding citizens?

5. If crime is seen as a product of innate, invariant individual traits, are permanent segregation of the criminal from society and capital punishment logical proposals?

Answers to Figure 12–1 (1) Alvin ''Old Creepy'' Karpis on his release from prison in 1968 after serving a thirty-year term for murder, robbery, and related crimes. Once labeled America's leading public enemy by then FBI director, J. Edgar Hoover. AP/Wide World Photos. **(2) Bruno Richard Hauptmann, the convicted kidnapper and murderer of the Lindbergh baby.** UPI/Bettman Newsphotos. **(3) The New York State police officer who arrested Bruno Hauptmann.** AP/Wide World Photos. **(4) FBI Special Agent Melvin Purvis, who was involved in the ''Pretty Boy'' Floyd case. He committed suicide in 1960.** AP/Wide World Photos. **(5) Famous news commentator, Walter Winchell.** UPI/Bettman Newsphotos. **(6) Louis ''Lepke'' Buchalter, head of Murder, Inc. His organization specialized in contract killings.** AP/Wide World Photos.

Notes

1. D. C. Gibbons, *The Criminological Enterprise.* Englewood Cliffs, N.J.: Prentice-Hall, 1979.

2. Frank H. Marsh and Janet Katz, eds., *Biology, Crime and Ethics.* Cincinnati, Ohio: Anderson, 1985.

3. Ashley Montagu, "The Sociobiology Debate: An Introduction," in F. H. Marsh and J. Katz, eds., *Biology, Crime and Ethics.* Cincinnati, Ohio: Anderson, 1985, p. 24.

4. T. Platt and P. Takagi. "Biosocial Criminology: A Critique," in F. H. Marsh and J. Katz, eds. *Biology, Crime and Ethics.* Cincinnati, Ohio: Anderson, 1985, p. 55.

5. R. Dugdale, *The Jukes: A Study in Crime, Pauperism, Disease, and Heredity.* New York: Putnam, 1910; and H. Goddard, *The Kallikak Family: A Study in the Heredity of Feeblemindedness.* New York: Macmillan, 1912.

6. J. Lange, *Crime as Destiny* (English translation). New York: Charles Boni, 1930; and H. H. Newman, F. H. Freeman, and K. J. Holzinger, *Twins: A Study of Heredity and Environment.* Chicago: University of Chicago Press, 1937.

7. D. C. Rowe, "Biometrical Genetic Models of Self-Reported Delinquent Behavior: A Twin Study," *Behavior Genetics,* vol. 13, 1983, pp. 473–489.

8. J. Ficara, "All about Twins," *Newsweek,* Nov. 23, 1987, pp 58–69.

9. Ficara, 1987:64, 69.

10. R. R. Crowe, "The Adopted Offspring of Women Criminal Offenders," *Archives of General Psychiatry,* vol. 27, no. 5, Nov. 1972, pp. 600–603.

11. B. Hutchings and S. A. Mednick, "Criminality in Adoptees and Their Adoptive and Biological Parents: A Pilot Study," in S. Mednick and K. O. Christiansen, eds., *Biosocial Bases of Criminal Behavior.* New York: Gardner, 1977.

12. S. A. Shah and L. H. Roth, "Biological and Psychophysiological Factors in Criminality," in D. Glaser, ed., *Handbook of Criminology,* Skokie, Ill.: Rand McNally, 1974.

13

Biological Inferiority and Body-Type Theories

CHAPTER HIGHLIGHTS

- Early inferiority theories presumed that unusual physical characteristics were evil.
- Inferiority theories paved the way for body-type research.
- Body-type theories of criminal behavior assume that the offender's constitution or physique is related to his or her behavior.
- Body type has been related to mental illness, temperament, and delinquency.
- There are different social reactions to different body types.
- Some inferiority theories focus on the criminal's low intelligence.
- There are many different kinds of intelligence.
- IQ tests generally measure a person's verbal and quantitative abilities.
- The average IQ of a randomly selected group is approximately 100.
- Early IQ studies indicated that low intelligence was inherited.
- Early IQ studies supported the notion that offenders had lower IQs than did nonoffenders.
- For many years criminologists generally supported the idea that criminals and noncriminals did not differ with regard to intelligence.
- Contemporary studies seem to support a link between criminality and low intelligence, with offenders scoring approximately 10 points lower than nonoffenders.
- There is some evidence that a person's IQ and the type of crime he or she commits are related.

KEY TERMS

Asthenic Type

Atavism

Dyplastic Type

Ectomorph

Endomorph

Idiot Savant

Intelligence

IQ

Mesomorph

Phrenology

Physiognomy

Pyknic Type

Social Darwinism

Somatype

T here are a number of biological theories of crime causation which indicate that, biologically speaking, the criminal is inferior to noncriminals. According to the inferiority theorists, it is the offender's inferiority that causes criminal behavior [1]. Inferiority theories can take the form of the offender being constitutionally inferior or inferior intellectually and mentally. The inferiority theories paved the way for research on body types. In this chaper we (1) trace the development of the inferiority theories, (2) examine the evolution of the body-type theories, and (3) explore the research on inferiority and body-type theories.

■ EARLY INFERIORITY THEORIES

The earliest inferiority theories focused on the offender's physical characteristics and made intuitive leaps regarding criminal behavior springing from physical characteristics. Unusual physical characteristics were presumed to be inherently evil. These theories are not taken seriously today; however, in their day they were accepted as valid.

Physiognomy and Phrenology

J. Baptiste della Porte (1535–1615) was one of the first persons to study the relationship between the criminal's physical characteristics and the type of crime he committed. He concluded that thieves had small ears, small noses, slender fingers, bushy eyebrows, and mobile eyes [2].

Physiognomy was the practice of judging a person's character from facial features and became popular in the second half of the eighteenth century. Facial features were related to conduct. John Caspar Lavater (1741–1801) published a work entitled *Physiognomical Fragments* in 1775. Lavater's work got a great deal of acclaim in its day, perhaps as much as Beccaria's *On Crimes and Punishments* discussed in Chapter 4.

Physiognomy gave way to phrenology, the study of head bumps and contortions and their relationship to behavior and personal characteristics. Franz Joseph Gall (1758–1828) and John Gaspar Spurzheim (1776–1832) were the two leading phrenologists of their day. Spurzheim authored *Phrenology in Connection with the Study of Phrenology* in 1826, and Gall and Spurzheim together authored *Anatomie et physiologie du système nerveux en général et du cerveau en particulier.* According to the theory of phrenology or crainology, "each function has an organic seat in the brain, and the external signs of these mental functions are observable in the skull" [3]. For instance, there is a bump on the cranium for theft, alcoholism, intelligence, violence, and so on.

Phrenology, as a science, was short-lived. It disappeared as a scientific discipline because no one was able to substantiate with verifiable data its conceptions of physiological organs of the mind or their relation to particular types of behavior. The public was also unwilling to accept phrenology's deterministic orientation. The views that human conduct was the result of organs of the mind and that the human future was in the hands of a genetic role of the dice were rejected and opposed by teachers, preachers, judges, and other leaders who influenced public opinion, "because it contradicted one of their most cherished ideas, namely that humans are masters of their own conduct and capable of making of themselves what they will" [4].

Lombroso's Criminal Anthropology

Cesare Lombroso's (1835–1909) theory of crime causation is discussed in Chapter 5. Our discussion here is limited to Lombroso's theory of criminal atavism.

Lombroso examined and measured many Italian prisoners' craniums before and after their deaths. He postulated, based on his research, that criminals were physically inferior to noncriminals and that criminals possessed certain physical stigmata that distinguished them from noncriminals. Lombroso believed that many criminals were born inferior and that for the most part, they were helpless to do anything about their differences. Criminals were atavistic beings, who resembled early evolutionary forms of human life. He drew analogies between the insane, criminals, and savages. In addition to believing that some criminality was a result of biological determinism, Lombroso believed that some criminality could also be caused by social determinism (see Chapter 5). The following statements, reported by Wolfgang, depict in Lombroso's own words how he felt when he stumbled upon the theory of atavism [5]:

> This was not merely an idea, but a revelation. At the sight of that skull, I seemed to see all of a sudden, lighted up as a vast plain under a flaming sky, the problem of the nature of the criminal—an atavistic being who reproduces in his person the ferocious instincts of primitive humanity and the inferior animals. Thus were explained anatomically the enormous jaws, high cheekbones, prominent superciliary arches, solitary lines in the palms, extreme size of the orbits, handle-shaped or sessile ears found in criminals, savages, and apes, insensibility to pain, extremely acute sight, tattooing, excessive idleness, love of orgies, and the irresistible craving for evil for its own sake, the desire not only to extinguish life in the victim, but to mutilate the corpse, tear its flesh, and drink its blood.

Lombroso also identified the criminal's distinct physical and mental stigmata. They include deviation in head size and shape from the type common to the race and religion from which the criminal came; asymmetry of the face; excessive dimensions of the jaw and cheek bones; eye defects and peculiarities; ears of unusual size, or occasionally very small, or standing out from the head as do those of the chimpanzee; nose twisted, upturned, or flattened in thieves, or aquiline or beaklike in murderers, or with a tip rising like a peak from swollen nostrils; lips fleshy, swollen, and protruding; pouches in the cheek like those of some animals toes; imbalance of the hemispheres of the brain (asymmetry of cranium) [6]. In conclusion, Lombroso's work supported the idea that the criminal was a biologically and physically inferior person.

Goring's Research

In 1913, Goring (1870–1919) conducted a study entitled *The English Convict* in which he studied traits of over 3000 English convicts. He statistically compared ninety-six traits among classes of criminals and among criminals and noncriminals. Goring's work is considered the classic example of the application of biometrics to the study of the criminal [7]. Goring refuted Lombroso's concept of criminal atavism but never rejected the idea that serious criminality was the result of a constitutional, physical, mental, and moral proclivity. He concluded that this proclivity was biological and inherited. He also concluded that criminals were physically smaller in stature and weight than the general population. He believed that criminal characteristics were inherited and recommended that people with such characteristics not be allowed to reproduce. According to Goring, persons with epilepsy, insanity, defective social instinct, and feeblemindedness, were among those who should not be allowed to have children. Goring did attempt to control for some environmental influences; however, many influences were ignored. As a result, Goring's work is considered only as evidence of an association between crime and heredity.

Hooton's Research

A more detailed analysis of Hooton's work is contained below in the section on body types. Hooton also believed that the criminal was biologically inferior to the noncriminal and that biological inferiority was inherited. During Hooton's time, some anthropologists still believed in the idea of Social Darwinism, the belief that societies, like human beings, began as primitive forms and evolved into modern, sophisticated forms. After Darwin's theory of human evolution became popular, anthropologists believed that the theory also applied to human societies. Now the anthropologists could understand why the primitive cultures that they studied were not interested in changing or becoming modern. These cultures were primitive, evolutionary forms. Social Darwinism was responsible for viewing people who were different as inferior. It was also partially responsible for cultural egocentricity and cultural and racial prejudices.

∎ INTELLIGENCE, IQ SCORES, CRIME, AND DELINQUENCY

Other theories which assume that the criminal is inferior to the noncriminal focus on intelligence. Prior to discussing the evolution of intelligence and IQ studies and their relation to criminality, a few comments need to be made about intelligence. Intelligence is a complex concept. When we use the term "intelligence" we may be talking about many different things in a person's adjustment to his or her environment. Intelligence is multifaceted and takes many forms. Some of the forms are analytical intelligence, creative intelligence, and even "street" intelligence. A number of years ago when one of the authors worked as a parole agent, she was assigned a parolee who was given a battery of IQ tests in prison. The IQ score assigned to the parolee was 70. The narrative information that accompanied the score indicated that the parolee was considered borderline defective and barely functional. It was interesting to watch the parolee, who was a drug addict and dealer, figure profits and losses on drug sales in her head. Most people would have needed adding machines and calculators to do such figuring, yet she had an IQ score of only 70.

For the most part, IQ tests measure only verbal and quantitative abilities. These tests generally measure a person's ability to use words and count, and probable success in an academic environment. In this sense the tests are limited. The unusual cases of people with savant syndrome who, severely retarded and without lessons, can innately play complex classical piano arrangements illustrate this point.

In 1904, Alfred Binet and Theodore Simon developed the IQ test to measure children's intelligence. The early tests were rough and crude. As time passed, the tests became more refined, and today they are considered to be sophisticated and fairly accurate instruments, although some experts still believe that standard IQ tests are crude, primitive measures of some aspect of human thinking [8].

Standard IQ tests generally arrange tasks starting from the easiest and ending with the hardest. The tasks are age-graded, with younger children able to accomplish the easiest tasks and adults able to accomplish the hardest tasks. A person's mental age is determined by the hardest task that he or she can accomplish. The mental age is then compared to the person's chronological age. The formula for IQ is mental age divided by chronological age times 100. This formula gives the person's intelligence quotient.

The average IQ of a randomly selected group is around 100. Approximately two-thirds of the population score between 85 and 115. About 11 percent of the population score above 120, and 1.6 percent score above 140. The IQ range is as follows [9]:

Very superior	140–169
Superior	120–149
High average	110–119
Normal	90–109
Low average	80–89
Borderline defective	70–79
Mentally defective	30–69

Early Views on Crime and Intelligence

The classic studies of the Juke and Kallikak families in the late nineteenth and early twentieth centuries were among the first to indicate that feeblemindedness or low intelligence was inherited and transferred from generation to generation (see Chapter 12). The development of IQ tests led to the application of testing procedures for offenders. The first results seemed to confirm that offenders had low mental abilities. They were found to be mentally impaired. Henry Goddard at the New Jersey Training School for the Feebleminded at Vineland gave IQ tests to inmates and reported that 25 to 50 percent of prisoners were feebleminded and mentally impaired. In short, prisoners were dull and were incapable of managing their affairs.

Nearly all early IQ tests of criminals were carried out without control groups and without knowing the average mental age of nonoffenders. The assumption was that the average citizen had a mental age of 16. In the early studies criminals were markedly deficient in IQ compared to the general population. Criminals were found to have average mental ages of approximately 13.

The errors of these studies came to light with the publication of IQ test results from the World War I draft. The test results showed that approximately one-third of the draftees were feebleminded. This resulted in more testing and it was found that the average mental age of the general population turned out to be 13.08, not 16 as had been assumed. The average citizen proved to be less intelligent than was supposed. When criminals were then compared to noncriminals, they tested at about the same level as the World War I draftees.

Current Views on Intelligence and Criminality

Bartol indicates evidence that intelligence is inherited [10]. Wilson and Herrnstein cited a number of studies that support the idea of a link between criminality and low intelligence. They state: "There appears to be a clear and consistent link between criminality and low intelligence" [11]. They also estimate that a 10-point gap exists on IQ tests between offenders and nonoffenders, nonoffenders scoring higher [12]. Wilson and Herrnstein also indicate that most offenders fall in the low-normal or borderline subnormal range (60–100 points). They also are of the opinion that IQ scores cannot be discounted as a measure of socioeconomic status or cultural advantage. Wilson and Herrnstein also cite studies that show that criminals' intellectual difficulties are mainly verbal, but they warn that a sharp line cannot be drawn between verbal and nonverbal intelligence.

Hirschi and Hindelang also provide support for the idea that delinquents have lower IQs than nondelinquents [13]. They believe that IQ does measure innate ability but argued that IQ affects delinquency by its affect on school performance. They also believed that IQ was as important a variable as socioeconomic status for predicting official delinquency. Finally, they advocated that those planning prevention and treatment programs for delinquents take into account the fact that delinquents have lower IQs than nondeliquents. Bartol cites research that suggests that higher-socioeconomic-status delinquents have lower IQs than do higher-socioeconomic-status nondelinquents [14]. Additionally, lower-socioeconomic-status delinquents score lower than lower-socioeconomic-status nondelinquents on IQ tests. Bartol also agrees that IQ is a better predictor of delinquency than social class or race. Bartol believes that criminologists have been too hasty in their reactions against IQ tests and states: "Until more evidence is collected and carefully sorted, we must assume that intelligence, or whatever concept IQ tests measure along with social class plays a role in the development of delinquency and crime."

There is limited evidence available on intelligence and criminal typologies. Wilson and Herrnstein cited studies which showed that forgery, bribery, securities violations, and embezzlement are crimes committed by offenders with higher IQs than those of offenders in the general population. They also state that assault, homicide, rape, and sex offenses are committed by offenders with lower IQs than those of offenders in the general population. High-frequency property offenders, such as burglars, car thieves, and drug and alcohol offenders, have IQs that correspond to general population offenders. (Offenders' IQs are lower than nonoffenders' IQs.) They also note that prison systems tend to place those who commit similar offenses in the same institutions. Therefore, prisons inadvertently segregate offenders by intelligence [15].

Evaluation of Intelligence and IQ Studies

The following is a summary of arguments from criminologists who reject the idea that criminals have lower IQs than noncriminals:

1. Low mentality is not a significant cause of most criminality. There are intelligent and stupid criminals and intelligent and stupid noncriminals. The proportions of high- and low-mentality citizens and lawbreakers are approximately equal.

2. Intelligence may be a factor in the type of crime committed rather than whether a person becomes a criminal. Persons who vary in mentality are likely to occupy different criminal role patterns. For example, who will become a white-collar offender and who will become a burglar?

3. There is little systematic evidence available on intellectual differences among prisoners and nonprisoners, or among different criminal types.

4. Standard IQ and intelligence tests do not measure innate ability but measure only cultural and socioeconomic status differences. Such tests are biased against the poor and minorities.

5. IQ tests do show that offenders do not score as high as nonoffenders. We also know that offenders generally come from lower-socioeconomic neighborhoods, where they have limited educational and cultural enrichment experiences. What comes first, low IQ or a lack of educational enrichment?

▌EVOLUTION OF BODY-TYPE THEORIES

Body-type theories of criminal behavior are popular with the layman, academician, and criminal justice professional alike. The public has been quick to accept certain ideas that have been perpetuated in our culture's folklore about the relationship between physical factors, personality, and behavior. For example, crippled hunchbacks appear in the literature as stereotypes of evil or as jesters. Fat people are presumed to be jolly. Thin persons are sad. Redheads are hot tempered. Cartoons commonly depict the criminal as middle-aged, hard in appearance, often with a malformation in general facial structure, or a scar.

Kretchmer's Study

In the 1920s, Kretchmer (1888–1964) studied the relationship between physique and mental illness. His research was based on a study of 4417 cases [16]. He concluded that bodies could be divided into three distinct types:

1. *Asthenic type:* a person with a thin and narrow build. The asthenic person generally had long, narrow arms and was delicate in bone structure and appearance. The asthenic body type could also be muscular and athletic. Kretchmer associated this body type with schizophrenia. A person with an asthenic body type tended to be idealistic, introverted, and withdrawn.

2. *Pyknic type:* a person whose body is round, fat, and fleshy. Such a body type is associated with manic-depressiveness. Kretchmer theorized that a person with a pyknic body type tended to exhibit moodiness, extroversion, joviality, and realism.

3. *Dyplastic type:* a person whose body type is part asthenic and part pyknic. Kretchmer did not indicate an identifiable mental illness for the dyplastic type.

Kretchmer also indicated that athletic types seem to be connected with violent crimes, asthenic types with larceny and fraud, and pyknics with deceptive crimes.

Hooton's Study

Hooton, a physical anthropologist from Harvard, published an elaborate study in which he compared 17,000 people, 13,873 of whom were prisoners incarcerated in jails and prisons. Hooton studied male prisoners from ten states. He was attempting to establish that Lombroso was correct in his biological theories, except that Lombroso had failed to categorize criminals by the types of offenses committed. Hooton concluded that there were differences between criminals and noncriminals. He concluded that criminals were more likely to have long, thin necks, thinner beards and body hair, more red-brown hair, and thinner lips than nonoffenders. He also theorized that criminals were inferior to noncriminals and they had low foreheads, compressed faces, and narrow jaws. Physical differences in body type were connected to mental differences and were due to hereditary factors. Hooton was severely criticized on the basis that his sample was not representative of the criminal and noncriminal populations. Hooton's book was published in 1939, the same year that Nazi Germany invaded Poland. Hooton's theories supported the Nazi belief of a "superior race." However, there was no evidence in his study that criminal inferiority was inherited [17].

Sheldon's Study

Prior to Sheldon's study, it was thought that body type was innately related to personality. In 1949, Sheldon studied 200 delinquent boys between the ages of 15 and 21 who had been referred by social agencies to a home for delinquent boys in Boston. He found that delinquents had greater mesomorphy (tendency to be big-boned and muscular) than did a group of 4000 college students [18]. In short, a higher percentage of delinquent than nondelinquent boys in Boston were found to be overwhelmingly insensitive, aggressive mesomorphs.

Sheldon was interested in relating body types to temperament. He developed his own method of body typing. He attempted to isolate three poles of physique, which he called somatypes. Sheldon's theory was based on embryology. The endoderm refers to the digestive viscera. The mesoderm refers to the bones, muscles, and tendons. The ectoderm refers to the connecting tissue of the nervous system. The three somatypes are as follows:

1. *Endomorph:* a person who is round, fat, and fleshy, with short, tapering limbs and small bones.

2. *Ectomorph:* a person who is thin, small, and bony, with a small face, sharp nose, fine hair, relatively little body mass, and relatively great surface area.

3. *Mesomorph:* a person who is big-boned and muscular and tends to have a large trunk, heavy chest, and large wrists and hands. If the person were lean, he or she would tend to have a hard rectangularity of outline.

Sheldon also indicated that temperaments accompany certain body types. By intuition he identified three clusters of traits that reflected three different temperaments. Endomorphs tended to have a

FIGURE 13–1

Sheldon's three basic body types. Note that the mesomorph is big boned, muscular with a large trunk, heavy chest, and large wrists and hands. The endomorph is round, fat, and fleshy with short, tapering limbs and small bones. The ectomorph is thin, small, and bony with small face, sharp nose, fine hair, relatively little body mass, and relative great surface area.

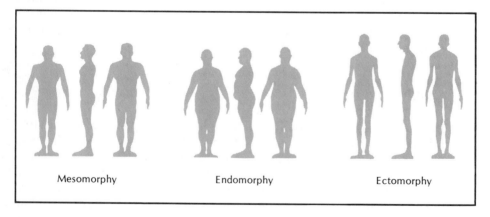

Mesomorphy   Endomorphy   Ectomorphy

relatively extensive development of digestive viscera and tended to put on fat. They also had soft, smooth, velvety skin. Their temperaments were labeled viscerotonic. This meant that they were relaxed, soft people who liked physical comfort, eating, and socalizing. They were essentially extroverted.

Mesomorphs had active, dynamic temperaments. They were labeled somatonic. They were people who tended to walk, talk, gesture, and behave aggressively. They were assertive, dominant, and tended to enjoy exercise and physical adventure.

Ectomorphs were people with cerebrotonic temperaments. They were introverted and full of functional complaints, allergies, skin troubles, chronic fatigue, insomnia, sensitivity to noise and distractions, and tended to shrink from crowds.

Sheldon's contributions include his system of body typing and his scale of temperament. Researchers who followed Sheldon utilized his instruments. Additionally, Sheldon went beyond other researchers and acknowledged that we all possess characteristics of all body types. He also said that a person's somatype, psychological characteristics, and culture interact to produce deviant behavior.

FIGURE 13–2

A prison classroom. Note the various body types. Courtesy of the office of the Comm. of Corrections, City of New York.

Gluecks' Study

The Gluecks, a husband and wife research team, also studied physical types and delinquency. They studied 500 delinquent boys and compared them to group of 500 nondelinquents. The researchers matched the groups for age, social class, and race. They found that 60 percent of the delinquents were mesomorphs compared to only 30 percent of a control group [19]. According to Montemayor, the Gluecks' research suggests that the strength, physical ability, and activity level of mesomorphy can, under certain conditions, become antisocial and criminal [20].

Both Sheldon and the Gluecks have been criticized for their methodological shortcomings. An analysis of their statistical data indicates that numerous statistical errors were made. In addition, people tend to live up to social expectations. It is not necessary to assume a direct causal relationship between body build and behavior to account for the correlations noted by Sheldon and the Gluecks.

Brodsky Study

Brodsky demonstrated that there are charactersitic social reactions to different male body types and builds [21]. He prepared fifteen-inch silhouettes of males representing endomorphs, ectomorphs, and mesomorphs. He also constructed a questionnaire containing such questions as "Which one would you like to have as your friend?" and "Which one would make the best leader?" His research population consisted of seventy-five male students from Howard University and fifty male students from George Washington University.

Brodsky's findings were that the mesomorph fared the best with regard to how others viewed him. The mesomorph was seen as the best athlete, the most successful, the best leader, the best soldier, the most self-sufficient, the most preferred as a personal friend, was seen as having many friends, and was seen as enduring pain the best. The endomorph fared the worst. He was seen as the poorest athlete, could endure pain the least, was least likely to be chosen as a leader, least aggressive, least preferred as a personal friend, and was seen as eating and drinking a lot. The ectomorph came out in the middle. He was seen as most likely to have a nervous breakdown, a heavy smoker, least self-sufficient, as having few friends, being a poor leader, and not able to hold liquor. Brodsky concluded that there are characteristic ways of relating to different types of male physique and that the trend is to favor the mesomorph.

Cortes and Gatti's Study

Cortes and Gatti administered Sheldon's temperament scale to adolescent boys and found a significant association between physique and self-descriptions of temperament [22]. Cortes and Gatti also studied and compared 100 delinquents with a group of nondelinquents. The researchers divided the boys into those who were fat, muscular, or thin based on their observations of what was dominant. They found that 57 percent of the delinquents tended to be mesomorphic, as opposed to 19 percent of the nondelinquents. Only 16 percent of the delinquents were thin, compared to 33 percent of the nondelinquents. Their research supports the notion that there is a relationship between delinquency and mesomorphy [23].

■ EVALUATION OF BODY-TYPE STUDIES

As interesting and popular as the body-type theories have been to the criminologist and layman alike, they have been criticized on several grounds:

1. The theory has not actually demonstrated the relationship between physique and behavior.

2. In nearly all studies, cultural factors are not considered or occupy a position subordinate to that of physical factors.

3. The contention that certain physical characteristics are by their very nature "inferior" is simply an assumption and nothing more.

4. Body-type studies have been conducted largely on institutionalized populations or very selective groups that probably do not represent a normal sample of the total population.

5. Most body-type studies have been conducted on males. There are also different female body types, and how they relate to criminal conduct has not been examined.

■ SUMMARY

Biological inferiority theories assume that the criminal is inferior to the noncriminal biologically. The offender can be constitutionally, intellectually, and/or mentally inferior. Physiognomy and phrenology were early inferiority theories that paved the way for Lombroso's theory of criminal atavism. Goring, who attempted to refute Lombroso's theory of atavism, did not reject the idea of the criminal being inferior to noncriminals. Other inferiority theories focus on the intelligence and IQ of offenders. Today the average IQ is considered to be 100 points, and there is evidence that delinquents and criminals tend to score lower than noncriminals on IQ tests. There is also some evidence that links a criminal's intelligence to the type of crime that he or she commits.

Body-type theories of criminal behavior are fascinating to the layman and the criminal justice professional alike. Such theories predominate in movies, literature, and popular culture. Some of the criminological theorists who have studied body types are Kretchmer, Hooton, Sheldon, the Gluecks, Brodsky, and Cortes and Gatti.

Body-type research has been criticized by many criminologists. Most research has been done on juveniles, not on adults or females. However, researchers have repeatedly found that mesomorphy generally appears to be positively related to juvenile delinquency.

■ MATCHING KEY TERMS AND DEFINITIONS

Match each key term with the correct definition

a. asthenic type
b. atavism
c. dyplasic type
d. ectomorph
e. endomorph
f. savant syndrome
g. intelligence

h. IQ
i. mesomorph
j. phrenology
k. physiognomy
l. pyknic type
m. social darwinism
n. somatype

_____ 1. A term that refers to the type of body structure a person has.

_____ 2. A term that refers to a person with a muscular, athletic body type.

_____ 3. A term that refers to a person with a thin, delicate body type. (Two answers)

_____ 4. A term that refers to a person with a round, fleshy, fat body type. (Two answers)

_____ 5. A person who has a body type that is round, fleshy, and delicate.

_____ 6. A term referring to a person with severe retardation who innately and without teaching possesses complex abilities such as playing complex arrangements on musical instruments.

___ 7. The term that refers to a person's ability to adjust to his or her environment.

___ 8. Intelligence Quotient.

___ 9. A term that refers to the idea that societies evolve from primitive beginnings and eventually become modern and sophisticated.

___ 10. A term that refers to a primitive throwback to an earlier evolutionary form.

___ 11. The study and science of cranial bumps and contortions.

___ 12. The study and science of assessing facial features to determine a person's character.

▌ DISCUSSION QUESTIONS

1. If criminals and delinquents have lower IQs than noncriminals, what changes would occur in the administration of justice? How would we have to approach the treatment of the offender?

2. If criminals were determined to be inferior to noncriminals and this inferiority was inherited, what types of social policies might emerge?

3. The mesomorphic body type is related to delinquency and criminality. What are some of the explanations for this occurrence?

Notes

1. Havelock Ellis, *The Criminal*, 2nd ed. New York: Scribner, 1900.

2. Stephen Schafer, *Theories in Criminology*. New York: Random House, 1969:113.

3. Marvin E. Wolfgang, "Cesare Lombroso," in H. Mannheim, ed., *Pioneers in Criminology*. Montclair, N.J.: Patterson Smith, 1973, pp. 232–291.

4. See Anthony M. Platt, *The Child Savers*. Chicago: University of Chicago Press, 1969, pp. 23–37.

5. Wolfgang, 1973:248.

6. See Gina Lombroso-Ferrero, *Criminal Man, According to the Classification of Cesare Lombroso*. Montclair, N.J.: Patterson Smith, 1911; and John L. Gillin, *Criminology and Penology*, 3rd ed. New York: Appleton-Century, 1945.

7. E. D. Driver, "Charles Buckman Goring," in Mannheim, 1973:429–442.

8. C. R. Bartol, *Criminal Behavior: A Psychosocial Approach*. Englewood Cliffs, N.J.: Prentice-Hall, 1980.

9. G. R. Lefrancois, *Psychology for Teaching; A Bear Always Faces the Front.* Belmont, Calif.: Wadsworth, 1972.

10. Bartol, 1980:27.

11. J. Q. Wilson and R. J. Herrnstein, *Crime and Human Nature.* New York: Simon and Schuster, 1985, p. 148.

12. Wilson and Herrnstein, 1985:154.

13. Travis Hirschi and M. J. Hindelang, "Intelligence and Delinquency," in L. D. Savitz and N. Johnston, eds., *Crime in Society.* New York: Wiley, 1978.

14. Bartol, 1980:126.

15. Wilson and Herrnstein, 1985:166.

16. Ernst Kretchmer, *Physique and Character* (translated by W. J. H. Sprott). London: Trubner, 1925.

17. E. A. Hooton, *The American Criminal: An Anthropological Study.* Cambridge, Mass.: Harvard University Press, 1939.

18. See W. H. Sheldon, *Varieties of Delinquent Youth.* New York: Harper, 1949; *The Varieties of Temperament.* New York: Harper, 1942; *Atlas of Men.* New York: Harper, 1954; and *The Varieties of Human Physique.* New York: Harper, 1940.

19. S. Glueck and E. Glueck, *Unraveling Juvenile Delinquency.* New York: Commonwealth Fund, 1950; and *Physique and Delinquency.* New York: Harper, 1956.

20. R. Montemayor, "Men and Their Body Types and Behavior," *Journal of Social Issues,* vol. 34, no. 1, 1978, pp. 48–64.

21. W. Shockley, "A 'Try Simplest Cases' Approach to the Heredity–Poverty–Crime Problem," *Proceedings of the National Academy of Sciences,* vol. 57, no. 6, June 15, 1967, pp. 1767–1774.

22. J. B. Cortes and F. M. Gatti. "Physique and Self-Descriptions of Temperament," *Journal of Consulting Psychology,* vol. 29, 1965, pp. 432–439.

23. J. B. Cortes and F. M. Gatti, "Physique and Motivation," *Journal of Consulting Psychology,* vol. 30, 1966, pp. 408–414; and J. B. Cortes and F. M. Gatti, *Delinquency and Crime: A Biopsychological Approach.* New York: Seminar Press, 1972.

14

Difference and Defectiveness Theories

CHAPTER HIGHLIGHTS

- The concept of biochemical imbalances was first established in 1828.
- One biochemical theory is that crime is a result of emotional disturbances caused by biochemical imbalances.
- A biochemical imbalance may be triggered by any number of factors, including nutrition.
- PMS/PMT is believed to affect approximately 40 percent of American women between the ages of 20 and 40.
- PMS symptoms normally begin ten to fourteen days prior to the onset of the menstrual period.
- Many women suffering from PMT have Dr. Jekyll and Mr. Hyde personality splits.
- It appears that the popularity of PMS theory far exceeds the empirical evidence supporting the theory.
- A relatively small percentage of the male population have sex chromosome abnormalities.
- The XYY chromosome abnormality has been linked to criminal behavior by some researchers.
- It appears that the higher rates of involvement in criminal conduct on the part of XYY males may be a function of lack of intelligence as opposed to chromosome imbalance.
- Many studies indicate that criminals have an excessive amount of slow-brain-wave activity compared to noncriminals.
- Some researchers contend that slow-brain-wave activity indicates that criminals have a low level of cortical stimulation.

- There is a general but unsupported belief tht epileptics are overrepresented in prison populations.
- Numerous studies indicate that a relationship exists between learning disabilities and criminal behavior.
- The anxiety reaction theory is based on the concept that people differ in the manner in which their bodies respond to fear of punishment.

KEY TERMS

Autonomic Nervous System
Central Nervous System
EEG
Extroversion
Introversion
Klinefelter's Syndrome

Learning Disability
Low-Cortical-Stimulation Theory
PMS/PMT
Slow-Brain-Wave Activity
XYY Males

In this chapter we examine the concept that criminals are biochemically different from noncriminals and therefore are defective. Linus Pauling, twice awarded the Nobel Prize in Chemistry, suggested that behavior disorders are caused mostly by "abnormal reaction rates" in the body which result from constitutional defects, faulty diets, and abnormal concentrations of essential elements. Pauling recommended establishing an optimal chemical state for the brain and nervous system in treating behavior disorders [1].

■ BIOCHEMICAL IMBALANCES

The concept of biochemical imbalances was established in 1928 by Fredrick Wöhler, a German chemist. Wöhler demonstrated that the organic compound "urea" could be synthesized. This achievement fostered the belief that people were chemical beings. In the middle of the nineteenth century, researchers were able to identify some physiological and psychosocial effects caused by the secretions of the endocrine glands (more commonly known as hormones). (*Note:* Urea is a substance found in the urine and other body fluids. The discovery

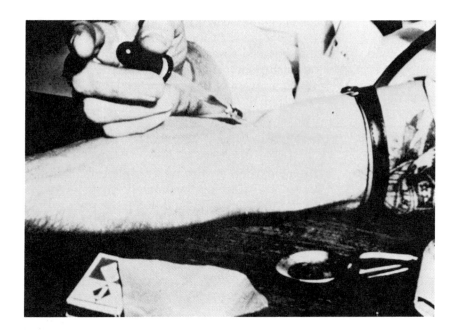

FIGURE 14–1
Drug addict "skin-popping." Courtesy of Donald O. Shultz.

of the fact that urea could be synthesized into various elements and was a chemical compound encouraged other chemists to look at other body substances as chemical compounds capable of being synthesized.)

In 1928, two criminologists, Max Schlapp and Edward Smith, presented the theory that crime was a result of emotional disturbances caused by a biochemical imbalance [2]. The imbalance, according to them, was in the secretions of the endocrine glands (hormones). If the secretions were the product of a chemical imbalance, the physiological and psychosocial effects of these secretions on a person could cause irrational behavior. Schlapp and Smith claimed that over 30 percent of all prison inmates suffered from irregular glandular functioning.

Similar research has been conducted on the relationship between high levels of testosterone and criminal conduct. This is based on the assumption that since males are more aggressive than females, males with high levels of testosterone would be more aggressive or assaultive than men with lower levels. (*Note:* Testosterone is the hormone secreted by the testes that stimulates the development of masculine characteristics.)

A biochemical imbalance may be triggered by any number of factors, including an inadequate diet. This is discussed in Chapter 15.

The glandular dysfunction theories are subject to the same criticisms as noted with the body-type theories: They fail to explain why most people with the dysfunctions do not commit crimes. In addition, the reported research fails to establish that there is any consistent relationship between criminal behavior and hormonal imbalance or varying levels of testosterone [3].

■ PREMENSTRUAL SYNDROME/PREMENSTRUAL TENSION

Premenstrual syndrome (PMS)/premenstrual tension (PMT) is believed to affect approximately 40 percent of American women between the ages of 20 and 40 [4]. Normally, the symptoms begin ten to fourteen days prior to the onset of the menstrual period and become progressively worse until the onset of menstruation. In some women it continues for several days after the onset. Common symptoms include:

Irritability	Migraine headaches
Anxiety	Fainting
Mood swings	Dizziness
Depression	Allergies

As one woman stated: "There is a pervasive sense of things always falling apart." Lark states that severely afflicted women are most vulnerable to extreme behavior during this period [5]. Katherine Dalton, an English physician, reports an increase in the likelihood of accidents, alcohol abuse, suicide attempts, and crimes committed by some women suffering from premenstrual tension [6]. Dalton states that in many cases, the affected women have Dr. Jekyll and Mr. Hyde personality splits (i.e., they are "mean," "witchy," and "irritable" during the PMT period). They often yell at their children, pick fights with their husbands, and snap at friends and coworkers. After the symptoms leave, they often spend the rest of the month trying to repair the damage done to the relationships.

One study of 249 female prison inmates indicated that 62 percent of female prison inmates' violent crimes were committed in the premenstrual week and only 2 percent were committed in the postmenstrual week [7]. (*Note:* The stress involved in committing the crime and the arrest could cause hormonal changes and trigger early menstruation with some women. Could this result in erroneous calculations regarding whether or not the female offender was in her premenstrual phase at the time the crime was committed?)

Lark divides the types of PMS into four major groups [8]:

1. *Type A (for anxiety).* Common symptoms are anxiety, irritability, and mood swings. (The most common type—occurs in approximately 80 percent of the cases involving PMS.)

2. *Type C (for carbohydrates).* Common symptoms are sugar craving, fatigue, and headaches.

3. *Type H (for hyperhydration).* Common symptoms are bloating, weight gain, and breast tenderness.

4. *Type D (for depression).* Common symptoms are depression, confusion, and memory loss.

The factors listed below increase the risk of a woman having PMS/PMT:

1. Being over 30 years (the most severe symptoms occur between 30 and 40)
2. Presence of significant emotional stress
3. Poor nutritional habits
4. Side effects from birth control pills
5. Lack of exercise

The popularity of the PMS theory far exceeds the empirical evidence supporting the theory. The PMS/PMT defense was successful in reducing murder to manslaughter in two English cases. (*Note:* The fact that a jury or judge accepts the defense as justification for criminal conduct is not evidence of its validity.)

The Case of Sandie Smith

Sandie Smith, an English barmaid, was convicted of carrying a knife and threatening a police officer. At the time of her last offense, she was on probation for stabbing another barmaid to death. Smith's background included nearly thirty convictions for assault and battery and eighteen attempted suicides. A review of her background established that her outbursts of erratic behavior always occurred several days prior to her menstrual period. Her attorney was successful in getting the British court to accept PMT as a mitigating factor. Since the trial, Smith receives a daily injection of progesterone. It appears that she has not been involved in any violent criminal behavior since she has been on the progesterone treatment.

Evaluation of PMS/PMT

Consider the following implications when evaluating PMS/PMT:

1. If PMS/PMT explains female crime, why are most violent crimes committed by males?
2. What is the potential effect of accepting the fact that women become more criminally prone during certain periods of the month?
3. Does this debase women's status as human beings? Are women victims of biology? Do women have diminished capacity?
4. Does this mean that women are criminal by nature?
5. Since only a small percentage of women suffer the extreme effects of PMS/PMT, does it provide any great assistance in solving the crime problem?

■ CHROMOSOMAL ABNORMALITY

In the normal person, there are twenty-three pairs of chromosomes in most cells, including a pair of sex chromosomes. In the normal woman, the sex chromosomes are alike. Women have two X chromosomes. In the normal male, the sex chromosomes are different and men have an X chromosome and a Y chromosome.

XYY Chromosome Abnormality

A relatively small percentage of the male population has a XYY chromosomal abnormality (i.e., an extra Y chromosome). According to the XYY theory, the extra Y chromosome causes more aggressive behavior. This is based on the assumption that men are innately more aggressive than women and that the absence of a Y chromosome in women explains woman's less aggressive nature [9].

The XYY theory is of recent origin. The first male with this chromosomal pattern was not discovered until 1961, and he was not violent or abnormal. Shortly after discovery of the XYY pattern, cases involving the XYY condition were reported in Australia, France, and the United States. In 1968 and 1969, the presence of the abnormality was presented, without success, as a defense in several highly publicized criminal trials.

Patricia Jacobs and her associates conducted a chromosome study of patients at a Scottish maximum security institution for violent and mentally ill patients [11]. In her examination of 315 males, she detected

IN FOCUS

H. A. Witkins and his associates screened all males born in Copenhagen between 1944 and 1947 who were over six feet tall. A total of 4139 were examined. Of this group, twelve were determined to be XYY males and sixteen XXY males. Forty-three percent of the XYY males had criminal convictions compared to 19 percent of the XXY males and only 9 percent of the XY males (normal). Witkins concluded that the differences were more a result of intelligence than of chromosome differences [10]. He also concluded that because of the rarity of the abnormality, XXY and XYY males had little influence on the crime rates.

that nine patients had the extra Y chromosome. Since the abnormality occurs in only 0.15 percent of the male population, detecting nine cases was unexpected. Jacobs' study received a lot of publicity and resulted in hundreds of similar studies in jails, prisons, and mental hospitals. Many of the researchers claimed that they had also found larger than expected percentages of XYY cases. In one case, Richard Speck (who in 1968 was convicted of killing eight student nurses in Chicago) was falsely diagnosed as having the XYY abnormality.

In 1972, the California Center for the Study and Reduction of Violence established a program to test California junior-high boys for the XYY chromosome abnormality. At the Boston Hospital for Women, a group of doctors started a screening program with newborn males for the XYY condition [12]. The popularity of the theory was probably based on the public's desire to find a single, simple cause of criminal behavior.

There have been over 200 research projects on the XYY condition and the research results do not support the thesis that XYY men are more aggressive and violent than XY men. The methodological problems, such as inadequate control groups, lack of double-bind studies, and researcher bias, have created serious doubts regarding the accuracy of many of the XYY studies. Since males with XYY tend to be mildly retarded at a higher-than-normal rate, many researchers contend that the higher rates of involvement in criminal conduct may be a function of lack of intelligence rather than chromosomal imbalance. In addition, even if the theory that XYY males ar more crime prone than non-XYY males, the small number of XYY males in the general population would have only a slight impact on crime rates [13].

Critical Evaluation of XYY

In evaluating the XYY theory, the following factors should be considered:

1. The XYY condition is so rare in the population that it cannot be a major factor in criminality.
2. XYY males tend not to be violent or aggressive.
3. How the XYY condition may cause deviance is unclear.
4. The XYY theory is a modern version of demonism.

Klinefelter's Syndrome (XXY)

Klinefelter's syndrome is another chromosome abnormality and involves the presence of an extra X chromosome in certain males. In most cases, males with the XXY condition are mildly retarded and have some degeneration of certain sex characteristics [14]. Common features found in XXY males include anomalism of body and facial hair and breast development. The XXY males appear to have a higher rate of alcoholism than other males. There are several studies which indicate that XXY men also have a higher rate of involvement in criminal behavior than XY men (normal) [15]. This difference, similar to the XYY men, also appears to be more related to intelligence than to chromosome abnormality. (*Note:* Other types of sex chromosome abnormalities include XY/XXY and XXYY males. There is limited research on the relationship between those types of males and criminal behavior. It appears that the results are similar to those noted for XYY males.)

∎ CENTRAL NERVOUS SYSTEM

The central nervous system includes the brain and the spinal column. It is involved in conscious thought and voluntary motor activities. Some criminological theories are based on the central nervous system. Four of those theories are discussed below:

1. Criminals have an excessive amount of slow-brain-wave activity compared to noncriminals.
2. There is a positive relationship between epilepsy and criminal behavior.
3. Criminal behavior is the result of brain damage.

IN FOCUS

People v. *Tanner*
California Court of Appeals, Second District (1970)

Tannner was charged with kidnaping, forcible rape and assault with intent to commit murder. He pled guilty to the charge of assault with intent to commit murder and was sent to the Atascadero State Hospital in California for further study as a possible mentally disordered sex offender. While at Atascadero, the appellant was discovered to possess cells with an extra male or Y chromosome. He petitioned for a withdrawal of his guilty plea, so that he could enter a plea of not guilty by reason of insanity based on his XYY condition.

Judge Cobey in his opinion stated:

> Appellant's (Tanner) sole contention on appeal is that this evidence (of the extra male chromosome) was sufficient to support a change of plea by him from "guilty" to "not guilty by reason of insanity."

> The studies of the XYY individuals . . . are rudimentary in scope, and their results are at best inconclusive. . . . The behavioral effects of this abnormal condition, the testimony of appellant's expert witnesses suggests only that aggressive behavior may be one manifestation of the XYY Syndrome. The evidence collected by these experts does not suggest that all XYY individuals are by nature involuntarily aggressive. Many identified XYY individuals have not exhibited such behavior. . . . The experts could not determine whether appellant's aggressive behavior, namely, the commission of an assault with the intent to commit murder, resulted from his chromosomal abnormality. The deficiencies in the geneticists' testimony renders the testimony that his chromosomal abnormality made him legally insane at the time he committed the assault unconvincing.

The judgment of conviction of assault with the intent to commit murder is affirmed (approved). (*People* v. *Tanner*, reported in California Reporter, vol 91, p. 656–70)

4. There is a definite relationship between learning disabilities and criminal behavior.

Slow-Brain-Wave Activity

By use of the electroencephalograph (EEG), the electrochemical processes of the central nervous system can be measured. Abnormal measurements have been associated with criminal behavior. Many studies indicate that criminals have an excessive amount of slow-brain-wave activity compared to noncriminals [16].

Since young childrens' brain waves are slower than adult brain waves, many researchers contend that the excessive amount of slow-brain-wave activity in criminals indicates that their brains are not fully developed. Other researchers contend that the data do not support the brain immaturity theory, but instead, a low-cortical-stimulation theory. The latter theory holds that the slow-brain-wave activity indicates that criminals have a low level of cortical stimulation and tend to be drowsy in dull experimental settings [17]. This theory is discussed in detail later in our discussion of the autonomic nervous system. (*Note:* An EEG does not measure extensive brain activity or the complicated interrelationships between the brain and the entire nervous system [18].)

Epilepsy

Another aspect of the central nervous system that has been associated with criminal behavior is epilepsy. There is a general but unsupported belief that epileptics are overrepresented in prison populations. Some researchers contend that it is more accurate to speak of epilepsies as symptoms rather than as disorders. There are four major types of epilepsy [19]:

1. The grand mal is the most common and dramatic type and features severe motor convulsions and an interruption or loss of consciousness.

2. The petit mal is rare in adults over 21. It features a disruption of consciousness and is difficult to recognize.

3. Jacksonian epilepsy resembles the grand mal; attacks begin with spasmodic muscular contractions in an arm or leg, which normally extend to the entire side of the body on which it started.

4. Psychomotor epilepsy features a disruption of consciousness, but the epileptic often manages to perform some fairly complicated patterns of behavior during seizures. During such seizures the person is considered to be capable of violence. (*Note:* Reportedly, the painter Vincent Van Gogh was in such a state when he sliced off his ear with a razor, packed it carefully in cotton, and presented it to a French prostitute.)

Epilepsy research has also failed to establish that there is a clear relationship between being epileptic and involvement in criminal behavior [20].

Brain Damage

A third aspect of the central nervous system's role in criminal behavior is that such behavior may be the result of brain damage or brain dysfunction [21]. Many studies indicate that criminals suffer from a higher-than-normal number of brain dysfunctions.

Learning Disabilities

"Learning disability" is a phrase used to describe a type of minimal brain dysfunction that prevents otherwise normal and intelligent children from learning in a normal classroom setting [22]. The National Advisory Committee on Handicapped Children describes the condition as follows [23]:

> Children with special learning disabilities exhibit a disorder in one or more of the basic psychological processes involved in understanding or using spoken or written languages. These may be manifested in disorders of listening, thinking, talking, reading, writing, spelling, or arithmetic.

Numerous studies have established a relationship between delinquency and learning disabilities. The estimates of learning disabilities in the delinquent population range from 30 to 90 percent. In most cases, the research designs of the studies were so poorly developed that their findings are seriously questioned. [*Note:* Most of the research on learning disabilities and criminal behavior have focused on children with "special learning disabilities" (SLDs). The classification of "general learning disabilities" (GLDs) is normally reserved for those children who have been diagnosed as being mentally retarded.]

If we accept the fact that there is a positive relationship between delinquency and learning disability, this does not necessarily mean that the relationship is caused by biological factors. The causation could be due to social factors. The primary social role of children in our society is to attend school. Accordingly, those children with learning disabilities who do not fare well in school are social misfits and may be pushed into delinquency by social fators. Often, a student with a poor academic record is perceived as a disciplinary problem.

▌AUTONOMIC NERVOUS SYSTEM

The autonomic nervous system (ANS) is that part of the nervous system which controls many of the body's involuntary functions. The ANS is especially active in "fight or flight" situations. There are two concepts involving the relationship between crime and ANS:

1. The anxiety reaction to anticipated punishment
2. The introversion/extroversion orientations of personality

The Anxiety Reaction

Sarnoff Mednick believes that people differ as to the manner in which their bodies respond to the inhibition and consequent reduction of fear [24]. Mednick based his conclusions on the differences noted in the rate of skin conductance response (SCR) recovery times. What is measured is the rate at which anxiety is reduced and disappears. (Note: This is one of the primary responses measured when conducting a polygraph examination.) The key points of his theory are summarized below:

1. The time periods between individuals' peak skin conductance amplitude and their return to normal levels can be used, according to him, to measure general rates of recovery of the ANS after stimulation. (The rate of recovery measures how rapid a person's ANS returns to normal after experiencing fear or anxiety. A person whose ANS has a rapid recovery rate will also have a rapid response rate to fear.)

2. People differ in the extent to which they are rewarded for not committing antisocial behavior. This difference is caused, in part, by the autonomic nervous system (ANS). An individual with an ANS that responds quickly to fear has a greater fear of punishment for antisocial behavior and therefore learns acceptable behavior more quickly. (Note: Mednick contends that fear reduction is the most powerful known reinforcer to human behavior.)

3. A major assumption of the theory is that if a person fears punishment sufficiently, the person will not commit antisocial acts.

IN FOCUS

Inhibiting Antisocial Behavior

According to the ANS theory, the relationship between ANS and anti-social behavior is evident in the following example. John and Robert, two young male children, commit aggressive behavior toward Jane, a young female. Both John and Robert are punished by their parents. If John and Robert's ANS respond differently, giving the same punishment to both will not have the same effect. Suppose that John's ANS reacts quicker than Robert's; then the following sequence of events could occur:

1. John and Robert contemplate new aggressive antisocial behavior.

2. Because of the ANS differences, John fears punishment more than Robert does.

3. The greater fear of punishment suffered by John may deter him from committing the contemplated antisocial behavior.

4. Since Robert's ANS reacts more slowly, he does not fear punishment as much as John does; accordingly, Robert is more likely than John to commit the antisocial behavior.

---

4. If a person's ANS responds at a slower-than-normal rate, the person will fear punishment less. In this case, punishment to inhibit antisocial behavior will have less effect than in cases involving persons who demonstrate an ANS that responds quickly.

Under Mednick's theory, it appears that punishment will deter normal persons from committing crime but will not deter people with abnormally slow responding ANS. Mednick bases his conclusions on his research, which indicates that most persons who commit criminal acts have slow ANS values.

Introversion and Extroversion

Eysenck used Jung's concepts of introversion and extroversion as the major orientations of a person's personality and Pavlov's concepts of excitation and inhibition to develop his theory. Eysenck contended that the two sets of concepts were connected [25]. According to Eysenck:

1. Introverts are characterized by higher levels of excitation and/or lower levels of inhibition.
2. Extroverts are characterized by lower levels of excitation and/or higher levels of inhibition.

The introvert is oriented toward the inner, subjective world. He or she tends to be quiet, cautious, and controlled. The extrovert is the opposite. He or she craves excitement, takes chances, and tends to lose his or her temper more easily. Eysenck hypothesized that the orientation toward introversion or extroversion is determined by degree or amount of stimulation reaching the cortex [26]. Introverts, according to him, receive higher levels of stimulation and thus need lower levels of stimuli. Since extroverts are less sensitive to pain, they need greater stimuli. Extroverts are therefore stimuli hungry. Accordingly, they tend to seek out prohibited activities in their quest for stimuli.

According to Eysenck, psychopaths are extreme extroverts and fail to develop adequate consciences because of the dysfunctioning of the ANS (see Chapter 18). He contended that since extroverts are less sensitive to pain, the possibility of punishment for criminal conduct does not have the same effect on extroverts as it would have on introverts.

Eysenck relied on Pavlov's classical conditioning-response for his explanation of criminal behavior. Critics contend that Eysenck's theory reduces antisocial behavior to uncontrolled responses to insufficient conditioning and deemphasizes social choices of rational behavior. Many criminologists consider Eysenck's reliance on classical conditioning response and the discounting of other learning forms as major weaknesses of his theory.

■ SUMMARY

There are many criminological theories that attribute criminal behavior to biochemical imbalances. One theory is that crime is due to the emotional disturbances caused by the biochemical imbalance. Several researchers contend that PMT/PMS causes violent and irrational behavior in some women. It appears, however, that the popularity of the PMS theory exceeds the empirical evidence supporting it. Another theory links criminal behavior to the XYY chromosome abnormality. The relatively small percentage of the male population who are XYY males minimizes the importance of this theory. Excessive slow-brain-wave activity is considered by some researchers as the cause of criminal behavior. Numerous studies have reported a relationship between learning disabilities and juvenile delinquency. However, the studies fail to explain the causal connection.

There is lack of clear evidence that aggressive criminal behavior is a direct result of brain or body dysfunction. It appears that the existence of a biological dysfunction under certain circumstances may trigger criminal behavior in a person. At most, it may be stated that some criminals are indirectly affected by biological abnormalities.

∎ MATCHING KEY TERMS AND DEFINITIONS

Match each key term with the correct definition.

a. autonomic nervous system
b. central nervous sytem
c. EEG
d. extroversion
e. introversion
f. Klinefelter's syndrome

g. learning disability
h. low-cortical-stimulation theory
i. PMS/PMT
j. slow-brain-wave activity
k. XYY males

____ 1. Is believed to be present in approximately 40 percent of women between the ages of 20 and 40.

____ 2. A relatively small percentage of the male population who have an extra male chromosome.

____ 3. A chromosome abnormality in certain males who possess an extra X chromosome.

____ 4. That part of the nervous system composed of the brain and the spinal column.

____ 5. The electroencephalograph.

____ 6. A condition used to support the "brain immaturity" theory.

____ 7. A phrase used to describe a type of minimal brain dysfunction that prevents otherwise normal and intelligent children from learning in a normal classroom setting.

____ 8. That part of the nervous system which controls many of the body's involuntary functions.

____ 9. A person who tends to be quiet, cautious, and controlled.

____ 10. A person who craves excitement.

____ 11. A theory which states that slow-brain-wave activity indicates that criminals have a low level of cortical stimulation.

◼ DISCUSSION QUESTIONS

1. If PMS/PMT were accepted as a valid cause of female criminal behavior, does this exclude women from some occupations? Should women become police officers?

2. If evidence were established conclusively that the majority of criminals are biologically different from the majority of non-criminals, how would we then explain the causal linkages to criminal behavior?

3. If we accept the assumption that criminal behavior is biologically caused, does this mean that a person inherits an uncontrollable desire to commit rape or robbery?

Notes

1. A. Hoffer, "Some Theoretical Principles Basic to Orthomolecular Psychiatric Treatment," in L. J. Hippchen, ed., *Ecologic–Biochemical Approaches to Treatment of Delinquents and Criminals.* New York: Van Nostrand Reinhold, 1978.

2. Max G. Schlapp and Edward H. Smith, *The New Criminology.* New York: Boni, 1928.

3. Sarnoff Mednick and Jan Volavka, "Biology and Crime," in Norval Morris and Michael Tonry, eds., *Crime and Justice.* Chicago: University of Chicago Press, 1980.

4. Susan Lark, *Premenstrual Syndrome Self-Help Book.* Los Angeles: Forman, 1984, p. 19.

5. Lark, 1984:20.

6. Katherine Dalton, "Menstruation and Crime," *British Medical Journal,* vol. 3, 1961, pp. 1752–1753.

7. J. H. Morton, et al., "A Clinical Study of Premenstrual Tension," *American Journal of Obstetrics and Gynecology,* vol. 65, 1953, pp. 1182–1191.

8. Lark, 1984:27.

9. Patricia Jacobs et al., "Aggressive Behavior, Mental Subnormality and the XYY Male," *Nature,* vol. 208, 1965, pp. 1351–1358.

10. H. A. Witkin et al., "XYY and XXY Men: Criminality and Aggression," *Science,* vol. 193, 1976, pp. 547–555.

11. Jacobs et al., 1965:1351.

12. Richard Fox, "The XYY Offender: A Modern Myth," *Journal of Criminal Law, Criminology, and Police Science,* vol. 62, 1971, pp. 59–73.

13. William J. Chambliss, *Exploring Criminology.* New York: Macmillan, 1988, p. 186.

14. Fox, 1971:72.

15. W. H. Price et al., "Criminal Patients with XYY Sex-Chromosome Complement," *The Lancet,* vol. 1, Mar. 1966, pp. 565–566.

16. Sarnoff Mednick et al., "Biology and Violence," in Marvin Wolfgang and Neil

Alan Weiner, eds., *Criminal Violence*. Beverly Hills, Calif.: Sage, 1982, pp. 46–52.

17. Mednick et al., 1982:51.

18. Mednick and Volavka, 1980.

19. Harold J. Vetter and Ira J. Silverman, *Criminology and Crime*. New York: Harper & Row, 1986, p. 416.

20. Mednick et al., 1982:49.

21. Mednick et al., 1982:52.

22. H. R. Myklebust, "Learning Disabilities: Definitions and Overview," in H. R. Myklebust, ed., *Progress in Learning Disabilities*, Vol. I. New York: Grune & Stratton, 1968.

23. National Advisory Committee on Handicapped Children, *Special Education for Handicapped Children, First Annual Report*, Washington, D.C.: U.S. Government Printing Office, 1968.

24. Sarnoff Mednick, "Biosocial Factors and Primary Prevention of Antisocial Behavior," in Sarnoff Mednick, ed., *New Paths in Criminology*. Lexington, Mass.: Lexington Books, 1979.

25. H. J. Eysenck, *Crime and Personality*. Boston: Houghton Mifflin, 1964.

26. Eysenck, 1964:102.

15

Nutrition and Criminal Behavior

CHAPTER HIGHLIGHTS

- Considerable attention has been focused on the relationship between vitamins, preservatives, sugar, diet, and criminal behavior.
- The study of nutrition as a causative factor in criminal behavior can be traced to biochemical imbalance theories.
- One of the primary causes of chemical imbalance is a lack of proper nutrition.
- Various researchers contend that malnutrition is a causative factor in criminal behavior.
- Poorer children are more likely to have vitamin deficiencies because their parents cannot afford well-balanced diets.
- Subdivisions of nutrition theory include: low blood sugar, vitamin deficiencies, and food allergies.
- Hypoglycemia, according to many nutritionists, is caused by a high consumption of large quantities of refined sugar and starches, and to poisonous food additives.
- Lack of sufficient levels of certain vitamins is considered by some to be the cause of many juvenile delinquency problems.
- Studies of institutionalized criminals indicate that most of them have vitamin deficiencies.
- Various researchers are of the opinion that food allergies can trigger violent behavior.
- Dairy products, corn, eggs, and wheat products are food groups with high incidents of food allergy problems.
- Neuroallergy is an allergic condition that affects the body's central nervous system.
- Many research reports on causes of hyperactivity in children focus on nutrition.

KEY TERMS

Allergy   Hypoglycemia
Biochemical Imbalance   Neuroallergy
Cyclic Food Allergies   Nutrition
Fixed Food Allergies   Taraxein
Hyperkinesis   Vitamin

■ YOU ARE WHAT YOU EAT

A popular saying in the 1970s and 1980s is: "You are what you eat." Since the 1970s, the roles of vitamins, preservatives, sugar, and diet in human behavior have been researched, particularly in relationship to juvenile behavior [1].

The study of nutrition as a causative factor in criminal behavior can be traced to the biochemical imbalance theories. According to these theories, criminal behavior is a direct result of imbalances in a person's "biochemical balance" [2]. For example, many researchers contend that schizophrenic behavior, which often results in criminal behavior, is caused by a biochemical abnormality within the body [3]. Although the biochemical abnormality may be caused by factors other than nutrition (e.g., genetic factors), improper nutrition is considered the primary reason for the chemical imbalance [4].

One of the causes of chemical imbalance is a lack of proper nutrition (improper diet). An additional impetus in the study of the relationship between criminal behavior and nutrition is the research that links crime to poverty and economic inequality. According to this research, malnutrition is a causative factor in criminal behavior. Poorer children are more likely to have vitamin deficiencies because of the inability of their families to afford well-balanced diets. The vitamin deficencies, in turn, may trigger violent and irrational behavior.

Another rationale used by theorists who place blame on nutrition as a cause of criminal behavior is that "hunger drives a person to crime" [5]. An example of this is the classic dilemma by Grotius of the man who steals bread to feed his children. Subareas of the nutrition theory include:

1. Hypoglycemia (low blood sugar)
2. Vitamin deficiencies
3. Food allergies

■ HYPOGLYCEMIA/LOW BLOOD SUGAR

The study of the relationship between low blood sugar and criminal behavior can be traced to 1927 and the research of J. La Barre. He and his associates performed a series of experiments on the role of the central nervous system in the control of pancreatic secretions [6]. Inadequate sugar metabolism (hypoglycemia) refers to the condition in which blood glucose levels are insufficient for proper brain and body functioning. This is important, for if the brain does not function, rationality and decision making will be affected. (*Note:* The brain weighs 2 to 4 percent of body weight and consumes 25 percent of the body's glucose supply.)

According to many nutritionists, hypoglycemia is caused by a

FIGURE 15–1
Note the junk-food items for sale in this prison canteen. Courtesy of the Iowa Department of Social Services.

high consumption of refined sugar and starches, and to poisonous food additives. Nutritionists contend that eating patterns of many youths in today's society consist of a large intake of refined sugar and starches, which results in major fluctuations in blood sugar levels.

Hypoglycemia (a low-blood-sugar disorder) is a common medical problem with institutionalized delinquents [7]. (*Note:* Hypoglycemia is a symptom rather than a disease.) Some criminologists contend that there is a relationship between low blood sugar and criminal behavior. They see this disorder as a probable cause of sudden, violent, unexplained behavior in some persons. According to the medical reports, hypoglycemia produces in some people symptoms of lethargy and depression and in others irritability, suspiciousness, bizarre thinking patterns, hallucinations, extreme mania, anxiety, and violent behavior. According to Hippchen, persons with low blood sugar are capable of stealing, rape, arson, assault, and homicide [8]. He also states that a high percentage of persons convicted of criminal homicides who are diagnosed as paranoid schizophrenics are, in reality, suffering from hypoglycemia. (*Note:* In the 1950s, a famous criminal attorney, Samuel Segal, successfully defended a woman charged with murder based on the fact that she was suffering from hypoglycemia.) D'Asaro studied inmates confined to a local jail and concluded that inmates having indications of hypoglycemia committed significantly more violent crimes than did inmates without any indications of hypoglycemia [9].

Kelly cites a study that suggests hypoglycemia as a cause of the aggressive behavior in the Qolla in Peru [10]. In a village with about 1200 persons, 50 percent of the heads of households have been involved in homicides. According to Kelly, the Qolla have one of the highest homicides rates in the world. The Qolla's blood sugar levels were tested and the results were that 50 percent of those tested had low blood sugar levels. Kelly indicates: "The hypoglycemic may suffer from temporary diminished responsibility because his or her brain does not function rationally, presenting alternatives among which he or she could actually choose."

Virkkunen conducted a glucose tolerance test (GTT) on sixty-eight male habitually violent offenders and twenty control subjects (employees of the hospital) [11]. He concluded that the GTT readings of the habitually violent offenders were significantly different from those of the control group. He noted the presence of hypoglycemic conditions more frequently in offenders and that they had a slower recovery rate from sugar intake than did nonoffenders. Kelly cites an article that stated: "A very large number of inmates suffer from hypoglycemia, which aggravates and perpetuates criminal behavior" [12]. Fredericks found that the removal of sugar from the diet, with necessary changes in the intake of starch, protein, and fat to meet the needs and tolerances of the person, will reduce depression, hyperactivity, and schizophrenia [13].

▊ VITAMINS

The recent decade could be described as the decade of the vitamin, as vitamin deficiencies are blamed for all types of human behavior, including criminal behavior. Leonard Hippchen conducted a study of the relationship between vitamin deficiencies and juvenile delinquency [14]. He concluded that the lack of sufficient quantities of certain vitamins was the cause of many juvenile delinquency problems, including truancy and running away. According to Hippchen, a person with a vitamin deficiency can suffer severe distortions in sight, hearing, and other senses. The deficiency can also cause violent behavior and other "antisocial" actions.

A number of studies have concluded that the majority of alcoholics and drug addicts suffer from vitamin deficiencies. Similar studies estimated that most acute schizophrenics and persons with behavior disorders also suffer from vitamin deficiencies. In addition, studies of institutionalized criminals indicate that most of them also have vitamin deficiencies [15]. (*Note:* The studies fail to indicate which comes first, the disorder or the deficiency. The deficiency may be the result of the disorder, not the cause of it.)

According to the vitamin deficiency theorists, the chain of events is as follows:

1. Malnutrition or vitamin deficiency
2. Disordered brain chemistry
3. Thought disorders or changes in perception
4. Pathological (abnormal) interaction with society and people
5. Mental, emotional, and spiritual deterioration, pain, personality defects, depression, and coping problems
6. Violent criminal behavior

Many researchers have contended that in some people, the lack of nicotinic acid (vitamin B_3) causes the body to produce an abnormal amount of taraxein (a protein ingredient). They also presume that taraxein causes the body to convert epinephrine (a neurotransmitter) into toxic substances, which produce hallucinations and cause schizophrenia [16]. Hoffer noticed that many of the symptoms of schizophrenia were similar to those of pellagra, a niacin (B_3) deficiency. After he treated patients with huge doses of vitamin B_3, they recovered and remained nonschizophrenic as long as they continued the vitamin B_3 treatment [17]. Other researchers have contented that the inability of a schizophrenic to suppress hallucinogenic substance production is caused by inadequate levels of vitamins C and E in the body [18].

FOOD ALLERGIES

Some researchers are of the opinion that food allergies can trigger violent behavior. (Allergy is an unusual or excessive reaction of the body to a foreign substance.) Various researchers contend that food allergies can cause a variety of problems, from hyperactivity to arthritis. In addition, certain food groups can cause perceptual distortions due to "allergies." The perceptual distortions often result in violent and irrational behavior. According to these researchers, perceptual distortions were highest in a test group that had a diet high in wheat, corn, and milk products [19]. Alex Schauss concluded that many chronic criminal offenders drank twice as much milk as cokes. According to him, some chronic offenders drink a quart of milk every two or three hours. Schauss noted that one 16-year-old juvenile delinquent drank milk at every meal but ate few vegetables. One 10-year-old arsonist with five prior offenses reported regularly eating a breakfast of presweetened cereal along with twenty ounces of milk and twenty ounces of soda [20]. Dairy, corn, eggs, and wheat products are food groups that frequently result in food allergy problems.

Allergic reactions may occur within seconds, minutes, or up to seventy-two hours after intake. One of the problems with food allergies is that often the person will feel better after eating food to which he or she is sensitive. According to Bonnet and Pfeiffer, the best diagnostic clue of food sensitivity is the evaluation of the food cravings of a person [22]. For example, a person who craves ice cream may be sensitive to milk.

IN FOCUS

Carlton Fredericks has asserted that during World War II in Greece, when the Nazi occupation made bread, a staple of the Greek diet, scarce, there was a marked improvement in Greek schizophrenics and paranoids [21].

IN FOCUS

Eighty percent of all the colorings and additives in foods cause emotional problems, as well as arthralgia, macroglossia, etc. (Benjamin F. Feingold, Chief Emeritus of the Department of Allergy, Kaiser–Permenta Medical Center of San Francisco)

There are two types of food allergies, fixed and cyclic. With the fixed allergy, the person will have a reaction each time he or she eats food to which he or she is sensitive. With cyclic food allergies, a reaction to the food may not result immediately each time the food is eaten, but may be delayed.

Fixed allergies are normally easy to diagnose because of this direct reaction. Cyclic food allergies are more common but are more difficult to diagnose. An additional problem with cyclic food allergies is that the delayed reaction may often be relieved temporarily by additional intake of the food to which the person is allergic.

▊ NEUROALLERGY

Neuroallergy is an allergic condition that affects the body's central nervous system. If the allergy directly affects the brain, it is also known as a cerebral allergy. It interferes with a person's thought patterns, planning, reasoning, reading, vision, and the ability to get along with others. The symptoms of a neuroallergy condition include the following [23]:

Headaches	Shortened attention span
Fatigue	Irritability
Slowness in thinking	Hyperactivity
Inability to concentrate	Perceptual problems

According to Wunderlich, the symptoms above may lead to paranoia, antisocial behavior, excessive dependence on others, fear of change, loss of self-esteem, and feelings of insecurity. The neuroallergy may be caused by nutritional deficiencies or reactions to food. A common cause of neuroallergy is a diet lacking in variety. Accordingly, when a person eats certain foods in large amounts, in a chronic

**FIGURE 15–2
Nicotine can also
affect behavior.** Randy
Matusow/Monkmeyer
Press.

repetitive pattern, neuroallergy may result [24]. It can be acute or chronic. The central nervous system allergy begins when a person loses his or her tolerance to certain foods. This is especially true of dairy products. The allergy pattern often begins in early childhood.

Wunderlich reports a case involving a 14-year-old juvenile delinquent who had a history of theft, malicious destruction of property, and tantrum throwing [25]. His progress in school was unsatisfactory and he was known as being clumsy and uncoordinated. He was two years behind in school and was considered a troublemaker by the local police. The juvenile's diet consisted of sweetened cereals, cokes, and an assortment of refined carbohydrates, with few other foods. A glu-

IN FOCUS

If improper diet causes criminal behavior, consider these facts: in one two-week period, the inmates of the San Diego County Jail bought 2485 bags of potato chips, 2918 candy bars, and 4983 sugar packets.

IN FOCUS

"We don't need to worry about Communism taking over the world. We are now getting the Russians to drink Pepsi-Cola. What a masterful stroke!" [26] The author was referring to the fact that colas are about 10 percent sugar. He made that statement in 1974. At that time about 30,000 cases of Pepsi-Cola were being sold each year in the Soviet Union. In 1987, over 1 million cases were sold. In 1988, more Pepsi-Cola was sold than vodka.

cose tolerance test using his normal diet indicated a flat curve with a decline two and six hours after eating. It was determined that he was allergic to refined sugar and the allergies affected his central nervous system. Wunderlich reports that with treatment and proper diet, the antisocial behavior ceased, and as time passed, the juvenile became more interested in helping himself.

▪ HYPERKINESIS

Hyperkinesis is seen as an "antisocial" form of behavior and is associated with unwarranted and sometimes criminal behavior in juveniles. Hippchen states that hyperkinesis has been identified as the primary cause of restlessness among youth and leads them into such activity as alcohol and drug use, running away, truancy, vandalism, violence, delinquency, and crime [27]. The primary cause of hyperkinesis, according to Hippchen, is vitamin B_3 dependency, and the secondary cause is hypoglycemia (low blood sugar).

Many of the research reports on causes of hyperactivity in children focus on nutrition. The idea that food additives cause behavioral and learning impairments in children has popular support in the United States. In this regard, considerable attention has been focused on the adverse effects of sugar and food additives on the hyperactivity of juveniles [28].

Many researchers claim that changes in diet for hyperactive children will result in "improved behavior" [29]. However, recent research evaluation indicates that there are questions regarding the reliability of the data used. Several recent studies indicate that sugar and food additives may not have the significant adverse impact on behavior as earlier believed. Prince, Thomsen, and McLaughlin concluded that: "The causes of hyperactivity are not known but it is apparent from the literature that diet is not a related cause or cure of kinetic behavior" [30].

The "Twinkie" Defense

When considering nutrition and criminal behavior, consider also the fact that Americans buy 700 million Twinkies a year, 80 percent of them on impulse. Over 50 billion Twinkies have been sold in the past sixty years.

On May 22, 1979, Dan White, a former San Francisco, California County Supervisor, was convicted of voluntary manslaughter for the November 1978 killing of San Francisco Mayor George Mascone and Supervisor Harvey Milk. White was originally charged with first-degree murder (a capital offense). The prosecutor argued to the jury that White was guilty of cold-blooded murder. It was established that White had gone to city hall to talk to the mayor. He had entered through a window to avoid the metal detector at the main entrance. At the time, he was carrying a snub-nosed revolver. He shot Mayor Moscone and Harvey Milk nine times with the weapon, killing both of them. (Note: White readily admitted killing the mayor and supervisor Milk, who was his most vocal opponent on the San Francisco Board of Supervisors.)

White's defense attorney, Douglas Schmidt, presented evidence to establish that White had suffered from "diminished capacity" caused by a "biochemical change" in his brain. According to the defense's theory of the case, White was incapable of the premeditation, deliberation, and malice required to obtain a murder conviction. Evidence at the trial indicated that White was a manic-depressive with a high degree of stress caused by financial and other personal problems. A defense medical expert testified that White suffered from a "genetically caused melancholia" and, at the time, was "discombobulated." Defense witnesses, who included family members, friends, and experts, testified about White's moods and his diet. One defense psychiatrist testified that White's compulsive diet of candy bars, Twinkies, and cokes was evidence of a deep depression and resulted in excessive sugar, which either caused or aggravated a chemical imbalance in his brain. In finding White guilty only of manslaughter, not of first-degree murder, the superior court jury apparently accepted the Twinkie defense.

■ ALCOHOLISM AND CRIMINAL BEHAVIOR

Associated with the nutrition theories of crime causation is the study of alcohol and its relationship to criminal behavior. Alcohol affects criminal behavior in three ways [31]:

1. Direct criminal activities that result from the fact that alcohol is a regulated and taxed substance

2. Indirect behavioral effects of alcohol acting as an anesthetic, with the potential to frustrate social goals

3. Acts resulting from alcohol addiction and physical dependence on alcohol

Some of the basic facts regarding the relationship between alcohol and criminal behavior are as follows:

1. One-third of all arrests are for alcohol-related crimes.

2. A significant number of violent crimes involve alcohol.

3. Research on the relationship between alcohol and crime show that both offenders and victims are often drinking at the time of the offense.

4. With the crime of robbery, approximately 75 percent of the offenders and 67 percent of the victims had been drinking at the time of the offense.

5. With criminal homicides, four out of five homicides involve a drinking offender and/or victim.

6. As many as 83 percent of those arrested for criminal conduct admit to having a drinking problem.

7. The "skid-row" alcoholic is arrested on the average 3.7 times for offenses other than alcohol-related crimes.

For many people, alcohol acts as a social lubricant and relaxes normal inhibitions. Therefore, it chemically dissolves a person's behavioral restraints. Since alcohol depresses the central nervous system and the inhibition control of the brain by causing localized loss of oxygen being carried to the base of the brain, it disrupts the communicative aspects of the brain. As depression of the inhibition control of the brain occurs, the drinker becomes more talkative, active, and aggressive. It is at this point that a person is more likely to commit a crime.

FIGURE 15–3
The devastating effects of alcoholism may remain hidden.

Alcohol also causes toxic brain systremma. Under these conditions, the brain releases higher levels of adrenaline-like substances. The higher levels of adrenaline often produces a hostile, hyperactive, paranoid state. With the paranoia, the person has impaired judgment and heightened aggression, often resulting in violent criminal behavior [32]. A related problem with alcohol is that it tends to suppress the appetite in many people and thus creates nutrition problems.

A drug known as antabuse has been used in the treatment of alcoholics. Antabuse, which is taken orally, causes headaches, nausea, and vomiting within three days of any alcohol consumption. The long-term effectiveness of antabuse has not been established. It appears, however, that antabuse works against impulsive drinking. Research is now being conducted on antabuse implants, which release the drug slowly into the body for several weeks.

IN FOCUS

Robinson v. California
Supreme Court of the United States, 1962
(370 U.S. 660)

Mr. Justice Stewart delivered the opinion of the court:

A California statute makes it a criminal offense for a person to be addicted to the use of narcotics. This appeal draws into question the constitutionality of [the statute] . . .

The broad power of a State to regulate the narcotic drug traffic within its borders is not here in issue . . . There can be no question of the authority of the State in the exercise of its police power to regulate the administration, sale, prescription and use of dangerous and habit-forming drugs. . . . The right to exercise this power is so manifestly in the interest of the public health and welfare, that it is unnecessary to enter upon a discussion of it beyond saying that it is too firmly established to be successfully called in question.

This statute . . . is not one which punishes a person for the use of narcotics, for their purchase, sale or possession, or for antisocial or disorderly behavior resulting from their administration. It is not a law which even purports to provide or require medical treatment. Rather, we deal with a statute which makes the "statue" of narcotic addiction a criminal offense, for which the offender may be prosecuted "at any time before he reforms." California has said that a person can be continuously guilty of this offense, whether or not he has ever used or possessed any narcotics within the State, and whether or not he has been guilty of any antisocial behavior there.

It is unlikely that any State at this moment in history would attempt to make it a criminal offense for a person to be mentally ill, or a leper, or to be afflicted with a venereal disease. A State might determine that the general health and welfare require that victims of these and other human afflictions be dealt with by compulsory treatment, involving quarantine, confinement, or sequestration. But, in the light of contemporary human knowledge, a law which made a criminal offense of such a disease would doubtless be universally thought to be an infliction of cruel and unusual punishment in violation of the Eighth and Fourteenth Amendments.

. . . We hold that a state law which imprisons a person thus afflicted as criminal . . . is cruel and unusual.

Questions: Do you agree with the Supreme Court that it is cruel and unusual to label a person a criminal because the person is afflicted with a disease? Does the case imply that the Supreme Court is of the opinion that narcotic addiction is a disease?

[Note: In *Powell v. Texas*, (1968) 392 U.S. 514 the U.S. Supreme Court held that a Texas statute punishing a person for being drunk in a public place was constitutional.]

▌LEAD POISONING

Although lead poisoning is not related to nutrition, its symptoms and resultant behaviorial problems are similar to those caused by nutrition problems. Lead poisoning can also cause bizarre, violent, and anti-social behavior. Many of the interior paints used in homes and other buildings in the 1950s and 1960s were lead-based. Since lead is a toxic heavy metal, lead poisoning can result. There are a variety of psychological symptoms with lead poisoning similar to those associated with hyperactivity and schizophrenia. Lead acts as a pollutant in the body. (*Note:* Some lead in the blood is normal, but when it exceeds 20 parts per million in an adult, lead poisoning is possible.) The usual sources of unwanted lead include paint, leaded gasoline exhaust, and food grown near heavily traveled roads [33].

▌CAFFEINE

Most of us drink coffee, tea, or soda with caffeine and do not commit violent crimes. However, in some persons, caffeine may aggravate a low-blood-sugar condition. It stimulates the body to dump sugar into the bloodstream at a faster-than-normal rate. The same reactions that result from the intake of caffeine may also occur from the intake of too much sugar and starch. Caffeine is an alkaline of the xanthine family. It is a stimulant that causes the heart and lungs to work at an abnormally fast rate. Caffeine causes the kidneys to excrete more fluid and the stomach to excrete more acid.

■ EVALUATION

In evaluating the nutrition theories, several problems are apparent, the major ones are as follows:

1. Most of the research is based on after-the-fact studies of criminal behavior and involve the effects on selected individuals, not on large groups of people.

2. The theories fail to explain the extent to which nutritional conditions are related to criminal behavior.

3. Those studies that report positive results generally lack scientific rigor and fail to use carefully controlled statistical measures in establishing their success.

4. Most studies read like testimonials, and not like objective, empirical endeavors.

Except for the association between sex hormones and criminal activity (discussed in Chapter 14), there has been a general failure to establish any systematic connection between crime and chemical imbalance.

■ SUMMARY

Various researchers are of the opinion that there is a direct relationship between nutrition and criminal behavior. The study of nutrition can be traced to the biochemical imbalance theories. The subareas of nutrition theory include: low blood sugar, vitamin deficiencies, and food allergies.

Some researchers believe that low blood sugar is a probable cause of sudden violent and unexplained behavior. According to many nutritionists, hypoglycemia (low blood sugar) is caused by a high consumption of large quantities of refined sugar and starches, and to poisonous food additives.

A lack of sufficient quantities of certain vitamins is seen by some as the cause of many juvenile delinquency problems. The deficiencies can also cause violent behavior and other social problems. Studies of institutionalized criminals indicate that most of them have vitamin deficiencies. A vitamin deficiency may cause the body to produce taraxein, which, in turn, causes hallucinogenic experiences and schizophrenia.

Some criminologists contend that food alergies can trigger criminal conduct. Certain food groups can, in some cases, cause perceptual distortions, which, in turn, can trigger violent and irrational behavior. There are two types of food allergies, fixed and cyclic. Cyclic allergies are the most common and are the most difficult to diagnose. Neuroallergy is an allergic condition that affects the body's central nervous system.

Hyperkinesis (hyperactvity) is seen as an antisocial form of behavior and is often associated with criminal behavior. The primary causes of hyperkinesis are vitamin B_3 dependency and hypoglycemia.

■ MATCHING KEY TERMS AND DEFINITIONS

Match each key term with the correct definition.

a. allergy
b. biochemical imbalance
c. cyclic food allergies
d. fixed food allergies
e. hyperkinesis

f. hypoglycemia
g. neuroallergy
h. nutrition
i. taraxein
j. vitamin

____ **1.** One of the causes of chemical imbalance.
____ **2.** Low blood sugar.
____ **3.** The substance that causes the body to convert epinephrine into toxic substances.
____ **4.** An unusual or excessive reaction of the body to a foreign substance.
____ **5.** The most common type of food allergy.
____ **6.** A reaction that occurs each time a particular food is eaten.
____ **7.** An allergic condition that affects the body's central nervous system.
____ **8.** Hyperactive behavior.
____ **9.** A deficiency of this substance has been blamed for violent and irrational behavior.
____ **10.** A condition that some researchers contend causes criminal behavior and is the direct result of imbalance in a person's biochemical balance.

■ DISCUSSION QUESTIONS

1. If poor nutrition were accepted as a major cause of criminal behavior, how would this fact change our crime prevention programs?
2. If criminal behavior is the result of poor nutrition, hypoglycemia, vitamin deficiency, and so on, should the offender be responsible for his or her behavior? How should the administration of justice be restructured?
3. If the premise of question 2 is correct, how do we change offenders' eating habits?
4. Do we need to train our probation officers, institutional personnel, and so on, regarding the treatment of nutrition problems?

Notes

1. See Alexander Schauss and C. Simonson, "A Critical Analysis of the Diets of Chronic Juvenile Offenders," *Journal of Orthomolecular Psychiatry*, vol. 8, 1979, pp. 222–226, 1949–1957.
2. Louis Berman, *The Glands Regulating Personality*. New York: Macmillan, 1921.
3. Kayla F. Bernheim and Richard R. J. Levine, *Schizophrenia*. New York: W. W. Norton, 1979, p. 17.
4. Leonard J. Hippchen, "The Need for a New Approach to the Delinquent-Criminal Problem," in Leonard J. Hippchen, ed., *Ecologic–Biochemical Approaches to Treatment of Delinquents and Criminals*. New York: Van Nostrand Reinhold, 1978, pp. 3–19.
5. Macklin Fleming, "A Short Course in the Causes of Crime," *Prosecutor's Brief*, May–June 1979, pp. 8–25.
6. E. M. Abrahamson and A. W. Pezet, *Body, Mind and Sugar*. New York: Avon Books, 1977, p. 113.
7. J. A. Yaryura-Tobias and F. Neiziroglu, "Violent Behavior, Brain Dysrhythmia, Glucose Dysfunction and New Syndrome," *Journal of Orthopsychiatry*, vol. 4, 1975, pp. 182–188.
8. Hippchen, 1978.
9. Gary H. Bachara and William R. Lamb, "Intervention with Juvenile Delinquents," in Hippchen, ed., 1978:352–388.
10. H. E. Kelly, "Biology and Crime," in F. H. Marsh and J. Katz, eds., *Biology, Crime and Ethics*. Cincinatti, Ohio: Anderson, 1985.
11. M. Virkkunen, "Reactive Hypoglycemic Tendency among Habitually Violent Offenders," *Neuropsychobiology*, vol. 8, 1982, pp. 35–40.
12. Kelly, 1985:192.
13. Carlton Frederick, *Psycho-Nutrition*. New York: Grosset & Dunlap, 1976, p. 99.
14. Hippchen, 1978:12.

15. Hippchen, 1978:14.

16. R. G. Heath et al., "Effect on Behavior of Humans with the Administration of Taraxein," *American Journal of Psychiatry*, vol. 114, 1957, pp. 14–24.

17. Kelly, 1985:190.

18. Bernheim and Levine, 1979:135–136.

19. Hippchen, 1978:15.

20. Kelly, 1985:191.

21. Fredericks, 1976:26.

22. Phillip L. Bonnet and Carl C. Pfeiffer, "Biochemical Diagnosis for Delinquent Behavior," in Hippchen, ed., 1978:183–205.

23. Ray C. Wunderlich, "Neuroallergy as a Contributing Factor to Social Misfits: Diagnosis and Treatment," in Hippchen, ed., 1978:229–253.

24. Wunderlich, 1978:241.

25. Wunderlich, 1978:249.

26. Glen Green, "Treatment of Penitentiary Inmates," in Hippchen, ed., 1978:269–283.

27. Hippchen, 1978:14.

28. Michelle Prince, Valerie Thompsen, and T. F. McLaughlin, "Hyperkinesis and Feingold's K-P Diet," *Corrective and Social Psychiatry and Journal of Behavior Technology Methods and Therapy*, vol. 34, no. 2, Apr. 1988, pp. 13–17.

29. C. K. Conners, *Food Additives and Hyperactive Children*. New York: Plenum Press, 1980.

30. Prince et al., 1988:14.

31. Russell Smith, "Alcoholism and Criminal Behavior," in Hippchen, ed., 1978:21–30.

32. Smith, 1978:27.

33. Bonnet and Pfeiffer, 1978:191.

PSYCHOLOGICAL THEORIES

Chapters 16 to 19 deal with the psychological theories of crime causation. Chapter 16 covers the Freudian theories of crime causation and the Freudian explanation of criminal behavior. In Chapters 17 to 19 we discuss four different categories of psychological theories of crime causation. There are numerous ways to classify psychological theories; however, when studying theories relating to the etiology of crime and criminals, it is practical to divide them into:

1. Emotional problem theories
2. Mental disorder theories
3. Sociopathic personality theories
4. Thinking pattern theories

The psychological crime causation theories have a common assumption that there is something wrong with the mind of the offender which causes him or her to commit crimes. Some mental disorder theorists contend that there may be organic problems with the offender's brain and therefore a discernible biological basis for criminal behavior exists. However, other mental disorder theorists indicate that a functional disorder causes the person to commit criminal acts. The emotional problem theorists indicate that the criminal is not a separate psychological type but rather has emotional problems similar to the emotional problems that any nonoffender may have. These emotional problems render the offender unable to cope, and hence he or she acts out criminally. Sociopathic personality theorists support the idea of the criminal as a unique personality type known as the "sociopath," "psychopath," or "antisocial personality." These terms are used interchangeably. Finally, there are the thinking pattern theorists, who contend that the criminal and/or delinquent has different thinking patterns and cognitive processes from those of nonoffenders and nondelinquents.

All of the psychological theories, however, assume that there is something wrong with the mind or mental faculties of the criminal that causes him or her to commit crimes. According to these theories, the cause of crime lies within the person. The criminal is not considered normal and is thought to be different from the rest of us. The cause of criminal behavior is, therefore, internal, not external. The theorists are not always clear, however, on just what causes the mind to be defective.

16

Psychological Theories of Crime Causation

CHAPTER HIGHLIGHTS

- The psychological theories of crime causation are largely the result of the work of Sigmund Freud in the early twentieth century.
- Freudian theorists view criminal and delinquent behavior as largely caused by guilt, unconscious conflicts, repression, inadequate personality development, traumatic developmental stages, and weak superego development.
- Standardized psychological tests tend to show differences between offenders and nonoffenders.

KEY TERMS

Anal Stage	Neophallic Stage
CPI	Oedipus Complex
Ego	Oral Stage
Electra Complex	Phallic Stage
Id	Pleasure Principle
Latency Stage	Reality Principle
MMPI	Superego

This chapter focuses on Sigmund Freud's contributions to psychological theories of crime causation. Although many of Freud's ideas have been discounted, he has been responsible for the spirit and impetus behind the psychological and psychiatric movements. Topics discussed in this chapter are as follows: (1) the development of the psychological theories, (2) how the psychological theories interface with criminology, (3) Freud's contributions to criminological theory, and (4) the psychoanalytic theory of criminal behavior.

■ THE PSYCHOLOGICAL APPROACH

The psychological approach developed from the fields of psychiatry and psychology in the early twentieth century and is based primarily on the works of Sigmund Freud (1856–1839) [1]. Psychological theories have had a dominant influence on the treatment and rehabilitation philosophy embraced by correctional systems in the United States. Psychological theories were also a major impetus in the growth of corrections and penology in the United States.

Criminology has been deficient, however, in adequately addressing the importance and significance of the psychological forces and personality factors in crime and delinquency. Gibbons has stated that most criminologists tend to berate psychological theories by attacking the theory and methodology advanced by the psychological community [2].

Most criminologists contend that there is a lack of evidence that psychological factors such as mental and emotional difficulties are important in criminal behavior [3]. There are many, however, who feel that psychological variables are important in understanding criminal behavior. A large proportion of criminal justice professionals consciously or unconsciously use some form of psychoanalytic theory in explaining criminality [4]. Inkeles stated that institutions are often influenced by personality and other psychological variables of persons who are found within them [5]. For example, researchers have contributed a great deal of prison violence to prisoners with volatile personalities. Sutherland and Cressey also are of the belief that psychological factors contribute to criminality [6]. They contended that mental

IN FOCUS

Allen Kearbey: Normal or Different?

On January 20, 1985, Allen Kearbey, a 14-year-old ninth-grader carried an automatic rifle and a revolver to school. When the high school principal asked him why, he shot and killed the principal. He also wounded three other people. He was described as quiet, inoffensive, and a loner.

Was he normal or different from other children his age?

Was his conduct the product of a rational choice to commit a crime, or was he a victim of his defective psychological makeup?

Did he have different thinking patterns?

Did he have an emotional disorder?

Was he sociopathic?

FIGURE 16–1

Law enforcement authorities unearth a buried moving van in which twenty-six children and their school bus driver had been held captive after their July 1976 abduction in California. Curt R. Bartol, *Criminal Behavior: A Psychosocial Approach,* © 1980, p. 301. Reprinted by permission of Prentice Hall, Inc., Englewood Cliffs, NJ.

retardation and psychoses are important causal factors in lawbreaking. James Q. Wilson and Richard Herrnstein also state [7]:

> People who break the law are often psychologically atypical. This is not to say that they are necessarily sick (although some are), or that atypicality of any sort characterizes every lawbreaker. Rather, the evidence says that populations of offenders differ statistically in various respects from populations of nonoffenders.

Thorton, Voigt, and Doerner cite studies that have identified personality traits most commonly associated with crime and delinquency [8]. Some of the common traits associated with crime and delinquency are maturity level, poor ability to conceptualize, poor ability to assume different roles, poor attachment to families, and poor ability to accept authority figures.

Most attempts to study offenders' psychological variables have involved the administration of psychological tests and personality inventories to determine whether offenders' scores are different from nonoffenders' scores. The results of these tests have been confusing, to say the least. As testing procedures became more sophisticated and standardized tests became more widely applied, results began to show personality and psychological differences between offenders and nonoffenders. Two tests that have been widely administered to offenders and nonoffenders and have discriminated between these groups over 90 percent of the time are the Minnesota Multiphasic Personality Inventory (MMPI) and the California Psychological Inventory (CPI) [9].

■ FREUD ON VIOLENCE

Sigmund Freud believed that aggression and violence have their roots in instinct [11]. According to him, violence is a response to thwarting the pleasure principle [12]. He developed the idea that each of us has a "death wish" that is a constant source of aggressive impulses and that this wish tries to reduce the organism to an inanimate state. The

FIGURE 16-2

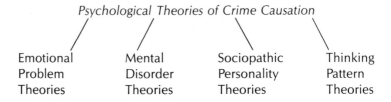

Psychological Theories of Crime Causation

Emotional Problem Theories | Mental Disorder Theories | Sociopathic Personality Theories | Thinking Pattern Theories

IN FOCUS

Sigmund Freud: The Person (1856–1939)

Freud was born in Freiberg, Moravia, on May 6, 1856 of Jewish parents. In his youth he was interested in philosophy and humanities. His parents impressed on him, however, the need to balance those interests with rigorous scientific training. He was a distinguished student at the University of Vienna, where he graduated in 1881 with a medical degree. From 1881 to 1885 he did pure research in physiology and was on the staff of the Vienna General Hospital. For the next two years, he worked with a leading French neurologist in Paris. From 1887 to 1902, he was in private practice, emphasizing neurology.

In 1902, Freud was appointed professor of neuropathology at the University of Vienna School of Medicine. He remained there until 1923, when he was forced to retire because of cancer in his jaw. During the remainder of his life, he worked incessantly on his research until his death in London in 1939. In 1938, he was forced to leave Vienna and escape to London when the Nazis took over Austria. He had an apparently normal home life, a happy marriage, and six children.

Sigmund Freud was one of the most controversial and influential persons of the twentieth century. He was a person of great industry and learning, and extraordinary eloquence. He was witty and expansive. He shrank, however, from those who opposed him. For the most part, he worked in isolation until about 1900. During the next ten years he gathered around him famous scholars in psychology and psychiatry, two of whom were Carl Jung and Alfred Adler. Later in life, he considered them bitter enemies [10].

In addition to Freud's contributions to psychology and criminology, which are discussed below, he had a profound influence on the literature of the period, as noted in the writings of Eugene O'Neill and Tennessee Williams. There are many popular misinterpretations of his writings, which people have used to justify strange behavior in everyday life. Although his observations and theories are widely disputed, it is clear that Freud has had a significant impact on our concept of human behavior.

death wish may be expressed directly, manifested indirectly as in hunting, or sublimated into sadomasochism. He also believed that "guilt" arising from the Oedipus conflict was the basis of criminal activity. (The phrase "Oedipus conflict" is taken from the name of a character in Greek mythology who kills his father and marries his mother.)

Freud contended that we have a hidden desire to act out behavior similar to that of Oedipus. The equivalent complex for girls is known as the Electra complex and is taken from a classic tragedy in Greek mythology. (*Note:* The Oedipus and Electra complexes are based on the Freudian premise that incest is a basic human desire.) The individual, feeling guilty about his or her Oedipus or Electra fantasy, seeks to punish himself or herself. The criminal, according to Freud, wants to be caught and punished to be relieved of his or her guilt. Accordingly, the criminal takes such foolish risks that he or she appears to be trying to get caught. Criminals therefore unconsciously project on the environment their need and desire to be punished. Criminals are, in fact, their own worst punishers [13]. As Freud stated in *The Ego and the Id* [14]:

> [I]t was a surprise to find that an increase in a sense of guilt can turn people into criminals. But it is undoubedly a fact. In many circumstances, especially youthful ones, it is possible to detect a very powerful sense of guilt which existed before the crime, and is therefore not its result but its motive.

Freudian Theory of Personality

Sigmund Freud focused on the pathological, not the healthy part of human beings. His emphasis was on the unconscious mental life of the individual. He believed that a great deal of human behavior was hereditary and predetermined. Freud was concerned with the elements that were significant in personality development. He focused on the individual's motivational factors, his or her efforts to resolve conflicts, and the unconscious aspects of the various forces behind behavior.

Freud's major contributions to psychology involve his theory of personality structure and his theory concerning human developmental stages. Well known to all are Freud's concepts of the id, ego, and superego. These concepts form the basis of personality. Also noteworthy are Freud's concepts of the oral, anal, phallic, latency, and neophallic or genital stages. These concepts are fundamental to understanding the Freudian explanation of crime and delinquency.

The id, according to Freud, was the primary, rash, impulsive part of the personality and was unconscious. It was governed by what Freud termed the "pleasure principle." The id was hedonistic and had no regard for responsibility and sensible things. The id consists of impulses and/or drives that are present at birth. The id impulses are not social and must be repressed or adapted so that they are socially acceptable. As a result, human beings experience a frustration of drives. The impulses or drives remain in the person's unconscious. The offender may be a person who has failed to keep his or her impulses in the unconscious, a person who is symbolically expressing repressed desires, or a person whose ego has become maladjusted [15].

The ego was considered to be the sensible and responsible part of the personality and was governed by what Freud termed the "reality principle." The ego appraises the external situation and then enables the person to make rational decisions. The ego is the objective, rational part of the personality. It is a barometer of the real world and allows the person to see his or her behavior according to others. It is the ego that represses the unacceptable social impulses and/or drives into the unconscious.

The superego is also termed the "conscience" and is unconscious. The superego is the part of the personality that allows a person to feel pride, shame, and/or guilt. The superego is often structured by our parents' attitudes and it incorporates the ideas of right and wrong as taught by our parents. The superego is the human being's moral faculty and it is largely responsible for making a person follow the moral codes of society. It sets moral and ethical standards. It evaluates thoughts and actions and is the primary socialization force for the human being.

Freudian Concept of Developmental Stages and Delinquent Behavior

The contribution of human developmental phases that Freud made is also important. The oral stage is the first stage with which a person has to deal in life. This stage occurs during infancy and the first year of life. According to Freud, the child enters the world as a criminal who is totally antisocial and laden with primitive urges. During this stage the infant is beset by a variety of oral urges, often satisfied by nursing. The infant's oral urges can be sadistic, cannibalistic, and antisocial.

The next stage of life, known as the anal stage, lasts until the child is about 3 years old. The child during this stage is usually stubborn, spiteful, and cruel. Children at this age sometimes seem to be motivated by a desire to hurt and destroy simply for the sake of the behavior. The phallic stage is the next stage to occur and genitals are a major focus, according to Freud. This stage generally occurs during early childhood and continues until approximately age 6. During this stage the child begins to develop strong erotic feelings toward the parent of the opposite sex and, at times, experiences strong feelings of jealousy and hostility toward the parent of the same sex (Oedipus complex in boys and Electra complex in girls). The Oedipus complex disappears at approximately age 6 because of internal prohibitions against incest and parricide. Boys also tend to develop fear of their fathers and fear of castration. These conflicts are often resolved by identifying with the parent of the same sex and unconsciously enjoying the parent of the opposite sex. Freud felt that these prohibitions were at the core of the superego.

By age 6 the child internalizes his or her image of its parents, and it is this image that controls the child's behavior internally just as his or her parents controlled the child's behavior in earlier years. Also internalized are the attitudes and feelings of the parents toward antisocial behavior. This becomes the core of the superego's control over the person. The next period is the latency period, which lasts from age 6 to puberty. It appears that no urges are present during the latency period. During this period the oral, anal, and phallic urges are dormant. However, right before puberty at approximately age 12 there is an reawakening of the impulses that were activated earlier in life. This is known as the neophallic or genital stage. The pre-teenager is again obsessed with his or her genitals, sex, oral urges, and anal urges.

Puberty and its attendant behavioral problems are viewed by the psychoanalytic theorists as a struggle between the newly resurrected oral, anal, and phallic urges and the superego. The superego's main role is to control the new urges [16].

Schoenfeld continues to point out that for the most part, the upsets of puberty, such as sudden enthusiasms, depressions, rebellions, self-indulgence, and moodiness, are symbolic of the struggle for control between the resurrected oral, anal, and phallic urges and the superego. The adolescent who is likely to commit delinquent or criminal acts is a person whose superego has criminal tendencies and does not oppose the antisocial instincts of early childhood. An example is an adolescent who has parents who do not respect the law. The adolescent's superego internalizes the attitudes and feelings of the parents. In such a case the superego does not exert control over the reactivated antisocial urges. This young person is simply doing what his or her early childhood impulses have instinctively told him or her to do.

Delinquent behavior may also occur in a youngster whose superego is rigid, prim, and proper. This child's superego is so offended by the reactivated urges that his or her superego becomes guilty. To deal with the overwhelming guilt, the youth commits crimes, with the unconscious aim of being caught and punished. Schoenfeld indicated that this would explain why certain criminals make it so easy for the police to apprehend them [17].

The essence of Schoenfeld's theory of juvenile delinquency is that the superego is weak, defective, or incomplete, and it cannot control the powerful resurgence of the adolescent's antisocial early childhood urges. Some of the factors that play a role in determining whether an adolescent's superego will be strong enough to empower him or her to resist the reactivation of early childhood antisocial impulses are parental affection and love, consistent discipline, and good parenting and child-rearing practices. In summary, Schoenfeld focused on the superego's role in controlling delinquent behavior.

There are other theorists who believe that juvenile delinquency arises from unresolved Oedipal complexes. For example, a boy hates or resents his father but is afraid to act against him, so he acts out against substitute targets and commits crime. Most psychoanalytic theorists take the position that criminality and delinquency are caused from conflict within the person, insecurity, inadequacy, inferiority, and unconscious motivation and conflict within the person [18].

Yablonski and Haskell summarize how psychoanalytic theory views the cause of criminal and delinquent behavior. They state:

1. Inability to control criminal drives (id) because of a deficiency in ego or superego development. Because of faulty development, the delinquent or criminal is believed to possess little capacity for repressing instinctual (criminal) impulses. The individual who is dominated by his id is consequently criminal.

2. Antisocial character formation resulting from a disturbed ego development. This occurs during the first three years of life.

3. An overdeveloped superego, which makes no provision for the satisfaction of the demands of the id. Offenders of this type are considered neurotic.

Franz Alexander, a disciple of Freud, in applying Freud's concepts to criminal behavior, contended that criminality is a part of human nature. He believed that the difference between a criminal and a "normal" person is that the normal person can control his or her criminal drives and find other socially acceptable outlets for them, whereas the criminal cannot [19]. Franz Alexander and Hugo Staub, in The Criminal, the Judge, and the Public, presented another Freudian view of crime and punishment [20]. They contended that every person is born criminal and would run rampant if his or her id were not restrained. Human beings enter the world totally unsocialized and criminal. This criminality lasts until the end of the latency period of development and until the Oedipus conflict is resolved. They also believe that unless the Oedipus compelx is resolved sucessfully, the person will act out criminally. Finally, they hold that the unconscious mind and the first rebellious act that a person commits in early childhood will serve as a prototype of criminal behavior later in life. Alexander and Staub focused their analysis on males.

Critique of Freud

Freud's theoretical superstructure is considered faulty by today's standards of scientific rigor. In addition, his theory and empirical observations were not always consistent. He is noted for his attempt to find hidden connections between apparently unrelated symptoms. Freudian explanations of the hidden connections are challenged in many cases because of lack of empirical evidence to support relationships. Another criticism of Freud and Freudian positions is that the language used is vague, unscientific, and nonempirical, and that Freudians use circular reasoning. They constantly cite the "unconscious mind" as the primary cause of odd behavior. Also, Freudian methodology does not lend itself to empirical verification. Only the patient or client knows the facts of a particular situation. In addition, Freud's ideas, with the exception of the Oedipus complex, were not supported in cross-cultural studies.

The Freudian position has also been criticized for its overemphasis on the sexual aspects of behavior and motivation and for underemphasizing the nonsexual aspects of behavior and motivation. Freud and the psychoanalysts have been attacked for not dealing adequately with the social factors affecting human behavior. They are accused of minimizing social factors and emphasizing instincts, drives, and biology. Psychoanalysts are also accused of overemphasizing the impact of early infancy experiences.

Freud's Contributions

Although Freud wrote no books or articles on crime or criminals per se, his contributions to the psychological theories of crime causation are great. He introduced the concept of repression, the means whereby threatening experiences are banished into the unconscious. He introduced the concept of the unconscious mind. He also believed that the instinctual drives were so strong that if a person were not able to integrate them satisfactorily into his or her personality, the drives would find expression by indirect means, such as deviant behavior or abnormal character traits. Drives could also reveal themselves in slips of the tongue (known as Freudian slips), dreams, and emotional reactions.

One important contribution was a demonstration of the fact that we need to study the mental life of the criminal as a whole and consider the impact of early experiences on later mental development. Accordingly, the adult criminal must be understood and treated in relation to the child that he or she has been.

An additional contribution is the realization that often the reasons for committing crimes may not be known to the criminal. Does this mean that as we trace the development of criminal behavior backward from the crime to the cause, we cannot rely on traditional causation concepts, and that retrospective approaches often produce erroneous results?

■ SUMMARY

There are many ways to classify the psychological theories of crime causation. Some of the theories emphasize emotional problems, mental disorders, sociopathy, and thinking patterns. The psychological theories have the common assumption that there is something wrong with the mind of the offender which causes him or her to commit crimes.

The psychological theories have had a dominant influence on the treatment and rehabilitation emphasis embraced by correctional personnel in the United States. Criminologists, however, are deficient in addressing adequately the role of psychological forces in crime and delinquency. Sophisticated standardized tests, such as the MMPI and the CPI, have shown differences in psychological and personality variables between offenders and nonoffenders.

Psychoanalytic theory dealing with crime and delinquency has evolved from the theories of Sigmund Freud. Among Freud's contributions are the concepts of unconscious mind, repression, instinctual drives and impulses, guilt, personality structure, and developmental stages.

■ MATCHING KEY TERMS AND DEFINITIONS

Match each key term with the correct definition.

a. anal stage

b. CPI

c. ego

d. Electra complex

e. id

f. latency stage

g. MMPI   k. phallic stage
h. neophallic stage   l. pleasure principle
i. Oedipus complex   m. reality principle
j. oral stage   n. superego

---- 1. The Minnesota Multiphasic Personality Inventory.
---- 2. The California Psychological Inventory.
---- 3. A theory that boys have a secret desire to kill their fathers and have sex with their mothers.
---- 4. A theory that girls have a secret desire to kill their mothers and have sex with their fathers.
---- 5. This part of the personality is primary, rash, and impulsive.
---- 6. This is the first human developmental stage that a person encounters.
---- 7. The sensible and responsible part of the personality.
---- 8. The part of the personality that allows a person to feel pride, shame, and/or guilt.
---- 9. The ego is governed by this principle.
---- 10. The id is governed by this principle.
---- 11. The stage of a person's life that lasts until the person is approximately 3 years old.
---- 12. At this stage in a person's life, the genitals are a major focus.
---- 13. The stage of a person's life that lasts from age 6 to puberty when all urges appear to be dormant.
---- 14. The stage of a person's life when all the oral, anal, and phallic urges begin again.

∎ DISCUSSION QUESTIONS

1. Explain the importance of Freud's work on the development of psychological crime causation theories.
2. What is the Freudian theory of crime and delinquency?
3. In what Freudian developmental stage is a person most likely to commit crimes? Why?
4. How are psychological theories applied by criminal justice professionals?
5. Describe how a Freudian would describe the personality of a criminal.

Notes

1. Sigmund Freud, *A General Introduction to Psychoanalysis*. New York: Boni & Liveright, 1920; and *Civilization and Its Discontents* (translated by Joan Riviere). Garden City, N.Y.: Doubleday, 1930.

2. Donald Gibbons, *The Criminological Enterprise*. Englewood Cliffs, N.J.: Prentice-Hall, 1979, p. 212.

3. Gibbons, 1979:214.

4. Edwin H. Sutherland and Donald Cressey, *Criminology*, 9th ed. Philadelphia: J. B. Lippincott, 1974, p. 168.

5. A. Inkeles, "Sociological Theory in Relation to Social Psychological Variables," in J. C. McKinney and E. A. Tiryakian, eds., *Theoretical Sociology*. New York: Appleton-Century-Crofts, 1970.

6. Sutherland and Cressey, 1974:170.

7. James Q. Wilson and Richard J. Herrnstein, *Crime and Human Nature: The Definitive Study of the Causes of Crime*. New York: Simon and Schuster, 1985, p. 173.

8. William Thorton, Lydia Voight, and William Doerner, *Delinquency in Justice*, 2nd ed. New York: Random House, 1987, p. 115.

9. Wilson and Herrnstein, 1985:185–186.

10. G. F. M. Russell and L. Hersov, *Handbook of Psychiatry*, Vol. 4, *The Neuroses and Personality Disorders*. Cambridge: Cambridge University Press, 1983, p. 78.

11. Freud, 1930.

12. Freud, 1920.

13. S. Yochelson and S. E. Samenow, *The Criminal Personality*. Northvale, N.J.: Jason Aronson, 1976, pp. 80–82.

14. Reported in Yochelson and Samenow, 1976:81.

15. Sutherland and Cressey, 1974:169.

16. C. G. Schoenfeld, "A Psychoanalytic Theory of Juvenile Delinquency," in E. Peoples, ed., *Correctional Casework and Counseling*. Pacific Palisades, Calif.: Goodyear, 1975, p. 22.

17. Schoenfeld, 1975:23.

18. L. Yablonski and M. R. Haskell, *Juvenile Delinquency*. New York: Harper & Row, 1988, p. 355.

19. Yochelson and Samenow, 1976, p. 81.

20. F. Alexander and H. Staub, *The Criminal, the Judge, and the Public*. New York: Free Press, 1956.

17

Emotional Problem and Mental Disorder Theories

CHAPTER HIGHLIGHTS

- Emotional problem theories assume that the offender is unable to cope with life situations.
- Emotional problems that render the offender unable to cope can spring from everyday-life situations.
- The way an offender perceives how he or she looks can create emotional problems.
- There is evidence that offenders are seen as less attractive than nonoffenders.
- There is evidence that attractive people are given more lenient punishments than those given to unattractive people.
- There is evidence that for some offenders, plastic surgery has reduced recidivism.
- The mental disorder theories emphasize the neuroses, psychoses, and personality disorders.
- Mental disorders can be organic or functional.
- There are several neuroses that have been linked with deviant, delinquent, and/or criminal behavior.
- The two main psychoses that have been linked with deviant, delinquent, and/or criminal behavior are schizophrenia and paranoia.
- Few offenders are classified as psychotic upon being admitted to jails and prisons.
- Many criminologists believe that the more bizarre criminal offenses are committed by psychotics.

KEY TERMS

Acting Out

Anxiety

Coping Mechanisms

Depression

Explosive Disorder

Histrionic Behavior

Hysteria

Impulse Disorder

Kleptomania

Mental Disorder

Neurasthenia

Neurosis

Obsessive-Compulsive Behavior

Paranoia

Pathology

Phobia

Psychosis

Pyromania

Schizophrenia

In this chapter we discuss both the emotional problem theories and the psychological disorder theories. The emotional problem theories view the offender as having the same psychological makeup as the nonoffender. There is no disease or psychological disorder present in the offender. The offender does not cope well with his or her environment, and this creates frustration that results in crime. The mental disorder theories assume that the offender has a disorder or pathology that makes the offender different in psychological makeup from the nonoffender.

■ EMOTIONAL PROBLEM THEORIES

The emotional problem theories assume that the lawbreaker does not have a gross pathology that causes him or her to commit crimes but rather, he or she commits crimes because of everyday emotional problems that render him or her unable to cope. Instead of possessing a gross pathology, the offender is responding to very subtle psychological factors that make him or her unable to function normally. The offender becomes unable to cope. As a result of the offender's inability to cope, he or she acts out criminally. These theorists therefore see the offender as being normal in psychological makeup. Offenders are not

FIGURE 17–1
**Emotional problems
can be devastating.**
Courtesy of Laima Druskis.

psychotic, neurotic, or sociopathic. They are normal human beings whose coping skills have deteriorated. If offenders commit crimes as a result of having emotional problems that cause them to be ineffectual copers, any human being who was not coping adequately could become a criminal. Emotional problems could spring from any number of events: relationships, crises, finances, employment, sickness, self-concept, and so on. The criminal is not different in psychological orientation from the noncriminal, and after the offender's coping mechanism is functioning again, the person is not likely to commit crimes.

The way a person perceives how he or she looks can create emotional problems, especially if the person feels bad about how he or she looks. We have chosen to present selected research that deals with attractiveness and criminality to illustrate the emotional problem theories.

■ ATTRACTIVENESS AND CRIMINALITY

In today's society, physical beauty and attractiveness are given a high premium. In the United States approximately 100,000 people per year pay impressive amounts of money for elective reconstructive and plastic surgery. Why? People want to look better and feel better about themselves. The way a person looks to others may affect his or her self-concept. A number of researchers have indicated that physically attractive people benefit from their looks in a number of ways. Attractive people are liked better and are seen as having more socially desirable traits and as having more potential for happiness than are physically unattractive people [1]. A number of studies have shown that physically attractive people possess an advantage over physically unattractive people. Dion, Berscheid, and Walster have indicated that a stereotype exists that attractive people are assumed to have more socially desirable personalities, will be happier, and will attract the world's material benefits [2]. Even at an early age, attractiveness appears to have benefits. Dion found that the attractiveness of a child who misbehaves influences the adult's perception of him or her. How a child looks also influences how the adult sees the misbehavior (i.e., whether the offense is seen as mild or severe). Accordingly, an attractive and unattractive child can engage in the same misdeed and the attractive child's transgression will be viewed as less undesirable than will the unattractive child's transgression. Such findings could have an impact on children's self-concepts.

There have been several studies that have dealt with offenders and physical attractiveness. Bartol noted that inmates in prison are seen as physically unattractive by correctional personnel [3]. Monahan noted the following [4]:

> Even social workers accustomed to deal with all types often find it difficult to think of a normal, pretty girl as being guilty of a crime. Most people, for some inexplicable reason, think of crime in terms of abnormality in appearance, and I must say that beautiful women are not often convicted.

Sigall and Ostrove conducted a study where they attempted to determine what effects attractiveness of a criminal defendant might have on juror's decision making. They found that physically attractive people had an advantage over physically unattractive people. Simulated jurors were more lenient on attractive criminals than on unattractive ones [5].

Another study took place at New York's Rikers Island on inmates who had various disfigurements. The inmates who were selected for plastic surgery had obvious disfigurements, such as protruding ears, broken noses, skin tracks, and tatoos. The researchers screened the inmate candidates closely and gave them counseling. There were 425 male inmates, mostly addicts, who took part in the study. The inmates were assigned to one of four groups: (1) surgery and social and vocational services, (2) surgery, (3) no surgery but social and vocational services, and (4) no treatment. Groups 3 and 4 did not receive plastic surgery. Follow-up occurred on the inmates approximately nine months after release from prison. If an offender was convicted of a new crime or returned to prison during the time he was followed up, he was considered a recidivist. It was found that the nonaddict group benefited the most from plastic surgery, especially those offenders who had major facial disfigurements. Addicts seemed to benefit more from vocational and psychological services than from plastic surgery [6].

■ MENTAL DISORDER THEORIES

The mental disorder theories explain criminal behavior by using certain diagnostic categories, such as psychosis, neurosis, and personality disorders. The sociopathic personality is discussed in Chapter 18. The impulse and explosive personality disorders are discussed in this chapter. The *Diagnostic and Statistical Manual of Mental Disorders* (DSM), published by the American Psychiatric Association, contains the psychiatric profession's diagnostic labels and the types of behavior

FIGURE 17–2

Are persons with emotional problems more inclined to frequent these places?

Courtesy of Mike Kagan/ Monkmeyer Press

associated with mental disorders. However, the label "mental disorder" does not mean that the person behaves in an exactly predictable pattern. In addition, many disturbed people will exhibit overlapping behaviors found in several diagnostic categories. There are many categories of neuroses and psychoses. Generally speaking, neuroses are disorders that do not manifest themselves by divorcing the person from reality, whereas psychoses are disorders that do divorce the person from reality.

There are two general types of mental disorders. First, there are the organic disorders, which have an identifiable physiological cause, such as head injuries that leave the mind blank, senility, Parkinson's disease, Huntington's chorea, and Alzheimer's disease. Organic disorders refer to brain pathologies. Second, there are the functional disorders, which are characterized by strange or bizarre behavior that cannot be traced to any known organic disease. Functional disorders are characterized by no apparent brain pathology that can be identified by existing techniques. (Note: This does not mean that brain pathologies do not exist but currently we have no technology for detecting such pathologies.) Examples of functional disorders would be people with no apparent brain pathologies who hear voices that others do not hear or who see things that others do not see. In other words, a person's cognitive, perceptual, and memory functions do not operate normally.

Bartol has summarized the research dealing with psychoses and neuroses and criminal behavior [7]:

> The problem here is the popular tendency to view deviant, seemingly irrational behavior as psychologically abnormal behavior. The public confuses socially deviant behavior with "mental illness," and in this sense, the psychotics, the schizophrenics, and the personality disordered are guilty by association. Unpredictable, irrational, bizarre, disoriented people are frightening and, thus, dangerous. It is important to note, however, that murderers and violent offenders, although socially deviant, are not necessarily psychotic or "crazy." In fact, the research literature is highly consistent in pointing out that psychotic or severely disturbed individuals are no more likely to commit serious crimes against others than the general population. . . .

Bartol continues his discussion with a summary of research conducted by various other researchers who have concluded that psychotics are no more likely to commit crime than the general population in the United States and in Germany. It must also be noted that if a criminal is psychotic, it does not suggest that his or her particular criminal behavior was caused by his or her psychosis. However, Bartol states: "It is possible, however, as some clinicians believe, that although the incidence rate of violent offenses among psychotic people is about equivalent to that found in the general population, the more bizarre violent offenses are committed by psychotics." There is a tendency for criminal justice officials to label antisocial behavior as mental disorders when the offenders are not mentally disordered. It is difficult to determine the type and quantity of mental disorders that exist among offenders [8].

Selected neuroses, psychoses, and impulse disorders are described below. The purposes of the remainder of this chapter are (1) to describe and explain the popular types of mental disorders that have been related to criminality, and (2) to summarize the research relating criminality to neuroses, psychoses, and impulsive behavior.

The concept of neurosis was popular during the early part of the twentieth century and it has generally been referred to hysteria and neurasthenia. Some of the more common neuroses are anxiety, obsessive/impulsive behavior, hysteria, phobias, and depression. Some of the more common psychoses are schizophrenia and paranoia. Some of the more common impulse disorders are kleptomania, pyromania, and explosive behavior.

Mental disorders have been studied for many years but there is still much disagreement regarding definitions, classifications, causes, methods of identification, diagnoses, and treatment. There is also difficulty in determining the extent of the disorders in the general population and the criminal population. Therefore, any conclusions should be made with caution.

▌ NEUROSES

Neurosis is a common type of mental disorder used to explain criminal behavior. The word "neurosis" was first used to cover a class of diseases that referred to "affections of the nervous system" [9]. (Note: Neuroses have no demonstrable organic cause. This does not mean that organic causes do not exist, only that we lack the means to identify them.) Neurotic behaviors are behaviors that do not grossly violate social norms or represent severely disorganized personalities. Most neurotics are aware of their problems and may not seek professional help. Neurotics, for the most part, do not require hospitalization but are guilty, unhappy, anxious people. Several of the more common neuroses offered as explanation for criminal or delinquent behavior are as follows:

1. *Neurasthenia.* This is a condition of weakened nerves. This condition manifests itself in fatigue and nervousness and sometimes in physical symptoms such as pain. It has also been called an American disease, brought about by rapid urbanization [10]. The term was originated by Beard in 1880 and was generally used to describe an irritable weakness. Today the term refers to nonspecific disorders in which exhaustion is a prominent feature.

2. *Anxiety.* This neurosis is also known as "anxiety state" or "anxiety reaction." This condition manifests itself in the person feeling anxious, fearful anticipation or apprehension. The person may be irritable; have chronic tension, worry, poor concentration, and overreaction to noise; and/or feel restless. For example, a person who feels his or her heart beating rapidly whenever he or she is anxious may believe it to be the onset of a heart attack [11]. Sometimes the anxiety manifests itself in somatic symptoms such as hyperventilation and difficulty in falling asleep. Generally, anxiety neuroses arise when there is unusual stress in a person's life. Both offenders and well-adjusted, law-abiding people may experience anxiety neurosis.

3. *Obsessive-compulsive behavior.* Obsessions are unwanted, repetitive, irresistible thoughts or urges. Generally, the person knows that they are senseless, but he or she is unable to make them go away. Compulsions are stereotyped repetitive behaviors that are thought to produce or prevent something that is thought to be magically connected to the behavior [12]. People who suffer from this neurosis have unwanted, intrusive repetitive thoughts and/or behaviors. Obsessional behaviors are sometimes called compulsions.

4. *Hysteria.* Hysteria has two forms: true hysteria and histrionic behavior [13]. Hysterics can be defined as morbid or senseless emotionalism and is characterized by emotional frenzy and sometimes violent emotional outbreaks. Hysteria is manifested differently in men and women [14]. Female hysterics are generally characterized as relating easily to others and as keeping warm and long-term relationships. They tend to be highly dramatic and prone to emotional crises. They are usually extroverted, outgoing, and involved with others. Male hysterics also tend to be dramatic emotionally but are more prone to temper tantrums and infantile behavior when involved intimately.

Histrionic women tend to be self-centered and self-indulgent. They tend to be clingy, dependent, and to form immature involvements. They overidentify with others and project unrealistic, fantasized intentions onto others. Male histrionics tend to have poor control over their impulses. They tend to be manipulative, severely promiscuous, and antisocial [15].

5. *Phobia.* Phobias are generally called exaggerated fears of things that normal people fear to some degree, and fears of things that ordinary people do not fear. Some examples would be the fear of spiders, snakes, flying, guns, knives, stores, theaters, and so on.

6. *Depression.* People who suffer from depressive neuroses generally have feelings of pain, hurt, unpleasantness, sadness, dejection, self-reproach, helplessness, despair, boredom, pessimism, and rejection. When these feelings become pervasive and affect all aspects of a person's life, depression is said to occur. This neurosis is characterized by more than occasional "blue" feelings. Depression is a depressed mood that occurs in people who have difficulty dealing with anger, a tendency toward self-reproach, excessively high expectations, and a need for total positive regard of others to maintain self-esteem [16].

In conclusion, there are a variety of different neuroses with a myriad of different symptoms. The neuroses have been related to criminal acts and/or criminal tendencies. Most people are neurotic and most people are not criminals. However, there are those whose neuroses drive them to commit criminal acts.

■ PSYCHOSES

Psychosis is a common category of mental disorder used to explain criminal behavior. Note that psychoses can be functional and/or organic. Psychotic people loose contact with reality and have difficulty distinguishing reality from fantasy. They often have severe breakdowns in their ability to communicate. Also, many psychotics become isolated from others. Only a small percentage of the persons who are classified as psychotic are dangerous, and many are not hospitalized [17]. Sutherland and Cressey suggest that of prisoners sent to state prison, not more than 5 percent are diagnosed as psychotic, and in many institutions less than 1 percent are diagnosed as psychotic. They also show that offenders admitted to jails and houses of correction have a slightly higher rate of psychoses than those admitted to prisons, but the rate is rarely higher than 5 percent and is usually 2 percent. Usually, the offenders in jails and houses of correction have alcoholic psychoses, from which they may quickly recovery.

In the *Diagnostic and Statistical Manual of Mental Disorders*, psychoses are subdivided into several types of schizophrenia, severe mood disorders, and several types of paranoia. Selected common types of psychoses used to explain criminality and delinquency and their definitions are described below.

1. *Schizophrenia.* To be identified as schizophrenic, a person must have delusions or hallucinations or a clear-cut thought disorder. The condition must persist for at least two weeks. Schizophrenia characteristically develops in adolescence or early adulthood. The delusions that a person experiences can be varied. Examples include a person who feels that police cars are following him or her and a person who feels that his or her skin is turned inside out. Hallucinations experienced by schizophrenics can be equally varied. Some people hear voices that others cannot hear. Some may see or taste things that others do not. Some people may see things that others do not see. Sometimes schizophrenics are not logical in their thoughts, as manifested by their language usage. Generally, schizophrenics' behaviors are odd and bizarre. Most of the time the person withdraws from contact with others [18]. It should also be noted that schizophrenia does not always have clear symptoms and often lacks a demonstrable organic origin.

2. *Paranoia.* This term is derived from the Greek and is roughly translated to mean "a mind beside itself." Common lay definitions of the term include suspiciousness and a feeling that others are against oneself or that one is being persecuted. It is also used to refer to psychotic delusions. Diagnostic categories for paranoia are numerous. Generally speaking, paranoid disorders are psychoses characterized by delusions, which are incorrect or unreasonable ideas and are seen as absolute truth by the paranoid. In the paranoid's mind the delusional system is firm and is accompanied by clear and orderly thinking. Paranoid persons can generally give clear, rational, and distinct reasons for his or her thoughts. The paranoid is difficult to treat because he or she is often suspicious and hostile [19].

■ IMPULSE DISORDERS

Impulse disorders are sudden, explosive, and driven to action. They are considered personality disorders, like the sociopathic personality disorder discussed in Chapter 16. The person who has an impulse disorder does not necessarily lose touch with reality or lose communication, and the person does not necessarily become isolated from others. The following are the common impulse disorders that are used to explain some types of antisocial behavior.

1. *Kleptomania.* This impulse disorder has been called compulsive thievery. Generally, kleptomaniacs steal things that are not for immediate use or monetary gain. Kleptomaniacs have great tension before stealing. They have a sense of pleasure or relief during the theft. The theft is done without planning or assistance from others. Frosche states: "Kleptomania must be distinguished from ordinary stealing. . . . Most shoplifters are not kleptomaniacs" [20]. The disorder tends to be more common in women than in men. Female kleptomaniacs tend to be middle-aged, married, and professional. Frosche also cites a study by Bradford and Balmaceda dealing with fifty shoplifters. They found only two kleptomaniacs in their study. Out of the total shoplifter population, it is estimated that between 3.8 and 8 percent are kleptomaniacs [21].

2. *Pyromania*. This impulse disorder manifests itself in an irresistible impulse to burn, with no other motive than to set fires. The person cannot control impulses to set fires. Pyromaniacs commit arson but are different from other types of nonpsychologically motivated fire-setters, who are motivated by profit. It has been estimated that as many as 40 percent of fire-setters may be pyromaniacs, but recent investigations show that pyromania may be a rare condition. Lewis and Yarnell studied 1584 fire-setters and only found 50 true pyromaniacs [22].

3. *Explosive disorder*. This disorder is identified by sudden assaultive or other destructive behavior that occurs in a person who otherwise shows good control. Generally, people feel that they are impelled to such outbursts and are surprised at them. If the consequences are negative, people usually feel regret. According to Frosche, these disorders are more common in men than women and generally develop in a person's twenties and thirties. Frosche also suggests that men with this disorder generally end up in correctional institutions and women end up in mental health facilities [23].

∎ SUMMARY

The emotional problem theories view the offender as having the same psychological makeup as the nonoffender. The offender is not seen as having a psychological disorder; rather, he or she is seen as not being able to cope with his or her environment. The inability to cope then results in frustration and criminal behavior. Many things can cause emotional problems. Some examples of common causes of emotional problems are relationships, crises, finances, employment, lack of employment, sickness, and self-concept. Once emotional problems are resolved and the offender is coping again, criminality is not likely to occur. As illustrations of the emotional problem theories, attractiveness and criminality were discussed.

The mental disorder theories explain criminal behavior by using the diagnostic categories of psychosis, neurosis, and personality disorder. It is generally held that neurotic disorders do not manifest themselves by divorcing a person from reality. Organic disorders are dis-

The Case of John Hinckley

On March 30, 1981, John W. Hinckley, Jr., shot and wounded President Ronald Reagan as the president was walking to his limousine at the Hilton Hotel in Washington, D.C. Hinckley's shots hit three other people, including press secretary James Brady, who was gravely injured by a wound in the head. The shooting was observed by many eyewitnesses and also by millions of others on television. Hinckley was immediately apprehended by federal law enforcement officials. There was no question that Hinckley was the one doing the shooting.

Hinckley was charged with thirteen crimes. His trial, which started on May 4, 1982, lasted seven weeks. The transcript of the trial extends to 7342 pages, most of which are devoted to testimony on Hinckley's primary defense: that at the time of his conduct he was legally insane. Of June 21, after three days' deliberation, the jury returned a verdict of not guilty by reason of insanity. This verdict extended to each of the thirteen crimes that Hinckley was accused of committing. Hinckley was then committed to Saint Elizabeth's Hospital.

Low, Jefferies, and Bonnie described the public reaction to the acquittal as follows [24]:

> The general reaction to Hinckley's acquittal was outrage and disbelief. Many people could not understand how Hinckley could be found "not guilty"—and could escape punishment—for a planned assassination attempt resulting in serious injury to three people. This issue was fully ventilated in the press and remains the subject of continuing debate.

The experts who evaluated Hinckley agreed that Hinckley was psychotic at the time that he committed his offense and was said to be schizophrenic. The experts did not agree on the precise diagnosis, however. As noted in Chapter 4, the "insanity" defense is based on the concept of "free will." The inability to reason, in most cases, is considered the result of a mental disorder. Until the 1980s the insanity defense was rarely invoked and even more rarely successful. In the 1980s, with the advancement of theories regarding mental disorders, insanity pleas have increased sixfold [25].

To what factors besides the advancement of mental disorder theories do you attribute the increased use of insanity pleas in the 1980s?

orders that have identifiable physiological causes; functional disorders are disorders that cannot be traced to an identifiable physical basis. There is evidence that the most bizarre violent offenses are committed by psychotics. However, to date, it is difficult to determine the types and quantity of mental disorders that exist among offenders. Therefore, any conclusions should be made with caution.

Of the neuroses, neurasthenia, anxiety, obsessive-compulsive behavior, hysteria, phobia, and depression have been related to criminal acts and or criminal tendencies. Of the psychoses, schizophrenia and paranoia have been related to criminal acts. Of the impulsive disorders, kleptomania, pyromania, and explosive disorder have been linked to criminal behavior.

■ MATCHING KEY TERMS AND DEFINITIONS

Match each key term with the correct definition.

a. acting out

b. anxiety

c. coping mechanisms

d. depression

e. explosive disorder

f. histrionic behavior

g. hysteria

h. impulse disorder

i. kleptomania

j. mental disorder

k. neurasthenia

l. neurosis

m. obsessive-compulsive behavior

n. paranoia

o. pathology

p. phobia

q. psychosis

r. pyromania

s. schizophrenia

___ 1. An impulse disorder identified by sudden, assaultive, destructive behavior.

___ 2. An impulse disorder that manifests itself in an irresistible impulse to burn objects.

___ 3. A personality disorder that is sudden and driven to action.

___ 4. A term derived from the Greek that means "a mind beside itself."

___ 5. A mental disorder manifested by delusions, hallucinations, or a thought disorder.

___ 6. A mood precipitated by those who have difficulty in dealing with anger and have a tendency toward self-reproach and high expectations, manifested by pain, hurt, and unhappiness.

___ 7. Exaggerated fears of objects, animals, people, and situations.

___ 8. Affected, dramatic, theatrical behavior.

___ 9. Unwanted, repetitive, irresistible thoughts or urges.

___ 10. A condition that manifests itself in fearful anticipation and/or apprehension.

___ 11. A condition that manifests itself in fatigue and nervousness.

___ 12. A psychosis, neurosis, and/or impulse disorder.

___ 13. A mental disorder that does not grossly violate social norms.

___ 14. A mental disorder that manifests itself in a loss of reality.

___ 15. A psychological term that refers to behaving in ways that are not characteristic for the person.

___ 16. A term that refers to what enables a person to function normally.

___ 17. The study of diseases.

___ 18. A morbid or senseless emotionalism characterized by emotional frenzy and possible violent emotional outbreaks.

___ 19. An impulse disorder that manifests itself in an irresistible impulse to take things.

■ DISCUSSION QUESTIONS

1. What are differences and similarities among psychoses, neuroses, and impulse disorders?

2. How should psychotic and neurotic offenders be handled by the U.S. criminal justice system?

3. What are some of the problems involved in using psychosis as an explanation of criminal conduct?

4. What are the relationships that exist between crime and mental disorders?

5. How does attractiveness or unattractiveness cause a person to become criminal?

6. What type of emotional problems would cause a person to commit criminal acts?

Notes

1. H. Sigall and N. Ostrove. "Physical Attractiveness and Jury Decisions," in L. Savitz and N. Johnson, eds., *Justice and Corrections*, New York: Wiley, 1978, p. 322; and S. L. Halleck, *Psychiatry and the Dilemmas of Crime: A Study of Causes, Punishment and Treatment*. New York: Harper & Row, 1967.

2. K. Dion, E. Berscheid, and E. Walster, "What Is Beautiful Is Good," *Journal of Personality and Social Psychology*, vol. 24, 1972, pp. 285–290; and K. Dion, "Physical Attractiveness and Evaluations of Children's Transgressions," *Journal of Personality and Social Psychology*, vol. 24, 1972, pp. 207–213.

3. C. R. Bartol, *Criminal Behavior: A Psychosocial Approach*, Englewood Cliffs, N.J.: Prentice-Hall, 1980, p. 125.

4. F. Monahan, *Women in Crime*. New York: Washburn, 1941, p. 103.

5. Sigall and Ostrove, 1987.

6. R. L. Kurtzberg, W. Mandell, M. Levin, H. Safer, D. S. Lipton, and M. Shuster, "Plastic Surgery on Offenders," in Savitz and Johnson, 1978:679–700.

7. Bartol, 1980:157.

8. Bartol, 1980:159.

9. A. M. Cooper, A. J. Frances, and M. H. Sacks, *The Personality Disorders and Neuroses*, Vol. 1. New York: Basic Books, 1986; p. 317.

10. J. E. Helzer and S. B. Guze, *Psychoses, Affective Disorders, and Dementia*, Vol. 12. New York: Basic Books, 1986, p. 5.

11. G. F. M. Russell and L. Herzov, eds., *Handbook of Psychiatry*, Vol. 4, *The Neuroses and Personality Disorders*. Cambridge, Cambridge University Press, 1983, p. 213.

12. K. M. Shear and W. A. Frosch, "Obsessive-Compulsive Disorder," In Cooper et al., 1986:353.

13. O. F. Kernberg, "Hysterical and Histrionic Personality Disorders." in Cooper et al., 1986.

14. Cooper et al., 1986:231–241.

15. Cooper et al., 1986:235.

16. M. H. Sacks, "Introduction to the Neuroses," in Cooper et al., 1986:399.

17. Edwin H. Sutherland and D. R. Cressey, *Criminology*, 9th ed. Philadelphia: J. B. Lippincott, 1974, p. 155.

18. R. E. Kendell, "Schizophrenia: Clinical Features," in J. E. Helzer and S. B. Guze, *Psychoses, Affective Disorders, and Dementia*, Vol. 2. New York: Basic Books, 1986, pp. 25–44.

19. N. Retterstol, "Paranoid Disorders," in Helzer and Guze, 1986:245–251.

20. Cooper et al., 1986:278.

21. W. K. Frosche, James P. Frosche, and John Frosche, "The Impulse Disorders," in Cooper et al., 1986:278.

22. Frosche et al., 1986:279; and Nolan Lewis and Helen Yarnell, *Pathological Firesetting*, New York: Nervous and Mental Disease Monographs, 1951.

23. Frosche et al., 1986:279–280.

24. P. W. Low, J. C. Jefferies, and R. J. Bonnie, *The Trial of John W. Hinckley, Jr.: A Case Study in the Insanity Defense*. New York: Foundation Press, 1986, p. 68.

25. Bennett H. Beach, "Picking between Mad and Bad," *Time*, Oct. 12, 1981, p. 68.

18

Sociopathic Personality Theories

CHAPTER HIGHLIGHTS

- According to the sociopathic personality theorists, the sociopath does not have a psychological disorder but rather, a unique personality structure.
- There are several labels for the sociopathic personality. Psychopath and antisocial personality are two of the more popular labels.
- There is evidence of a positive correlation between sociopathy and criminal behavior.
- Sociopathic personality structures can be identified in criminal and non-criminal populations.
- Sociopathic personalities are identified by many traits and characteristics.
- All sociopathic traits and characteristics need not be present and manifested for a person to be a sociopath.
- There is no consensus about the cause of sociopathy. Some believe it to be caused by biology. Others believe it to be caused by faulty personal development. Still others believe it to be caused by sociological factors.
- Contemporary research on the cause of sociopathy focuses on brain wave patterns and central nervous system deficits.
- Selected research reveals that at roughly age 40 or 50, many sociopathic personality characteristics go into remission.
- Sociopathy is difficult to treat successfully.
- Some researchers believe that sociopathy causes criminality, and others think that criminality contributes to the sociopathic personality.

KEY TERMS

Antisocial Personality	Disorganized Slum Neighborhood
Autonomic Nervous System	EEG
Core Sociopath	Egocentricity

Emotional Isolation   Psychopath
Hostility   Sociopath
Impulsive Behavior   Violent Gang Structure

Some theorists assume that criminal and/or delinquent behavior is the result of a particular personality structure known as the "sociopathic personality." The terms "sociopathy," "psychopathy," and "antisocial personality" are interchangeable and refer to the same personality disorder. We have chosen to use the term "sociopath" because of its descriptive quality. The term "antisocial personality" is ambiguous and bland, and the term "psychopath" tends to conjure images of a crazed, psychotic person with glassy eyes, an imagery that is totally misleading. Other older, medical labels for the personality disorder are "psychopathic inferiority," "moral imbecility," "semantic dementia moral mania," and "moral insanity." The most current term for the personality disorder is "antisocial personality" [1]. Some criminological theories and empirical studies suggest a connection between criminal behavior and sociopathy.

In this chapter we (1) describe the theory of sociopathy, (2) examine the research on sociopathy and criminal behavior, and (3) discuss how some predispositional patterns of personality structure may contribute to certain types of criminal behavior.

■ THE THEORY OF SOCIOPATHY

The term "sociopathy" usually refers to a pattern of behavior exhibited alike by many offenders and nonoffenders. Some theorists believe that the sociopath is mentally ill; however, others do not. The problem is caused in part because some persons with sociopathic personalities do not engage in criminal behavior, and others, who are not sociopathic, do engage in criminal activity. Wilson and Herrnstein state: "Psychopathy only overlaps with criminality; it is not identical with it. If for no other reason than the vagaries of the criminal justice system, there would be many non-psychopathic offenders and many psychopathic non-offenders" [2].

314

IN FOCUS

L.A. Gangs: A Home For Sociopathic Youths?

Yablonski concluded that youths who were more likely to join violent gangs were youths from disorganized slum communities who had defective socialization because of "sociopathic" personalities [4]. He stated that the inability to function in normal social structures, lack of empathy and guilt for his destructive actions, and the lack of social conscience toward others are dominant personality characteristics of violent gang members.

Does this help explain the recent violent gang activity in Los Angeles?

Another problem exists in attempting to diagnose the sociopathic personality disorder. The method of diagnosing the sociopath is not standardized or objective. As in most diagnoses, the person making the diagnosis is the one who decides whether or not a particular person is sociopathic. It is often the case that the diagnostician's preconceptions about sociopathy will determine whether the person in question will be labeled as sociopathic. It is not easy to define or identify a sociopath, and as a result, the label can be applied to almost anyone. Sometimes people will exhibit sociopathic symptoms while under great stress, and after the stress is reduced, the symptoms will diminish and/or disappear. Is such a person a sociopath? Can sociopathy come and go intermittently?

As a result of the difficulty in defining and labeling sociopathy and the vagueness of the term, the concept is often called a "wastebasket category." Such a category is a convenient place to toss otherwise inexplicable criminal behavior [3].

■ SYMPTOMS OF SOCIOPATHIC PERSONALITY

Hervey Cleckley, in *The Mask of Sanity*, was one of the first persons to describe the pivotal characteristics of the sociopath. He was also one of the first people to acknowledge sociopathy as a serious illness. According to Hervey Cleckley and H. G. Gough, the sociopathic personality is identified by many characteristics or symptoms [5]:

1. *Egocentricity.* The sociopath is self-centered and "me" oriented. His or her world is himself or herself. The goal in any interaction is to serve only himself or herself. The sociopath seeks immediate pleasure for himself or herself and is absorbed in his or her own needs all the time. An example of this would be the popular television character, J. R. Ewing in "Dallas."

2. *Asocial behavior.* The sociopath is often a loner. He or she behaves without regard for social norms. He or she does what he or she wants. McCord and McCord state the following [6]:

> Society cannot ignore the psychopath, for his behavior is dangerously disruptive. He may be robbing a store or knifing another man; he may be peddling drugs or forging a check. No rule, however important, stops him. Since the bizarre, erratic behavior of the psychopath antagonizes society, he is often found in the social waste baskets: the prisons or the mental hospitals.

However, just because a person behaves antisocially or criminally, he or she is not necessarily a sociopath. Also, long-term criminal behavior does not suggest sociopathy. To be a sociopath, a person must have chronic symptoms or characteristics.

3. *Insensitivity to others.* The sociopath is unable to take the role of others and experience how others may be feeling. He or she is unable to empathize.

4. *Hostility.* Often sociopaths are angry at "others." They often have chips on their shoulders and get angry when things do not go their way. They are also aggressive people. They often throw temper tantrums when things do not work in the ways that they may expect.

5. *Lack of concern for the rights and privileges of others.* The sociopath is concerned only with his or her rights and privileges. He or she lives by a double standard; what is a rule for others is not necessarily a rule for himself or herself.

6. *Impulsive behavior.* The sociopath is not a planner. He or she is spontaneous in his or her actions and words. The sociopath gives in to his or her whims repeatedly. McCord and McCord state: "His life seems an erratic series of unconnected acts, first leading one way, then another" [7].

7. *Poor loyalty and social relations.* Sociopaths generally do not have close friends. Few people are allowed to know them. They also do not have loyalty to those persons to whom most people feel loyal (i.e., parents, siblings, and spouses).

8. *Poor planning and judgment; failure to learn from experience.* Sociopaths generally make the same mistakes over and over.

9. *Projection of blame onto others.* If things go wrong for the socio-path, instead of accepting responsibility, he or she places the blame on others. Sociopaths often see themselves as victims of the situations in which they find themselves.

10. *Lack of responsibility.* The sociopath does not see himself or her-self as having a duty or obligation to anyone or anything.

11. *Emotional poverty.* The sociopath has feelings and emotions but only to the extent that they apply to him or her. The sociopath feels hurt, sadness, joy, and pain but is not able to project those feelings onto others. He or she is unable to take the role of others and does not feel remorse or shame. In addition, the sociopath does not feel much guilt [8].

12. *Meaningless lying.* The sociopath lies for the sake of lying, even when the truth would serve him or her better. According to Wilson and Herrnstein, lie detection tests are not very effective with socio-paths [9]. Yochelson and Samenow state that a sociopath's "lies may come easily for roughly the same reasons that they are not readily de-tected by measures of autonomic arousal" [10].

13. *Punishment does not deter.* The sociopath does not learn from punishment. Punishment is not a mechanism for social control. Legal punishment appears to deter psychopaths less than it does others be-cause it is delayed and aversive, and aversive stimuli are especially ineffective for psychopaths if they are delayed [11].

14. *Lack of inner feeling for what he or she does to others.* The socio-path does not seem to have a "conscience" and appears to be guiltless. Joe Hunt, age 23, was the founder and leader of the Billionaire Boy's Club, a business and social fraternity composed of young men from some of southern California's most prominent families. The club mem-bers frequented Los Angeles's trendiest spots, while operating increas-ingly shady business ventures out of swank West Hollywood offices. Joe Hunt kidnapped, extorted, and murdered Hedayat Eslaminia, a former close associate of the late Shah of Iran. Hunt's plan was to torture Eslaminia until he transferred $30,000,000 to the group, and then kill him. Is Joe Hunt sociopathic? Would a professional contract killer and/or an assassin be sociopathic?

15. *Expresses verbally appropriate affective responses but shows cal-lous indifference to others.* The sociopath is very believable. He or she can make others feel that he or she understands. He or she is an ex-cellent rapport maker and actually responds as though he or she cares about others, but internally is indifferent to others. In short, the so-ciopath is a manipulator and is manipulative.

16. *No distress over his or her maladjustment.* The sociopath knows that he or she is different from others but does not care. Most people

IN FOCUS

60 Minutes Interview With Joe Hunt

Joe Hunt was accused of killing Ron Levin based on a seven-page list of notes that Ron Levin's father stumbled across in his son's apartment. The list was in Joe's own handwriting and detailed the elimination of Ron Levin. The list included items such as "tape mouth," "handcuff," "put gloves on," "scan for tape recorder," and "kill the dog." Ed Bradley, interviewer for "60 Minutes," confronted Joe Hunt with the list and he admitted to writing it as a prop to extort from and scare Ron Levin, but not to murder him. Listed below are excerpts from the CBS News "60 Minutes" interview after he admitted to drawing up the list:

Mr. Hunt: I drew it up as a prop in a plan to try and keep Levin from taking advantage of the BBC for a third time.

Bradley (voice-over): Hunt says he and several of the BBC members drew up the list merely in an effort to scare Levin, not to hurt him. [interviewing] So you went over with this list.

Mr. Hunt: Yes, I did.

Bradley: The seven pages which said, "tape mouth, handcuff, put gloves on, kill dog [emphasis]."

Mr. Hunt: Yes, we tried to—

Bradley: Handcuff?

Mr. Hunt: It was supposed to be very lurid. And that was about as lurid of things that we could think of.

Bradley: To frighten him into what? Coming up with the bucks for you?

Mr. Hunt: No absolutely not. See, this was just Levin, get out of our lives.

Bradley: The bottom line with this list here was that I'm involved with some guys who are prepared to kill you?

Mr. Hunt: No sir. That was a prop to indicate there was a plan of extortion, not murder.

Is Joe Hunt sociopathic? What sociopathic characteristics are present in the interview?

Reprinted courtesy of CBS News, *60 Minutes.*

confronted with being different are usually worried about their differences; however, the sociopath has little worry, anxiety, or inner conflict in this regard or in any regard.

17. *A warped capacity for love or lovelessness.* The sociopath tends not to feel affection toward others [12]. He or she tends not to have close attachments with others. When the sociopath does form attachments to others, the attachments are fleeting and lack emotional depth.

18. *An ability to be charming.* He or she projects the image of a happy, well-adjusted person who has poise, is articulate, and appears to be intelligent [13]. They are often good con artists and have the ability to make others like them and trust them.

A person does not have to possess all of the foregoing characteristics to be considered sociopathic. If a person has several major characteristics that are chronic, the sociopathic personality may well be present. According to Wilson and Herrnstein, every human being may possess the characteristics of sociopathy to some degree. Characteristics are manifested by degrees. The more full blown the characteristics of sociopathy, the more likely it is that the person will exhibit criminality. They state [14]:

> Instead of a sharply defined entity, psychopathy is made up of deviations along some of the common dimensions of personality. In a medical metaphor, it is more like anemia than a broken bone. Everyone has a red blood count; the anemic's is just too low. Likewise, everyone has a rate of discounting future events; the psychopath's is relatively high. Everyone has some level of internal arousal or emotionality and a susceptibility to the conditioning of internalized inhibitions; the psychopath's are relatively weak. Everyone has his or her own habitual level of internal speech; the psychopath's level tends to be minimal. People who deviate toward psychopathy, but not as much as the full-blown psychopath, will suffer a smaller risk of asocial behavior, but more than average.

Children, adolescents, and adults have all been labeled as being sociopathic. Some people have cautioned not to apply the label lightly to young people, for they may be going through periods of stress whereby they exhibit behavioral symptoms but do not have the true sociopathic personality [15]. Two to three percent of human beings are estimated to be sociopathic, with the rate twice as high among those who live in fragmented families and the poverty of the inner cities [16]. One common opinion in this area is that certain occupations at-

A Famous Person with Sociopathic Personality Behavior

One of the most famous persons who has been diagnosed as suffering with sociopathic personality behavior disorder was Robert Franklin Stroud (1887–1963), better known as the "Birdman of Alcatraz" [17]. In 1909, while a pimp, Stroud killed a bartender in Alaska for failing to pay for a night of fun with one of Stroud's girls. Shortly before his parole date in 1916, he killed a guard at Leavenworth for no apparent reason. When asked the reason for the killing, Stroud stated: "The guard just took sick and died all of a sudden." He was sentenced to death for the killing. The sentence was later commuted to life imprisonment. He died of old age in prison in 1963. Stroud was made famous by Gaddis's book about him and a movie of his life starring Burt Lancaster. At the time of his death, he had served 54 consecutive years in prison.

While in prison he developed an interest in sick sparrows and canaries. He became an expert on bird diseases. He never developed an adequate or significant relationship with another human being [18]. Stroud was always hostile and angry to anyone in authority. He had an unfavorable self-image and considered his appearance to be a disgrace. Stroud was unable to communicate with others, especially those in authority.

tract sociopathic personalities. For example, politicians, bureaucrats, recreational skydivers, mercenaries, and law enforcement officers tend to need greater stimulation than the average person and tend to seek occupations that can provide more stimulation to their nervous systems. This notion supports the sociopathic-personality low-arousal hypothesis discussed more fully later in the chapter. It may be that some persons with sociopathic personalities commit crime to satisfy the need for high stimulation.

THE CAUSES OF SOCIOPATHY

There are several theories concerning the cause of sociopathy. Some researchers believe that the sociopathic personality disorder is biological, physical, and/or genetic. Others think that the personality disorder is a result of the person's emotional development (i.e., poor relationships and faulty child–parent relationships in the early years).

Still others are of the opinion that the personality disorder is the result of the person's social environment (i.e., poverty, racism, disrupted family life, poor housing, and limited education).

EEG (electroencephalographic) research on the sociopath has been interesting. Elliot reported frequent EEG abnormalities in aggressive patients [19]. Schulsinger has shown that sociopaths have an excess of abnormal EEGs compared to the general population [20]. He has also showed that the more violent or impulsive the sociopaths, the greater the number of EEG abnormalities [21]. Others have also found altered or abnormal brain wave functions for sociopaths [22]. One of the best discussions in the literature about EEG research and sociopathy is by Bartol [23], an advocate of the theory of EEG differences between sociopaths and nonsociopaths. In his book *Criminal Behavior: A Psychosocial Approach*, he summarizes the research in this area [24]:

1. Most aggressive sociopaths have abnormal EEGs compared to nonsociopaths.

2. The abnormality of the EEG waves are of a slow-wave variety, mainly delta and theta waves, as opposed to alpha and beta waves.

3. The delta and theta waves are typical of children, not adults.

4. Sociopaths' central nervous systems are immature and "don't grow up" until roughly age 40.

5. At middle age, sociopathic behavior patterns tend to disappear.

EEG studies are, however, in their infancy and have not rendered definitive results; therefore, these studies and conclusions should be approached with caution. Authorities can be found who agree and disagree with the EEG difference theory. For example, Reid shows that the sociopath's characteristics and symptoms can change as the person approaches middle age; however, he does not accept that there is enough evidence to say that sociopathy will remit of its own accord by the time a person reaches 40 or 50 years of age [25]. He contends that most sociopaths just "burn themselves out" physically and emotionally. They become too tired to maintain such an exacting pace. They are still sociopathic but are just less successful sociopaths.

Another promising area of sociopathy research is related to central nervous system deficits. Many of these studies measure psychological arousal by electrical skin conductance tests. Some research has revealed that sociopathic personalities have lowered levels of baseline anxiety, lessened autonomic reaction to some forms of stress, and changes in speed of autonomic recovery from such stress. This means that the sociopath confronts danger or the threat of danger without the rise in bodily responses to anxiety that normal people would show.

The inference from such findings has been that sociopath has different responses to fear and anxiety and does not learn from experience as does the nonsociopath [26].

Robert Hare, a psychologist, has conducted research on sociopaths for more than twenty years. He has found that the sociopath's impaired understanding may be related to an unusual neurological pattern. The language center of right-handed people is almost always in the left hemisphere of the brain. However, in right-handed sociopaths, language is controlled as much by the right hemisphere as by the left. These findings suggest that the sociopath may have a failure of neurological development [27]. Bartol offers an excellent summary of the research in this area and concludes that the autonomic functioning of the sociopath is as follows [28]:

1. The sociopath is autonomically and cortically underaroused.
2. The sociopath does not learn to avoid pain.

IN FOCUS

Commonwealth v. Marshall
(Supreme Court of Pennsylvania, 1974; 318 A. 2d. 724)

Justice Manderino:

The appellant, Eugene Marshall, allegedly shot his estranged wife in full view of several eyewitnesses. . . . He was given a psychiatric examination . . . The psychiatric report diagnosed the appellant as a "Schizophrenic Reaction, Paranoid Type—Acute," and recommended his incarceration in the Institute for Criminally Insane . . . The diagnostic formulation in the report of that examination said "this man is seen at this time as continuing in a schizophrenic reaction of the paranoid type with inappropriate affect, delusional ideation and apparently hallucinatory phenomenon of a religious nature." The report also said the appellant "displayed poor judgment . . . and it was obvious that he was in reality unable to understand or fully appreciate his situation because of the degree of his present illness."

The mental competence of an accused must be regarded as an absolute and basic condition of a fair trial. The conviction of an accused person while he is incompetent violates due process . . . and . . . state procedures must be adequate to protect this right.

3. If the sociopath's emotional arousal can be induced by adrenaline, he or she learns from his or her experiences and avoids pain.

There appears to be no one identifiable early developmental experience that is highly predictive of sociopathy. However, some have postulated that sociopathy is related to maternal deprivation, traumatic and turbulent mother–child relationships, and lack of parental bonding. The fact of the matter is that no one is sure of the cause of the personality disorder. Some say that it is a result of lack of intimacy, trust, and security in early life and other psychosocial factors. Others say that it is the result of biological factors.

■ TREATMENT OF SOCIOPATHY

It is not impossible for the sociopath is be treated; however, it requires unusual motivation by the sociopath and his or her therapists. Since there appears to be no definitive answer to what causes sociopathy, it follows that the appropriate treatment is difficult to pinpoint. It has been noted that traditional forms of therapy such as group therapy and brief forms of individual therapy generally do not work. Also, institutionalization generally does not cure sociopathy. There are only about six special hospitals devoted to the treatment of sociopathy in the world [29]. Medications and drugs are often not used in such facilities. The focus of treatment in such facilities is to make the person responsible for his or her behavior and learn to feel, trust, and empathize by creating a special milieu. Milieu therapy is considered best for sociopaths with higher levels of maturity, and those with less maturity often respond to authoritarian regimes [30]. It is thought that the best therapy for sociopaths is therapy that will help the sociopath to reach the stage of psychological development that will give him or her an adult sense of responsibility. Often, this treatment will take months or even years. In short, the treatment of sociopathy is often an inexact science with no guarantees of success. Sociopathy is considered chronic.

■ SOCIOPATHY AND CRIMINALITY

There are many studies that have linked sociopathy with criminality. Results of these studies are confusing. Sutherland and Cressey reviewed the literature and concluded that no relationship exists [31].

FIGURE 18–1
**Are inmates on death
row sociopathic?**
Courtesy of the Kentucky
Department of Corrections.

On the other hand, many authorities accept the argument that socio-paths appear in the population of offenders in excessive numbers and that there is a personality structure that occurs before criminal be-havior emerges and that this personality structure contributes greatly to criminal and delinquent behavior. The sociopath is not necessarily a criminal. Criminal and delinquent sociopaths generally make poor or average sociopaths in that they generally get caught. Pure or ideal sociopaths (if they exist) would probably behave such that they would never get caught and no one would suspect that they had a personality disorder. Wilson and Herrnstein have suggested that the sociopath has a number of characteristics that make him or her more susceptible to criminal behavior [32]. Eysenck has found that the sociopath is ex-traverted in his or her personality and states: "The psychopath pre-sents the riddle of delinquency in a particularly pure form, and if we could solve this riddle in relation to the psychopath, we might have a very powerful weapon to use on the problem of delinquency in gen-eral" [33]. We have selected for review several of the most noteworthy studies dealing with sociopathy and criminality.

Sociopaths and the Violent Gang

In Yablonski's classic study of the violent gang, a major hypothesis was that the violent-gang structure recruited its participants from sociopathic young people who lived in disorganized-slum communities. Such communities, according to Yablonski, do not socialize young people adequately. Yablonski states: "At hardly any point is he [the slum youth] trained to have human feelings of compassion or responsibility for another. The youth with this type of sociopathic personality syndrome living in the disorganized-slum neighborhood is most prone to participation in the violent gang" [34].

Violent-gang members tend to be unable to emphasize, identify, and take the role of others. This is what enables the sociopath to commit senseless violence without guilt. Yablonski relates a comment made by a young male sociopath who had committed murder as a member of a gang [35]. The sociopath's statement was made in response to being asked what he was thinking as he was killing a young man with a bread knife. He stated: "What was I thinking about when I did it? Man, are you crazy. I was thinking about whether to do it again!" In addition, sociopathic youths are egocentric, self-seeking, and manipulative in that they exploit others for immediate self-gratification. The gang is a place where they appear successful and competent when, in fact, by mainstream societal standards, such sociopathic youths are painfully inadequate people. Yablonski states that the more sociopathically disturbed the youth, the greater the probability that he will become the gang leader [36]. He calls the gang leader a "core" member of the gang and suggests that the core members are heavily committed to gang activity.

According to Yablonski, in the violent gang the core sociopath is usually the leader. This young person achieves and finds success in gang activity. He achieves status, notoriety, and fame within the gang. Outside the gang in mainstream society, he would have nothing. Yablonski believed that the violent gang's sociopathic leader was "socially ineffectual" as a human being and could not transfer his energies to mainstream society. Yablonski states [37]:

> Contrary to many widely held misconceptions that these leaders could become "captains of industry if only their energies were redirected," the gang leader appears as a socially ineffectual youth incapable of transferring his leadership ability and functioning to more demanding social groups. The low-level expectations of the violent gang, with its minimal social requirements,

is appropriate to the leader's ability. Given his under-socialized personality attributes, he could only be a leader of a violent gang.

Sociopathic gang members also have difficulty with interpersonal relationships. Yablonski addresses this difficulty in his analysis of the sociopathic sex pattern of the gang. The sociopathic gang member engages in "egocentric, exploitative heterosexual relations." The sociopathic youth is not involved in warm, loving, human relationships. Instead, there is fear of responsibility, emotional isolation, manipulation for self-gratification, and often violence in the gang members' relationships with women. Yablonski states: "The girl becomes a target for hostility and physical brutality, which when reported back to the gang confers prestige on the violator" [38].

These sociopathic youth are looking to imitate success in extra-gang society but are failures in any environment other than the violent gang. The sociopathic personality disorder renders sociopaths difficult people with which to deal and they do not fit in easily. Therefore, gangs provide a safe haven for such youth. Violent gangs may very well attract sociopathic personalities as members.

Sociopathy and Juveniles

In *Deviant Children Grown Up*, Lee Robins has conducted a longitudinal study of the sociopathic personality [39]. The study revolved around 524 patients who were identified and studied as deviant children and then restudied as adults thirty years later. Ninety percent of Robin's population was located and restudied after thirty years had passed. She found that subjects could be found after such a long period and that through records and personal interviews she could obtain significant information about their adults lives. She found that 86 percent of the sociopaths interviewed talked so freely about themselves and their deviant adult behaviors that they could be classified as sociopaths by the psychiatrists who interviewed them without having to go to their records for further information.

Robins expected that the children that were seen in child guidance clinics would yield a high rate of diagnosed adult sociopathy. She found that the children who were seen were more maladjusted as adults than were the control subjects. Maladjustment manifested itself in high rates of arrests, low occupational achievement, greater numbers of mental hospitalizations, high divorce rates, alienation from friends and community, frequent moves, abuse of alcohol, and transmission of behavior problems to children [40].

Sociopathy was found almost exclusively in boys who had been referred to the clinic for theft, incorrigibility, running away from home, truancy, associating with bad companions, sexual activities, and staying out late. These boys were described as "aggressive, reckless, impulsive, slovenly, enuretic, lacking guilt, and lying without cause." The sociopaths tended to have fathers who were sociopaths and/or alcoholics [41].

As adults the sociopaths have the following characteristics:

1. Poor work histories
2. Financial dependence on social agencies or relatives
3. Marital problems
4. Multiple arrests, culminating in prison
5. Heavy drinking patterns
6. Impulsiveness
7. Sexual promiscuity
8. Vagrancy
9. Hostility
10. Poor credit
11. Social isolation

Robins found that improvement in sociopathy was most likely to occur between ages 30 and 40 [42]. This improvement has been noted by other researchers cited earlier in the chapter.

The best single childhood predictor of sociopathy was the degree of juvenile antisocial behavior exhibited by the child. With children who had a wide variety of antisocial behaviors, the best predictor of sociopathy was whether the child was ever placed in a correctional institution.

In short, Robins concluded that children who were child guidance clinic patients had a strikingly higher rate for sociopathy than did control subjects. She also underscored the role of the father in predicting the child's sociopathy and antisocial behavior. She stated: "Antisocial behavior in the father, in addition, was the only childhood variable which predicted that sociopathic persons would not decrease their antisocial behavior with aging" [43].

Sociopathy and Hereditary

There are researchers who conclude that concerning crime, innate tendencies play a large role [44]. Karl O. Christiansen conducted a major study in Denmark in which he studied nearly 6000 pairs of twins born in Denmark between 1881 and 1910 [45]. About 900 pairs of twins were entered into the Central Police Register and/or into local penal registers. Christiansen found greater rates of sociopathy in one-egg twins as opposed to two-egg twins. In one-egg twins the genetic makeup is identical, and if one twin is sociopathic, the other twin is more likely to be sociopathic. In fraternal twins the genetic makeup is not identical and if one twin is sociopathic, the other twin is not as likely to be sociopathic.

Schulsinger noted that the results of several Third Reich researchers (i.e., Berlit, Riedel, and Stumpfl) have unanimously shown that heredity plays a role in the causation of sociopathy [46]. Slater and Cowie also suggests that there is a genetic component to sociopathy [47]. Schulsinger embarked on a study in Denmark to attempt to discover whether sociopathy was inherited. He studied 854 biological and adoptive relatives of 57 sociopathic adoptees and found the frequency of mental disorders to be higher in the biological relatives of the sociopaths than among their adoptive relatives or than among either group of relatives of the controls. He also found that the difference was greater when only sociopathic disorders were considered. He stated: "The study supports a hypothesis of heredity as an etiological factor in psychopathic spectrum disorders"[48].

Consider the following quotation [49]:

> I would only remark that in a situation where individualism is trump, the psychopath is powerfully equipped to survive, if not always to succeed. That is if the operational basis of the culture requires projecting a good image while watching out for oneself, it encourages pursuit of material pleasure and the merchandizing of people, then far from being a mask of sanity or a moral imbecile, the psychopath is the reasonable one and those of us who are trusting, reliable, and empathic are out of phase with reality.

There are adult, juvenile, male, and female sociopaths within our society and within our criminal justice system. We find them at the arrest stage, as defendants in the legal system, and in our correctional institutions. Perhaps the values taught to our young encourage the development of the sociopathic personality structure, and as long as the sociopath does not break the law, he or she does not come to the attention of criminal justice officials. Perhaps there are many sociopaths walking around who have channeled their sociopathy in socially accepted ways. Sociopathy does not manifest itself as an obvious mental disorder and therefore is not readily identified.

∎ SUMMARY

The sociopath does not have a psychological disorder but rather has a unique personality structure. There are several labels for the sociopathic personality. Psychopath and antisocial personality are two of the more popular labels. There is evidence of a positive correlation between sociopathy and criminal behavior. Sociopathic personality structures can be identified in criminal and noncriminal populations. Sociopathic personalities are identified by many traits and characteristics. All sociopathic traits and characteristics need not be present and manifested for a person to be a sociopath. There is no consensus about the cause of sociopathy. Some believe it to be caused by biology. Others believe it to be caused by faulty personal development. Still others believe it to be caused by sociological factors. Contemporary research on the cause of sociopathy focuses on brain wave patterns and central nervous system deficits. Selected research reveals that at roughly age 40 to 50, many sociopathic personality characteristics go into remission. Sociopathy is difficult to treat successfully. Some researchers believe that sociopathy causes criminality, and others think that criminality contributes to the sociopathic personality.

∎ MATCHING KEY TERMS AND DEFINITIONS

Match each key terms with the correct definition.

a. antisocial personality   g. emotional isolation
b. autonomic nervous system   h. hostility
c. core sociopath   i. impulsive behavior
d. disorganized slum neighborhood   j. psychopath
e. EEG   k. sociopath
f. egocentricity   l. violent gang structure

_____ 1. Three common terms used to suggest a personality disorder that manifests itself by many characteristics that render the individual asocial and difficult to relate to. (Three answers)

_____ 2. A group of nerves and ganglia which are involuntary and lead from the spinal cord and brain to glands, blood vessels, muscles, and viscera and control involuntary functions.

_____ 3. Electroencephalogram.

    —— **4.** A term referring to a person who is self-centered and "me" oriented.

    —— **5.** A term referring to aggressive anger.

    —— **6.** A term referring to spontaneity and giving into whims.

    —— **7.** A term referring to the organizational hierarchy of violent gangs.

    —— **8.** An environment that does not socialize its youth adequately.

    —— **9.** The violent gang leader.

   —— **10.** The lack of involvement in warm, loving, human relationships.

∎ DISCUSSION QUESTIONS

1. How do American social values contribute to the development of sociopathy?
2. If sociopathic offenders are resistant to treatment, what are the implications for the American criminal justice system?
3. What are the best ways of handling the sociopathic offender?
4. What are the positive aspects of the sociopathic offender's personality? How can they be used in making him or her a law-abiding citizen?
5. Distinguish between the emotional problem theories and sociopathic personality theories.

Notes

1. A. M. Cooper, A. J. Frances, and M. H. Sachs, *The Personality Disorders and Neuroses.* Philadelphia: J. B. Lippincott, 1986, p. 251.
2. James Q. Wilson and Richard J. Herrnstein, *Crime and Human Nature: The Definitive Study of the Causes of Crime.* New York: Simon and Schuster, 1985, p. 199.
3. Edwin H. Sutherland and Donald R. Cressey, *Criminology,* 9th ed. Philadelphia: J. B. Lippincott, 1974, p. 159.
4. L. Yablonski, *The Violent Gang.* New York: Macmillan, 1962.
5. H. M. Cleckley, *The Mask of Sanity.* St. Louis: C. V. Mosby, 1941; and H. C. Gough, "A Sociological Theory of Psychopathy," *American Journal of Sociology,* vol. 53, 1948, pp. 359–366.
6. W. McCord and J. McCord. *The Psychopath: An Essay on the Criminal Mind.* Princeton, N.J.: D. Van Nostrand, 1964, p. 8.
7. McCord and McCord, 1964:10.

8. McCord and McCord, 1964:12–15.

9. Wilson and Herrnstein, 1985:200.

10. S. Yochelson and S. Samenow, *The Criminal Personality*, Vol. 1, *A Profile for Change*. Northvale, N.J.: Jason Aronson, 1976.

11. Wilson and Herrnstein, 1985:207.

12. McCord and McCord, 1964:15–16; and W. McCord and J. McCord, *Psychopathy and Delinquency*. New York: Grune & Stratton, 1956.

13. R. J. Smith, *The Psychopath in Society*. New York: Academic Press, 1978, pp. 19–20.

14. Wilson and Herrnstein, 1985:207.

15. Cooper et al., 1986:252.

16. D. Goleman, "Brain Defect Linked to Amoral Behavior of Psychopaths," *Daily Journal*, July 30, 1987, p. 9.

17. Vernon Fox, *Introduction to Criminology*. Englewood Cliffs, N.J.: Prentice-Hall, 1976, p. 181.

18. T. Gaddis, *Birdman of Alcatraz*. New York: New American Library, 1956.

19. F. A. Elliott, "Neurological Aspects of Antisocial Behavior," in W. H. Reid, ed., *The Psychopath: A Comprehensive Study of Antisocial Disorders and Behaviors*. New York: Brunner/Mazel, 19l78.

20. F. Schulsinger, "Psychopathy: Heredity and Environment," *International Journal of Mental Health*, vol. 1, 1972, pp. 190–206.

21. Schulsinger, 1972:194.

22. K. Schneider, *Psychopathic Personalities*. London: Cassell, 1958.

23. C. R. Bartol, *Criminal Behavior: A Psychosocial Approach*. Englewood Cliffs, N.J.: Prentice-Hall, 1980.

24. Bartol, 1980:64–66.

25. W. H. Reid "Antisocial Personality," in Cooper et al., 1986:256.

26. R. D. Hare, *Psychopathy: Theory and Research*. New York: Wiley, 1970; and R. D. Hare and D. N. Cox, "Psychophysiological Research on Psychopathy," in Reid, 1978.

27. Goleman, 1987:9.

28. Bartol, 1980:72–76.

29. Cooper et al., 1986:257.

30. Cooper et al., 1986:257.

31. Sutherland and Cressey, 1974.

32. Wilson and Herrnstein, 1985:207.

33. H. J. Eysenck, *Crime and Personality*. Boston: Houghton Mifflin, 1964:41.

34. Yablonski, 1962:196.

35. Yablonski, 1962:198.

36. Yablonski, 1962:201.

37. Yablonski, 1962:171.

38. Yablonski, 1962:199.

39. Lee Robins, *Deviant Children Grown Up*. Baltimore: Williams & Wilkins, 1966.

40. Robins, 1966:292–293.

41. Robins, 1966:293.

42. Robins, 1966:296.

43. Robins, 1966:301.

44. J. Lange, "Verbrechen als Schicksal," *Studien an Kriminellen Zwillingen*. Leipzig: Georg Thieme, 1929.

45. Karl O. Christiansen, "Crime in a Danish Twin Population," *Acta Genetical Medical Gemellologial*, 1970, 19:323–326.

46. Schulsinger, 1972:1939.

47. E. Slater and V. Cowie, *The Genetics of Mental Disorders*. London: Oxford University Press, 1971; and S. Guze, *Criminality and Psychiatric Disorder*. New York: Oxford University Press, 1976.

48. Schulsinger, 1972:204.

49. Smith, 1978:115.

19

Thinking Pattern Theories

CHAPTER HIGHLIGHTS

- Thinking pattern theories are psychological theories that deal with the criminal's cognitive processes, intellect, logic, mental structure, rationality, and language usage.
- According to the thinking pattern theorists, how an offender processes things, objects, events, and situations in his or her mind will ultimately determine the offenders behavioral choices.
- Thinking pattern theories of crime causation are related to developmental psychology theories.
- Human thinking structures may develop in stages; simple thinking structures develop early in life, and more complex thinking structures develop in the early teen years.
- Some thinking pattern theorists advocate the existence of a separate and distinct criminal mind.
- Other thinking pattern theorists advocate that the criminal's mind is no different from noncriminal minds.
- The criminal adheres to certain rationalizations which become justifications that allow him or her to commit crimes.
- Criminals are concrete thinkers.
- The criminal's thinking is characterized by "fragmentation," fluctuations in mental state that occur within very short periods.
- The criminal operates with a rigid, closed mind.
- Criminals view themselves as unique and one-of-a-kind beings who emphasize their differences from other people.
- The criminal believes that there are those in the world for him or her or against him or her.

- The way a criminal thinks is erroneous only to mainstream society.

- Thinking errors are the mental processes necessary for the criminal to live his or her life and achieve his or her objectives.

- Before real change can occur in a criminal's life, the criminal must adopt a new lifestyle.

KEY TERMS

Cognitive Processes

Concrete Operations

Criminal Pride

Formal Operations

Phenomenological Reporting

Piaget

Preoperational Stage

Sensory Motor Stage

Shutoff Mechanism

Stage Theory of Thinking

Techniques of Neutralization

Thinking Errors

Transductive Reasoning

Yochelson and Samenow

Zero State

The thinking pattern theories are psychological theories that deal with the offender's cognitive processes. These theories focus on the offender's intellect, logic, mental processes, rationality, and language usage. The mind of the offender is affected by his or her cognitive process, and it is, in turn, the cognitive process that influences behavior. The way that offenders think and what they tell themselves in their minds will determine the offender's behavioral choices. The internal messages we give ourselves ultimately influence our self-image and actions.

■ BACKGROUND

Thinking pattern theories of crime causation are directly related to developmental psychology theories. Jean Piaget, a developmental psychologist, devoted his life to understanding how people learn to think. Some of the highlights of Piaget's theory are presented below.

■ THE STAGE THEORY OF JEAN PIAGET

Piaget, a Swiss psychologist, studied human intelligence, perception, and how human beings think. Perhaps the aspect of Piaget's theory that has received greatest attention is his stage theory of learning and thinking. According to him, people cannot think and comprehend certain things until they have gone through a sequential process. Piaget described developmental stages of human thinking as follows:

1. *Sensory-motor stage.* This stage characterizes the human being from birth to 2 years of age. During this stage the person's world is "here-and-now" oriented. If the object cannot be seen, heard, touched, tasted, or smelled, it does not exist for the person. In addition, the human child learns the idea of objects during this stage. This concept is that objects can continue to exist even if they are not seen, heard, touched, tasted, or smelled. The beginning of symbolization, the development of the reality, and the idea of cause and effect are also developed during this stage of development.

2. *Preoperational stage.* This stage characterizes the person from 2 to 7 years of age. The child does not acquire operational thinking until around 7. During the preoperational stage, the child cannot reverse his or her thoughts. The child's thinking structure, according to Piaget, does not have "reversibility," the ability to reverse or undo actions and thoughts that are not logical. The child is not able to govern his or her thinking according to logical outcomes [1]. Perhaps some offenders' thinking structures are fixed at this stage of development?

The human being between 2 and 4 years of age has preconceptual thought. An example of preconceptual thinking is the child who sees five Santa Clauses in one day and still thinks there is only one Santa Claus. The child also has transductive reasoning. Transductive reasoning is reasoning that goes from particular instances to other particular instances. An example of the transductive reasoning process is A is furry, B is furry; therefore, A is a B.

Between the years of 4 and 7, the person develops intuitive thought governed by perception and egocentricity [2]. Problems are, however, interpreted solely from the child's point of view. The person has an egocentric view of everything. Children are also unable to classify during this stage. Intuition, not logic, is relied on for problem solving during this stage. Many criminals have egocentric views of the world. Perhaps their thinking structures never evolved past the preoperational stage of development?

3. *Concrete operations.* This stage characterizes human thought between the ages of 7 and 11. It is during this stage that the human being

begins to apply rules of logic to classes, to relations, and to numbers. The human being's thinking becomes less egocentric and perception-oriented. However, the human being is still unable to apply rules of logic to objects or events that are not concrete. The person can deal only with what is real or what he or she is capable of imagining [3].

4. *Formal operations.* This stage of thinking occurs between the ages of 12 and 15. The human being during this stage of development begins to deal with hypotheticals and can apply formal sets of logical rules. Human beings can also engage in idealistic and abstract thinking. It is at this stage that people can place themselves in the role of others and can experience what it might be like to be in another person's shoes. Many offenders never learn to do this.

Piaget was not necessarily concerned with the questions of whether development could be accelerated; however, his theory implies that enriched experiences may lead to the appearance of thought structures characteristic of different stages.

Many adult offenders think like young children. They are egocentric and often illogical. Many offenders are unable to think abstractly, a prerequisite for placing themselves in the role of another person. Also, many offenders do not possess reversibility in their thinking. They are often unable to let go of ideas that others view as illogical.

∎ THINKING PATTERNS OF OFFENDERS

One of the most detailed studies conducted on the way offenders think and the criminal's mind in general was Samuel Yochelson and Stanton E. Samenow's *The Criminal Personality.* This longitudinal study took place over a fifteen-year period and involved intensive interviews, therapy, and follow-up studies. Yochelson left private practice to do more reflection and writing and to contribute something important to society. Samenow joined him later. The study took place at Saint Elizabeth's Hospital, a Washington, D.C. facility that treats criminals with psychological problems. At Saint Elizabeth's it was thought that patients would be around for long time spans because of their psychological diagnoses. Also, Saint Elizabeth's Hospital had good research and treatment facilities and the hospital authorities promised the researchers that they would not have to testify in court against the offenders with whom they would be working [4].

The 255 male criminals who were the subject of treatment and research came from a wide variety of backgrounds. The subjects had different socioeconomic statuses, religions, races, and ages. Some were from stable family environments and backgrounds and others did not have family stability. Some were substance abusers and others had no substance abuse history. All the subjects were of average intelligence.

Yochelson and Samenow isolated certain character traits that all their criminal subjects manifested [5]:

1. Fearfulness. Their fears were in greater number and intensity than the fears of noncriminals. One of the major fears that the offenders had was that others would see weakness in them.
2. The inclination to view oneself as worthless.
3. Lying.
4. The "shutoff mechanism." The researchers defined this as a process of pushing fears away from conscious consideration.
5. Successive changes in mental states.
6. Refusal to view themselves as criminal.

The researchers concluded that the traditional psychiatric ideas and techniques that worked with noncriminals did not work on criminals. They learned that they were dealing with a different type of person with a different mental makeup. The researchers concluded that criminals also used language differently, and to better understand them, the researchers became students of semantics. At times they thought they grasped what a criminal was saying, and later found out that the criminal had meant something quite different. According to the researchers, the criminal has a different frame of reference. If the criminal says that he is "lonely," it does not refer to a lack of companionship. The criminal knows nothing of companionship based on a community of interest and experiences.

> Lonely meant having no one to control and exploit. In addition, much of our descriptive terminology was inadequate or meaningless when applied to criminals. Saying that a man was "manipulative" reflected his effect on us more than it indicated how his mind worked; the criminals did not view themselves as manipulative, we thought that we were being manipulated by their tactics [6].

Yochelson and Samenow eventually rejected the more traditional psychological interventions and approaches that they embraced earlier because they concluded that the traditional insight therapy that they were using was providing criminals with additional excuses for crime. They theorized that to reform the criminal, we would need to change the criminal's ways of thinking and behaving. Before a real change could occur, the offenders needed to adopt a new lifestyle [7]. The criminal's new lifestyle would include a total alteration in thinking and behavior. The criminal would have to become something and not just live in a vacuum.

Phenomenologic reporting, an intense probe of a criminal's stream of thinking, was the major research tool used to understand the criminal's mind. The researchers gathered data on how their subjects thought throughout the day.

Yochelson and Samenow were able to isolate fifty-two criminal thinking errors. Thinking errors are the mental processes necessary for the criminal to live his life and achieve his or her objectives. These thinking patterns are not errors to the offenders, but are the core of their personalities. From the criminal's perspective, the way he thinks is an error only to society. Yochelson and Samenow concluded that criminals' thinking patterns were manifested and ingrained into them by an early age. Thinking patterns and irresponsibility make a criminal. Criminality will continue indefinitely unless the offender abstains completely from criminal activity [8].

Yochelson and Samenow recognized that criminals told self-serving stories and told those in authority what they wanted to hear. Yochelson and Samenow recognized that most offenders were aware of society's ways of thinking, but many used life's adversities to justify their behavior.

Eventually, the researchers isolated three general categories of "thinking errors": (1) general criminal thinking patterns, (2) obvious thinking patterns that are mostly labeled and ignored, and (3) thinking patterns that are manifested during criminal activity. The thinking errors are present everywhere in the criminal's life and involve not taking responsibility for behavior [9]. The following are some of the common thinking errors held by criminals; they are patterns of thought and action.

1. The criminal has a mental life that includes fantasies of triumph, power, and control.

2. The criminal's idea of normal energy differs from that of the non-criminal population. "If he [the criminal] is not full of vitality and energy and ready to go, he thinks that something is wrong with him" [10].

3. The criminal is preoccupied and fears death.

4. The criminal thinks about and is fearful of being put down, being a "zero," being rejected, and being criticized. He believes that his or her "zero state" will last forever. He believes that everyone can see how worthless he or she is.

5. The criminal experiences such intense anger that spreads so quickly that the criminal loses his or her perspective and his or her thinking becomes defective.

6. The offender has an unyielding "criminal pride" that manifests itself in the idea that he is better than and above others, even when this is decidedly not the case. This idea manifests itself in not being accountable to others.

7. Criminals think that there are no limits to what they can do and that the world is theirs to do with as they please. They believe that there is no limit to their power and control over others.

8. Nearly all criminals are sentimental toward their mothers, children, animals, and the helpless, disabled, and underprivileged, but they believe that showing their sentimentality is an admission of being weak. "Sentimentality never eliminates 'patterns' of criminal thought action. In fact, it contributes to their continuation. The criminal's kindness, charity, and aesthetic interests and talents enhance his opinion of himself and add to his belief that he is a good person" [11].

9. Criminals view the teachings of religions literally. However, religion can provide the offender with greater license for crime in that religious people are likely to tell the criminal that he or she is a good person although his behavior has been bad.

10. Criminals are concrete thinkers. They tend to think in terms of isolated events. Young children tend to think concretely also. Conceptual thinking is more sophisticated thinking and involves recognizing the similarity between situations and learning from experience.

11. The criminal's thinking is characterized by "fragmentation," fluctuations in mental state that occur within very short periods. Fragmented minds change quickly and capriciously, maybe in a matter of minutes. The criminal's fragmentation is not psychotic, irrational, or unconscious. He knows what he or she is doing. Fragmentation is manifested in a pattern of starting something and then doing something else. One offender stated it in the following way. "When I'm in church, I think 'church.' When I'm in crime, I think 'crime.'" According to the researchers, the offender never stopped to think about the relationship between crime and church. The researchers contend that fragmentation of thinking is a necessity for criminality [12].

12. Criminals view themselves as unique and one-of-a-kind beings who emphasize their differences from others. They believe that other people are not like them. What applies to other people could not apply to the criminal because the criminal is in a class unto himself or herself.

13. Criminals believe that they must be perfect in those things that they value.

14. A criminal is suggestible depending on what he or she wants.

15. Criminals believe that there are those in the world for them or against them. The offender sees the world in a polarized way. Criminals have a "loner" quality and are loners by choice who set themselves apart by secrecy.

16. Criminals believe themselves to be sexually irresistible.

17. Lying and being untruthful are incorporated into the criminal's basic makeup. It is essential and is justified. It is automatic. It is the way of dealing with the world. The criminal knows that he or she is lying and lying is under his or her control. The criminal knows right from wrong but goes by what is right for him or her at the time. The person does not view himself or herself as a liar but merely doing what needs to be done to reach his goals. The criminal believes that given similar circumstances, everyone would lie.

18. The criminal operates based on a closed channel. He or she is secretive, self-righteous, and has a closed mind. This is what makes change impossible for the criminal [13]. In addition, criminals fail to disclose, are not receptive, and do not engage in self-criticism.

19. The "I can't" theme is apparent in the criminal's refusal to act responsibly. According to Yochelson and Samenow, it really means "I don't want to" or "I won't."

20. Criminals believe that they are victims when they get caught. They tend to blame everyone but themselves for their behavior. The researchers state: "If the criminal can half-believe that what he did was attributable to forces outside himself, this can help him to hang on to the idea that he is basically good" [14].

21. The criminal's time perspective is in the present instant and pervades the criminal's thinking. The criminal is not future-oriented, nor does he or she postpone immediate gratification. They want everything now. Offenders are unable to develop responsible time perspectives.

22. Criminals do not mentally allow themselves to place themselves in another's role, be sensitive to others, or be empathetic to others. The only apparent exception to this is the criminal's sentimentality shown to mothers, children, animals, and the helpless. (*Note*: Compare this concept with the one stated as characteristic 8.)

23. The criminal has a limited view of injury to others. The criminal does not conceptualize the emotional damage done to victims of his or her criminal behavior and society as a whole.

24. The idea of "obligation" is foreign to the criminal's thinking.

25. Criminals have initiative but not in socially acceptable directions. They do not think in terms of taking responsible initiatives because they do not believe that there is anything in it for them.

26. Criminals think that they can own anything that they want or any person they want. Ownership is a part of the offender's view that his or her rights are unlimited [15].

27. Criminals do not trust others, because when they trust, it is thought that trust will be betrayed.

28. Criminals do not believe that dependence on others is necessary. They believe that it is a sign of weakness.

29. Concerning interest, criminals generally think: "If I like it, O.K. If not, to hell with it" [16].

30. The criminal's thinking is pretentious. He or she tends to think of himself or herself as being superior to others.

31. Criminal thinking attempts to avoid adversity.

32. Criminals no not have sound, objective, rational, careful thinking patterns. Generally, criminals make decisions based on the way that they feel at the time.

Yochelson and Samenow suggest that criminals have little understanding of how noncriminals think and therefore make bad decisions [17]:

> Society's error is to believe that a man totally unfamiliar with the thinking patterns that are necessary for responsible living can become responsible simply by schooling, work, or a change in environment. This is similar to expecting a plane to fly. It is just not equipped for that.

The results of Yochelson and Samenow's research revealed that thirteen of thirty hard-core offenders functioned responsibly after being taught noncriminal thinking patterns. After intensive and long-term treatment, thirteen of their parents had little, if any, criminal thoughts left. These patients were successful in changing their lifestyles completely.

Reactions to *The Criminal Personality* have been strong. O. J. Keller reacted to Yochelson and Samenow's ideas by suggesting that the researchers were advocating a "hate syndrome" [18]. Keller thinks that the researchers did corrections a disservice in that their research supports an attitude of public nihilism about rehabilitation. Keller also takes exception to the researcher's thesis that there is a separate criminal personality. Keller believes that "crime is not the providence of a select or unusual group."

Samenow responded to Keller by stating that his research offers hope in a climate of rehabilitation nihilism [19]. He also responded that the research that he and Yochelson did, did not advocate a genetic theory of crime causation. Their research was not a search for crime causation but simply a study of criminals' thinking patterns. Samenow is adamant in that "intensive and prolonged efforts are necessary to help career criminals make a significant and lasting change in their personalities." He also suggests that their program can be carried out in a community where it will be less expensive then incarcerating criminals.

▌CRITIQUE OF *THE CRIMINAL PERSONALITY*

In an evaluation of Yochelson and Samenow's work, the following four points are evident:

1. Yochelson and Samenow do not answer the questions "Why do some criminals think in certain ways and others do not?" and "What causes criminal thinking patterns?" They are more concerned with a description of criminal thinking.

2. Yochelson and Samenow do not offer a satisfactory validation method. Their data were derived from personal interviews and case studies. There was no attempt to validate data with formal, concurrent measures.

3. The study from a methodological perspective cannot provide an adequate basis for drawing clear cause-and-effect conclusions. Additionally, there were no control groups.

4. The theory suffers from the use of vague terminology [20].

5. The researchers looked only at criminals confined to institutions. What about all the other criminals who were never confined to institutions?

▌TECHNIQUES OF NEUTRALIZATION

Sykes and Matza's techniques of neutralization were discussed in Chapter 8. It is mentioned here because such rationalizations support the thinking pattern theorists' conclusions that the criminal's mind works differently.

Sykes and Matza set out to answer the question, "Why do people violate laws in which they believe?" Techniques of neutralization are justifications or rationalizations for deviance that is seen as valid by the offender but not by the mainstream society. There are five major techniques of neutralization. (For a more detailed discussion, see Chapter 8.) They are a part of the way the criminal thinks about the

FIGURE 19-1
Do the thinking patterns of criminals differ from those of noncriminals before they are incarcerated? Or does incarceration cause different thinking patterns?
Courtesy of the Kentucky Department of Corrections.

world and they function to enable the person to commit criminal acts. The techniques of neutralization are as follows:

1. *Denial of responsibility.* The offender denies himself or herself as having responsibility for his or her behavior.

2. *Denial of injury.* This refers to injury or harm to victims. The offender denies that injury occurs to the victim despite the evidence.

3. *Denial of the victim.* This refers to the idea that the injury is not wrong considering the circumstances.

4. *Condemnation of the condemners.* In a sense this is a rejection of the rejecters in the mind of the offenders. Whenever a public figure falls from grace by committing questionable behaviors, incarcerated prisoners openly express hostility. They do not understand why they are in prison and public figures remain in society at large.

5. *Appeal to higher loyalties.* The gang, peer group, or friendship clique is more important than the individual.

■ SUMMARY

Thinking pattern theories are psychological theories of crime causation that emphasize the criminal's cognitive processes. Thinking pattern theories are related to developmental psychology theories such as those developed by Jean Piaget. Yochelson and Samenow spent 15 years studying the criminal mind and found that the criminal thinks differently from the noncriminal. There has been considerable opposition to Yochelson and Samenow's notion of a criminal mind separate and distinct from a noncriminal mind because it promotes antitreatment attitudes and policies. Techniques of neutralization support the idea of a separate thinking structure for criminals.

■ MATCHING KEY TERMS AND DEFINITIONS

Match each key term with the correct definition.

a. cognitive processes
b. concrete operations
c. criminal pride
d. formal operations
e. phenomenological reporting
f. Piaget
g. preoperational stage
h. sensory-motor stage
i. shutoff mechanism
j. stage theory of thinking
k. techniques of neutralization
l. thinking errors
m. transductive reasoning
n. Yochelson and Samenow
o. zero state

____ 1. Rationalizations that justify criminal behavior.

____ 2. The researchers who advocate the idea of a criminal mind.

____ 3. One of Piaget's stages that emphasizes the development of idealistic and abstract thinking.

____ 4. One of Piaget's stages that emphasizes the development of the ability to apply rules of logic.

____ 5. One of Piaget's stages that emphasizes that thinking is egocentric and intuition is the major force used in solving problems.

____ 6. One of Piaget's thinking stages that emphasizes the development of the "object concept," reality, and cause and effect.

____ 7. People cannot think and comprehend in more complex ways unless they develop along a sequential process.

____ **8.** A developmental psychologist who devoted his life to understanding how people think.

____ **9.** The way an offender thinks is characterized by not taking responsibility for his or her behavior.

____ **10.** The process of pushing fears away from conscious consideration.

____ **11.** A research tool that involves an intense probe of a criminal's stream of thought.

____ **12.** The belief that the offender holds that he or she is better than and above others.

____ **13.** The application of logic and rationality to problem solving.

____ **14.** A thinking process that goes from particulars to particulars.

____ **15.** The belief that the criminal has of being put down, rejected, criticized, and being worthless.

∎ DISCUSSION QUESTIONS

1. Perhaps certain criminals' thinking structures are arrested at the preoperational stage or concrete operations' stage of development. What are the implications of this idea for corrections?

2. Why do some criminals think in certain ways and others do not?

3. What causes criminal thinking patterns?

4. Assume that criminal thinking patterns do exist. What type of treatment would you recommend for the offender?

5. Distinguish between the emotional problem theories and the thinking pattern theories.

NOTES

1. C. R. Lefrancois, *Psychology for Teaching*. Belmont, Calif.: Wadsworth, 1972, p. 206.
2. Lefrancois, 1972:208.
3. Lefrancois, 1972:215.
4. S. Yochelson and S. Samenow, *The Criminal Personality*, Vol. 1, *A Profile for Change*. Northvale, N.J.: Jason Aronson, 1976.
5. Yochelson and Samenow, 1976:21–22.
6. Yochelson and Samenow, 1976:31.
7. Yochelson and Samenow, 1976:36.
8. M. T. Nietzel, *Crime and Its Modification: A Social Learning Perspective*. New York: Pergamon Press, 1979, p. 82.

9. Yochelson and Samenow, 1976:117.

10. Yochelson and Samenow, 1976:257.

11. Yochelson and Samenow, 1976:297.

12. Yochelson and Samenow, 1976:310–313.

13. Yochelson and Samenow, 1976:360.

14. Yochelson and Samenow, 1976:368.

15. Yochelson and Samenow, 1976:385.

16. Yochelson and Samenow, 1976:397.

17. Yochelson and Samenow, 1976:405–406.

18. O. J. Keller, "O. J. Keller Answers," *American Journal of Correction*, vol. 40, no. 6, Nov.–Dec. 1978, pp. 29–31; and R. J. Wright, "ACA Past President Disagrees with Content of Book Entitled 'The Criminal Personality,'" *American Journal of Correction*, vol. 40, no. 6, Nov.–Dec. 1978, p. 28.

19. S. E. Samenow, "Author/Researcher Takes Issue with O. J. Keller," *Corrections Today*, vol. 41, no. 3, May–June 1979, pp. 12–19; and "Dr. Samenow Responds," *American Journal of Correction*, vol. 40, no. 6, Nov.–Dec. 1978, pp. 28–29.

20. Nietzel, 1979:82–83.

THE PAST
AND THE FUTURE

In Chapter 20 we discuss the crime problem. Included are topics on the costs of crime, career criminals, recidivism, reporting of crime, and victimology. Also included in Chapter 20 is an introduction to the concept of criminal behavior systems. In Chapter 21 we discuss crime typologies. Chapter 22 ends the book with a review of the major crime causation theories and concepts.

20

The Crime Problem

CHAPTER HIGHLIGHTS

- Sutherland and Cressey contend that certain types of criminal behavior have their own "behavior systems."
- Sutherland and Cressey contend that "the behavior system" is a group way of life and it is not merely an aggregation of individual acts.
- Criminals who commit certain types of offenses have a feeling that they belong together.
- Sutherland and Cressey state that if the behavior system can be isolated, the problem would then be to study and explain the system as a unit.
- Sesnowitz concluded that taking all factors into consideration, the average burglar would make more money from legitimate employment.
- Plate concludes that criminals work on commissions. The criminal's income therefore depends to some extent on how hard the criminal works at crime.
- Plate also points out that the criminal's income is tax-free, and this saves the criminal a nice sum of money each year.
- The average career criminal is normally in and out of prison or jail all of his or her life.
- Most career criminals live at or below the poverty level.
- The career criminal is usually a property offender.
- The crimes most susceptible to recidivism are forgery, auto theft, robbery, burglary, and assault.
- Actual recidivism rates are difficult to measure.
- It appears that less than two-fifths of all crimes are reported to authorities.
- Except for rape, the more serious the crime in terms of economic loss or physical injury, the more likely it is to be reported.
- The science of victimology is the study of crime from the victim's viewpoint, with emphasis on the relationship between the victim and the offender.
- Hans Von Hentig concluded that in many respects the victim shapes and molds the criminal and the crime.

KEY TERMS

Behavior Systems

Career Criminal

Compulsive Recidivist

Duet Frame of Reference

Dysocial Recidivist

Impulsive Recidivist

Inadequate, Dependent Repeater

Penal Couple

Tat Twam Asi

Victimology

In earlier chapters we have discussed attempts to explain or locate the origins of criminal behavior. In this chapter we examine the economics of crime, victim issues, and other problems associated with criminal behavior.

■ BEHAVIOR SYSTEM

Sutherland and Cressey contended that certain types of criminal behavior have their own behavior system [1]. They stated that a behavior system can be described by three characteristics.

1. *The behavior system is an integrated unit.* This unit includes individual acts, codes of behavior governing the acts, traditions surrounding the acts, social relationships among the participants, and the indirect participation of other persons. Sutherland and Cressey contended that the "behavior system" is "a group way of life" and is more than an aggregation of individual acts. As examples of "behavior systems," they cite professional theft, organized crime, and racketeering. For example, professional thieves make a regular business of theft, they have codes of behavior, look down on amateur thieves, and tend to associate with other professional thieves.

2. *The behavior that occurs in a behavior system is not unique to any particular individual.* According to Sutherland and Cressey, behavior in the commission of criminal acts is common behavior to persons in that system and is not unique to any particular individual. For example, professional thieves have their own ways of behaving in the principal situations that they encounter in their criminal activities. In

Rank	Offense	Estimated Number of Arrests
1	All other offenses (except traffic)	2,489,200
2	Driving under the influence	1,788,400
*3	Larceny-theft	1,348,400
4	Drunkenness	964,800
5	Drug abuse violations	811,400
6	Disorderly conduct	671,700
7	Simple assaults	637,600
8	Liquor law violations	548,600
*9	Burglary	443,300
10	Fraud	342,600
*11	Aggravated assault	305,390
12	Vandalism	259,600
13	Weapons: carrying, possessing, etc.	180,900
14	Runaway	161,200
*15	Robbery	136,870
*16	Motor vehicle theft	133,900
17	Stolen property: buying, receiving, possessing	127,100
18	Prostitution and commercial vice	113,800
19	Sex offenses (except forcible rape)	100,600
20	Forgery and counterfeiting	87,600
21	Curfew and loitering law violations	81,500
22	Offenses against family and children	58,800
*23	Forcible rape	36,970
24	Vagrancy	33,800
25	Gambling	32,100
*26	Arson	19,500
*27	Murder and nonnegligent manslaughter	18,330
28	Suspicion	12,900
29	Embezzlement	11,400

*UCR Index Crimes.

FIGURE 20-1

A total of 11.9 million arrests were reported by law enforcement agencies in 1985.

most cases, the behavior of one professional thief in a given situation will be similar to the behavior of another professional thief in a similar situation (i.e., they all tend to act the same in most situations).

3. *There is a feeling of identification of those who participate in the behavior system.* Criminals who commit certain types of offenses have a feeling that they belong together. For example, Sutherland and Cressey suggested that a professional forger and a professional confidence man would feel that they belong together because they have common interests and standards, whereas an embezzler and an automobile thief lacking common interests and standards would not have the feeling of belonging together.

According to Sutherland and Cressey, if the behavior system can be isolated, the problem would then be to study and explain it as a unit. Concerning the study of a system, Sutherland and Cressey explain [2]:

> This is similar to an attempt to explain baseball in America. It does not consist primarily of explaining why a particular person becomes a baseball player, in fact the explanation of why a particular person becomes a baseball player merely assumes the existence and persistence of baseball as a system. By taking the behavior system as a problem it is possible to avoid some of the methodological difficulties which arise when the act of a specific person is taken as the problem.

Sutherland and Cressey admitted that not all crimes may be considered as part of a behavioral system. According to them there are certain crimes that stand isolated and separate from any system. (*Note:* They fail to provide any examples of crimes that are not a part of any behavior system. However, for those crimes that are part of a behavior system, Sutherland and Cressey point out that they may be better understood as part of a system than as individual crimes.)

■ CRIME DOES NOT PAY OR DOES IT?

As children, we are taught that "crime does not pay." A closer examination of crime and its rewards appears to establish that the saying may not be correct. If crime pays, maybe criminals are rational beings.

W. E. Cobb conducted research on the material benefits of grand larceny and burglary using FBI statistics for Norfolk, Virginia, for the years 1964 and 1966 [3]. His study, though dated, provides insight on the material benefits of criminal behavior. Cobb estimated the value of the property stolen (discounted for sale to fences) times the number of property offenses suspected to have been committed by each criminal during the period under study and compared this to the estimated incomes in wages that criminals would likely make if legally employed. He also considered the income lost through imprisonment and concluded that thieves in general make "slightly" more from crime than they would if legally employed. (*Note:* He did not consider in his study the loss of freedom and other intangible costs of imprisonment.)

A similar study was made of burglars in Chicago by Krohm [4]. Krohm estimated the net annual income for the average burglar, including the chances of being caught and serving time in prison. Krohm concluded that burglary is a "highly superior" source of income when compared to the types of legitimate employment the average burglar could hope to obtain.

Sesnowitz also conducted a study of burglaries in Pennsylvania for the year 1967 [5]. He concluded that taking all the factors into consideration, such as the loss of time from imprisonment if convicted and the reduced value received from the stolen property, the average burglar would make more money from legitimate employment.

Thomas Plate conducted a study of "successful" criminals. He concluded that criminals work on commissions [6]. The criminal's income therefore depends to some extent on how hard the criminal works at crime. Plate also points out that the criminal's income is tax-free, and this saves the criminal considerable money each year. He estimated criminal salaries of successful criminals (1975 levels) as follows:

Pickpocket	$ 20,000
Bank robber	$ 24,000
Loan shark	$150,000
Hit man	$ 75,000
House burglar	$ 26,500
Numbers runner	$ 26,000
Mob lieutenant	$125,000

■ ECONOMIC COST OF CRIME TO VICTIMS

According to the Bureau of Justice Statistics, burglary, household larceny, and motor vehicle offenses had the largest economic cost per offense. (*Note:* Embezzlement, white-collar, and business crimes were not included in this study.) Approximately 35 percent of the losses were recovered or reimbursed within six months after the offense. Most of the costs were from losses of property or cash and medical expenses resulting from the offense. (*Note:* The cost of the justice system: The federal, state, and local spending for all civil and criminal justice activities in the United States for fiscal year 1987 was $5.6 billion [7].)

■ CAREER CRIMINALS

The term "career criminal" refers to a person who makes or attempts to make a living by committing crime. The average career criminal is normally in and out of prison or jail all of his or her life. Most career criminals live at or below the poverty level. The career criminal is usually a property offender.

FIGURE 20-2

Two out of five prison inmates reported that they were under the influence of drugs or were very drunk around the time of their offenses.

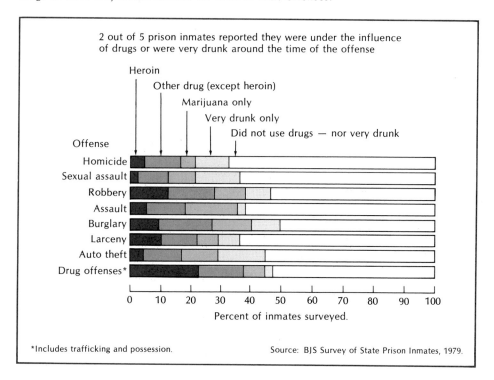

■ RECIDIVISM

The crimes most susceptible to recidivism are forgery, auto theft, robbery, burglary, and assault. Actual recidivism rates are difficult to measure because they depend on the length of time under consideration [8]. For example, if the period of study is ten years, more repeat offenders will be found than if the period of study was five years.

Sheldon and Eleanor Glueck did a study of 510 inmates released from a Massachusetts Reformatory during 1921 and 1922 [9]. The inmates were examined every five years over a fifteen-year period. Only 418 could be traced for the entire period. Of those, 80 percent were considered as "unrehabilitated" after five years. About one-third of the inmates were considered recidivists. Less than 25 percent of the inmates did not have any conflicts with the law.

The study by the Gluecks focused on behavior that occurred over sixty years ago. How relevant are the results today? The most comprehensive current study on recidivism was conducted by the Rand Corporation under the direction of Stephen P. Klein in 1986. The findings of the Rand study are very similar to those noted by the Gluecks. Accordingly, it appears that the prevalence of recidivism has changed little in the past sixty years despite the changes in society. The Rand Study's findings include [10]:

1. Habitual offenders usually do not specialize in one crime but commit a variety of different offenses.

2. Habitual offenders commit an average of 10 to 20 crimes per arrest (note that this varies across crime types and offenders).

3. A small number of offenders are responsible for a disproportionately large number of crimes.

4. The habitual offender usually has a background that includes involvement in crime as a young juvenile and a poor employment record.

Additional general conclusions regarding recidivism include:

1. Recidivists generally outnumber first-timers in major prison populations. This is probably due to our tendency not to confine first-time offenders.

2. Recidivists tend to be a small but persistent minority with "hardcore" problems in terms of socialization.

3. The majority of recidivists' personalities can be classified as:

a. The inadequate, dependent repeater. This is the person who is arrested over and over for drunk and disorderly conduct, vagrancy, petty larceny, and so on.

b. The dysocial or subcultural repeater. This is a person who is engaged in illegal business in which arrest is an occupational hazard (e.g., the pimp or the gambler).

c. The compulsive recidivist, who repeats the same crime again and again. This is a person who starts early in life and repeats the same offense. Glaser considers these offenders as "adolescent recapitulators" [11]. The recidivist rapist would fit in this classification.

d. The impulsive recidivist, who may repeat a variety of crimes over and over. The sociopath, psychopath, or person with an antisocial personality disorder who is impulsive, without anxiety, and is willing to do anything without feeling for others is an example of this type of recidivist. (See Chapter 18 for further discussion of the sociopath.) The impulsive recidivist's asocial outlook allows him or her to commit property and assaultive offenses [12].

Allen Beck and Bernard Shipley, Bureau of Justice Statistics, traced the criminal activities over a six-year period of a sample of young adults paroled from 22 state prisons in 1978. As a result of the study, they concluded [13]:

- Approximately 69 percent of the parolees were rearrested for a serious felony within the six-year period.
- Recidivism rates were highest in the first two years after release from prison.
- Recidivism rates were higher among men, minorities, and persons who had not completed high school.
- Seventy-five percent of those paroled for property offenses were rearrested, compared to about 66 percent of those paroled for violent personal crimes.
- The longer the parolee's prior arrest record, the higher the rate of recidivism.
- The earlier the parolee's first adult arrest, the more likely the chances for rearrest.
- The length of time served in prison had no consistent impact on recidivism rate. Those who had served six months or less were rearrested at the same rate as those who had served more than two years.
- Over 20 percent of the rearrests occurred in states other than those in which the offenders were paroled.

▌ FEAR OF CRIME

Society has traditionally not collected data on the fear of crime. There are some isolated studies that have attempted to measure the public's fear of crime and the extent of that fear. The most comprehensive report on this subject is *The Figgie Report on Fear of Crime* [14]. That report noted that:

- Two-fifths of those surveyed reported that they were "highly fearful" that they would become victims of crime.
- Most of those surveyed felt uneasy walking streets in their own neighborhoods.
- The highest level of fear was reported by elderly women.
- The least afraid group were young males.

According to various Gallup Polls, high school students appear to be more worried about crime than about hunger and poverty, drug use, nuclear war, pollution, population growth, and energy shortages. The elderly also appear to be more worried about crime than most other problems. The majority of adults state that they feel safe in their own neighborhoods. Almost 90 percent of the adults questioned stated

The Coconut Grove Fire

The Coconut Grove was a popular Boston nightclub. One evening, a bus boy was replacing a burned-out bulb in the corner of a downstairs lounge. He lit a match to illuminate the area. Paper decorations caught fire and the blaze spread quickly. Patrons unable to find an exit or an exit that was not blocked, panicked. As the result of the fire many people died. It was later established that there were numerous fire hazards, including defective wiring, flammable decorations, overcrowding and blocked or concealed exits.

Questions: If it were established that the owner was responsible for creating and permitting the conditions to exist that produced the fire and prevented people from escaping, is he a murderer? How different is his degree of guilt, for causing the death of many, from that of a robber who kills only one victim? Aren't both crimes motivated by economic reasons?

that they felt safe at their place of employment [15]. (*Note:* The odds are 2 in 100,000 that a male worker will be murdered at work. There are about 1600 homicides on the job annually in the United States.)

■ REPORTING CRIME

It appears that less than two-fifths of all crimes are reported to official authorities. Except for rape, the more serious the crime in terms of economic loss or physical injury, the more likely it is to be reported. Murder appears to be the most reported crime, based on the fact that the presence of a body or the absence of a person must be explained. Excluding murder, the most frequently reported crimes are motor vehicle theft (over 70 percent reported), aggravated assault (about 60 percent reported), and robbery (about 55 percent reported). The overall reporting rate for violent personal crimes is about 50 percent, whereas it is only 25 percent for personal crimes of theft [16].

Demographic characteristics (age, sex, and race) make less difference in reporting rates than does the type of crime. Most crimes are reported by the victim or a member of the victimized household. Crimes against teenagers are less likely to be reported to the police than crimes against adults. This fact may be explained by a lack of trust and confidence that many teenagers have for the criminal justice system.

The reasons most often given for reporting property crimes include:

1. To establish proof of loss (for insurance or taxes)
2. Desire to recover the property

The reasons most often given for not reporting property crimes include:

1. Not important enough to report
2. Police would be ineffective
3. Too busy

The reasons most often given for reporting violent personal crimes include:

1. Desire to see offender punished
2. To prevent crime from recurring

The reasons most often cited for not reporting violent personal crimes include:

1. Offender was a member of household
2. Matter was private or personal
3. Embarrassment

■ CRIMES AND DRUGS

While there is considerable evidence of a relationship between drug and/or alcohol use and the involvement in criminal behavior, the strength of the relationship and how it operates are not clear [17]. Some of the common conclusions regarding this link include:

1. Drugs or/and alcohol may stimulate aggressiveness or weaken inhibition of offenders.
2. Obtaining money to buy drugs or alcohol may be motivating offenders to commit other crimes.
3. Drug use is much greater among criminal offenders than among nonoffenders.
4. Prison inmates used alcohol more than their counterparts in the general population.
5. There is indication that involvement in crime may precede drug use.

■ FEMALE CRIMINALS

Women constitute less than 6 percent of the adult prison population. The ratio of arrests is generally about one female to every five males. The most popular reasons advanced for the differences involve social and cultural factors. In addition to the differences in crime rates for male and female offenders, the following is a list of other differences noted between male and female criminal behavior patterns:

1. Women seldom commit robbery and burglary.
2. Women seldom kill strangers. The majority of victims of female killers and husbands, lovers, rivals, and children.
3. Women criminals are more likely than male criminals to be married.

4. Female offenders are normally older than male offenders. Most male offenders are between the ages of 12 and 24; most female offenders are between the ages of 20 and 35.

5. In recent years arrest rates for women have increased at a much higher rate than arrest rates for men.

▌VICTIMOLOGY

For me, as a matter of fact, this was the most notable quality of his confession—that Gary White, who had brutally assaulted and murdered Theresa Dunn a few hours after meeting her in a Manhattan singles spot called Mr. Goodbar, had a very clear sense of himself as the victim of the woman he had murdered . . . [18].

The science of victimology is the study of crime from the victim's viewpoint, with emphasis on the relationship between the victim and the offender. Most textbooks on criminology overlook the impact of the victim in crime causation. The manner in which a question is asked limits and disposes the answer. Researchers have traditionally asked questions regarding the crime problem in such a manner that the resultant body of knowledge about crime has been largely about the criminal, especially the conditions that produced the criminal [19]. Research indicates that the victim plays a significant role in the crime causation process in many crimes. Historically, we have been quick to blame the rape victim for being raped but have ignored the victim's part in other crimes. (Note: It appears that in most cases, the rape victim is less involved, if involved at all, in the causation process than the victim is in the majority of other crimes.)

Schafer described crime as a social phenomenon, not an individual act [20]. In his study, Schafer described the problems of the criminal–victim relationship and assigned to the victim complementary functional responsibility for his or her part in the relationship.

The Penal-Couple

Mendelsohn, a Romanian barrister, claims to have made the first in-depth criminological study of the victim and the victim–offender relationship [21]. He used the term "penal-couple" to describe the relationship between the victim and the criminal. At the time he coined the term, Mendelsohn was a practicing attorney. He required his clients in criminal cases to answer some 300 or more questions regarding the crime and the victim. As the result of his study, he concluded that a "parallelity" exists between the biopsychosocial personality of the offender and that of the victim. He viewed the total set of criminal factors as one set that includes the victim. Mendelsohn established "potential of victimal receptivity" to measure a person's unconscious aptitude for being victimized.

The essence of Mendelsohn's studies was the realization of the value of looking at the crime problem from a new direction by focusing on the victim and his or her relationship with the offender. Thus Mendelsohn's perspective involves looking at familiar facts from an unfamiliar perspective.

Hans Von Hentig

Hans Von Hentig published a victim-centered study of crime in which he concluded that in many respects the victim shapes and molds the criminal and the crime [22]. In an earlier law review article, Hentig stated that while in many cases, a person may be killed without his conduct affecting the final determination, in many other cases there is reciprocal action between the perpetrator and the victim [23]. Frequently, he concluded that a mutuality between the perpetrator and the victim can be observed. He also contended that this phenomenon of criminal interaction has escaped the attention of sociopathologists. Hentig theorized that if there are born criminals, it is evident that there are "born victims" who are self-harming and self-destroying through the medium of a pliable outsider. This concept is similar to Mendelsohn's concept of "potential of victimal receptivity." Thus it would appear that both Mendelsohn and Von Hentig agree with the theory that certain people are "victim-prone."

Von Hentig concluded that there were four categories of persons who make perfect murder victims: the depressive type, the greedy person, the wanton type, and the tormentor. He determined that the depressive type is at the top of the list. He sees the depressive type as dominated by a secret desire to be annihilated, and states that a study of accidents would reveal that many depressive persons are killed in accidents. In addition, he determined that the depressed person's instinct for self-preservation is weakened. The depressed, according to Von Hentig, are not bold, simply unsuspecting and careless. He points out that melancholy murderers are caught with less trouble by the police and are more easily induced to plead guilty.

Von Hentig also noted that the greedy person shows an inclination to be victimized and that the expectation of easy money affects some individuals like drugs, removing their normal inhibitions and deadening any well-founded suspicions. As to the wanton type, Von Hentig sees this type as victims not only to an aggressor but also to their own special conditions. For example, he notes a number of cases involving youthful victims and middle-aged women victims, who, approaching the climacteric period, fall victims to aggressors and their "own critical conditions." By "critical conditions" Von Hentig is referring to the situational stresses that are normally present during critical times of a person's life (e.g., approaching old age). The tormentor type was his final class of perfect murder victims. In these cases, when some form of oppression, whether parental, marital, and so on, has existed for some time, the oppression becomes tyrannical and insufferable. At this point, in many cases, a final explosion occurs, with the tormentor becoming the victim, as in the case where the wife-beating husband is killed by his wife (e.g., "the burning bed syndrome").

Hentig's chief contribution to the study of crime causation was the elevation of social interaction to the central unit of analysis. He stressed the "duet frame of reference" and limited his study to an analysis of specific encounters and their immediate outcomes. "Duet frame of reference" refers to the process of considering the victim and offender as a duet in the criminal process.

The Concept of a Hidden Unity

In 1954, Henri Ellenberger of the Menninger Foundation introduced the concept of a hidden fundamental unity in crime between the offender and the victim. Under Ellenberger's concept there is neither guilt nor innocence, neither criminal nor victim. He based his concept on the Brahmian philosophy. According to the Brahmian philosophy, all is illusion or deceptive manifestation of a hidden fundamental unity. As a result, there is neither guilt nor innocence. The concept is expressed in the formula of Tat Twam Asi (thou art that). Thus, according to this concept, "it is ourselves who lie hidden in all people who appear to us." Ellenberger contrasts this concept of crime from the popular view of crime, which is that the criminal and the victim are as different as night and day [24]. Thus the wicked Cain kills the good Abel.

According to Ellenberger, this hidden unity concept was first expressed not by criminologists or social scientists, but by literary writers such as Ralph Waldo Emerson in *Brahma* and Kahlil Gibran in *The Prophet* [25].

Ellenberger noted that it is frequently difficult to draw a distinction between the psychological makeup of the offender and the victim

IN FOCUS

> The murdered is not unaccountable for his own murder, and the robbed is not blameless in being robbed. . . . Yea, the guilty is oftentimes the victim of the injured. And still more often, the condemned is the burden bearer for the guiltless and unblamed.   (Kahlil Gibran, *The Prophet*, pp. 47–48)

[26]. He concludes that many criminals are predisposed psychologically to achieve the role of a victim. As he notes, the Bible tells of Cain being marked by a sign on his forehead to prevent him from being killed by his fellow man. He sees this act as a recognition of the concept that as a criminal, he was also predisposed to be a victim.

According to Ellenberger, a person may be the criminal and the victim simultaneously. He noted the psychoanalytic studies of Karl Menninger on suicide [27]. In those studies, Menninger had stated that in many cases, the wish to die, the wish to kill, and the wish to be killed existed at the same time in the person, with the predominance in each particular case of one or the other of these forces. Ellenberger stated that in many cases, it is sheer chance whether the subject becomes the criminal or the victim. For example, the same person, when he or she is sober, might rob his or her neighbor, and when drunk, might be robbed by the neighbor.

Ellenberger, like Mendelsohn and Von Hentig, recognized that certain persons have special characteristics which make them victim-prone. However, Ellenberger described this condition as a "special predisposition" on the part of the person to be a victim [28].

William Frank McDonald

William Frank McDonald made an analysis of a survey conducted by the American Transit Association regarding the causes and nature of assaults and robberies on bus drivers [29]. He interviewed 1065 bus drivers in five major cities. Of the drivers interviewed, 59 percent expressed the opinion that drivers participate in their own victimization.

During the period of the study, three bus drivers were killed in three different cities. Looking into each case, McDonald felt as if the same case were being described for a second and a third time. Each driver had a reputation for being critical of the permissiveness of mod-

IN FOCUS

If the red slayer thinks he slays,
Or if the slain thinks he is slain,
They know not the subtle ways
I keep, and pass, and turn again.
(Ralph Waldo Emerson, *Brahma*)

ern society. Each had also been critical of how the courts and the transit systems were handling the crime problem and let it be known that they were not going to let any "punk kid" rob them. Each carried a gun in violation of company rules, and finally, each had attempted to use the gun to prevent the robbery, despite clear company policies against such heroism. Each victim tended to identify himself with the need for public order movement and wanted to do what the formal agencies of social control were not doing (i.e., bring the criminal to justice).

McDonald also found that bus drivers who had taken precautionary measures against assaults and robberies, such as watching the passengers with rear-view mirrors, rather than traffic, were in fact assaulted and robbed more often than drivers who had not taken any precautionary measures. His findings suggest that there is a definite relationship between the perception of risk and concern for crime and the experience of being victimized. It may be that this phenomenon is caused by subconscious feedback being transmitted to the offender that the victim can be intimidated.

Marvin Wolfgang's Study of Criminal Homicides

Marvin Wolfgang conducted a study of criminal homicides in Philadelphia [30]. One part of the study considered victim-precipitated homicides. Wolfgang stated that Hentig's concept of the "duet frame of crime" provided the basis for his analysis of the victim-prone relationship. He noted the importance of the social interaction concept of crime in his studies. Wolfgang concluded that a number of would-be murderers became victims. In many cases, the victim had the same major characteristics as the offender (e.g., socioeconomic standing in the community and prior criminal records). Wolfgang concluded in an article published eleven years after his original study that many

IN FOCUS

Comments on Victim Interaction

There is so much talk about crime in the streets and the rights of the criminal that little attention is being paid to the victims of the crime. But there is a current of opinion that our courts are being too soft on the victims, and many of them are going unpunished for allowing a crime to be committed against them.

One man who feels strongly about this is Professor Heinrich Applebaum, a criminologist who feels that unless the police start cracking down on the victims of criminal acts, the crime rate in this country will continue to rise.

"The people who are responsible for crime in this country are the victims. If they didn't allow themselves to be robbed, the problem of crime in this country would be solved," Applebaum said.

"That makes sense, Professor. Why do you think the courts are soft on victims of crimes?"

"We're living in a permissive society and anything goes," Applebaum replied. "Victims of crimes don't seem to be concerned about the consequences of their acts. They walk down a street after dark, or have cash registers right out where everyone can see them. They seem to think that they can do this in the United States and get away with it."

"You speak as if all the legal machinery in this country was weighted in favor of the victim, instead of the person who committed the crime."

"It is," Applebaum said. "While everyone is worried about the victim, the poor criminal is dragged down to the police station, booked and arraigned, and if he's lucky, he'll be let out on bail. He may lose his job if his boss hears about it and there is even a chance that if he has a police record, it may prejudice the judge when he's sentenced."

"I guess in this country people always feel sorrier for the victim than they do for the person who committed the crime."

"You can say that again. Do you know that in some states they are even compensating victims of crimes?"

"It's hard to believe," I said.

"Well, it's true. The dogooders and the bleeding hearts all feel that victims of crimes are misunderstood, and if they were treated better, they would stop being victims. But the statistics don't bear this out. The easier you are on victims, the higher the crime rate becomes."

"What is the solution, Professor?"

"I say throw the book at anybody who's been robbed. They knew what they were getting into when they decided to be robbed, and they should pay the penalty for it. Once a person has been a victim of a crime and realizes he can't get away with it, the chances of his becoming a victim again will be slim."

"Why do people want to become victims of crime, Professor?"

"Who knows? They're probably looking for thrills. Boredom plays a part, but I would think the biggest factor is that victims think they can still walk around the streets of their cities and get away with it. Once they learn they can't, you'll see a big drop in crime statistics.

"You make a lot of sense, Professor. Do you believe the American people are ready to listen to you?"

"They'd better be, because the criminal element is getting pretty fed up with all the permissive coddling of victims that is going on in this country."

Source: The Washington Post, Feb. 4, 1969, p. 6; reprinted courtesy of Art Buchwald, Los Angeles Times Syndicate.

victim-precipitated homicides were, in fact, caused by the subconscious desire of the victims to commit suicide [31].

Wolfgang's study was partially replicated by Pokorny for criminal homicides occurring in Houston, Texas; by Voss and Hepburn for criminal homicides occurring in Chicago; and by Roberson for criminal homicides occurring in San Francisco [32]. Their findings support Wolfgang's conclusion that in many criminal homicides the victim plays a significant role in the causation process.

■ SUMMARY

Sutherland and Cressey contend that there are criminal behavior systems. They hold that a criminal behavior system can be described by three characteristics. The three characteristics are (1) the "behavior system" is an integrated unit, (2) the behavior that occurs in a system is not unique to any particular individual, and (3) there is a feeling of identification on the part of those who participate in the system. Criminals who commit certain types of offenses have a feeling that they belong together. Sutherland and Cressey admitted that not every crime may be considered part of a "behavioral system." According to them, certain crimes are isolated and separate from any system.

As children, we are taught that "crime does not pay." A closer examination of crime and its rewards appears to establish that the saying may not be correct. If crime pays, maybe criminals are rational beings.

The term "career criminal" is used to identify the person who makes or attempts to make a living committing crime. The average career criminal is normally in and out of prison or jail all of his or her life. Most career criminals live at or below the poverty level. The career criminal is usually a property offender.

The crimes most susceptible to recidivism are forgery, auto theft, robbery, burglary, and assault. Actual recidivism rates are difficult to measure because they depend on the length of time under consideration.

It appears that less than two-fifths of all crimes are reported to official authorities. Except for rape, the more serious the crime in terms of economic loss or injury, the more likely it is to be reported. Murder appears to be the most reported crime based on the fact that the presence of a body or the absence of a person must be explained. Demographic characteristics (age, sex, and race) make less difference in the reporting rates than does the type of crime. Most crimes are reported by the victim or a member of the victimized household.

The science of victimology is the study of crime from the victim's viewpoint, with emphasis on the relationship between the victim and the offender. Research indicates that in many crimes, the victim plays a significant role in the crime causation process.

■ MATCHING KEY TERMS AND DEFINITIONS

Match each key term with the correct definition.

a. behavior systems
b. career criminal
c. compulsive recidivist
d. duet frame of reference
e. dysocial recidivist

f. impulsive recidivist
g. inadequate, dependent repeater
h. penal couple
i. Tat Twam Asi
j. victimology

——— 1. A person who is arrested over and over for drunk and disorderly conduct, vagrancy, petty larceny, and so on.

——— 2. A person who is engaged in illegal business in which arrest is an occupational hazard (e.g., the pimp or the gambler).

——— 3. A person who starts early in life and repeats the same offense.

    ___ 4. The recidivist who repeats a variety of crimes over and over whose asocial outlook allows him or her to commit property and assaultive offenses.

    ___ 5. Mendelsohn used the term to describe the relationship between the victim and the criminal.

    ___ 6. The study of crime from the victim's viewpoint, with emphasis on the relationship between the victim and the offender.

    ___ 7. The term used to identify the person who makes or attempts to make a living committing crimes.

    ___ 8. Described by its characteristics, which are: (1) it is an integrated unit; (2) the behavior that occurs in it is not unique to any particular person; and (3) there is a feeling of identification for those who participate in it.

    ___ 9. According to this concept, "it is ourselves who lie hidden in all people who appear to us."

    ___ 10. The process of considering the victim and offender as a duet in the criminal process.

▋ DISCUSSION QUESTIONS

1. Regarding the question "Does crime pay?", does income tax evasion or employee theft "pay"? Explain your answer.

2. In your opinion, what role does the victim play in the crime causation process?

3. Explain the concept of crime "behavior systems."

Notes

1. Edwin H. Sutherland and Donald R. Cressey, *Criminology*, 8th ed. New York: J. B. Lippincott, 1970.
2. Sutherland and Cressey, 1970:281.
3. W. E. Cobb, "Theft and the Two Hypotheses," in S. Rottenberg, ed., *The Economics of Crime and Punishments.* Washington, D.C.: American Enterprise Institute for Public Policy Research, 1973.
4. G. Krohm, "The Pecuniary Incentives of Property Crimes," in Rottenberg, 1973.
5. M. Sesnowitz, "The Returns of Burglary," *Western Economic Journal*, vol. 10, 1972, pp. 477–481.
6. Thomas Plate, *Crime Pays.* New York: Simon and Schuster, 1975.

7. U.S. Department of Justice, *Data Report*, 1987:28.

8. Vernon Fox, *Introduction to Criminology*. Englewood Cliffs, N.J.: Prentice-Hall, 1976, p. 305.

9. Sheldon Glueck and Eleanor Glueck, *Criminal Careers in Retrospect*. New York: The Commonwealth Fund, 1943.

10. Stephen P. Klein, "Prevalence and Predictability of Recidivism," in *Prosecutor's Brief*. Sacramento: California District Attorney's Association, 1986, pp. 4–8.

11. Daniel Glasser, *Adult Crime and Social Policy*. Englewood Cliffs, N.J.: Prentice-Hall, 1972.

12. Fox, 1976:307.

13. U.S. Department of Justice, BJS, *Special Report: Recidivism of Young Parolees*. Washington, D.C.: U.S. Government Printing Office, May 1987.

14. *The Figgie Report on Fear of Crime: America Afraid*, Part I, *The General Public*. Willoughby, Ohio: Research and Forecasts, Inc., sponsored by A-T-O, Inc., 1980.

15. Vernon Fox, 1976.

16. U.S. Department of Justice, BJS, *Special Report*, 1987.

17. U.S. Department of Justice, BJS, *Report to the Nation on Crime and Justice*, 2nd ed. Washington, D.C.: U.S. Government Printing Office, 1988.

18. Judith Rossner, *Looking for Mr. Goodbar*. New York: Simon and Schuster, 1975.

19. William Frank McDonald, "The Victim: A Social Psychological Study of Criminal Victimization," unpublished Ph.D. dissertation, University of California, 1970.

20. Stephen Schafer, *The Victim and His Criminal*. New York: Random House, 1968.

21. B. Mendelsohn, "The Origin of Victimology," *Excerpta Criminologica*, vol. 3, Fall 1963, pp. 239–256.

22. Hans Von Hentig, *The Criminal and His Victim*. New Haven, Conn.: Yale University Press, 1948.

23. Hans Von Hentig, "Remarks on the Interaction of Perpetrator and Victim," *Journal of Criminal Law, Criminology and Police Science*, vol. 31, Sept. 1941, pp. 303–309.

24. Henri Ellenberger, "Psychological Relationships between Criminal and Victim," *Archives of Criminal Psychodynamics*, vol. 2, Aug. 1954, pp. 257–299.

25. Ralph Waldo Emerson, "Brahma," *The Harvard Classics*, Vol. 42. New York: Collier, 1938; and Kahlil Gibran, *The Prophet*. New York: Alfred A. Knopf, 1923.

26. Ellenberger, 1954:288.

27. Karl Menninger, *Man against Himself*. New York: Harcourt, Brace, 1938.

28. Ellenberger, 1954:298.

29. McDonald, 1970.

30. Marvin E. Wolfgang, *Patterns in Criminal Homicide*. Philadelphia: University of Pennsylvania Press, 1958.

31. Marvin E. Wolfgang, "Victim-Precipitated Criminal Homicide," in M. E. Wolfgang, ed., *Studies in Criminal Homicide*. New York: Harper & Row, 1969.

32. Alex D. Pokorny, "A Comparison of Homicide in Two Cities," *Journal of Criminal Law, Criminology and Police Science*, vol. 105, Dec. 1965, pp. 479–497; Cliff Roberson, "Patterns of Victim Involvement in Criminal Homicide," unpublished Ph.D. dissertation, U.S. International University, 1976; and H. L. Voss and J. R. Hepburn, "Patterns of Criminal Homicide in Chicago," *Journal of Criminal Law, Criminology and Police Science*, vol. 109, Dec. 1968, pp. 499–508.

21

Crime Typologies

CHAPTER HIGHLIGHTS

- Typologies refer to the study of different types of crime.
- Typologies examine the patterns of particular types of criminal behavior and make statements about personal and environmental factors in crime causation.
- As people grow older, they are less likely to commit crimes.
- The majority of offenders who commit crimes are between the ages of 16 to 24 years of age.
- Although minorities tend to commit more common crimes, they are also more likely to be victims of common crimes.
- Offenders tend to commit crimes against victims of their own races.
- Most common crimes are committed by male offenders.
- Violent personal crime victimization rates are highest for black males and lowest for white females.
- Most bank robbers appear to be unsophisticated, unprofessional criminals.
- Calling the police when a domestic violence incident occurs may reduce the risk of one spouse attacking the other spouse again within six months by about 60 percent.
- Black women are more likely to be raped than are nonblack women.
- It is estimated that only about half the rapes or attempted rapes are reported to the police.
- Alcohol-related automobile crashes kill approximately 25,000 persons each year.
- Women constitute less than 6 percent of the adult prison population.

KEY TERMS

Common Crimes   Domestic Violence
Criminal Homicide   DUI
Date Rape   Embezzlement

Incest　　　　　　　　　　　　　　Typologies
Naive Check Forgers　　　　　　　Victimless Crimes
Organized Crime　　　　　　　　　Violent Personal Crimes
Pilfers　　　　　　　　　　　　　　White-Collar Crimes
Serial Murderers

In this chapter the differential expressions of criminal behaviors are examined. Crime typologies are used to link individual criminal conduct together in clusters in order to study the clusters as a whole. Typologies help classify and group large numbers of crimes into easily understood categories. Typologies are also models of "typical" criminals who commit particular crimes: the property offender, violent personal offender, white-collar criminal, and so on. Typologies examine the patterns of particular types of criminal behavior and make statements about personal and environmental factors. (*Note:* When dealing with crime rates and criminal justice statistics, it is easy to get lost in statistics. Accordingly, in many cases we have presented generally accepted conclusions regarding crime patterns and offenders without presenting the detailed statistical data to substantiate the conclusions.)

■ COMMON CRIMES

Often when we talk about the "crime problem" we are considering "common crimes." Common crimes are, for the most part, violent personal offenses, petty property crimes, theft, burglary, and robbery. Looking at the age, race, and sex characteristics of those who commit common crimes, the following conclusions are apparent:

- *Age.* As people grow older, they are less likely to commit common crimes. The majority of common crime offenders are between the ages of 16 and 26. Common crimes, therefore, are normally crimes of the youth. It also appears that the earlier a person gets involved in the criminal justice system as an offender, the greater the chances that he or she will continue a pattern of criminal behavior.

371

IN FOCUS

Average Age of Offenders at Arrest By Type of Crime

Crime	Average Age at Arrest
Murder	30
Robbery	24
Arson	22
Rape	28
Motor vehicle theft	22
Common theft	22

Source: U.S. Department of Justice, BJS, Report to the Nation on Crime and Justice, 2nd ed. (Washington, DC.: U.S. Government Printing Office, 1988).

■ *Race.* There is an overrepresentation of minorities involved in common crimes, both as victims and as offenders. While minorities tend to commit more common crimes, they are also more likely to become victims of common crimes. Offenders tend to commit crimes against victims of their own races.

■ *Sex.* Males commit most of the common crimes. The sex of a person is one of the best predictors of whether or not the person will be involved in criminal behavior as an offender. For example, over 90 percent of people arrested for robbery and burglary are male. Shoplifting, however, is a female-dominated crime.

Social and Economic Characteristics of Offenders

There appears to be a lack of consensus regarding the relationship between crime and various social and economic factors. The common social and economic characteristics of common offenders include the following:

■ A high proportion of offenders grow up in single-parent homes.
■ Most offenders are not married. However, most have dependent children (71 percent of the women inmates and 52 percent of the male inmates).

- Prison and jail inmates are likely to have relatives who have served time in prisons or jails.
- The educational level of incarcerated offenders is several grades below the national average.

■ VIOLENT PERSONAL CRIMES

According to data collected by the National Crime Survey (NCS), it appears that violent personal crime rates increased during the 1970s but fell sharply in the 1980s. Most of the rise in rates in the 1970s was for victims under age 35. The violent personal crime rates for victims age 35 and older remained fairly stable during the 1970s and 1980s

FIGURE 21-1

Measures of recidivism vary; more offenders are rearrested than reconvicted, and more are reconvicted than reincarcerated.

	Percent of Young Parolees Who Within Six Years of Release from Prison Were:		
	Rearrested	Reconvicted	Reincarcerated
All parolees	69	53	49
Sex			
Men	70	54	50
Women	52	40	36
Race/ethnicity			
White	64	49	45
Black	76	60	56
Hispanic	71	50	44
Other	75	65	63
Education			
Less than 12 years	71	55	51
High school graduate	61	46	43
Some college	48	44	31
Paroling offenses			
Violent offenses	64	43	39
Murder	70	25	22
Robbery	64	45	40
Assault	72	51	47
Property offenses	73	60	56
Burglary	73	60	56
Forgery/fraud	74	59	56
Larceny	71	61	55
Drug offenses	49	30	25

Source: *Recidivism of young parolees,* BJS Special Report, May 1987.

[1]. It is unclear why the rise and then the fall in violent personal crime rates.

Violent crime victimization rates are highest for black males and lowest for white females. Unemployed persons are victims of violent crime at a higher rate than employed persons. (*Note*: minorities also have a higher unemployment rate than nonminorities.) Teenage victimization rates for violent personal crimes are approximately twice that of persons over the age of 20. If the current crime rates continue, four out of five of today's teenagers will become victims of a violent crime during their lifetimes.

The chances of being the victim of an assault is much greater than the chances of being the victim of robbery. For women, the chances of being robbed are greater than the chances of being raped.

Most violent personal crimes are committed by strangers (57 percent, including 11 percent where the offender was known by sight only). Most violent crimes committed by strangers are committed against males (70 percent). Violent personal crimes tend to be intra-

FIGURE 21-2
Riot damage.
Courtesy of the
Washington State
Department of
Corrections.

racial (i.e., committed against victims who are of the same race as the offenders). About 80 percent of the violent personal crimes committed against nonminorities are committed by nonminorities. About 85 percent of the crimes against minorities are committed by minorities. Most violent crimes occur in the general location where the victims live [2].

Criminal Homicide

Criminal homicide is defined as a death where the killer is determined to have intentionally killed someone without legal justification or to have accidentally killed someone as a consequence of reckless or grossly negligent conduct. Many homicides are precipitated by another crime, such as robbery, rape, or battery.

Criminal homicide is the second-highest killer of young people between the ages of 15 and 24; the highest is automobile accidents. Murder, a type of criminal homicide, is used to indicate intentional killing without legal justification. Murder most often results from arguments or the commission of another felony. There are four general categories of murderers:

1. *Subcultural murderer.* This is a person who accepts violence as a problem-solving technique.

2. *Deliberate antisocial lifestyle murderer.* This is a murderer who exhibits an antisocial lifestyle (e.g., the person who kills during a robbery to avoid identification). The serial murderer discussed later in this chapter fits into this category.

3. *One-time offender.* This is a person who leads an otherwise uneventful life and kills because of the circumstances or situation.

4. *Mentally ill or deranged killer.* This is a person who suffers from severe psychiatric disorders.

IN FOCUS

To completely fathom the secret processes of the mind of a man which impels him to kill another human being has not yet been vouchsafed to even the most profound student on the mainsprings of human action [3].

IN FOCUS

Motives Behind Murders

Murder was the result of:	Percent of all murders
Arguments	39
Robbery	9
Narcotics	3
Sex offenses	2
Arson	1
Other felonies and suspected felonies	5
Other motives	18
Unknown motives	23

Serial Murderers

The phrase "serial murderer" is used to describe a murderer who over a period of time commits a series of motiveless murders. Since 1800 there have been at least 143 "known" serial murderers and 1647 "known" victims. Eric W. Hickey conducted a study of serial murderers [4]. His findings included:

1. Twenty-four of the known serial killers were women and 119 were male.

2. Twenty-eight percent used accomplices.

3. Serial killers averaged nine to twelve victims.

4. The majority of victims were strangers to the killers.

5. Sex and money were the motives in at least 85 percent of the killings.

6. There are three types of serial killers:

   a. *Transient killer.* 47 "known" killers were transient killers.

   b. *Single-area killer.* 58 "known" killers fit this category.

   c. *Specific-site killer.* 38 "known" killers always killed their victims at a specific site.

7. Only about 5 percent of the serial killers have visible mental problems.

FIGURE 21–3
Contraband weapons found in a shakedown of a California prison.
Louis P. Carney, *Corrections: Treatment and Philosophy,* © 1980 p 189. Reprinted by permission of Prentice Hall, Inc., Englewood Cliffs, NJ.

In 1982–1983, the Training Division of the Federal Bureau of Investigation conducted an in-depth study of thirty-six convicted sexual serial murderers. Despite the limited number of subjects, the findings tend to point out general characteristics of the offenders. The characteristics noted in the FBI study include [5]:

1. Offenders were predominately white (92 percent).

2. Their intelligence appeared to be above average (measured by IQ tests).

3. They had a history of poor academic performance (65 percent).

4. They had a poor employment history (80 percent).

5. Most often, the mother was the dominant parent in the household (66 percent).

6. Seventy-two percent reported a "cold" relationship with their fathers.

7. Most admitted to having homicidal sexual fantasies in their pre-teens, and a fetish for things such as underwear.

8. Most reported at least one experience of physical or sexual abuse as a child.

Helen Morrison spent more than 4000 hours researching serial murderers [6]. She contended that serial killers are "formed" (both by biology and environment) by their twelfth month of life. Her other findings include:

1. Victims are selected because they have a "certain look" (e.g., long black hair and fair complexion).

2. Most serial killers display an early consistent pattern of minor crimes, such as "peeping Tom" episodes, although they may not have a criminal record.

3. Most serial killers have above-average intelligence and have an interest in law enforcement.

4. Serial killers tend to be overweight, but otherwise look ordinary.

IN FOCUS

How Do Victims of Violent Crime Protect Themselves?

- Rape victims are more likely than victims of other violent crimes to use force, try a verbal response, or attract attention, and they are less likely than the others to use a gun or knife, use nonviolent evasion, or do nothing to protect themselves.

- Robbery victims are the least likely to try to talk themselves out of being victimized and the most likely to do nothing.

- Assault victims are the least likely to attract attention and the most likely to attempt some form of nonviolent evasion.

- Compared with simple assault victims, aggravated assault victims are more likely to use a weapon, less likely to use other means of force, less likely to try to talk themselves out of the incident, and less likely to do nothing to defend themselves.

Source: U.S. Department of Justice, BJS, *Report to the Nation on Crime and Justice,* 2nd ed (Washington, D.C.: U.S. Government Printing Office, 1988).

5. The biological factor in the causation process (according to Morrison) is sex related.

6. By the time serial killers are caught, many have been killing for as long as fifteen years.

7. Morrison contends that serial killers are, for the most part, not insane, but rather, "evil" or "bad."

Rape

There are approximately 1.5 million rapes or attempted rapes reported each year in the United States. Approximately 65 percent of the victims are unmarried and about the same percentage are under 25 years. Black women are more likely to be raped than nonblack women. About 50 percent of the rape victims are from low-income families. Two-thirds of the rapes or attempted rapes occur at night, with the majority of them between 6 P.M. and midnight. Eighty percent of the victims reported that they attempted to use self-protective measures, such as reasoning with the offender, fleeing, screaming, kicking, scratching, and/or using a weapon.

During the twelve-year period 1973–1984, reported rapes occur at a higher average rate in July than in any other month. The lowest average monthly rates occur in February.

It is estimated that only about half the rapes or attempted rapes are reported to the police. Reasons given for not reporting rape include [7]:

1. The incident was too private or personal.
2. The victim felt that the police would be insensitive or ineffective.

The reasons given for reporting rape include:

1. To keep it from happening again or to others
2. To punish the offender

Although rape is often listed as a sex crime, most criminologists consider it as a violent crime in the same category as murder, assaults, and batteries. Rape is also a crime that is closely linked to cultural standards and sex roles. It is linked to cultural standards by the fact that men have always been in more powerful positions relative to women, and rape is a reflection of that power. It is linked to sex roles since rape is seen by many rapists as a means of keeping women in their places (i.e., in subservient roles) [8].

A common classification of rapes by types is as follows [9]:

1. *Power-assertive.* The offender uses rape as an expression of power and dominance.

2. *Power-reassurance.* The offender uses rape in an effort to resolve doubts about his sexual adequacy and masculinity.

3. *Anger-retaliation.* The offender uses rape as an expression of his hostility and rage toward women.

4. *Anger-excitation.* The offender finds pleasure and thrills in the suffering of his victim.

Groth, Burgess, and Holmstrom contend that approximately 65 percent of the rapes are "power rapes" and 35 percent are "anger rapes." According to them, the least common rape is the "anger-excitement," which accounts for only about 6 percent of rapes [10].

DATE RAPES.   An area of increasing concern on college campuses is date rape. One study indicated that approximately one in five college women are victims of rape or attempted rape. In appears that coercive sexual encounters occur frequently in dating situations. Thomas Meyer estimated that less than one in ten date rapes are reported to the police. He contends that many of the date rape victims do not view their experiences as real rapes since it did not involve a stranger "jumping out of the bushes" [11].

MARITAL RAPE.   Traditionally, a husband could not be convicted of raping his wife. A common element of the crime of rape was that the woman was not the spouse of the offender. Until recently, if a woman was forced to have sex with her husband, he could be prosecuted for assault and battery but not rape. Ten states now have statutes that permit husbands to be convicted of rape for having forced sex with their wives. Other states have replaced their rape crimes with sexual assault crimes. The sexual assault crimes include homosexual rape. These statutes are designed to be sexually neutral.

Domestic Violence

The National Crime Surveys indicate that almost 500,000 cases of family violence are reported each year. Domestic violence appears to be a crime that is largely unreported. Common reasons given for not reporting domestic violence include: (1) it's a family or private matter; (2) victims are ashamed or embarrassed to report it; (3) fear of reprisal; and (4) many victims do not view their victimization as crimes. The most common reason given for reporting domestic violence was to prevent future recurrences.

In about 90 percent of all domestic violence cases, men are the offenders. About 25 percent of the victims reported that they had been the victim of at least three similar crimes in the previous six months. It appears that once a woman has been victimized by her spouse or live-in boyfriend, her risk of being victimized again is high.

Until recently, most criminologists thought that the police could do little to prevent domestic violence. The opinion was that since it occurs in private residences inaccessible to the police, there was no way the police could prevent it. A 1977 study by the Police Foundation of domestic violence cases that occurred in Detroit and Kansas City found that in over 50 percent of the cases involving serious domestic assaults or homicide in the two years preceding the crime, the police had been called to the residence at least five times [12]. The Minneapolis Police Department in 1981 conducted an experiment in minor domestic assault cases. Under the experiment, when police were called to the scene of a domestic assault, the officers used one of three random responses:

1. Give advice only.
2. Order the offender to leave the residence for at least eight hours.
3. Arrest the offender.

Six months later, the victims were reinterviewed to determine whether there were repeat assaults by the same offenders. The researchers concluded that calling the police when a domestic violence incident occurs may reduce the risk of a husband attacking his wife again within six months by about 50 percent [13]. For example, 37 percent of the suspects who were only advised and 33 percent of those ordered off the premises for at least eight hours committed a new assault. However, only 19 percent of those who were arrested committed a new offense. As the results of the study, the researchers concluded that in domestic assault cases reported to the police, "an arrest should be made unless there are good, clear reasons why an arrest would be counterproductive" [14].

Child Sexual Abuse and Incest

It is estimated that only a small fraction of child sexual abuse offenses are known to the police. Accordingly, it is difficult to determine the extent of the problem. A 1965 survey of 1000 college-aged women indicated that 25 percent of them had a sexual experience with an adult

IN FOCUS

Victim–Offender Relationship
In Domestic Violence Cases

Offender is:	Percent of incidents
Spouse	40
Ex-spouse	19
Parent or child	1
Sibling	2
Other relative	3
Boyfriend or ex-boyfriend	10
Live-in friend	9
Other nonrelative	16

Source: U.S. Department of Justice, BJS, *Special Report: Preventing Domestic Violence against Women* (Washington, D.C.: U.S. Government Printing Office, 1986).

before age 13, and only 6 percent of the offenses were reported. Another study indicated that one of every four females will be sexually abused before reaching the age of 18 [15].

Robert Berry conducted a study of child sexual abuse. He concluded that the following myths concerning incest are false [16]:

- The aggressor (the father in most cases) is inferior in intelligence and is psychotic. [Berry concluded that the incestuous father is usually a churchgoer, a decent provider, and of average intelligence. Often, it is not until he is discovered that he displays neurotic behavior.]
- The incestuous father is often seduced by a promiscuous daughter. [According to Berry, a promiscuous or seductive daughter is often the result but never the primary cause of an incestuous relationship.]
- Incest is less traumatic than rape or other types of sexual molestation. [Berry disagrees and states that unlike rape or molestation, incest occurs within the home, leaving the victim no escape from the assaults.]

- Children born of incestuous relationships will be retarded or handicapped. [Although this is a possibility, Berry concludes that not all children born out of this type of relationship are abnormal.]
- Incest is always confined to one child. [Although a father will usually target one child, there are numerous cases in which the father has had sexual contact with more than one daughter.]
- Incest is harmless. [Berry concluded that although there is often no use of physical force, studies indicate that emotional damage is usually done. About 25 percent of disturbed children have been involved in incestuous relationships.]

Characteristics of incest include:

- Incest usually develops in multiproblem families. Family members are often emotionally isolated from each other.
- Brother-sister incest is the most common.
- The incestuous parent is often confused regarding family roles and attempts to escape from adult realities.
- The typical incestuous family is character disordered and within a situation that fosters narcissistic and self-centered individuals.
- About 70 percent of the father–daughter incest situations last longer than one year.
- The incestuous father is often authoritarian, domineering, and inspires fear in his family. Often he was sexually abused as a child. Usually, he has strong unmet needs for personal warmth.
- The incestuous father often is a chronic alcoholic.

▌ DRUNK DRIVING

Driving under the influence of alcohol or drugs is considered a serious crime because of the public concern for traffic safety. Drunk driving differs from most other crimes in the following aspects:

1. It lacks the usual criminal motives of gaining property, harming another person, or trafficking in contraband.

2. Physical tests are used by the police to determine whether or not a crime has been committed.

3. Administrative sanctions, such as suspension of drivers' licenses, are also used in an effort to control this crime.

IN FOCUS

Is Drunk Driving America's Only Socially Acceptable Crime?

Alcohol-related automobile crashes kill approximately 25,000 persons each year. In over 50 percent of traffic fatalities, alcohol is involved. About 300,000 people are seriously injured each year in alcohol-related automobile crashes. Between the hours of midnight and 4 A.M., 80 percent of all fatally injured drivers have been drinking.

The Presidential Commission on Drunk Driving concluded that programs to prevent drunk drinking should include at least the following six key elements [17]:

1. Drunk driving must be recognized as being socially unacceptable. We must focus on bringing about changes in society's attitude of toleration toward drunkenness and drunk driving. The public must realize the grave consequences of driving under the influence, and each of us must take personal responsibility for prevention in our own social circles.

2. Since attitudes about drinking and driving are largely shaped within the community, and because the primary administrative responsibility for our efforts to combat drunk driving rests with groups and governments at that level, efforts must have a community focus.

3. Because attempts to deal with the problem involve a large number of governmental agencies and private groups, a systems approach must be employed to ensure that the activities of these groups are coordinated and interrelate smoothly to enhance their effectiveness.

4. To ensure that our laws play their proper role in discouraging the largest possible number of potential drunk drivers, states and localities should take a general deterrence approach in developing short-term remedies to the problem, with the focus on increasing the perception of risk of arrest.

5. To help develop personally responsible drinking and driving behavior and to build a community consensus behind effective countermeasure programs, citizen support through grass-roots groups must be encouraged.

6. Because drivers under the influence are responsible for this problem with its great resulting human cost, it is appropriate that offenders should defray the costs of enforcement, prosecution, adjudication, treatment, and education.

Recommendations of the commission included:

- Mandatory confinement for DUI (driving under the influence) offenders
- DUI cases be concluded within sixty days of the arrest
- Preconviction diversion programs be eliminated
- Required restitution to victims

States have used a variety of methods in an attempt to reduce drunk driving offenses, the methods including the following:

1. Taking administrative sanctions against repeat offenders by suspending or revoking their driver's licenses

2. Requiring drivers to submit to physical tests or lose their driver's licenses

3. Requiring convicted offenders to attend educational programs

4. Raising the drinking age to 21 (*Note*: Public Law 98–363 requires states to raise the drinking age to 21 or lose a percentage of national highway construction funds.)

IN FOCUS

From the steps and recommendations of the Presidential Commission on Drunk Driving listed above, can you detect a prevailing crime causation approach used by the members of the commission?

ROBBERY

Robbery occurs when one or more offenders threaten to use force to take property from a person or the person's immediate presence. Included within the category of robbery are holdups, stickups, and muggings involving thefts. Robbery is both a violent personal crime and a property crime. Like murder and rape, robbery is feared because of its potential for violence or actual violence to the victims. Like property crimes, robbery involves an attempted or completed theft of personal property. Robberies are often committed in conjunction with other crimes, such as homicide and rape.

Over one-half of all robbery victims were also physically attacked. Female robbery victims are more likely than male victims to be physically assaulted. Many female victims are also raped. About one-half of the robberies take place during hours of darkness. Robberies involving injuries to the victims are more likely to occur during the hours of darkness. About four of ten robberies occur on the street.

IN FOCUS

Characteristics and Trends for Robbery

The general characteristics and trends for robbery include:

- There are approximately 1.5 million robberies in the United States each year.
- One in 12 robbery victims experiences serious bodily injury during commission of the crime.
- About one-half of the completed robberies involved losses of less than $82.
- Weapons were used in about half of all robberies.
- Ninety percent of known robbery offenders are male.
- Blacks are victimized by robberies more than twice the rate of whites.
- Robbery rates reached a high in 1973 and have since declined.
- Eighty percent of the robbery victims were robbed by strangers or offenders known only by sight.
- Victims who suffer both injury and property loss were more likely to have tried to protect themselves than victims who lost only property.

Source: U.S. Department of Justice, BJS, *Data Report* (Washington, D.C.: U.S. Government Printing Office, 1987).

About 20 percent occur at or inside the victim's home. Most of the robberies occurring inside victims' residences are committed by offenders who had no right to be there. Few robberies occur on public transportation or in commercial establishments. Victims are less likely to be injured in robberies occurring in commercial establishments [18].

There are approximately 10,000 bank robberies in the United States each year. Most bank robbers appear to be unsophisticated, unprofessional criminals. About 75 percent of them used no disguise despite the popular use of surveillance equipment. Over 85 percent of the robbers arrested indicated that they never inspected the bank prior to the robbery. About 95 percent of them had no long-range plans to avoid capture and to spend the money without being detected. The average dollar loss from a bank robbery is less than $5000. Only about 20 percent of the money is recovered. Police clear (solve) approximately 65 percent of the bank robberies with an arrest. Of the offenders tried for bank robbery, the majority had histories of prior arrests and convictions for felonies. About 45 percent of the robbers had served at least one year in prison prior to committing the offense [19].

■ BURGLARY

As noted in Chapter 3, burglary is the unlawful entry of a building or other structure with the intent to commit a felony or theft. In most states, a locked automobile may be subject to burglary. Also, under modern statutes, there is no requirement that the entry into the building or structure be a forcible entry. Burglary, like robbery, is an offense against the person (sanctuary of the home) and against property.

Burglars commit three-fifths of all rapes and robberies of the home and a third of all household assaults. In approximately 85 percent of the household burglaries, no one is home at the time of the offense. When someone is home, however, the commission of a violent personal crime on the occupant occurs approximately 30 percent of the time. About one-third of the burglaries are forcible entries. Theft is involved in about 75 percent of the cases. Urban household families are more likely than suburban or rural household families to be victims of forcible entries. (*Note:* In the cases where no force is used in the entry, the victimization rates for burglary are very similar in urban, suburban, and rural households.)

Burglary occurs more often in warm weather than in cold weather. A possible explanation for higher burglary rates in warm weather is the greater tendency to leave windows and doors open during warm months, thus creating an opportunity for easy entry. About one-half of burglaries occur during daylight hours.

ARSON

Arson is the willful and illegal burning of real property (i.e., homes, buildings, etc.). Juveniles account for about 40 percent of the arrests for arson. One in every 15 persons arrested for arson is under the age of 15. One-half of the arrestees are under the age of 18. Arson appears to be a white-male-dominated crime. Approximately 80 percent of "known" arsonists are white and 90 percent are male. Arson is the largest single cause of property damage by fire in the United States. Approximately 50 percent of the arson cases involve residential property. The average loss per arson exceeds $50,000 [20].

THEFT CRIMES

Theft crimes discussed in this section include larceny/theft, shoplifting, check offenses, credit card offenses, and embezzlement. Burglary and robbery also normally involve an element of theft. They were discussed earlier in conjunction with violent personal crimes due to the high incidence of personal injuries in their commission.

Larceny/Theft

In early common law, larceny was the wrongful taking of personal property of another with the intent to deprive the owner or person permanently of the right of possession of the property. It is one of the oldest crimes under English common law. It is a crime against the possession of property. For example, if one thief (first thief) has possession of stolen property and a second thief takes it from the first thief, the second can be convicted of theft. Being a crime against possession, the English judges who originally created the crime of larceny were concerned with possible disturbance of the peace if someone attempted to take property from the possession of another.

Larceny/theft offenses constitute approximately 55 percent of all index crimes recorded each year by the FBI. Less than 20 percent are cleared (solved) by an arrest. The larceny/theft offenders constitute a wide range of persons. Accordingly, no general assumptions regarding these offenders are feasible. It is actually an All-American crime.

Shoplifting

Shoplifting is the illegal taking of merchandise from retail stores by persons posing as customers. It is estimated that merchants lose approximately $26 billion a year from this crime. It is estimated that most

FIGURE 21–4
A pilfer shoplifting.
Courtesy of Mike Kagan/
Monkmeyer Press.

shoplifters are women, and over 90 percent of them have never been convicted of another criminal offense. Shoplifting comprises about 15 percent of all theft cases reported to the police.

The classic study on shoplifting was conducted by Mary Cameron. The key findings of her study include [21]:

- Most shoplifters are pilfers or snitches.
- Pilfers do not think of themselves as criminals.
- Most women who shoplift are from families with limited budgets.
- Most women shoplifters are not employed outside the home.
- Most of the women who shoplift do not steal items that they usually buy, but luxury items that they cannot afford on a modest budget.
- Most women shoplifters rationalize that the department store will not suffer from the loss of the items.
- The act of apprehension is usually sufficient to deter most pilferers from further shoplifting offenses.
- Only about 10 percent of shoplifters are professional thieves.

Check Offenses

Edwin Lemert conducted a study of check forgers. He concluded that most forgers are "naive check forgers" who do not believe that their conduct will harm anyone. Most of the naive check forgers are from middle-class backgrounds and have had little contact with criminal subcultures. They cash bad checks in an attempt to resolve a financial crisis. He concluded that the naive check forgers were socially isolated people who have unsuccessful personal relationships and are risk-prone. Not all check forgers are amateurs according to Lemert. He noted that there was a small segment of check forgers who are systematic forgers. These forgers make a substantial living by passing bad checks [22].

Credit Card Offenses

Credit card offenses are generally committed by two basically different types of offenders: the professional credit card gang members and amateurs. Most credit card offenses are committed by amateurs who acquire credit cards through theft, muggings, and so on. The amateurs use the cards for a few days, then discard them. The professional credit card gangs are highly organized and use techniques such as establishing phony businesses to maximize the return from credit cards.

Embezzlement

Embezzlement is the taking of property that has been entrusted to the offender. For example, a teller at a bank who steals money the teller has received on behalf of the bank is guilty of embezzlement. Embezzlement is generally a white-collar crime since it occurs within the business setting. It is primarily a crime of the middle- and upper-income levels of society.

IN FOCUS

Theories of Corruption

Why do public officials violate the laws they have been selected to implement or enforce and often become the instruments of organized crime? This question has been debated for many years, and a variety of explanations–some conflicting, some complementary–have been offered. Some of these explanations focus on the individuals involved and their backgrounds and personalities; others focus on the situations in which corruption arises and their relationship to broader social and political environments. This report will not provide a complete statement of these theories, or even select one that seems superior; all the explanations have a degree of validity and are useful in explaining some facets of the problem. As in any complex human behavior, the reasons for and reactions to the situation are multifaceted and, therefore, not subject to simple labeling or explanations. . . .

Examinations of corruption have differed in their conclusions in part because they have analyzed different factors. Some authors have focused on the acts of corruption, seeking to ascertain whether they are isolated events or parts of systemic patterns of illegality. A second set of studies looked at the characteristics of the participants in the corruption. In some cases they are merely the few "rotten apples" that one might, on a statistical basis, expect to find in any group; in other cases they seem to be average persons representative of their society. Finally, a third body of research attempted to measure the significance of the settings in which corruption occurs, asking whether it arises from the ways in which governments conduct their business. . . .

Corrupt Acts: Premeditated Greed or Crimes of Opportunity?

For over a century, criminologists and psychologists have sought explanations of criminality in family relationships, personalities, medical histories, job and educational skills, friendships, and other characteristics of offenders. During the past decade, scholarly attention also has been directed at the nature of the crimes committed, distinguishing between premeditated crimes and the so-called "crimes of opportunity." For example, one homicide may be a carefully planned gangland execution, while another the unfortunate consequence of an overheated barroom brawl.

In terms of corruption, some acts involve systematic looting of the public till–often by organized crime–using the skills of many conspirators and developing complicated procedures to conceal the frauds. By comparison, the decision of a traffic officer to accept $10 in lieu of writing a ticket might be made on the spur of the moment. The latter type of corruption presumably could be reduced by removing the opportunities. However, the reduction of planned corruption, including that perpetrated by organized crime, will require more complicated steps to alter the costs and benefits perceived by potential offenders. . . .

What determines whether a particular governmental activity might be seen as an opportunity for a potential corrupter or corruptee? Among the factors that first come to mind are legal constraints, surveillance and supervision practices, and market demand for the activity.

Whether some public employees succumb to the temptation to abuse their offices may depend on the degree to which they are bound by legal constraints and citizen attitudes. Are government purchases left to the discretion of purchasing agents or do they require advertisements, competitive bidding, and independent auditing? Do the laws and regulations governing the officials' conduct–those the police officer enforces or the bureaucrat implements–allow substantial or even excessive discretion, or are they specific?

One of the major facilitators of official corruption is secrecy, and those governmental activities that go unnoticed are most susceptible to abuse by organized crime and other corrupting influences. . . . Few people are likely to notice the approval of a minor zoning variance, a technical amendment to the tax code, or a police officer's on-the-street evaluation of a drug purchase. . . . This situation suggests that, to maximize both the possibility and the probability of detection, a comprehensive program to reduce corruption must include accountability and supervision.

The level of demand for the goods and services controlled by public officials—the funds, jobs, contracts, programs, privileges, and restrictions that can be allocated as prescribed by law or the highest bidder—also can determine the frequency of corruption. . . . If an office supply contract with city hall offers no greater reward than that available from other business opportunities, a stationery supply house would have no incentive to offer a bribe to get the contract.

THE PARTICIPANTS. Whenever corruption is uncovered, the first impulse is to question the character of the people involved. . . . One must avoid simplistic theories that offer easy explanation of why people are or may become corrupt. Many grafters act simply on the basis of greed, while others seek prestige or power. Some may be coerced into cooperating–because of threats by organized crime figures, for example–and then subjected to threats or blackmail. Others may rationalize their behavior by thinking that they will be subject to enforcement by organized crime. And still others may be involved in corruption or organized crime activities to advance the interests of relatives or friends. . . .

SETTINGS FOR CORRUPTION. A final set of theories addresses the environment of corruption, the broader political and structural settings that may determine whether specific reforms will succeed. The first theory argues that corruption will thrive in a setting in which the public does not support the laws or is divided about their values. The second is that a weak government, one that is poorly organized to carry out its duties, is less able to mount an effective fight against the major source of corruption–organized crime.

(Excerpt from Law Enforcement Assistance Administration, *Report of the Task Force on Organized Crime*, GPO: Washington, D.C., 1976).

❚ ORGANIZED CRIME

The President's Task Force Report on Organized Crime defined "organized crime" as follows [23]:

> Organized crime is a society that seeks to operate outside the control of the American people and their governments. It involves thousands of criminals, working within structures as complex as those of any large corporation, subject to laws more rigidly enforced than those of legitimate governments. The actions are not impulsive but rather the result of intricate conspiracies, carried

on over many years and aimed at gaining control over whole fields of activity in order to mass profits.

The definition above is a set of conclusions regarding organized crime more than a definition. The conclusions listed above include:

1. Organized crime is a society.
2. It involves thousands of criminals.
3. It has structures as complex as large corporations.
4. It has its own laws that are rigidly enforced.
5. The course of conduct is deliberate and planned rather than impulsive.
6. It is carried on over many years.
7. Its goal is to amass huge profits.
   Question: Can organized crime be considered a "behavior system" of crime?

Economics is the driving force behind organized crime. Organized crime is especially active in those goods and services that are scarce and illegal but have a strong market demand (i.e., drugs, prostitution, etc.). The motive is simple: profit.

▐ CRIMES IN THE BUSINESS SETTING

"Crimes in the business setting" is a phrase used to designate crimes committed by people in the course of legitimate occupational endeavors. Other terms used for this category include "white-collar" crime and "occupational" crime. Typical crimes in the business setting in-

IN FOCUS

Socioeconomic Status and Crime

The majority of common crime offenders are from lower socioeconomic classes, and most white-collar criminals are from middle or upper socioeconomic classes. Is a person's socioeconomic class more a factor in what type of crime the person will commit rather than a factor in whether or not the person will commit a crime?

The Ford Pinto

On August 10, 1978, a Ford Pinto was rear-ended. The Pinto burst into flames, killing three teenage girls. In September 1978, the Ford Motor Company was indicted in Elkhart, Indiana, on three charges of reckless homicide. Ford was charged with recklessly designing and manufacturing the Pinto in such a manner as would be likely to cause the automobile to flame and burn upon rear-end impact. If convicted, the maximum punishment would be a fine of $30,000. Since the company was a corporation, it could not be incarcerated. (*Note:* At the time Ford was the fourth largest corporation in the world.)

Ford contended that the company was not sociopathic and did not randomly victimized its customers, but rather, was a responsible citizen that obeyed federal regulations and carefully weighed all factors in manufacturing a product that the public wanted: a small, affordable American car [24]. The Ford Motor Company was found not guilty by a jury on March 13, 1980.

1. If the death penalty is appropriate for premeditated murder, should corporations be liable to suffer a similar fate (i.e., the dissolution of the corporation and all assets turned over to the state)?

2. Since the maximum penalty if convicted was $30,000, why did Ford spends millions in legal fees and expenses defending this case?

clude embezzlement, computer crime, employee thefts, medical fraud, and consumer fraud.

Unlike common crimes, the white-collar criminal tends to be mature, middle-class or higher, white, and male. Sutherland, in his famous work on white-collar crime, observed [25]:

Those who become white-collar criminals generally start their careers in good neighborhoods and good homes, graduate from college with idealism, and, with little selection on their part, get into particular business situations in which criminality is practically a folkway, becoming inducted into that system of behavior just as into any other folkway.

Recent evidence indicates, however, that women and minorities are becoming more involved in white-collar crime as they move more into the business world. The victims of white-collar crimes are the employers of the offender and the employers' customers.

Counterfeit Ball Bearings

In a civil lawsuit filed in the U.S. District Court in Los Angeles in August 1988, an airplane parts manufacturing company was alleged to have sold counterfeit and substandard ball bearings to be used in 737, 747, and 757 Boeing aircraft. A former Federal Aviation Administration official stated that if the allegations contained in the law suit were correct, airplanes with the counterfeit ball bearings installed would be unsafe and could crash. (*Note:* In early 1988, a Boeing 737 made an emergency landing at Houston's Hobby Airport because of "erratic movement of its stabilizer trim wheel" apparently caused by failure of the same type of ball bearings. No one was injured.)

If the allegations are correct, are the company officers who committed such acts or who allowed the acts to be committed any different from common murderers? Would it make any difference as to the criminality of the acts if instead of landing safely, ninety-two people were killed in an airplane crash due to the defective bearings?

■ VICTIMLESS CRIMES

The phrase "victimless crimes" is used to describe crimes that do not have traditional victims. In most cases, the person against whom the crime is committed is an active and willing participant in the process. Victimless crimes are also referred to as "consensual crimes." Rarely in these cases are there victims who seek prosecution. The most common victimless crimes are gambling, voluntary sexual practices, and drug usage.

Prosecution of victimless crimes is expensive and time consuming. The rationale for prosecution includes:

1. It is a proper function of government to regulate morality by criminal sanctions.

2. Prosecution would be effective if laws were strictly enforced.

3. Society is the victim in victimless crimes, and failure to prosecute will lead to a moral decline in our society.

The rationale against prosecution of victimless crimes includes:

1. It is not the proper function of government to regulate private morality.

2. Prosecution is not cost-effective.

3. There is no evidence that decriminalization of victimless crimes will lead to an increase in immoral behavior.

4. Individual rights include the right to live as one desires as long as no one else is harmed.

■ SUMMARY

Typologies refer to the study of different types of crimes. Typologies examine the patterns of particular types of criminal behavior and make statements about personal and environmental factors in crime causation.

As people grow older, they are less likely to commit crimes. The majority of known criminal offenders are between the ages of 16 and 24 years. Most common crimes are committed against victims of the same race as the offenders. The violent personal crime victimization rates are highest for black males and lowest for white females.

Calling the police in a domestic violence incident may reduce the risk of one spouse attacking the other spouse again within the next six months. Only a small fraction of the child sexual abuse and incest cases are reported to the police. One in every four females will be sexually abused before reaching the age of 18.

Alcohol-related automobile crashes kill approximately 25,000 persons each year. During the hours between midnight and 4 A.M. 80 percent of all fatally injured drivers in automobile accidents have been drinking. To reduce the DUI problems, social attitudes must be modified.

Robbery is both a violent personal crime and a crime against property. Over 50 percent of the female robbery victims are also physically attacked. Many female victims are also raped. Robberies involving injuries to the victims are more likely to occur during hours of darkness. Most bank robberies are committed by unsophisticated, unprofessional criminals.

Burglars commit three-fifths of all rapes and robberies in the home and a third of all household assaults. In most burglaries, no one is present at the time the crime is committed. Burglaries occur more frequently in warm weather than in cold weather. About 50 percent of burglaries occur during hours of darkness.

Most shoplifters are women who have no prior criminal record. Shoplifting comprises about 15 percent of all theft cases reported to the police. Most shoplifters do not think of themselves as criminals. Only about 10 percent of shoplifters are professional thieves.

■ MATCHING KEY TERMS AND DEFINITIONS

Match each key term with the correct definitions.

a. common crimes
b. criminal homicide
c. date rape
d. domestic violence
e. DUI
f. embezzlement
g. incest
h. naive check forgers

i. organized crime
j. pilfers
k. serial murderers
l. typologies
m. victimless crimes
n. violent personal crimes
o. white-collar crimes

____ 1. Crimes that do not have traditional victims.
____ 2. Crimes committed in the course of legitimate business endeavors.
____ 3. The taking of property that has been entrusted to you.
____ 4. A crime system that is clearly profit motivated.
____ 5. The study of crime categories.
____ 6. Amateur check forgers.
____ 7. Engaging in sexual relations with your daughter or son.
____ 8. Driving under the influence of drugs or alcohol.
____ 9. A problem on college campuses.
____ 10. Physical spouse abuse.
____ 11. A person who commits a series of motiveless murders.
____ 12. Murder.
____ 13. Violent personal offenses, petty property crimes, thefts, burglary, and robbery.
____ 14. Amateur shoplifters.
____ 15. Rapes, assaults, and murders.

■ DISCUSSION QUESTIONS

1. Why is the study of crime typologies important?
2. What steps can be taken in your community to reduce the DUI problem?
3. How would you classify rape, as a sexual offense or as an assaultive offense? Why?

4. Why are minorities more likely than nonminorities to be crime victims?

Notes

1. U.S. Department of Justice, BJS, *Special Report: Violent Crime Trends.* Washington, D.C.: U.S. Government Printing Office, 1987.

2. U.S. Department of Justice, *Data Report, 1987.* Washington, D.C.: U.S. Government Printing Office, 1988.

3. Emil Frankel, "One Thousand Murders," *Journal of Criminal Law and Criminology,* vol. 29, Jan. 1939, pp. 672–688.

4. Vernon Fox, *Introduction to Criminology.* Englewood Cliffs, N.J.: Prentice-Hall, 1976.

5. Robert K. Ressler, Ann W. Burgess, Ralph D'Agostino, and John E. Douglas, "Serial Murder: A New Phenomenon of Homicide," paper presented at the tenth triennial meeting of the International Association of Forensic Sciences, Oxford, England, Sept. 18–25, 1984.

6. Helen Morrison, interview with Kathy McCarthy, Associated Press on July 6, 1984 (Seattle, Wash.), reported in *Los Angeles Times,* July 8, 1984.

7. U.S. Department of Justice, BJS, *Data Report, 1987.* Washington, D.C.: U.S. Government Printing Office, 1987, p. 8.

8. William B. Sander, *Criminology.* Menlo Park, Calif., Addison-Wesley, 1983.

9. Nicholas A. Groth, Ann W. Burgess, and Lynda L. Holmstrom, "Rape: Power, Anger and Sexuality," *American Journal of Psychiatry,* vol. 134, 1977, pp. 1239–1243.

10. Groth et al., 1977:1240.

11. Thomas Meyer, "Date Rapes: A Serious Campus Problem That Few Talk About," *Chronicle of Higher Education,* vol. 29, Dec. 5, 1984, p. 15.

12. Police Foundation, *Domestic Violence and the Police: Studies in Detroit and Kansas City.* Washington, D.C.: Police Foundation, 1977.

13. U.S. Department of Justice, *Data Report, 1987,* 1987.

14. Lawrence W. Sherman, and Richard A. Berk, "The Specific Deterrent Effects of Arrest for Domestic Assault," *American Sociological Review,* vol. 49, 1984, pp. 261–272.

15. Florence Rush, *The Best Kept Secret: Sexual Abuse of Children.* Englewood Cliffs, N.J.: Prentice-Hall, 1980.

16. Robert Berry, "Incest: The Last Taboo," *FBI Law Enforcement Bulletin,* Jan. 1984, pp. 2–9.

17. *Report of Presidential Commission on Drunk Driving, Final Report, Nov. 1983.* Washington, D.C.: U.S. Government Printing Office, 1984.

18. U.S. Department of Justice, *Special Report: Robbery Victims.* Washington, D.C.: U.S. Government Printing Office, 1987.

19. U.S. Department of Justice, *Data Report, 1987,* 1988:18.

20. U.S. Department of Justice, *Data Report, 1987,* 1987; *Data Report, 1987,* 1988.

21. Mary O. Cameron, *The Booster and the Snitch.* New York: Free Press, 1964.

22. Edwin Lemert, "An Isolation and Closure Theory of Naive Check Forgery," *Journal of Criminal Law, Criminology and Police Science,* vol. 44, 1953, pp. 297–299.

23. President's Commission on Law Enforcement and the Administration of Justice, *Task Force Report: Organized Crime*. Washington, D.C.: U.S. Government Printing Office, 1967, p. 15.

24. Francis T. Cullen, William J. Maakestad, and Gray Cavendar, *Corporate Crime under Attack*. Cincinnati, Ohio: Anderson, 1987, p. 251.

25. Edwin H. Sutherland, "White-Collar Criminality," *American Sociological Review*, vol. 5, 1940.

22

Conclusion

This book provides students with a general overview of the development of Western criminological theories of crime causation. We have examined the important ideas of the past and present as well as the noteworthy sociological, biological, and psychological theories of crime causation. There is no doubt that the body of knowledge dealing with theories of crime causation is proliferating and becoming more sophisticated. In this chapter we summarize the major concepts presented in the text.

OVERVIEW OF THE DEVELOPMENT OF WESTERN CRIMINOLOGICAL THEORIES

Criminology includes a practical study of why people commit crimes. Criminological theories are, for the most part, practical and applied. Crime theories also tend to be descriptive and explanatory. Crime is a major industry in our society, and many criminologists contend that crime serves a functional role. This raises the question: Since crime is functional, is complete elimination of it desirable?

Law and the Definition of Crime

The law is a formal expression of our value system. The leading concepts on the nature of law include: law has a supernatural origin, law is justice, law is a function of the sovereign, law is a utilitarian concept, and law is an instrument of the ruling class. There is no general agreement as to what constitutes a crime. Frequently used definitions of crime include the social definition, the strictly legal definition, and the less rigid legal definition. There is also a problem in defining who is a criminal. The common definition of a "criminal" is one who has been convicted of a crime. The problem with this definition is that much crime is undetected and/or unsolved. The failure, however, to convict a person who has committed a crime does not make his or her actions any less criminal.

Criminology is best described as a social science dealing with the functional aspects of human behavior. Since crime does not occur in a vacuum, the search for the causes of crime includes a study of social movements and trends.

Early Study of Crime Causation

Criminology developed as a separate field of inquiry in Europe during the late eighteenth century. The early criminologists at that time were physicians, philosophers, physical scientists, social reformers, and so on. The Code of Hammurabi was the first major attempt to codify laws. It was also the beginning of state-administered punishment for criminal behavior. The ancient Hebrews, Greeks, Romans, and early Western Europeans made the initial theoretical contributions to the study of crime causation. Criminology in America was influenced by European Enlightenment ideas. American criminology came into its own in the nineteenth century. It evolved from the fields of sociology and psychology.

Classical School

The classical school is considered one of the first attempts to organize a view of criminal causation and pinpoint the significant concepts in understanding the crime problem. The classical school was an outgrowth of the Age of Enlightenment. The Age of Enlightenment promoted optimism, certainty, reason, toleration, humanitarianism, and the belief that all human problems could be solved. Its influence is noted in the U.S. Constitution.

The leaders of the classical school were Cesare Beccaria and Jeremy Bentham. The main points of the classical school are as follows:

- The doctrine of free will is used to explain human behavior.
- Criminals are responsible for their behavior.
- Crime reduction can be accomplished by inflicting a sufficient amount of pain upon the offender.
- The purposes of punishment should be to deter others from committing criminal acts.
- The type and amount of pain to impose on the offender should be determined by focusing only on the crime itself.
- Punishment to be effective should be prompt, certain, and serve a useful function.

Neoclassical School

The neoclassical school of criminology, while based on the concept of free will, recognizes that some people, such as juveniles and persons with unstable mental conditions, cannot reason. Accordingly, these people may not be completely free to make a choice, and this should be considered when determining and imposing punishment. Neoclassical thinking is alive and well in many of our present criminological theories.

Positivist's School

The positivist's school of criminology was the leading school of criminology during the latter half of the nineteenth century. The school was a product of the "realism" movement and a reaction to the harshness of the classical school. Auguste Comte is considered the founder of the positive school. According to this school, crime can be studied as an empirical science, and the causes of crime can be determined. The most famous of the positive theorists was Cesare Lombroso, who is considered the "father of modern criminology."

The concept of determinism is an important part of the positive theory. The theory is based on the concept that a person is propelled by social, biological, emotional, and or spiritual forces beyond his or her control. The school discounts the punitive approach to crime and instead advocates treatment. In addition, treatment should be individually tailored to meet the needs of the individual offender.

■ SOCIOLOGICAL THEORIES OF CRIME CAUSATION

Strain Theories

Strain theories of criminology assume that people commit crimes as a result of extreme pressures or strains on them. They also believe that people are innately moral and want to be law-abiding. Strain theorists attempt to isolate the type of strain that causes people to break laws.

Emile Durkheim, one of the first strain theorists, contributed theories on anomie, suicide, criminality, and punishment to the field of criminology. Robert Merton believed that the "goals–means dysjunction" caused strain or pressure on the individual. He also believed that people responded to strains and pressures in different ways. They could conform, innovate, engage in rituals, retreat, and/or rebel.

Albert Cohen applied anomie theory to delinquency. He believed that boys from working classes had strains and pressures on them that were products of being taught values different from those being taught to middle-class boys. The working-class boys had a disadvantage in middle-class schools. This resulted in the working-class boy joining gangs to relieve the pressures or strains on them.

Cloward and Ohlin also offered an explanation of subcultural delinquency. They believed that lower-class boys did not have the same "opportunity structures" or access to legitimate means to attain their goals as did middle-class boys. This produces frustration and pressure that make them look for illegitimate opportunity structures to deal with their frustrations and pressures.

Control Theories

The control theorists hold that crime occurs whenever a person's bond to society becomes weak or severed. Our bonds to society are formed primarily by our socialization experiences. Control theorists also believe that people are not born good or bad but rather, have the inclination to do whatever they can get away with. People are prevented from doing anything they like by their bonds to family, friends, school, church, and so on.

Emile Durkheim, who is also considered as a control theorist, believed that there were greater controls on human deviance in small, homogeneous, mechanistic societies, where people knew each other and were able to keep an eye on everyone, as opposed to larger, heterogeneous organic societies, where people were anonymous to one another. Albert Reiss contended that control was related to the attachment people had for others to whom they were attached. Gresham Sykes and David Matza indicate that delinquents do not have a particularly strong commitment to delinquent/criminal or conventional norms and values. Instead, delinquents adhere to the norms and values in both groups and pick and choose norms and values that are convenient. Delinquents therefore drift from one set of norms and values to other sets of norms and values.

Sykes and Matza also developed the idea that in order to commit crimes criminals know are wrong, they have to rationalize, justify, and make the wrong behavior acceptable before they can go through with it. This is known as their "techniques of neutralization" theory. Techniques of neutralization are critical in lessening the effectiveness of social controls that lie behind a large amount of criminal and delinquent behavior.

Walter Reckless's containment theory holds that people have a number of containments or protective barriers that help them in resisting pressures that attract them to crime. Travis Hirschi's social bond theory maintains that only when a person has attachment, involvement, commitment, and belief to people and society's institutions will he or she not break the law.

Radical and Conflict Theories

There are two major approaches used by sociologically based criminological theorists when considering societal norms: (1) the consensus approach and (2) the conflict approach. Conflict theorists contend that there is an implicit ideology of our criminal justice system which conveys a subtle, powerful message in support of our present criminal justice system. Austin Turk held that criminologists should study the differences between the status and role of legal authorities and subjects. According to the conflict theorists, by concentrating on individual wrongdoers, we are diverted away from consideration of whether our society is just or unjust.

Radical criminology is but one of a new group of criminological theories that are based on the economic determinism thesis of Karl Marx. The central theme of the radical theories is that criminal behavior can be explained in terms of economic conditions and is an expression of class conflict. Karl Marx and Friedrich Engels believed that crime is a product of capitalism. The capitalist economic system encourages people to be greedy and selfish and to pursue their own benefits without regard to the needs and wishes of others. The criminal justice system criminalizes the greed of the poor but allows the rich to pursue their selfish desires.

Richard Quinney stated that the traditional notion of the causes of crime should be abandoned and we should attempt to understand what "could be," not "what is." He stated that criminology, as the scientific study of crime, has served a single purpose: legitimation of the existing social order. According to Quinney, by asking the question "What causes crime?" we have focused our study on the criminal rather than understanding that crime is a product of the authority that defines behavior as criminal.

The criminal justice system, according to the critical criminologists, is used for the purpose of maintaining the status quo for the powerful members of society or as a means of serving the self-interests of those who operate the criminal justice agencies.

Cultural Deviance Theories

Cultural deviance theories assume that most people are not capable of committing deviant acts; acts are deviant only by mainstream standards, not by the offender's standards. The Chicago School researchers studied people in their own natural habitats in an attempt to understand their behavior. Social disorganization theorists indicate that a positive relationship between increasing crime rates and social disorganization exists and is caused by increasing complexity of society. Ecological theorists hold that crime rates are highest in the center of the city, where there is greatest social disorganization. Culture conflict theorists contend that if a person's norms conflict with society's conventional norms, culture conflict will occur.

Subculture Theories

Subculture theorists believe that there are subcultures with value systems different from conventional value systems in society. Cultural deviance theorists hold that lower classes have a separate identifiable culture that is distinct from the middle-class culture. Subculture of violence theorists hold that lower classes in the United States have a value system that emphasizes aggression and violence in resolving problems. Criminogenic culture theorists believe that certain inherent social values and factors encourage criminal behavior on the part of its members.

Symbolic Interactionist Theories

The two leading symbolic interactionist theories of criminal causation are differential association and labeling. Both theories examine the process of becoming a criminal and locate the cause of behavior in our interpretations of reality. Differential association has been the most influential sociopsychological theory of crime causation for the past sixty years. According to differential association theory, criminal behavior is learned. It is learned with others in the process of communication. A person becomes a criminal, according to differential association, because of an excess of definitions favorable to violation of law compared to definitions unfavorable to violation of law. The processes of learning criminal behavior involves all the mechanisms that are involved in any other learning.

According to the labeling theory, no act is intrinsically criminal. A person becomes a criminal not by violation of the law alone, but by the designation of criminal by authorities. The "degradation ceremony" is used by labelists to describe the process whereby a person is separated from the rest of us and labeled a criminal. Lemert differentiates between "primary" and "secondary" deviance to explain the direct relationship between criminal behavior and the labeling processes. Primary deviance is that deviance committed prior to being labeled a criminal. Secondary deviance is deviance that is caused by the reaction to the labeling process.

■ BIOLOGICAL THEORIES OF CRIME CAUSATION

The biological theories of crime causation are popular because society is interested in concrete, simple, cause-and-effect answers to the crime problem. In the twentieth century alone there have been awesome technological and medical breakthroughs that have prolonged and saved lives. Medical techniques and drugs have also been discovered that have allowed us to alter antisocial behavior. Under these circumstances, why shouldn't we look toward biology for the answer to the crime problem?

Sociobiology is a relatively new field that looks toward genetics for the answers to social problems. Biosocial criminology looks toward the interaction of biology and environment for the answers to the crime problem.

The biological explanations of criminal behavior are based on the assumption that chromosomes, genes, chemistry, hormones, and/or body type can affect behavior, possibly causing antisocial or criminal behavior. There are four subdivisions of the biological theories: (1) inferiority theories, (2) body-type theories, (3) difference and defectiveness theories, and (4) nutrition and vitamin theories.

Two problems that plague any attempt to discover hereditary influences on criminal behavior are (1) keeping separate hereditary and environmental influences, and (2) understanding modern genetic theory. Much of the biological research focuses on twin, adoptee, and genotype/phenotype studies.

Biological inferiority theories assume that the criminal is inferior to the noncriminal biologically. The offender can be constitutionally, intellectually, and/or mentally inferior. Physiognomy and phrenology were early inferiority theories that paved the way for Lombroso's theory of criminal atavism. Goring, who attempted to refute Lombroso's theory of atavism, did not reject the idea of the criminal being inferior to noncriminals. Other inferiority theories focus on the intelligence and IQ of offenders. Today the average IQ is considered to be 100 points, and there is evidence that delinquents and criminals tend to score lower than noncriminals on IQ tests. There is also some evidence that links a criminal's intelligence to the type of crime that he or she commits.

There are many criminological theories that attribute criminal behavior to biochemical imbalances. One theory is that crime is due to the emotional disturbances caused by the biochemical imbalance. Several researchers contend that PMT/PMS causes violent and irrational behavior in some women. It appears, however, that the popularity of the PMS theory exceeds the empirical evidence supporting it. Another theory links criminal behavior to the XYY chromosome abnormality. The relatively small percentage of the male population who are XYY males minimizes the importance of this theory. Excessive slow-brain-wave activity is considered by some researchers as the cause of criminal behavior. Numerous studies have reported a relationship between learning disabilities and juvenile delinquency. The studies, however, fail to explain the causal connection.

There is lack of clear evidence that aggressive criminal behavior is the direct result of brain or body dysfunction. It appears that the existence of a biological dysfunction under certain circumstances may trigger criminal behavior in a person. At most, it may be stated that some criminals are indirectly affected by biological abnormalities.

Various researchers are of the opinion that there is a direct relationship between nutrition and criminal behavior. The study of nutrition can be traced to the biochemical imbalance theories. Subareas of nutrition theory include: low blood sugar, vitamin deficiencies, and food allergies.

Some researchers believe that low blood sugar is a likely cause of sudden violent and unexplained behavior. Hypoglycemia (low blood sugar), according to many nutritionists, is caused by the high consumption of large quantities of refined sugar and starches, and to poisonous food additives.

The lack of sufficient quantities of certain vitamins is seen by some as the cause of many juvenile delinquency problems. The deficiencies can also cause violent behavior and other social problems. Studies of institutionalized criminals indicate that most of them have vitamin deficiencies. A vitamin deficiency may cause the body to produce taraxein, which, in turn, causes hallucinogenic experiences and schizophrenia.

Some criminologists contend that food allergies can trigger criminal conduct. Certain food groups can, in some cases, cause perceptual distortions, which, in turn, can trigger violent and irrational behavior. There are two types of food allergies, fixed and cyclic. Cyclic allergies are the most common and are the most difficult to diagnose. Neuroallergy is an allergic condition that affects the body's central nervous system.

Hyperkinesis (hyperactivity) is seen as an "antisocial" form of behavior and is often associated with criminal behavior. The primary cause of hyperkinesis is vitamin B_3 dependency and hypoglycemia.

■ PSYCHOLOGICAL THEORIES OF CRIME CAUSATION

There are many ways to classify the psychological theories of crime causation. Some of the theories emphasize emotional problems, mental disorders, sociopathy, and thinking patterns. The psychological theories have the common assumption that there is something wrong with the mind of the offender which causes him or her to commit crimes.

The psychological theories have had a dominant influence on the treatment and rehabilitation emphasis embraced by correctional personnel in the United States. Criminologists, however, are deficient in addressing adequately the role of psychological forces in crime and delinquency. Sophisticated standardized tests, such as the MMPI and the CPI, have shown differences in psychological and personality variables between offenders and nonoffenders.

Psychoanalytic theory dealing with crime and delinquency has evolved from the theories of Sigmund Freud. Among Freud's contributions are the concepts of unconscious mind, repression, instinctual drives and impulses, guilt, personality structure, and developmental stages.

Emotional Problem Theories

The emotional problem theories view the offender as having the same psychological makeup as the nonoffender. The offender is not seen as having a psychological disorder; rather, he or she is seen as not being able to cope with his or her environment. The inability to cope then results in frustration and criminal behavior. Many things can cause emotional problems. Some examples of common causes of emotional problems are relationships, crises, finances, employment, lack of employment, sickness, and self-concept. Once emotional problems are resolved and the offender is coping again, criminality is not likely to occur. As illustrative of the emotional problem theories, a discussion of attractiveness and criminality was presented.

The mental disorder theories explain criminal behavior by using the diagnostic categories of psychosis, neurosis, and personality disorder. It is generally held that neurotic disorders do not manifest themselves by divorcing the individual from reality. Organic disorders have identifiable physiological causes; whereas functional disorders cannot be traced to an identifiable physical basis. There is evidence that the most bizarre violent offenses are committed by psychotics. However, to date, it is difficult to determine the types and quantity of mental disorders that exist among offenders. Therefore, any conclusions should be made with caution.

Of the neuroses, neurasthenia, anxiety, obsessive-compulsive behavior, hysteria, phobia, and depression have been related to criminal acts and or criminal tendencies. Of the psychoses, schizophrenia and paranoia have been related to criminal acts. Of the impulse disorders, kleptomania, pyromania, and explosive disorder have been linked to criminal behavior.

Sociopathic Theories

The sociopath does not have a psychological disorder but rather has a unique personality structure. There are several labels for the sociopathic personality. Psychopath and antisocial personality are two of the more popular labels. There is evidence of a positive correlation between sociopathy and criminal behavior. Sociopathic personality structures can be identified in criminal and noncriminal populations. Sociopathic personalities are identified by many traits and characteristics. All sociopathic traits and characteristics need not be present and manifested for a person to be a sociopath. There is no consensus about the cause of sociopathy. Some believe it to be caused by biology. Others believe it to be caused by faulty personal development. Still others believe it to be caused by sociological factors. Contemporary research on the cause of sociopathy focuses on brain wave patterns and central nervous system deficits. Selected research reveals that at roughly age 40 or 50, many sociopathic personality characteristics go into remission. Sociopathy is difficult to treat successfully. Some researchers believe that sociopathy causes criminality, and others think that criminality contributes to the sociopathic personality.

Thinking Pattern Theories

Thinking pattern theories are psychological theories of crime causation that emphasize the criminal's cognitive processes. Thinking pattern theories are related to developmental psychology theories such as those developed by Jean Piaget. Yochelson and Samenow spent fifteen years studying the criminal mind and found that the criminal thinks differently than the noncriminal. There has been vehement opposition to Yochelson and Samenow's notion of a criminal mind separate and distinct from a noncriminal mind because it promotes antitreatment attitudes and policies. Neutralization theory supports the idea of a separate thinking structure for criminals.

■ THE CRIME PROBLEM

Sutherland and Cressey contend that certain types of criminal behavior have their own "behavior systems." The behavior system is a group way of life and it is not merely an aggregation of individual acts. Accordingly, criminals who commit certain types of offenses have a feeling that they belong together. Sutherland and Cressey state that if the behavior system can be isolated, the problem would then be to study and explain the system as a unit.

Sesnowitz concluded that taking all factors into consideration, the average burglar would make more money from legitimate employment. Criminals work on commissions. The criminal's income, therefore, depends to some extent on how hard the criminal works at crime. The criminal's income is tax-free and this saves a nice sum of money each year. The average career criminal is normally in and out of prison or jail all of his or her life. Most career criminals live at or below the poverty level.

The career criminal is usually a property offender. The crimes most susceptible to recidivism are forgery, auto theft, robbery, burglary, and assault. Actual recidivism rates are difficult to measure. It appears that less than two-fifths of all crimes are reported to authorities. Except for rape, the more serious the crime in terms of economic loss or physical injury, the more likely it is to be reported.

The science of victimology is the study of crime from the victim's viewpoint, with emphasis on the relationship between the victim and the offender. Hans Von Hentig concluded that in many respects the victim shapes and molds the criminal and the crime.

Glossary

Actus Reus: An illegal act or the wrongful failure to act.

Adjudication: The judgment concerning criminal charges, for example, guilty or not guilty.

Adversarial System: The American procedure used to determine truth in civil and criminal trials, which pits the prosecution or plaintiff (civil) against the defendant, with the judge acting as the arbitrator of legal rules.

Age of Enlightenment: The movement that dominated European thinking for most of the eighteenth century. It promoted optimism, certainty, reason, toleration, humanitarianism, progress and the belief that all human problems could be solved.

Altruistic Suicide: A suicide that occurs when a person is closely identified with a social group and feels that it is necessary to sacrifice his or her life for the higher goal.

American Society of Criminology: One of the leading American professional societies in the criminology field.

Anger Rape: A rape that is motivated by the offender's desire to release pent-up anger and rage.

Anomic Suicide: A suicide that occurs when a person is totally alienated from society.

Anomie: The condition produced by normlessness where a person has few guides as to what is socially acceptable conduct.

Appeal: The review of lower-court proceedings by a higher-court.

Applied Research: Research that is concerned with solving practical problems.

Arrest: The taking of a person into physical custody for legal purposes.

Arrest Warrant: An order issued by a magistrate (judicial officer) directing the arrest of a person wanted to answer criminal charges.

Assault: An attempted battery. The unlawful intentional infliction, or attempted infliction, of injury upon the person of another.

Asthenic Body Type: A person with a thin, narrow build.

Atavistic: Criminal characteristics that are throwbacks to those of animals or primitive people. Used by Lombroso to help explain criminal behavior.

Autonomic Nervous System: The part of the nervous system that controls many of the body's involuntary functions.

Bad Seed Concept: The idea that criminality is inherited and that a person is born a criminal.

Beccaria, Cesare: An 18th century Italian philosopher who was a leader in the classical movement. He wrote *On Crimes and Punishment.*

Behaviorism: The psychological movement that is concerned with the study of observable behavior in lieu of unconscious motives. It focuses on the relationship between stimuli and human responses.

Bentham, Jeremy: A prolific writer and armchair philosopher whose writing covered a variety of topics. He is also considered as one of the founders of the classical school.

Binet, Alfred: A psychologist who together with Theodore Simon developed the I.Q. test to measure intelligence.

Biological Inferiority Theories: Theories that assume that a criminal's biology is inferior to the biology of noncriminals.

Biological Theories of Criminal Behavior: Theories based on the assumption that structure determines function.

Biosocial Criminology: The study of crime from a biological perspective.

Blumer, Herbert: A sociologist who coined the phrase "symbolic interactionism."

Body-type Theories: Theories that assume that a criminal's constitution or physique is different from that of the constitution or physique of a noncriminal, and that constitution or physique influences behavior.

Born Criminal: A term coined by Ferri to indicate that the criminal is a product of biology, and that treatment cannot change the criminal.

Burglary: The breaking and entering of a home or structure for the purpose of committing a felony or theft.

Capital Punishment: The use of the death penalty to punish criminals.

Career Criminal: A person who organizes his or her lifestyle around criminal behavior and attempts to make a living by committing crime.

Charge: In a criminal case, it is the specific crime that the defendant is accused of committing.

Chicago School: A group of researchers from the University of Chicago who studied people in their natural habitats in an attempt to understand their behavior. One recurring theme of the Chicago School was that human behavior was shaped by social and physical environments, and not simply by genetic structure.

Classical School: One of the first organized systems of thought, that viewed the criminal as having free will and individual choice.

Classical Theory: The theoretical perspective which contends that: (a) people have free will and therefore freely choose criminal or non-criminal behavior; (b) in most cases, the decision to commit a crime is based on greed or personal need; (c) crime can be controlled by the use of criminal sanctions.

Cleckley, Howard: One of the first psychologists to describe the pivotal characteristics of the sociopath.

Cloward, Richard: A sociologist who together with Lloyd Ohlin used the opportunity theory to explain subcultural delinquency.

Code of Hammurabi: The first known written criminal code. It was developed in Babylonia about 2000 B.C.

Codification: The grouping of criminal laws together in one unified code.

Cognitive Theory: The study of the perception of reality and the mental processes required to understand society.

Cohen, Albert: A strain theorist who applied the anomie theory to delinquency. His book, *Delinquent Boys: The Culture of the Gang,* is a classic.

Common Crimes: Common crimes are for the most part, violent personal offenses, petty property crimes, theft, burglary, and robbery.

Common Law: The early English law developed by judges and eventually incorporated into our system of American Law.

Community Treatment: The use of probation, parole and residential programs in the local community to correct criminals.

Complaint: The formal sworn allegation presented to a court accusing the defendant of the violation of criminal law.

Comte, Auguste: A philosopher who is considered the founder of positivism. His positivism repudiated the metaphysical and speculative methodology of classical thinking.

Concurrent Sentence: Prison or jail sentences for two or more separate criminal acts which are served simultaneously.

Conflict Theories: Theories that emphasize the conflicts within society.

Conflict View: The view that criminal behavior is shaped by interpersonal conflict and that those who maintain social control and power in a social structure will use their power and control to further their own needs.

Conformity: One of Merton's adaptations to deal with anomie. This adaptation accepts the cultural goals and institutionalized means of the society.

Consensus Theories: Theories that are based on the concept that there is a general agreement concerning societal norms within a society.

Containment Theory: A theory that holds that people have a number of social controls, containments, or protective barriers which help them in resisting pressures that draw them towards crime. There are two types of containment: internal and external.

Conviction: The judgment of guilt by a court.

Cooley, C. H.: A sociologist who originally conceived the concept of primary and secondary groups. He defined a primary group as a group that forms the person's character and makes society an integral part of the person. (See also: Secondary Groups)

Corporal Punishment: The use of physical punishment such as whipping.

Corporate Crime: White collar crime in the business setting, committed by members of a corporate entity, such as price-fixing and waste dumping.

Corpus Delicti: The elements of a crime. Often referred to as the body of the crime.

Countercultures: Subcultures whose mores run counter to the mores of the rest of society.

Cressey, Donald: A student and long-time associate of Edwin Sutherland. After Sutherland's death, he became the leading advocate for differential association.

Crime Control: One model of criminal justice that emphasizes the control of criminals and the protection of society. Crime control advocates contend that harsh punishments, such as the death penalty, should act as deterrents to crime.

Criminal: One who has been convicted of a crime.

Criminal Law: The group of statutes that define crimes and sets forth criminal sanctions for their commission.

Criminal Sanction: The punishment that is permissible for the commission of a crime.

Criminogenic Culture Theorists: Theorists who contend that certain inherent social values and factors encourage criminal behavior on part of society's members.

Criminologist: A person who studies crime.

Cultural Deviance Theories: Theories that assume that people are not capable of committing deviant acts; acts are deviant only by mainstream standards, not by offenders' standards.

Culture: Culture refers to the system of values and meanings shared by a group, including the embodiment of those values and meanings in material objects. Culture gives meaning to a society.

Culture Conflict: The condition brought about when the rules and norms of a person's subcultural affiliation conflict with those of conventional society.

Customs: Social norms that do not arouse the intensity of feelings that mores do, and generally their violation will result in less severe reactions.

Davis, Kingsley: Researcher who studied children that had been isolated from society.

Decriminalize: Changing the punishment for a criminal act to a noncriminal sanction.

Defendant: The accused in criminal proceedings or the party being sued in civil proceedings.

Degenerate Anomalies: According to Cesare Lombroso, degenerate anomalies are primitive physical characteristics that make criminals animalistic and savage.

Degradation Ceremony: The phrase used in conjunction with the labeling theory to describe the process whereby a person is separated from the rest of society and labeled a criminal.

Deinstitutionalization: The movement to remove as many offenders as possible from prison or jail confinement to community correctional programs.

Despotic Spirit: The aspect of human nature that is a part of every human being and if left unchecked would plunge society into chaos.

Determinate Sentence: Prison sentence that has a definite term of confinement, such as three years.

Determinism: The concept that behavior is governed by physical, mental, environmental, and social factors beyond the offender's control.

Deterrence: The act of preventing crime before it occurs by using the threat of criminal sanctions. There are two basic types of deterrence: individual and general.

Deviance: Behavior that violates social norms.

Difference and Defectiveness Theories: Theories that assume that there is something physiologically different or wrong occurring within the criminal's body.

Differential Association: A criminological theory developed by Edwin Sutherland. It has been the most influential sociopsychological theory of crime causation for the past sixty years.

Directed Verdict: When, without submitting the case to the jury, the judge enters a finding of not guilty. A directed verdict is used only when the state has failed to establish the guilt of the accused.

Discretion: The use of personal decision making in carrying out official duties.

District Attorney: The prosecutor who is responsible for prosecuting the accused in most states. The district attorney represents the state against the accused in court.

Diversion: The use of non-criminal alternatives in handling criminal cases.

Drift: The theory, espoused by David Matza, that youths move in and out of delinquency and that their lifestyles embrace both conventional and non-conventional values.

Due Process: A constitutional principle that is based on the concept of individual rights and governmental limitations. Included in the concept of due process is the right of a defendant to a fair trial.

Durkheim, Emile: A noted French sociologist who contended that crime was an integral part of our society. His theory of anomie was originally developed to explain suicide. He is also known for his theories on social solidarity.

Dysplastic Body Type: A person whose body type is part asthenic and part pyknic.

Ecological Theorists: Theorists who contended that crime rates are highest in the center of the city, where there is the greatest social disorganization.

Economic Crime: A crime committed for financial gain.

Ectoderm: Ectoderm refers to the connecting tissue of the nervous system.

Ectomorph: A person who is thin, small, and bony, with a small face, sharp nose, fine hair, relatively little body mass, and relatively great surface area.

Egoistic Suicide: A suicide that occurs when an individual is inadequately integrated into society; that person perceives society as rejecting him or her.

Electroencephalogram (EEG):   A machine that records electronic impulses produced by the brain (brain waves).

Ellenberger, Henri: A researcher from the Menninger Foundation who introduced the concept of a hidden fundamental unity between the crime victim and the offender.

Embezzlement: The stealing of property that has been entrusted to the embezzler. For example, a bank teller who takes money that has been entrusted to him by a bank customer is guilty of embezzlement.

Explosive Disorder: A disorder that is identified by sudden assaultive or other destructive behavior that occurs in a person who otherwise shows good control.

Emotional Problem Theories: Theories that assume that the lawbreaker does not have a gross pathology that causes him or her to commit crimes, but rather he or she commits crimes because of everyday emotional problems that render him or her unable to cope.

Endoderm: Endoderm refers to the digestive viscera.

Endomorph: A person who is round, fat, and fleshy, with short, tapering limbs, and small bones.

Erikson, Kai: A sociologist who contended that deviant behavior is an ingredient in the glue that holds a community together.

Etiology: The study of causes.

External Controls: According to the containment theorists, external controls are one of the two types of containment. External containments are strong social bonds or ties that prevent a person from committing criminal behavior.

Exorcism: The act of driving the devil out of a criminal.

Fatalistic Suicide: This suicide occurs when the individual feels that he or she is backed into a corner and that there is no way out.

Felony: A serious crime for which a convicted person may be sentenced to a year or more in prison, or death.

Focal Concerns: According to Walter Miller, focal concerns are the value orientations of the lower-class cultures. Focal concerns include fate, and the need for trouble, excitement, smartness and personal autonomy.

Folkways: Norms that when violated carry the least intense feelings when compared to customs and mores.

Formal Norms: Norms imposed on us from above or outside and often codified or written down.

Free Will: The doctrine that supports the idea that a person is considered rational and is free to choose his or her behavior.

Freud, Sigmund: A controversial and influential person who developed a theory of personality structure.

Functionalism: A sociological perspective which contends that each part of society makes a contribution to the whole. Functionalism stresses social consensus of values and beliefs among the majority of society's members.

General Deterrence: Criminal sanctions that are aimed at convincing potential offenders that the sanctions associated with crime outweigh its benefits.

Gluecks, Sheldon and Eleanor: A husband and wife research team who studied physical body types and delinquency. They studied 500 delinquent boys and compared them to a group of 500 nondelinquents.

Goffman, Erving: A sociologist who was a supporter of labeling theory and who developed the concept of stigma.

Goring, Charles: A researcher who conducted studies in biometrics. His book, *The English Convict*, is a classic example of the application of biometrics to the study of the criminal.

Grand Jury: A group of citizens that investigates suspected criminal activity and has the power to issue criminal indictments. The average size of a grand jury is from 16 to 23 persons.

Hawthorne Study: A study of the Western Electric Company which provides a classic example of the emergence of informal norms.

Homicide: Causing the death of another.

Hooten, Ernest: A physical anthropologist who believed that the criminal was biologically inferior to the noncriminal, and that biological inferiority was inherited.

Hirschi, Travis: A sociologist who developed the social bond theory.

Incapacitation: The policy of keeping criminals in confinement so that the risk of them committing additional crimes is eliminated.

Indeterminate Sentence: A sentence to confinement with a stated maximum and minimum length. For example, a sentence of three to five years.

Index Crimes: The eight crimes used by the FBI to measure the level of criminal activity in the United States. The eight crimes: murder, rape, assault, robbery, burglary, arson, larceny, and motor vehicle theft, were selected because of their seriousness and frequency.

Indictment: The written accusation returned by a grand jury charging a person with the commission of a criminal offense (felony).

Idiot Savants: A term once used to refer to persons exhibiting savant syndrome.

Innovation: One of Merton's ways to deal with anomie. This adaptation accepts the cultural goals and rejects the institutionalized means of the society.

Interactionist Perspective: The view that a person's perception of reality is influenced by his or her interpretations of the reactions of others to similar stimuli.

Internal Containments: One of the two containments of the containment theory. Internal containments are values that give a person inner strength and self-control, such as good self-image, conscience, strong ego and goal-directedness.

Justice Model: A philosophy of corrections that stresses the view that prisons are places of punishment and not of rehabilitation. The criminal owes a debt to society which he or she must repay by suffering the pain of imprisonment.

Justification: A defense to a criminal charge in which the accused contends that his or her actions were justified by the circumstances of the situation, and therefore he or she should not be held criminally liable for the act.

Juvenile Delinquency: Participation in criminal behavior by a person under the age of majority.

Kleptomania: An impulse disorder involving compulsive thievery.

Klinefelter's Syndrome (XXY):   A chromosome abnormality where there is the presence of an extra X chromosome in certain males.

Labeling: The process by which a person is labelled with a negative identity, such as criminal, and thereafter suffers the consequences of having an outcast status.

Larceny: The unlawful taking, or attempting taking, or property from the possession of another by stealth, without force or deceit, and with the intent to deprive the owner of the property permanently.

Laws: Formal proscriptive norms that when violated cause a formal and punitive reaction.

Learning Disabilities: A phrase used to describe a type of minimal brain dysfunction that prevents otherwise normal and intelligent children from learning in a normal classroom setting.

Lemert, Edwin: A theorist who suggested that American values are not always clear and that Americans tend to be value plural. He also contended that criminality is the result of a positive response to one set of subcultural values that happens to be out of tune with another set of subcultural values.

Looking-glass Self: A concept used in the labeling theory to explain criminal behavior. According to Cooley, the social self is made up of what a person perceives others see in himself or herself.

Lombroso, Cesare: An early positivist criminologist, who is considered as the father of modern criminology.

Lunatic: A term that means insane, mad, or crazy.

Macrotheories: Theories that are abstract and focus on crime rates.

Mala in se Crimes: Acts that are considered crimes because they not only violate criminal statutes, but also the accepted basic moral values of society. Mala in se crimes include rape, murder, arson, theft, and assaults.

Mala Prohibitum Crimes: Acts that are considered crimes because they violate criminal statutes, but not the accepted basic moral values of society. Mala prohibitum crimes include speeding, failing to file income tax returns, and license violations.

Matza, David: A control theorist who wrote *Delinquency and Drift*. He contended that delinquents have no commitment either to societal norms or to criminal norms.

McDonald, William Frank: A victimologist who conducted a study regarding the causes and nature of assaults and robberies on bus drivers.

McKay, Henry D.: A sociologist who together with Clifford Shaw compared juvenile court records of Cook County, Illinois for the purpose of determining the extent to which changes in delinquency rates are related to changes in the physical or social characteristics of the neighborhood.

Mead, George Herbert: A sociologist who originated the concepts that became known as symbolic interactionism.

Mechanistic Societies: Societies that are preliterate, homogenous, preindustrial and orderly. The norms and values are shared by all.

Mens Rea: The mental element of a crime or the intent to commit the offense.

Mental Disorder Theories: Theories that assume that the offender has a disorder or pathology that makes him or her different in psychological makeup from the nonoffender.

Merton, Robert: A sociologist who applied Durkheim's anomie to deviant behavior.

Mesoderm: Mesoderm refers to a person's bones, muscles, and tendons.

Mesomorph: A person who is big-boned and muscular and tends to have a large trunk, heavy chest, and large wrists and hands.

Microtheories: Theories that are concrete in nature and focus on individual conduct.

Middle-class Measuring Rod: A theory developed by Cohen that lower-class boys are measured or evaluated by the standards and aspirations of the middle class which they do not have the opportunity to fulfill.

Miller, Walter: A sociologist who studied the diffusion of delinquent values in the lower class and explained that delinquency is caused by the fact that the lower class had a separate, identifiable culture distinct from the middle-class culture.

Minnesota Multiphasic Personality Inventory (MMPI): A popular test used in attempting to discover the personality and psychological differences between offenders and nonoffenders.

Misdemeanor: A minor crime for which the maximum sentence is less than one year's confinement.

M'Naghten Rule: The legal definition of insanity based on the early English case, M'Naghten. This rule holds that persons are not responsible for their actions if they do not know what they are doing, or if they cannot distinguish between right and wrong.

Moral Development The theory that criminals have an underdeveloped moral sense that prevents them from making correct behavior choices in given situations.

Mores: Social norms that arouse intense feelings and are subject to extreme consequences when violated.

Multifactor Approach: An approach to the study of crime which assumes that crime is the result of many different factors.

National Crime Survey: The victimization studies conducted jointly by the Justice Department and Census Bureau that surveys victims about their victimization experiences.

Natural Law: The division of Aristotle's classification of law that reflects those values that are universally accepted as correct.

Neo-classical: The school of criminology that is based on the concept of free will, but which recognizes that some people cannot reason.

Neuroallergy: Neuroallergy is an allergic condition that affects the body's central nervous system.

Nolle Prosequi: The decision by the prosecutor not to continue the prosecution of a case after the accused has been formally charged.

Nolo Contendere: The plea by an accused in court, wherein the accused does not contest the charge, but does not formally admit his or her guilt. For prosecution purposes, a plea of nolo contendere is the same as a plea of guilty.

Non-index Crimes: Crimes reported by the FBI in this category are limited only to those cleared by arrest, prosecution, or those formally charged. They are Type II crimes.

Nuremberg Boy: A feral child found in a dungeon in 1828.

Nutrition Theories: Theories that assume that what a person eats or does not eat affects his or her behavior and thus may cause criminal behavior.

Ohlin, Lloyd: A sociologist who together with Richard Cloward used the opportunity theory to explain subcultural delinquency.

Order Maintenance: The function in which the police maintain order in the community.

Organic Societies: Societies that have dense populations, high division of labor and are heterogeneous (populated by many different ethnic, religious, and racial groups).

Parens Patriae: The concept that the state must act as parent for those who cannot take care of themselves.

Parole: The conditional release of a prisoner from a prison sentence prior to the completion of the assigned prison term.

Parson, Talcot: A sociologist who introduced Durkheim to a wider reading public by an analysis of his work.

Peacekeeping: The function in which the police operate to maintain peace within the community.

Penal-Couple: A term used by Mendelsohn to describe the relationship between the victim and the criminal.

Piaget, Jean: A Swiss psychologist, who studied human intelligence, perception, and thinking.

Plea: The answer to formal charges in court by the accused. The normal pleas are guilty, not guilty, nolo contendere, and not guilty by reason of insanity.

Plea Bargaining: An agreement between the state and the accused whereby the accused will plead guilty in return for a promised benefit. For example, an accused may enter into a plea bargain to plead guilty for a lesser sentence.

Positivism: The criminological school that discounts free will and contends that criminal behavior is the product of social, biological, or psychological forces beyond a person's control.

Power Rape: A rape that is motivated by the desire of the rapist to dominate the victim.

Primary Culture Conflict: According to Sellin, a primary culture conflict occurs when one's native cultural conduct norms conflict with those of the person's new culture.

Primary Groups: According to C. H. Cooley, primary groups provide for the person's need for intimate association. They are also important in socializing the person. They are characterized by feelings of closeness, consensus, and we-ness.

Prison: A state or federal confinement facility where a person may be confined for periods in excess of one year. In some states, the term, correctional facility, is used instead of prison.

Probation: A sentence whereby the offender is conditionally released into the community in lieu of serving time in confinement.

Process Theories: Theories that focus on how people become criminals.

Pro Se: The situation where a person serves as his or her own attorney.

Psychopath: A person who has a personality disorder which is characterized by the lack of proper emotional content. A psychopath is not affected by punishment and is insensitive to the suffering of others.

Pure Research: Research that is concerned with developing the theoretical knowledge of a discipline.

Pyknic Body Type: A person whose body is round, fat, and fleshy.

Pyromania: An impulse disorder that manifests itself in an irresistible impulse to burn, with no other motive than to set fires.

Rape: The act of unlawful sexual intercourse with a female, by force or without legal or factual consent.

Rebellion: One of Merton's ways to deal with anomie. This adaptation openly rejects both the cultural goals and the institutionalized means of the society.

Recidivism: A term used to refer to the committing of new crimes by offenders already punished by the criminal justice system.

Reckless, Walter: A containment theorist who contended that we all have pushes and pulls toward crime; however, not all people with the same pushes and pulls become criminal. A person's containments may prevent the person from committing criminal behavior.

Redfield, Robert: An anthropologist who compared folk societies to the modern, urban criminalistic societies.

Rehabilitation: The concept of treating criminals in order to reform them.

Reiss, Albert: A sociologist who conducted a Chicago study dealing with the characteristics of working-class boys. He contended that delinquency emerges from the failure of personal and social controls to produce behavior that conforms to the norms of the social system to which penalties are attached.

Resocialization: The concept that is related to socialization. It refers to an extreme change or shift in values, attitudes, and behaviors that were once an integral part of a person's life. Examples of resocialization are the shift from civilian to military status and the shift from a criminal lifestyle to a noncriminal lifestyle.

Restitution: This requires the defendant to repay the victims for the damage suffered as the result of his or her criminal conduct. Restitution is often a condition of probation.

Retreatism: One of Merton's ways to deal with anomie. This adaptation rejects both the cultural goals and the institutionalized means of the society.

Ritualism: One of Merton's ways to deal with anomie. This adaptation rejects the cultural goals, but accepts the institutionalized means of the society.

Robbery: The unlawful taking or attempted taking of property that is in the immediate possession of another, by force or threat of force.

Sadistic Rape: A rape that is motivated by the rapist's desire to torment and abuse the victim.

St. Thomas Aquinas: A theorist who believed that the soul is implanted in the unborn child.

Samenow, Stanton E.:   A thinking pattern theorist and co-author of *The Criminal Personality*.

Schizophrenia: A type of psychosis often identified by bizarre behavior, hallucinations, loss of thought control, and inappropriate emotional responses.

Secondary Culture Conflict: According to Sellin, a secondary culture conflict occurs in complex societies comprised of a variety of groups when the behavior required by one group's conduct norms violates the conduct norms of another group.

Secondary Groups: The secondary group, according to C. H. Cooley, are groups not bound together by intimate ties. They are characterized by bureaucracy, organization, heterogeneity, complexity, and impersonality.

Selective Enforcement: The practice of the police in selectively enforcing laws. For example, stopping only those persons driving more than ten miles above the posted speed limit.

Self-report Study: A study in which persons are asked to reveal their own participation in criminal conduct.

Sellin, Thorsten: A theorist who is credited with publishing the first systematic discussion of the relationship between culture conflict and crime.

Sentence: The criminal sanction imposed by a court on the conviction of the accused.

Serial Murderer: A murderer who commits a pattern of motiveless murders in a random pattern.

Sexual Abuse: Illegal sexual acts performed against a minor by an adult.

Shaw, Clifford R.:   A sociologist who together with Henry D. McKay compared juvenile court records of Cook County, Illinois for the purpose of determining the extent to which changes in delinquency rates are related to changes in the physical or social characteristics of the neighborhood.

Shelton, W. H.:   A theorist who contended that a person's body type was related to personality.

Shire Reeve: The senior law enforcement officer in early English counties. The forerunner of today's sheriff.

Shock Probation: A sentence that involves an initial sentence of imprisonment and then community corrections, used to shock the accused.

Social Bond Theorists: Theorists who contend that people are born to break laws but will refrain if attachment, commitment, involvement, and belief (social bonds) are present.

Social Control Theorists: Theorists who contend that criminal behavior occurs when a person's bonds to society are weakened or severed.

Social Definition of Crime: Behavior that is considered antisocial and unethical.

Social Disorganization: Defined as a breakdown in the bonds of relationship, coordination, teamwork, and morale among different groups in society that impairs the functions of society.

Social Norms: Basic sociological concepts frequently used to explain human behavior and crime causation. They are also used to define socially accepted and expected conduct.

Social Learning Theory: The theory that human behavior is modeled by what an individual observes in social situations.

Social Process Theory: The theory that criminal behavior is controlled by social processes such as parental relationships, education, and peer relations.

Socialization: The concept that refers to the learning process by which the person learns and internalizes the ways of society so that he or she can function and become an active part of society.

Sociobiology: The concept that genetic factors combine with environmental conditions to control the form and content of human behavior. Genetic drives are translated into everyday behavior choices.

Sociology: The study or science of the origin, development, organization, and functioning of human society.

Sociopathy: A term usually used to refer to a unique pattern of behaviors.

Somatypes: According to Sheldon, somatypes are the three poles of physique. The three somatypes are endomorph, ectomorph, and mesomorph.

Stare Decisis: A legal principle by which decisions in earlier cases are used as standards for later cases.

Status Frustration: The feelings of anger and frustration brought about by membership in a powerless segment of society (lower-economic class).

Stigma: According to Erving Goffman and the labeling theory, stigma refers to discrediting marks such as tattoos or deformities that tend to belittle a person.

Strain: The sense of anger and frustration created by the absence of opportunity to achieve conventional success through legitimate means.

Strain Theories: Theories that assume that excessive pressure or strain on the person often results in criminal conduct.

Stratified Society: The concept that society can be separated into levels based on socio-economic factors.

Street Crimes: Crimes involving violence and designed to prey on the public.

Structural Theories: Theories that focus on how society is organized.

Subcultural Murderer: A person who commits murder as a problem-solving technique.

Subculture: A group that is loosely connected to the dominant culture but has its own unique set of values, beliefs, and traditions.

Subculture Theorists: Theorists who contend that there are subcultures with value systems different from those of the mainstream or parent value system in society.

Sumner, William Graham: A researcher who developed the concept that norms should be divided into three categories: mores, customs, and folkways.

Superego: According to Freud, the aspect of the personality that is influenced by the moral imperatives learned from parents and others.

Sutherland, Edwin: The criminologist who developed the theory of differential association. He is also considered the Dean of American Criminology.

Sykes, Gresham: A leading control theorist who contended that people do not commit crimes when they are controlled by morals. When the morals are neutralized, however, the controls are lessened and people are more likely to commit criminal acts.

Symbolic Interactionism: A term originated by Herbert Blumer and currently used as a label for a distinctive approach to the study of human group behavior. Symbolic interactionism's position is that the meaning people place on things is central in its own right.

Tannenbaum, Frank: A theorist who helped develop and expand labeling theory.

Thinking Pattern Theories: Thinking pattern theories are psychological theories that deal with the criminal's cognitive processes, intellect, logic, mental structure, rationality, and language usage.

Thrasher, Frederic: A researcher who conducted a classic study of 1,313 gangs in Chicago in the 1920s.

Tort: A civil personal wrong usually based on negligence, libel, slander, assault or trespass.

Turk, Austin: One of the developers of the labeling theory.

Type I Offenses: Another term for index crimes.

Type II Offenses: Another term for non-index crimes.

Typologies: A term used to refer to the study of different types of crimes. Typologies examine the patterns of particular types of criminal behavior and make statements about personal and environmental factors in crime causation.

Uniform Crime Reports: Annual series of crime statistics developed from a 1927 effort by the International Association of Chiefs of Police to create a uniform system for gathering statistics on crimes known to the police. It is currently compiled by the FBI and divided into index (type I) and non-index (type II) crimes.

Urea: A substance found in the urine and other body fluids.

Utilitarian Principle: A principle developed by Jeremy Bentham stating that an act has utility if it produces happiness or prevents pain.

Verdict: The findings or decision of a jury.

Victimization Survey: A crime-measurement process that surveys citizens to ascertain their experiences as crime victims.

Victimless Crimes: Crimes with no direct victims, such as possession of cocaine or prostitution.

Victimology: The study of crime from the victim's viewpoint, with emphasis on the relationship between the victim and the offender.

Victim Precipitated: A crime in which the victim was the first to use force or whose behavior ignited the offense.

Von Hentig, Hans: A victimologist who contended that in many respects the victim shapes and molds the criminal and the crime.

White-collar Crimes: Crimes that occur in the business or occupational setting of the offender.

Wohler, Fredrick: A German chemist who first established the concept of biochemical imbalances.

Wolfgang, Marvin: A criminologist who developed the subculture of violence theory in an attempt to integrate a wide range of disciplinary approaches to understanding deviant behavior.

Wilson, Edward O.:   His book, *Sociobiology: The New Synthesis* directed attention to the field of sociobiology.

Yablonski, Lewis: A sociologist who conducted classic research on violent gangs. His hypothesis was that the violent-gang structure recruited its participants from sociopathic young people who lived in disorganized slum communities.

Yochelson, Samuel: A co-author of *The Criminal Personality* and a thinking-pattern theorist.

Bibliography

AKERS, RONALD, "Toward a Comparative Definition of Law," *Journal of Criminal Law, Criminology and Police Science,* 56 (September, 1965), pp. 301–306.

——, "Theory and Ideology in Marxist Criminology: Comments on Turk, Quinney, Toby, and Klockers," *Criminology,* February 1979, pp. 442–44.

ALLEN, FRANCIS A., "Raffaele Garofalo" in Hermann Mannheim, ed. *Pioneers in Criminology.* Montclair, N.J.: Patterson Smith, 1973:318–40.

ATKINSON, CHARLES MILNER, *Jeremy Bentham: His Life and Work,* 1905.

BARLOW, HUGH D., *Introduction to Criminology.* Boston: Little, Brown, 1984.

BARRON, MILTON L., "The Criminogenic Society: Social Values and Deviance," *Current Perspectives on Criminal Behavior.* ed. Abraham S. Blumberg, New York: Knopf, 1974:68–87.

BEACH, BENNETT H., "Picking Between Mad and Bad," *Time.* October 12, 1981, p. 68.

BECCARIA, CESARE, *Dei delitti e delle pene,* 1776. (An Essay on Crime and Punishments) (Translated from the Italian with the commentary by Voltaire.) 5th ed., London, 1804.

——, *On Crimes and Punishments,* (reprint for The Library of Liberal Arts Series) translated by Henry Paolucci, New York: Bobbs-Merrill, 1963.

BECKER, G. S., "Crime and Punishment: An Economic Approach," *Journal of Political Economy.* Vol. 76, 1968:169–217.

BECKER, HOWARD S., *Outsider: Studies in the Sociology of Deviance.* New York: Free Press, 1963.

BENTHAM, JEREMY, *An Introduction to the Principles of Morals and Legislation,* (corrected ed.) Oxford: Clarendon Press, 1823.

BIRENBAUM, ARNOLD and EDWARD SAGARIN, *Norms and Human Behavior.* New York: Praeger, 1976.

BONGER, WILLEM A., *Criminology and Economic Conditions.* trans. Henry Horton, Boston: Little, Brown, 1916.

BLUMER, HERBERT, *Symbolic Interaction: Perspective and Method.* Englewood Cliffs, N.J.: Prentice-Hall, 1969.

BULMER, MARTIN, *The Chicago School of Sociology,* Chicago: University of Chicago Press, 1984.

BURGESS, ERNEST W., "The Study of the Delinquent as a Person," *American Journal of Sociology,* 28 (May, 1923), pp. 657–80.

BURGESS, ROBERT L. and RONALD AKERS. "A Differential Association–Reinforcement Theory of Criminal Behavior," *Social Problems,* 14 (Fall, 1966), pp. 128–47.

BYRD, RICHARD E., *Alone*. New York: G. P. Putnam's Sons, 1938.

CALHOUN, GEORGE, *The Growth of Criminal Law in Ancient Greece*, Berkeley: University of California Press, 1927.

CHAMBLISS, WILLIAM J., *Exploring Criminology*. New York: Macmillan, 1988.

CHINOY, ELY, *Society*. New York: Random House, 1962.

CLAUSEN, JOHN A., ed. *Socialization and Society*. Boston: Little, Brown, 1968.

CLINARD, MARSHALL B., *Sociology of Deviant Behavior*. New York: Holt, Rinehart, & Winston, 1968.

CLOWARD, R. A. and LLOYD E. OHLIN, *Delinquency and Opportunity*. New York: Free Press, 1960.

COHEN, ALBERT K., *Delinquent Boys: The Culture of the Gang*. New York: Free Press, 1955.

——, *Deviance and Control*. Englewood Cliffs, N.J.: Prentice-Hall, 1966.

COLEMAN, JAMES WILLIAM, *The Criminal Elite*. New York: St. Martin's Press, 1989.

COOLEY, CHARLES H., *Human Nature and the Social Order*. New York: Charles Scribner's, 1902.

——, *Social Organization*. New York: Scribner, 1909.

COSER, LEWIS A., "The Sociology of Poverty," *Social Problems*, Vol. 13 (Fall, 1971).

CROWE, R. R., "The Adopted Offspring of Women Criminal Offenders." *Archives of General Psychiatry*, Nov. 1972, 27 (5), 600–603.

CULLEN, F. T., *Rethinking Crime and Deviance Theory: The Emergence of a Structuring Tradition*. Totowa, NJ.: Rowman & Allanheld, 1983.

DARWIN, CHARLES, *Decent of Man*. London: John Murray, 1871.

DAVIS, KINGSLEY, "Extreme Isolation of a Child," *American Journal of Sociology*, XLV (January, 1940), 554–65.

——, "Final Note on a Case of Extreme Isolation," *American Journal of Sociology*, LII (March, 1947), 432–37.

DELLA PORTE, J. BAPTISTLE, *The Human Physiognomy*, 1586.

DUGDALE, R., *The Jukes: A Study in Crime, Pauperism, Disease, and Heredity*. New York: Putnam, 1910.

DURKHEIM, EMILE, *The Division of Labor in Society*. (translated by George Simpson) New York: Free Press, 1965.

——, *Suicide*. (translated by J. A. Spaulding and G. Simpson ed.) New York: Free Press, 1951.

EDWARDS, CHILPERIC, *The Hammurabi Code*, New York: Kennikat Press, 1971.

ELLIS, HAVELOCK, *The Criminal*, 2d ed. New York: Scribner, 1900.

EMPEY, LAMAR T., *American Delinquency: Its Meaning and Construction*. Homewood, Il.: Dorsey, 1982.

ERIKSON, KAI, *Wayward Puritans*. New York: John Wiley, 1966.

FARIS, ROBERT, *Social Disorganization* 2d ed. New York: Ronald Press, 1955.

FERRI, ENRICO, *Criminal Sociology*, Boston: Little, Brown, 1917.

——, *The Positive School of Criminology*, ed. by Phillip Grupp, Pittsburgh: University of Pittsburgh Press, 1968.

FICARA, J., "All About Twins." *Newsweek*, Nov. 23, 1987, 58–69.

FLEMING, MACKLIN, "A Short Course in the Causes of Crime," *Prosecutor's Brief*, May–June, 1979, pp. 8–12.

FARRIS, ROBERT, *Chicago Sociology: 1920–1932,* Chicago: University of Chicago Press, 1970.

FRIEDRICH, CARL JOACHIN, *The Philosophy of Law in Historical Perspective,* Chicago: 1963.

FULLER, LON, *The Morality of Law,* New Haven, 1964.

GARFINKEL, HAROLD, "Conditions of a Successful Degradation Ceremony," *American Journal of Sociology.* Vol. 61, (March, 1956) pp. 420–24.

GAROFALO, RAFFAELE, *Criminology,* Boston: Little, Brown, 1914.

GIBBONS, DON, *The Criminology Enterprise: Theories and Perspectives.* Englewood Cliffs, N.J.: Prentice-Hall, 1979:65.

GODDARD, H., *The Kallikak Family: A Study in the Heredity of Feeblemindedness.* New York: Macmillan, 1912.

GOFFMAN, ERVING, *Stigma.* Indianapolis: Bobbs-Merrill, 1963.

GORDON, CYRUS H., *Hammurabi's Code: Quaint or Forward Looking,* New York: Rinehart, 1957.

GOULD, JULIUS, "Auguste Comte," in T. Raison, ed. *The Founding Fathers of Social Science,* Harmondsworth, England: Penguin, 1969.

GLUECK, SHELDON and ELEANOR GLUECK, *Unraveling Juvenile Delinquency.* New York: Commonwealth Fund, 1950.

——, *Physique and Delinquency.* New York: Harper, 1956.

HIGGINS, PAUL C. and RICHARD R. BUTLER, *Understanding Deviance,* New York: McGraw-Hill, 1982.

HIRSCHI, TRAVIS, *Causes of Delinquency.* Berkeley: University of California Press, 1969.

HOEBEL, E. ADAMSON, *The Law of Primitive Man,* Cambridge, Mass.: Harvard University Press, 1954.

HOMANS, GEORGE, *The Human Group.* New York: Harcourt, Brace, 1950.

HOOTEN, E. A., *The American Criminal: An Anthropological Study,* Cambridge, Mass.: Harvard University Press, 1939.

HULL, C. RONALD, "Conflict Theory in Criminology," in James A. Inciarci, ed. *Radical Criminology: The Coming Crises.* Beverly Hills, Ca.: Sage, 1980:61–78.

ITARD, JEAN MARC, *The Wild Boy of Aveyron.* New York: Appleton-Century Crofts, 1962.

JEFFERY, C. RAY, "The Structure of American Criminological Thinking," *Journal of Criminal Law, Criminology and Police Science,* Vol. 46, pp. 663–74, Jan.–Feb., 1956.

—— "The Development of Crime in Early English Society," *Journal of Criminal Law, Criminology and Police Science,* Vol. 47, 1957.

—— "The Historical Development of Criminology," in H. Mannheim ed., *Pioneers of Criminology,* London: Stevens, 1960.

JOHNSON, HERBERT, *A History of Criminal Justice.* Cincinnati: Anderson, 1988.

KLOCKARS, CARL B., "The Contemporary Crises of Marxist Criminology," *Criminology: An Interdisciplinary Journal,* Vol. 16, No. 4, February, 1979, pp. 477–526.

KORN, RICHARD R. and LLOYD W. MCCORKLE, *Criminology and Penology.* New York: Holt, Rinehart and Winston, 1966.

LANGE, J., *Crime as Destiny.* (English Translation) New York: Charles Boni, 1930.

LAUB, J. H., *Criminology in the Making: An Oral History*. Boston: Northeastern University Press, 1983.

LEMERT, EDWIN, *Social Pathology*. New York: McGraw–Hill, 1951.

———, *Human Deviance, Social Problems, and Social Control*. Englewood Cliffs, N.J.: Prentice-Hall, 1967.

LIEBER, ARNOLD and CAROLYN R. SHERIN, "Homicides and the Lunar Cycles: Toward a Theory of Lunar Influence on Human Emotional Disturbance," *American Journal of Psychiatry*, Vol. 129, July, 1972, pp. 101–16.

LOMBROSO, CESARE, *Crime, Its Causes and Remedies*, translated by H. P. Horton, Boston: Little, Brown, 1911.

LOMBROSO-FERREO, G., *The Criminal Man According to the Classification of Cesare Lombroso*, Montclair, NJ.: Patterson Smith, 1972.

MAINE, SIR HENRY, *Ancient Law, Its Connection with the Early History of Society and Its Relation to Modern Ideas*, London: John Murray, 1861.

MARCUS, STEVEN, *Engels, Manchester, and the Working Class*. New York: Random House, 1974.

MARSH, FRANK H. and JANET KATZ, *Biology, Crime & Ethics*. Cincinnati: Anderson, 1985.

MATZA, DAVID, *Delinquency and Drift*. New York: John Wiley, 1964.

McCAGHY, C. H., *Deviant Behavior: Crime, Conflict, and Interest Groups*. New York: Macmillan, 1976.

MERTON, ROBERT K., *Social Structure and Anomie*. New York: Free Press, 1938.

MICHALOWSKI, RAYMOND J., *Order, Law, and Crime*. New York: Random House, 1985.

MILLER, WALTER B., "Lower–Class Culture as a Generation Milieu of Gang Delinquency," *Journal of Social Issues*, Vol. 14, 1958 pp. 5–19.

MONTAGU, ASHLEY, "The Sociobiology Debate: An Introduction." In F. H. Marsh and J. Katz (ed). *Biology, Crime & Ethics*, Cincinnati: Anderson, 1985:24.

MORRIS, M. F., *The History of the Development of Law*, Washington, D.C.: John Byrne, 1909.

NETTLER, GWENN, *Explaining Crime*. 2d ed. New York: McGraw-Hill, 1978.

PARK, ROBERT E., and ERNEST BURGESS, *Introduction to the Science of Sociology*, 2d ed. Chicago: University of Chicago Press, 1924.

PARK, ROBERT E., *Human Communities: the City and Human Ecology*. Glencoe, Ill.: Free Press, 1952.

PACKER, HERBERT L., *The Limits of the Criminal Sanction*. Stanford, Ca.: Stanford University Press, 1968.

PARKER, DONN B., *Crime by Computer*. New York: Charles Scribner, 1976.

PELFREY, WILLIAM V., *The Evolution of Criminology*. Cincinnati: Anderson, 1980.

PHILLIPS, PAUL, *Marx and Engels on Law and Laws*. Totowa, NJ.: Barnes and Noble, 1980.

PLATT, A., "Prospects for a Radical Criminology," in I. Taylor, P. Walton, and Jock Young, eds. *Critical Criminology*, London: Routledge and Kegan, 1975.

POPENOE, DAVID, *Sociology*. 3rd ed. Englewood Cliffs: Prentice-Hall, 1977.

QUINNEY, RICHARD, *The Problem of Crime*. New York: Dodd, Mead & Co., 1971.

———, *Critique of Legal Order: Crime Control in Capitalist Society*. Boston: Little, Brown, 1973.

——, *Criminology: Analysis and Critique of Crime in the United States.* Boston: Little, Brown, 1974:38–42.

RECKLESS, WALTER, *The Crime Problem* (5th ed.), Englewood Cliffs, NJ.: Prentice-Hall, 1973.

REDFIELD, ROBERT, *The Primitive World and its Transformation.* Ithaca, N.Y.: Cornell University Press, 1953.

REIMAN, JEFFERY H., *The Rich Get Richer and the Poor Get Prison: Ideology, Class and Criminal Justice.* New York: John Wiley, 1979.

REISS, ALBERT J., "Social Correlates of Psychological Types of Delinquency." *American Sociological Review,* 1952, 17, pp. 710–18.

ROETHLISBERGER, FRITZ J. and WILLIAM J. DICKSON, *Management and the Worker.* Cambridge: Harvard University Press, 1939.

ROWE, D. C., "Biometrical Genetic Models of Self-Reported Delinquent Behavior: A Twin Study." *Behavior Genetics,* 13, 1983, pp. 473–89.

ROSZAK, T., *The Making of a Counter Culture.* New York: Anchor, 1969.

SCHAFER, STEPHEN, *Theories in Criminology,* New York: Random House, 1968.

SCHRAG, C., *Crime and Justice: American Style.* Washington: GPO, 1971.

SELLIN, THORSTEN, *Culture Conflict and Crime.* New York: Social Science Research Council, 1938.

SHAW, CLIFFORD R. and HENRY D. McKAY, *Juvenile Delinquency and Urban Areas.* Chicago: University of Chicago Press, 1942.

SINGH, A. L. and R. M. ZINGG, *Wolf Children and Feral Man.* New York: Harper, 1942.

STINCHCOMBE, ARTHUR, *Constructing Social Theories,* New York: Harcourt, Brace & World, 1968.

SUMNER, WILLIAM G., *Folkways: A Study of the Sociological Importance of Usages, Manners, Customs, Mores, and Morals.* Boston: Ginn, 1906.

SUTHERLAND, EDWIN H., "The Differential Association Theory," in Stephen Schafer and Richard D. Knudten, *Criminological Theory.* Lexington: Lexington Books, 1977.

SYKES, GRESHAM M. and DAVID MATZA, "Techniques of Neutralization: A Theory of Delinquency." *American Sociological Review.* 22: (Dec. 1957), pp. 667–70.

TAFT, DONALD R. and RALPH W. ENGLISH JR., *Criminology.* New York: MacMillan, 1964.

TANNENBAUM, FRANK, *Crime and the Community.* Boston: Ginn, 1938.

TAPPAN, PAUL, "Who is the Criminal?", *American Sociological Review,* (1947), Vol. 12, pp. 96–102.

TARDE, G., *Social Laws: An Outline of Sociology.* New York: Macmillan, 1907.

TAYLOR, IAN.; PAUL WALTON and JOCK YOUNG, *The New Criminology.* New York: Harper and Row, 1973:209–36.

THRASHER, FREDERIC M., *The Gang,* Chicago: University of Chicago Press, 1927.

TURK, AUSTIN T., *Political Criminology: The Defiance and Defense of Authority.* Beverly Hills: Sage, 1982.

VAN DEN HAAG, ERNEST, *Punishing Criminals.* New York: Basic Books, 1975.

VOLD, GEORGE B. and THOMAS J. BERNARD, *Theoretical Criminology* (3d. ed.). New York: Oxford, 1986.

WEISSER, MICHAEL R., *Crime and Punishment in Early Modern Europe.* Atlantic Highlands, N.J.: Humanities Press, 1979.

WESTERMARCH, EDWARD, *The Origin and Development of the Moral Ideas*, Vol. I, 2d ed., London: 1912.

WILKINSON, JOHN, *The Ancient Egyptians*, Vol. III, London: John Murray, 1978.

WILLIAMS, III, FRANK P. and MARILYN D. MCSHANE, *Criminological Theory.* Englewood Cliffs, N.J.: Prentice-Hall, 1988.

WILLIAMS, G., "The Definition of Crime." *Current Legal Problems*, 1955, Vol. 8, pp. 107–30.

WILSON, JAMES Q. and RICHARD J. HERRMSTEOM, *Crime & Human Nature*, New York: Simon & Schuster, 1986.

WOLFGANG, MARVIN and FRANCO FERRACUTI, *The Subculture of Violence*, London: Social Science Paperbacks, 1967.

WOLFGANG, MARVIN E., "Cesare Lombroso" in Hermann Mannheim, ed. *Pioneers in Criminology.* Montclair, NJ.: Patterson Smith, 1973:232–91.

WORMER, RENE A., *The Story of Law*, New York: Simon & Schuster, 1962.

Index

KALAMAZOO VALLEY
COMMUNITY COLLEGE

Presented By

Mike Stacy